General's Jottings

★ ★ ★ REARMED ★ ★ ★

National Security, Conflicts & Strategies
(Including Operation Sindoor)

General's Jottings

★ ★ ★ REARMED ★ ★ ★

National Security, Conflicts & Strategies
(Including Operation Sindoor)

Lt Gen KJ Singh

Title: General's Jottings Rearmed: National Security, Conflicts & Strategies (Including Operation Sindoor)
Author: Lt Gen KJ Singh

Edition: 2nd
ISBN: 978-93-49042-24-7

Published by:
JGS Enterprises Pvt Ltd
Imprint: The Browser

Publisher's Address:
SCO 14-15, FF, Sector 8-C, Chandigarh 160 009

Website: thebrowser.org
Email: service@thebrowser.org

© Layout and Cover Design by 99 beagles
99beagles.com

Publishers & Booksellers

Oral History and Military Publishing

Contents

PLA Organisation

Sino-Bhutan Border, Siliguri Corridor, and Dolam (Doklam)

Relevance of Mechanised Warfare – Countering Drones and Chinese Tanks in High Altitude

Two Front or Single Front Reinforced Threat

Pakistan Army – Ethos and Hierarchy

Pakistan – Descent into Chaos

Western Front – Countering Pakistan

Afghanistan-Pakistan and Taliban

Indus Water Treaty

Proxy War in J&K

About General's Jottings Rearmed

1.1 Intellectual March in Columns

***Generals Jottings* was first published in 2024 as a primer and reference book for those wanting to comprehend national security issues.** The title 'General's Jottings' is drawn from the banner of fortnightly columns published in the regional edition of *Times of India* (Chandigarh). The 'Rearmed' appended to the title of this revised 2025 edition signifies the inclusion of longer articles published in Year Books of USI, CLAWS, and compilations by think-tanks and other authors in the form of edited books. These longer articles have been utilised for theme setting and as consolidation papers for various subjects. Print media articles are drawn from various newspapers like *Times of India (TOI), Tribune, Indian Express*, etc. More importantly, the book is not a mere lazy compilation but is a curated or distilled one, with updated articles, arranged thematically. Important issues have been highlighted and key take-away points duly flagged. Updating of articles has also been done with amplification notes, along with the indication of the time of writing for better referencing. Please do browse through the tool-kit for Citizen Warriors (outlined in Section 1.2) to get a better macro understanding on the subject of national security.

For the re-attired soldier, it is another form of marching, an 'intellectual' one and in 'columns', articulated in print instead of physically marching in contingents in uniform. Since the first edition has sold out, it is appropriate to publish an updated version, hence the suffix 'Rearmed' in the title. It includes the initial part of Operation Sindoor-related coverage. We hope to continue the march with support and feedback from readers, and more updated versions would follow.

The idea of writing a column on national security in the Chandigarh edition of *TOI* was proposed to Mr Robin David in 2016. He liked the proposal and launched the weekly column in April 2017. More importantly, he mentored the project in the formative stages. When he left on a posting to Hyderabad, he passed the baton to Ms Sarju Kaul, who continued anchoring the column aided by Ajay Sura, Deputy Editor. We now have new incumbent, Mr Prasenjeet Mund. The weekly Sunday column series started with two columnists alternating every week. For me, it was a fortnightly responsibility, in this shared space. In this journey, starting in April 2017, I have had two very eminent partners, initially, Lt Gen HS Panag till September 2018 and Lt Gen DS Hooda, replacing him and contributing till August 2020. As we went along, both had other commitments and had to discontinue, so it became a fortnightly column, instead of a weekly one from September 2020. **In sum, it has helped me to learn, connect, reflect, and also hone my analytical and articulation skills spread over 200 odd columns and 50 other articles over eight years.**

Writing columns is an interesting, yet challenging task. While there is an assured medium available to columnist, obviating disheartening editorial rejection slips (now mails), yet maintaining reliability and addressing contemporary issues is the prime requisite. After the initial struggle, the process becomes addictive and it is reassuring to hear from readers about missing the column when it is not published. The columns, limited to 900–925 words, are an interesting way to address contemporary issues. Unlike longer format articles, there is hardly any latitude. **Ideally, a column has to be direct, sharp, incisive, and brief, yet it must cover all important aspects of the subject. The oft-quoted analogy regarding the length of skirt applies to columns also.** Newspaper columns are based on an honorarium system and payment remains nominal, except for a few acclaimed columnists, yet they provide an avenue to connect.

1.2 Tool-Kit/Template for Citizen Warriors

General's Jottings seeks to guide you into a journey of making sense of national security and defence studies. Readers have to delve into the study of the 'strategic' domain connected with national security, yet this can be simplified. The first question can be: but why should we even get into this domain reserved for soldiers? Is it even needed? Well, this is no longer valid with the COVID-19 pandemic shock, where we had health warriors and even sanitation warriors. **The revised paradigm is that the national security entails a 'whole-of-nation' approach. Even if you pretend to not be interested, national security includes you and affects you. Everyone has to be 'Nagrik Yodha' (Citizen Warrior), in the mode of an ever vigilant or 'Jagruk' Hindustani.**

So put your thinking-cap on and don't hesitate to have your jotting pad handy. Making notes and highlighting helps. The subject is invariably geo-centric, which is used as the prefix, along with politics, economics, and strategy, making them geo-political, geo-economic, within the overall ambit of geo-strategy.

For ease of analysis, a simple tool-kit or template to follow is: LED-P^{2}A^{2}L, an acronym for Location, Economics, Demography, Past, Power Balance, Adversaries, Alliances, and Leaders.

- **Location:** The first thing is to geographically situate the issue by understanding its location and proximity. Please look at the neighbours and weigh their inter-se importance, geographical (locational, resource wise, demographics, and other connected factors) in global and regional context. Just to illustrate, the Suez Canal, Strait of Hormuz, Red Sea, and Malacca Straits can be leveraged as choke points, even in vast open maritime environment. It will be relevant to take a careful look at the maps included in this explainer. In this context, it will be most relevant to quote, 'While nations can choose friends, they cannot change their neighbours.' India is saddled with two inimical ones, Pakistan and China, with both acting in collusive mode posing major challenges for us. An interesting exercise could be to acquire maritime orientation. Turn India's map around and assimilate peninsular India's maritime domination over the Indian Ocean or Indo-Pacific; it is probably the greatest blessing by geography on us. It bears reiteration that approximately 80% of global cargo and energy is transported on sea lanes.

- **Economics:** The second key parameter is geo-economics, which entails mapping resources, trading linkages, and supply lines. Resource mapping entails: natural, derived (manufacturing and services), and human resources. As an example, Qatar, having the largest proven gas reserves, has considerable out of proportion geo-economic clout, notwithstanding her size. The United States (US) intervention in Ukraine is mainly driven by mineral wealth, especially rare-earth minerals and its agricultural wealth.

- **Demographics:** The third important factor is demography: population and its size and distribution. Profiling should include ethnic, tribal, and theological fault lines like Islamic-Jews, Sunni-Shia, Punjabi-Baluchi-Pashtun-Sindhi in Pakistan, and Meitei-Kuki-Naga in Manipur.

- **Past:** It is invariably the history that drives the present and complicates it.

- **Power Balance:** Comparative power balance and its defining effects need to be factored in. Nuclear weapons provide nations with a great degree of protection. If Ukraine had not given up its nuclear weapons, it probably would not have faced Russian aggression.

- **Adversaries:** In keeping with Sun Tzu's seminal wisdom, it is critical to know your adversaries in detail.

- **Alliances:** The next important parameter is alliances and partnerships with adversaries. These vary from global ones like the North Atlantic Treaty Organisation (NATO) to regional ones like the Association of South East Asian Nations (ASEAN). It is important to understand their objectives (stated and unstated/covert) and membership. Some, like NATO, have a security orientation, whereas others, like ASEAN, may have purely economic cooperation as the focus. Shanghai Cooperation Organisation (SCO) was formalised with proper structure, whereas others, like G-20 and Quadrilateral Security Dialogue (QUAD), have rotational staffing. It is also relevant to reiterate that there are no permanent friends/allies, increasingly referred to as partners, but only permanent interests.

- **Leadership:** The factor is leaders at the helm as often ineptitude and sometimes arrogance has not only created challenges and conflicts but also prevented their resolution. Just to name a few, leaders like Hitler, Stalin, Saddam Hussain, and Fidel Castro have had defining influences. Added to this list now are Vladimir Putin, Zelinsky, and Xi-Jin Ping, but at the very top is the maverick, Donald Trump.

To sum up, the template for analysis is – LED-P^2A^2L. But this list is only indicative, and more factors relevant to the subject should be considered and factored in for comprehensive analysis. There can be no standard template to cover all eventualities yet empirical analysis, centred on these factors, can help to discern likely trends, scenarios, and outcomes.

LED-P^2A^2L

L – Location-Geography

E – Economics

D – Demography

P – Past-History

P – Power Balance

A – Adversaries

A – Alliances

L – Leadership

Suez Canal
Strait of Hormuz
INDIA
Bab-el-Mandeb
Malacca Strait
Sunda Strait
Lombok Strait
Mozambique Channel
Cape of Good Hope

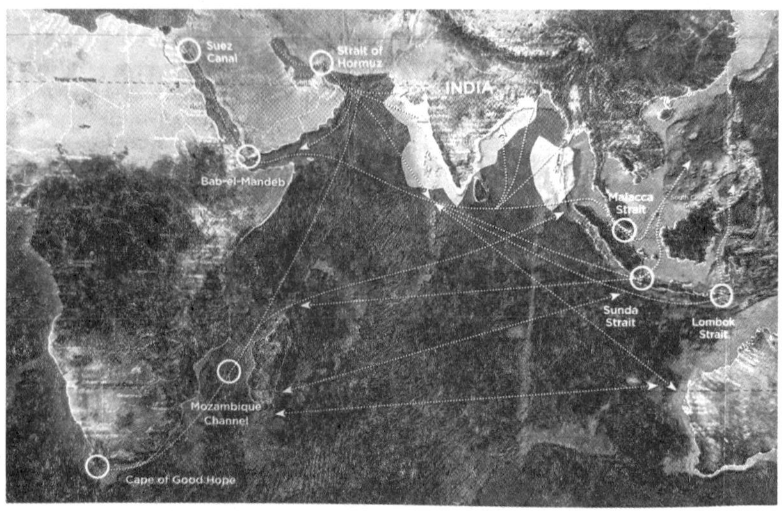

(Map source – www.sirjournal.org/research/2018/7/5/indias-indo-pacific-strategy-understanding/ indias-spheres-of-influence)

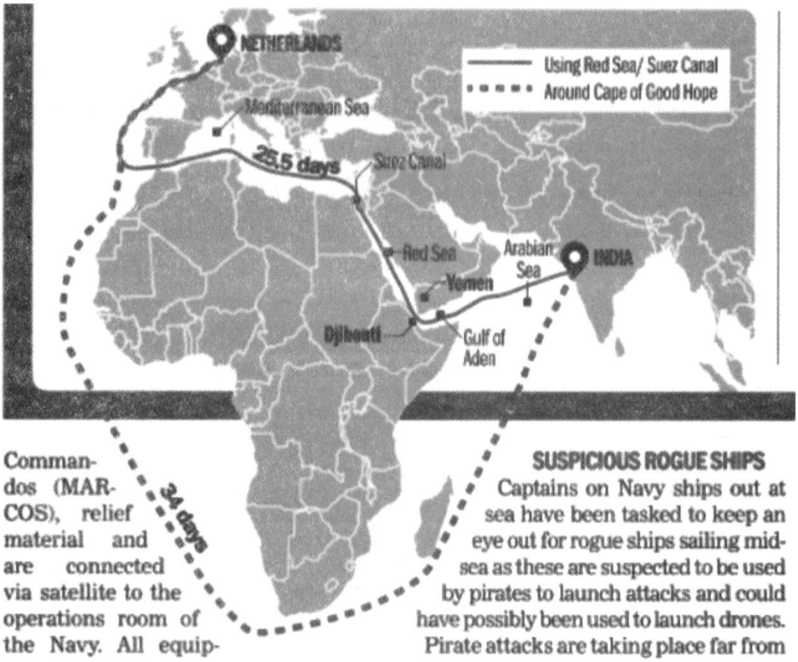

NETHERLANDS
Using Red Sea/ Suez Canal
Around Cape of Good Hope
Mediterranean Sea
25.5 days
Suez Canal
Red Sea
Arabian Sea
INDIA
Yemen
Djibouti
Gulf of Aden
34 days
Commandos (MARCOS), relief material and are connected via satellite to the operations room of the Navy. All equip-
SUSPICIOUS ROGUE SHIPS
Captains on Navy ships out at sea have been tasked to keep an eye out for rogue ships sailing mid-sea as these are suspected to be used by pirates to launch attacks and could have possibly been used to launch drones. Pirate attacks are taking place far from

(Map credit – www.tribuneindia.com/news/features/guarding-the-sea-indian-navy-has-fielded-12-anti-pirate-patrolling-ships-in-the-arabian-sea-581035)

Opening Perspectives

2.1 Pahalgam Terror Attack – Crafting a Response Strategy

Just when it appeared that the trajectory of economy in Kashmir had gathered traction with increasing influx of tourists, Baisaran Valley in Pahalgam was jolted by a dastardly terrorist attack. The attack, though denied by Pakistan, has unmistakable links to the deep state across. Consequently, the whole nation is angry and making strident demands for revenge. PM Narendra Modi has assured of stringent action against the perpetrators and securing justice for victims. Both sides have initiated a slew of politico-diplomatic measures. However, there is war hysteria building up and a cascading demand for kinetic-action by the Indian public. The Pakistan Army is scrambling to take up positions, and people across are nervous. The obvious questions are: when and how much of kinetics is likely? Unfortunately, ill-informed TV experts have sensed a Television Rating Point (TRP) opportunity and converted it into a somewhat comical side-show.

Missed Warnings

Lots has been written about the build-up to the attack and possible motivations of initiators of cowardly attack. It will be appropriate to accept that there has been failure on part of intelligence agencies, despite clearly articulated intransigence by Pakistan, coupled with gaps in our inter-agency coordination. However, post-mortem and correctives can be done discreetly and shared at the appropriate time, as long as we ensure that accountability is non-negotiable. The first signal was generated by Lt Gen Ahmed Sharif Choudhary, DG-ISPR (Director General of Inter-Services Public Relations), after the Jaffer-Express fiasco. He vowed *badla* (revenge) and blamed elements from India for train hijack. **This was accentuated by a highly provocative statement on the 'two-nation' theory by Army Chief Gen Aseem Munir.**

It may be appropriate to recount that a diabolic drift in the Pakistan Army was initiated by Gen Zia-ul-Haq. He gave a theological twist to its motto with 'Jihad-fi-Sablillah' and added the defence of ideological frontiers in its role. It was sustained by others like Gen Aslam Beg and Gen Pervez Musharraf. Gen Munir is a sort of an outlier, a 'dark horse', and a rare OTS achiever, with a somewhat ordinary track record. After two and half years at the helm, there is no point in getting surprised at his mullah orientation. Born to an imam, he had Madrasa education, supplemented with Hafiz (formal theological course) in Saudi Arabia, while on a military diplomatic assignment. **Ironically, all four—Zia, Aslam Beg, Musharraf, and Munir—are called Mohajirs as their families migrated from India during the Partition.** Even while describing Kashmir, as the jugular has been a constant theme across, Gen Kayani termed it as India's 'Shah rug'. The only difference is, Munir, surprisingly, called it Pakistan's jugular. In the long list of Pakistan Army Chiefs, somewhat moderate ones were Generals Jehangir Karamat and Qamar Javed Bajwa. The timing of Munir's uncalled-for diatribe was triggered by his yearning for an extension. He is unsettled by the growing dissent in junior ranks, coupled with recent statements by Karamat and other senior veterans calling for a review of the ongoing mismanaged operations, in Khyber Pakhtunkhwa (KPK) and Baluchistan.

Attack – Objectives and Challenges

In brief, the attack was designed to derail the booming tourism, which was reviving the economy and derail the process of normalisation in Kashmir. The targeting is also to exploit the festering fault line

in our society. Most regrettably, irresponsible politicians are only adding fuel to fire. It will be appropriate if we don't fall prey to this diabolic plot. The angst in the Kashmiri *awaam* is unprecedented and notwithstanding, it being driven by loss of livelihood, it is credible, with the possibility of strategic pay-offs. The bigger challenge is to revive tourism with assured security and incentives.

The government has initiated the first tranche of measures in the politico-diplomatic domain. However, people are demanding actions more lethal than surgical raids and the Balakot strike, along with verifiable evidence. Due to various factors, earlier measures resulted in a sort of a temporary stalemate, with limited deterrence value, which seems to have eroded. Unfortunately, expectations have hyped-up due to masochist declarations. It will be appropriate to recall that hysteria, whipped up after the Kandahar hijack, forced the government to release terrorists like Masood Azhar. The seminal wisdom is that governments and armed forces don't act in anger and haste. Retribution, unlike revenge, will have to be timed and calibrated to retain control on the escalation matrix. The other pivot of the matrix is not only a nuclear nation but, interestingly, one with self-proclaimed, cultivated irrationality in dealing with us.

Suspension of the Indus Water Treaty (IWT)

The most significant non-kinetic measure is holding IWT in abeyance. The notice on its review was given in January 2023 and reiterated in October 2024. Holding the treaty in abeyance is a well-thought-out escalation. After the commissioning of the Shahpur-Kandi project (with balancing reservoir) and repairs of the Hussainiwala barrage, we have established effective control on the waters of the eastern rivers—Ravi, Beas, and Sutlej. Even for the western rivers, stopping of sharing of hydrological data itself would accentuate psychological fear and uncertainty amongst Punjabi *Waderas* (large land holders), who are an extension of the military establishment. Though run-of-the-river, the Kishenganga project (on the Jhelum) and Salal and Baglihar (on the Chenab) have limited storage, which can be leveraged to upset crop-cycles in Pakistani Punjab. When Baglihar was filled in 2011, there was huge outcry in Pakistan, with reports of 30–40% drop in crop output. We have an urgent need to flush and de-silt the Kishenganga and Salal reservoirs, and this is the appropriate time to do it. We should expedite work on on-going projects on the Chenab and the Wullar Barrage on the Jhelum. **More importantly, Kashmir's water flowing across is diverted through link canals to Punjab, and it is time Kashmiris took ownership and drew benefits.**

Way Ahead

There are many more possibilities in the cyber, maritime, and aerospace domains besides conventional air-land options. Every action is likely to invite a seemingly equal and immediate response from Pakistan. Their sequencing and de-risking will have to be considered in great detail to ensure that it doesn't derail our journey to Viksit Bharat. In long term, we need to establish effective punitive deterrence.

2.2 Operation Sindoor – A Limited Operation with Potent Messaging

Operation Sindoor has been described by noted strategic expert, Brahma Chellaney, as shorter than the shortest—the six-day Arab-Israel war in 1967. Unless resumed, this paused conflict, has defied the recent global trend of unending and festering wars, notably, the Ukraine-Russia and Gaza conflicts. Yet, it cannot be dismissed as a mere skirmish because of the potency and significance of the messages delivered. These, of course, require consolidation. While signalling the new normal, it has also left few unanswered queries, which need to be examined. The most important one that many asked, using a cricket analogy—why declare when on the threshold of a century?

Characterisation of the Operation

It is difficult to propose the exact description for a mere 88-hour exchange triggered 14 days after a dastardly terrorist mayhem at Pahalgam, accounting for 26 innocent lives. **Notwithstanding its brevity, the conflict threatened to transition into the nuclear domain, bringing nuclear facilities in Kirana Hills in our daily debates. The operation was limited to the non-contact domain, with aerial delivery of lethal destruction adding kinetic dimension, more like a futuristic, sci-fi exchange.** Large formations were not even mobilised, so the intention to mount conventional offensive had not been firmed up. The navy was mobilised and deployed in coercive mode. Pakistan termed it's response as Operation Bunyan-un-Marsoos (Wall of Unity).

It was a short and intense operation, starting on the night of 6/7 May around 0130 hours with targeted strikes on nine terrorist hubs, including Bahawalpur [Jaish-e-Muhammad (JeM)], Muridke [Lashkar-e-Taiba (LeT)], and Mehmoona Zoya, Sialkot [Harkat-e-Mujahideen (HuM)]. In the second round, on the next night, on 7/8, Pakistan targeted military and civilian installations with large drone swarms. India responded in a proportionate manner. A significant target was the air defence (AD) installation at Lahore. On 8/9 night, Pakistan continued with indiscriminate targeting, which drew appropriate Indian response. On the final night, 9/10 May, in response to an escalation by Pakistan, Indian strikes covered 26 targets across Pakistan. Pakistan also fired missiles, targeting Delhi, which was intercepted at Sirsa. **India managed to retain control on the escalation ladder in all phases. There has been some discussion on the loss of two to three aircraft by India on the first night, including one or two Rafales.The loss of aircraft is an occupational hazard; however, it needs to be analysed. The Pakistan Air Force (PAF) also suffered considerable losses, including at least one Saab Airborne Warning and Control System (AWACS) aircraft.**

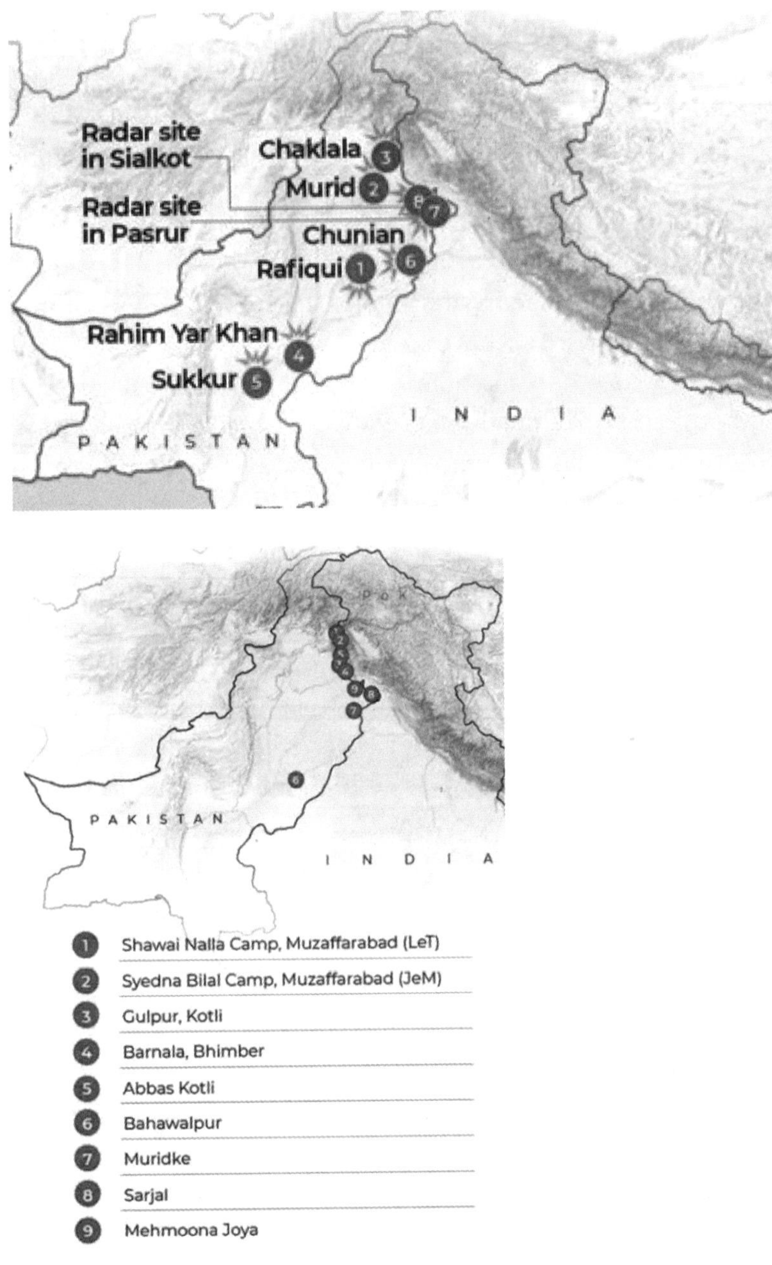
Radar site
in Sialkot
Radar site
in Pasrur
Chaklala
Murid
Chunian
Rafiqui
Rahim Yar Khan
Sukkur
INDIA
PAKISTAN
PAKISTAN
INDIA
Shawai Nalla Camp, Muzaffarabad (LeT)
Syedna Bilal Camp, Muzaffarabad (JeM)
Gulpur, Kotli
Barnala, Bhimber
Abbas Kotli
Bahawalpur
Muridke
Sarjal
Mehmoona Joya

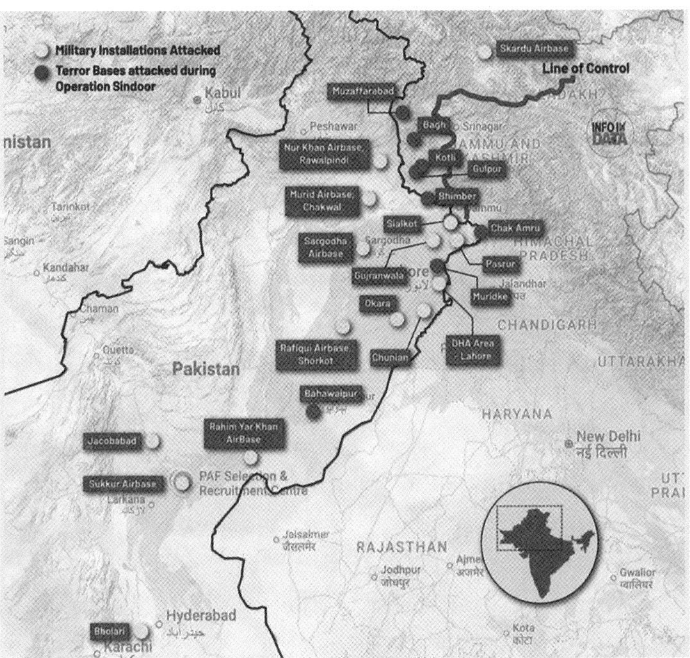

Missiles (beyond visual range) and drones were battling air-defence grids—HQ-9 based on the Pak side, and on our side—the Integrated Air Command and Control System (IACCS), Akash-Teer, and Counter-Unmanned Aircraft System (C-UAS). All three made an indigenous version of the Iron Dome, combining equipment of diverse origin—Russia, France, Israel, US—with indigenous developments. Defying the limitation of medium spatially, the geographic spread stretched from the north—Skardu—to the south—Bholari (Karachi). Most importantly, it touched the very heartland of Pak-Punjab-Rawalpindi, Lahore-Muridke, Sialkot, and Bahawalpur. Military targets that were degraded included key air-defence installations, command and control and logistics nodes, Sargodha, Chaklala, and Nur Khan bases (Rawalpindi).

The suspension of the IWT has given India a long-term, choke-hold leverage over the agro-economy of Pak Punjab. Pakistan is already pleading for reconsideration, and we need to remain focused on the pragmatic review. Politically, while India projected control and purpose, the Pakistani hierarchy displayed disparate voices and desperation. Pindi would certainly be in turmoil with the attack on terror hubs of Jamaat-ud-Dawa (JuD), LeT, JeM, and HuM, described by PM Modi as 'Universities of global terrorism'. All the bases/ determinants postulated in Pakistani nuclear expert Gen Kidwai's famous matrix of red lines for the nuclear threshold were attacked—spatial, military, economic, and political. Pakistan's nuclear sabre rattling was completely debunked once again. India has cemented space for conventional escalation created after Kargil and Balakot and enlarged it manifold.

India has also operationalised a refined, integrated response-matrix, synergising a large number of imported and indigenous platforms and systems. In mid-2016, when I retired, the considered view was that Pakistan had an edge over India in Air-Defence Control and Reporting (AD-C&R) with a dedicated AD Theatre Command. It is a great credit to our air-defence warriors that we not only fended off attacks but also degraded their defences, laying bare critical vulnerabilities. By some estimates, the PAF has lost 15 to 20% capability, largerly due to the deadly BrahMos strikes.

New Doctrine and Ceasefire

The new Modi doctrine has outlined three postulates. First, certainty of response: decisive retaliation on India's terms. Second, no tolerance for nuclear blackmail. Third, no distinction between terrorists and their sponsors/controllers. In his signature style, the Prime Minister ruled out terror and talks; terror and trade—further amplifying that blood and water will not be allowed to flow together.

There is a lot of chatter on the escalation ladder and suspension of exchange, which is sought to now be converted into ceasefire to conform to the agreements of 2003 and 2021. While we may not want to be seen to be pushed into ceasefire, yet, it is difficult to deny that a conflict between two nations armed with nukes will inevitably draw in global and regional powers. The ladder is a really complex matrix, and it would be influenced by the US, China, Russia, and even Arabs. With external dependencies, the stamina for extending conflict in the high-tech domain by both sides is limited. The ladder has become complicated with the addition of new domains of cyber and drones. The calibration of matrix and pace of escalation needs to be refined further. It appeared to have out-stripped the planned escalation in the current round. **The master stroke was the defining punishment delivered just before cessation. Strategically, we have achieved our objectives and avoided debilitating conflict, which could impede our journey towards Viksit Bharat.**

Way Forward

The country is galvanised with patriotic fervour, and it is time to build on national consensus. The government should go the extra mile to connect with sane elements in the opposition on the issues of national security. It is also time we addressed our internal fault lines, which are sought to be exploited by Pakistan. **To begin with, we need to redouble efforts towards socio-political initiatives in Jammu and Kashmir (J&K) and the North-East and fix accountability for lapses.**

While we have managed to put it across a prickly and persistent adversary, Pakistan, the primary one—the Dragon—lurks in the shadows. It would have mapped our capabilities and gathered electronic intelligence. It has also tested its weapons. **We need to prepare to dissuade China and Pakistan in a collusive mode.** Experts are referring to it as 'Single Front Reinforced' or even 'One Border-Three Adversaries' alluding to Pakistan assisted by China and Turkiye.

There is enough evidence that we cannot bank too much on external support. We need to revamp our diplomatic outreach to bolster support. 'Ekla Chalo Re' and 'Atma Nirbharta' are inspiring and even heady, but we can do with cooperative joint ventures what could be rebranded as 'Smart Atma Nirbharta'. **There is a definite and urgent imperative to refine our strategic communication. More**

importantly, rein in our electronic channels, who made a mockery of a refined operation.

In conclusion, one can only reiterate two guiding parameters. First, we need to adopt 'Josh with Hosh', as bigger challenges await us. Finally, for 'Viksit Bharat', we have to develop a culture of 'Viksit Samvad'.

2.3 Professional Analytics to Decipher Pakistan

The first time I met a Pakistani was in a UN Mission in Angola in 1992. He was a major with 15 years' service. I was a staff college graduate and had battled militancy in Punjab. Proxy war in the valley was in the nascent stage. In keeping with the requirements of military diplomacy, I drew on my reserve of Urdu, which I had picked up from movies like *Waqt*, *Taj Mahal*, and *Kanoon*, to strike conversation. He enquired if I knew Punjabi, and if so, why I was a Mohajir.That broke, in my mind, the entrenched stereotype of the Urdu-spewing Pakistani. It served as rude reality check. Every time he visited my HQ, I accommodated him in my container to understand his psyche.

The hijack of the of Jaffer-Express on 11 March was an incident that evoked much interest, and even celebrations, on social media. But it didn't wake up our intelligence experts, who should have anticipated immediate, violent reaction. After all, 380 passengers were taken hostage; 18 soldiers and 13 civilians were killed. It didn't take long, as within six weeks, we had the most dastardly Pahalgam attack.

The obvious question is: do we suffer from some sort of complacency in our analysis of intentions and capabilities of our neighbour? We have been following the objectives of no dialogue and minimum contact. It has been recently reiterated as—terror and talks/trade will not be permitted. Also, blood and water cannot be allowed to flow together. **Our broad game plan has been to render them irrelevant; keep them out of equation. These are indeed complex and difficult goals to achieve.** Objectively recounting, we negotiated the restoration of the ceasefire of 2003 on the Line of Control (LoC) in February 2021, aided by backroom parleys possibly facilitated by the UAE.

After Pahalgam, suddenly our experts discovered Gen (now FM) Syed Aseem Munir as the main culprit. The first signal was generated by Lt Gen Ahmed Sharif Choudhary, DG-ISPR, immediately after the Jaffer-Express fiasco. He vowed *badla* (revenge) and blamed the Research and Analysis Wing (R&AW) for the train hijack. This was accentuated by a highly provocative statement, on the 'two-nation' theory by Army Chief, Gen Munir. It may be appropriate to recount that diabolic drift in the Pakistan Army was initiated by Gen Zia-ul-Haq, Indian Military Academy (IMA)-trained, St Stephen's educated, hailing from Jullundur. He gave a theological twist with a new motto: 'Iman, Taqwa, Jihad-fi-Sabilillah' and, most surprisingly, added the defence of ideological frontiers in its role. Gen Aslam Beg, another a Mohajir from Azamgarh, triggered a proxy war in Kashmir. It was sustained by others like Gen Pervez Musharraf, a Mohajir with roots in Neharwali Haveli (Delhi). Gen Munir is a sort of an outlier and 'dark horse', a rare OTS achiever, with intelligence (Director General of Military Intelligence (DGMI) and Director General of the Inter-Services Intelligence (DGISI)) background. His posting profile is peppered with India-focused appointments.

After nearly two and half years at the helm, there is no point in getting surprised at his mullah orientation. Born to an imam father, hailing from Jullundur, he had Madrasa education. Like Zia, he is a Punjabi-Mohajir combo. Surprisingly, he earned the title of Hafiz by attending a Quran-recitation course in Saudi Arabia while on a diplomatic assignment. His description of Kashmir as the jugular has been a constant theme across Pakistani generals. Only a few years back, Gen Kayani called it India's 'Shah rug'. The only difference is that, Munir, inappropriately, termed it Pak's jugular. In the long list of Army Chiefs, somewhat moderate ones were Generals Jehangir Karamat and Qamar Javed Bajwa. The timing of Munir's uncalled-for diatribe was probably triggered by his yearning to recover his plummeting popularity. He was also unsettled by the growing dissent in junior ranks, coupled with recent statement by Gen

Karamat and other senior veterans, calling for a review of the ongoing mmismanaged operations in KPK and Baluchistan.

To quote Sun Tzu on enemies, 'Know the enemy and know yourself, in a hundred battles, you will never be in peril'. I would be audacious to add a few supplementaries to this seminal wisdom, reflecting our approach towards Pakistan. **First, all of us know them; they are not complicated like the Chinese; we don't need specialists. Second, they are irrelevant; there is no need to formally study them. In stark contrast, we have the China Study Group and multiple think-tanks. Even the Ministry of External Affairs (MEA) runs the Centre for Contemporary China Studies (CCCS).**

While China is the primary and complicated adversary, Pakistan is a persistent and prickly one. They consider us raison d'etre for their existence, and seek parity and attention. They certainly have the propensity to surprise us—unveiling the 6th Armoured Division in 1965—in Kargil (1999), and more recently, with their Chinese acquisitions. We have no formal study groups and think-tanks to analyse our western adversary except Twitter/TV channel warriors, who capture Karachi, Lahore, and PoK, periodically. **It is time we set up focused think-tanks and centres in universities to carry out meaningful analytics.**

In studying or influencing Pakistan, we have to differentiate target groups into—military establishment, mullahs (clergy), and awaam (public), customising content for each. Despite limiting contact, information and soft power continues to permeate through the Internet, as cognitive space does not allow vacuum. The common public in Punjab across the Radcliffe Line, communicates in Shahmukhi—Punjabi written in Persian-derived script. **Our attempts to set up Shahmukhi Linguistic Centre in Panjab University were dropped on the change of the Vice-Chancellor (VC) in 2018. Later, the counterpart university in Lahore set up a their Gurmukhi Department and chair. Expertise in dialects like Saraiki of South Punjab is also a critical requirement.**

PM Vajpayee said, 'We can choose friends but we cannot choose neighbours'. May I, most humbly, add to the seminal wisdom—

in order to render them irrelevant, we have to analyse them meaningfully.

Update: FM Munir managed to get invited for lunch with President Trump on 18 June. This raised speculation of Pakistan sneaking back into US's good books in exchange for providing bases and other concessions. The US would naturally return the favour.

2.4 Pakistan's New Great Game to Regain Strategic Depth

The array of targets, degraded by India during Operation Sindoor, unmistakably highlighted Pakistan's vulnerability in terms of the lack of geographical, strategic depth. At its broadest, the country is merely 450 km, with active insurgencies in its largest provinces—Baluchistan and Khyber Pakhtunkhwa. Hence, the options for secure basing and defensive deployment are severely constrained. Yet, it has always displayed significant measure of resilience, to retain relevance, in the traditional arena of the great geo-strategic game defined by the confluence of conflicting civilisations—Islamic (Arabic, Persian, and Turkic), Sinic, Slavic, and Indian.

Pakistan – A Balancing Expert

As early as 1963, Pakistan gifted the Shaksgam Valley to China and secured for itself the 'iron brother' relationship. In the Nixon-Kissinger era, it midwifed the courting of China by the US, which, despite proving disastrous, still gives Pakistan adequate balancing leverage in the US-China power play. It is indeed baffling to rationalise the courting of Pakistan by both. The US has thanked Pakistan for facilitating the apprehension of Mohammad Sharifullah, the mastermind of the Abbey Gate (Kabul Airport) suicidal attack on 26 August 2021, leading to the death of 13 marines. This Inter-Services Intelligence (ISI) ploy has been cashed many times, and it may be appropriate to recall Pakistan-vectored targeting of Al-Zawahiri in a Kabul safe house, on 31 July 2022. FM Aseem Munir recently attended the US Army's 250th anniversary parade. Central Command Commander Gen Michael E Kurilla, while briefing the Armed Services Committee, hailed Pakistan as a phenomenal partner in the fight against terror. It is indeed amazing to witness the continued, sinister manipulation by Pindi generals and the incredulous naivety of US top brass.

China, recently, in Operation Sindoor, staked her reputation and standing in the arms export market by providing Pakistan with not only platforms and munitions but, more importantly, seamless inter-operability. It extended access to BeiDou, and other surveillance systems. Chinese Foreign Minister orchestrated rapprochement between Pakistan and the Taliban by roping in Afghanistan in the China-Pakistan Economic Corridor (CPEC). It has the ominous portents of Taliban taking on the role of protectors and guarantors of the CPEC. Security has been the Achilles' heel despite the raising of two light divisions and the expansion of Frontier Constabulary and maritime security by Pakistan. The Mujahideen, who were once envisioned as pipeline police for Turkmenistan-Afghanistan-Pakistan-India (TAPI) energy grid may not be averse to becoming highway militia for the CPEC. It would also reduce the freedom of manoeuvre for Baloch and Pashtun insurgent groups. It could also revive Pakistan's long-term strategy of seeking strategic geographic depth in its western backyard. The Taliban will earn protection money as baksheesh (bribery), and shifting loyalties are rampant in this region. A quieter Durand Line and Iran border could enable Pakistan to turn its focus and mischief potential eastward. The US may even want to use Pakistan to keep Iran in check.

Strategic Depth – Multiple Dimensions

Pakistan's quest for strategic depth, often dismissed as floundering, merits a more nuanced consideration. Analysis cannot be driven by anger and moralistic considerations. PM Zulifkar Ali Bhutto and Gen Zia-ul-Haq can be described as two critical catalysts in Pakistan's endeavours. Bhutto steered an Islamic bomb projected as a collective security for the *ummah* (Islamic brotherhood). Iran's foray for a separate 'Shia' bomb, now degraded with Israeli attacks, could have further reduced the salience of the much-touted Pakistani capability. While it is right to infer that India has a reinforced space below the nuclear threshold, misguided and unsubstantiated narrative around Kirana Hills could well build sympathy for Pakistan in the Islamic block. It is imperative that this narrative is controlled and India continues to be respected as a responsible nuclear power.

Pakistan will certainly try and cobble at least a scaled-down version of the ballistic missile shield. Pakistan may resort to deeper and hardened tunnelling for basing and even for infiltration of the LoC. No defence-line or shield is impregnable, yet, it will certainly pose more stringent challenges in the next round. China now has access to a large amount of data gathered in Operation Sindoor, which could be weaponised against us.

Armies world over are committed to territorial frontiers and safeguarding them, but Gen Zia added 'ideological frontiers' as an additional commitment. The old motto, 'Ittehad, Yaqeen, Tanzeem' (Unity, Faith, Discipline) was jettisoned for 'Iman, Taqwa, Jihad-fi-Sablillah' (Faith, Piety, Struggle in the name of Allah (God)). *Quranic Concept of War* became the new guiding doctrine. The treatise is being misused to build a false notion of victory. In this conception, resilience and commitment to fight the next round defines the victory. We have witnessed the 1965 aggression being celebrated as Youm-e-Difa (day of defence), even when the reactionary, India, had an upper hand. Pakistan doesn't accept being defeated in the 1971 war, despite a humiliating defeat. India will have to be prepared to deal with terror.

Pakistan, afflicted with 'parity syndrome', utilised external balancing by joining the Central Treaty Organisation (CENTO) and Baghdad Pact in the 1950s. Unlike India, it has perfected the art of being a useful lackey on demand. The invitation to FM Munir by President Trump is indicative of Pakistan's continued relevance and utility. Currently, besides China, it has forged strategic Islamic alliance with Turkiye, Azerbaijan, and Qatar. The drift towards Ankara was anchored by Imran Khan even when India was steering Saudi Arabia and the Gulf nations towards a more balanced posture.

It is well known that the economy in Pakistan is on ventilator, yet, it has managed to establish a reasonable defence manufacturing ecosystem. Pakistan is leveraging Chinese technology for producing tanks, aircrafts, and missiles. It has even supplied artillery shells to Ukraine. There are already reports of projected collaboration in mining rare-earths and strategic minerals in Baluchistan. In sum, while we prepare for the next round of conflict, it will be pertinent to go beyond the geographical depth and give the devil its due. Like they say—forewarned is forearmed.

2.5 Taking Stock of Indian Defence Preparedness

Historical Perspective

India in Amrit-Kaal is gearing up to claim her rightful place on the global stage. This journey is marked by a multitude of challenges in the security domain—multiple wars and insurgencies. It is indeed appropriate to briefly map our conflicts to draw appropriate lessons.

To begin, the 1947–48 war by the Pakistan Army, masquerading as the Kabayali raiders, initially surprised the new nation. Analysts opine that the British were complicit in promoting the Pakistani plot to annex Jammu and Kashmir. It was also an attempt by Pakistan to gain salience and to emerge as a compliant buffer state for the colonial masters. India gained the upper hand due to its resilience and innovative responses. The fielding of Stuart tanks across Zojila by first stripping tanks and then re-assembling them across the pass surprised the enemy and stemmed raiders. Similarly, daring air support missions by basic aircraft defined our operational 'jugaad'. **The failure to press home the advantage and rush to the United Nations Organization (UNO) has left a festering Kashmir problem.**

The 1962 war caught us completely unprepared, but we can draw some solace from the bravery of our soldiers at Rezang La. **It was an all-**

around failure, and we didn't even use the air force, which could have stemmed the tide. Five years later, in 1967, Indian troops imposed heavy casualties on the People's Liberation Army (PLA) in localised conflicts at Nathu La and Cho La, to help us jettison the 1962 mentality.

The 1965 war was orchestrated by Pakistan, reportedly on the advice of US think-tanks, to take advantage of their technical asymmetry based on modern American equipment. The latest Patton tanks and Sabre jets were pitted against our obsolescent Centurion tanks and Gnats. Yet, our tank crews devised a three-round technique and the air warriors warded off the superior Sabre jets. The **1971 war remains a high point of our operational history, characterised by the sequencing of the campaign to preclude Chinese intervention, prioritisation of the Eastern Front, and bold application of air and naval forces.**

The Kargil war tested our capability to redeploy and marshal resources like Bofors guns and retain control on the escalation matrix. The war highlighted intelligence failure and the need to review our preparedness and organisations.

The recent **Balakot surgical strike and post-Uri coordinated surgical raids called off Pak's nuclear bluff and crafted space for conventional force application below the much-touted nuclear threshold.** The most notable trend was the nuanced selection of targets and the strategic messaging of Indian resolve to strike terror hubs beyond the Line of Actual Control (LAC), even beyond the PoK.

Proxy War and the Two-Front Connundrum

The first seeds of proxy war were sown in the misplaced use of Kabayalis and the instigation of revolt along religious lines in the J&K State Forces in the 1947 war. The same diabolic plan was repeated in December 1963 with the mysterious temporary vanishing of the Moi-e-Muqqadas (holy hair relic of the Prophet) to promote the uprising in J&K as a precursor to the 1965 war. It bears reiteration that task forces named after Islamic fighters like Salahuddin were deployed in the 1965 war. The Mujahideen narrative in Kargil in 1999 was another attempt to leverage persistent malfeasance. **The diabolic trend continues with the ISI-aided Khalistan separatist movement, the ongoing proxy war in Kashmir, and the K2 plot.**

Unknown to most, East Pakistan became a sanctuary for Naga rebels as early as the 1950s. Naga leader, Phizo, escaped to London via East Pakistan in 1956. Mowu Angami and other rebels had concurrently trekked to China for weapons and assistance. In the same period, Naga rebels were ferried from the Eastern to the Western wing for commando training. Pakistan gifted the strategic Shaksgam Valley to China without being in de facto possession and, more importantly, de jure jurisdiction. Both countries forged a strategic alliance, and China issued an ultimatum to India during the 1965 war when the tide turned against Pakistan. Notwithstanding these and other signals, there was a belief among the strategic community that China will stay out of Indo-Pak conflicts, despite late RM George Fernandes flagging China as the main enemy in 1990. There was a feeling that we needed to focus on hybrid war and deal with Pakistan in the short term.

Current Geo-Strategic Realities

India has recently been jolted by Chinese coercive salami-slicing deployments and fisticuff face-offs on the LAC, even while coping with the COVID-19 pandemic. A few defining trends that have emerged are:

- Firstly, **the two-front threat is real, besides internal fault lines. Bangladesh could pose another challenge.**
- Secondly, the **Chinese threat is the primary one, and the Northern Front is the main concern.**
- Thirdly, **collusive machinations have manifested between China and Pakistan, with Bangladesh joining them** in joint production of armaments, inter-operability, intelligence sharing, and strategic weapons, extending to other domains like the CPEC.

- Fourthly, **India has determination, political will, and resilience,** and if forced, it can successfully exercise Quid-Pro-Quo (QPQ) options, like the pre-emptive occupation of the Kailash Heights. Balakot and the coordinated surgical raids exemplify this determination.

- Fifthly, **coercive tactics have limits, and China simply cannot push its way through.** The de-escalation process on the LAC is indicative of this.

- **Most importantly, we have to remain focused on infrastructure development and force modernisation, as it is a long-term challenge.**

- The COVID-19 pandemic reinforced the **need for 'whole-of-nation' resolve and resilience, which was displayed in abundance. It also brought home the need to reduce dependencies and adopt a smart Atma Nirbhar approach.** Consequently, considerable headway has been made in this direction. There is also renewed thrust to develop infrastructure and ecosystem in border areas, such as the Vibrant Villages Programme (VVP).

Force Rebalancing

India has undertaken force rebalancing to match the Chinese posture on the northern border. One Strike Corps and additional formations, along with weapon systems, have been re-deployed on the northern borders. Orders for the raising of an infantry division and pullback of Rashtriya Rifles (RR) formations from Leh have been issued. **With this, India has created dedicated corps-sized reserves for the Ladakh and Arunachal sub-theatres. In addition, the Central and Sikkim sectors have dedicated reserves.** While retaining a defensive posture, the capability of QPQ, as also timely and effective offensive-defense responses—as witnessed in Yangtze and Doklam—is well as in place. Enough mechanised forces are deployed, and the Zorawar light tank is being developed.

Infrastructure development is on course and connectivity to forward areas has substantially improved under the Parvatmala project. The air force has also upgraded and developed new airfields in forward areas coupled with the deployment of the latest platforms, like Rafales. Drones and surveillance systems, are being inducted. Long missile systems like BrahMos and Pralay, are being positioned to match the Chinese Rocket Force. The navy is also modernising to tackle the increased Chinese forays in the Indian Ocean, consequent to the PLA acquiring the Djibouti naval base and the development of Gwadar as part of the CPEC.

India has joined alliances like QUAD and is trying to leverage others, like the Shanghai Cooperation Organisation (SCO), BRICS and the Bay of Bengal Initiative for Multi-Sectoral Technical and Economic Cooperation (BIMSTEC) to build deterrence and dissuasive influences. India has also established an enviable reputation in peace-building, disaster relief, and multi-national exercises. However, alliances have limited utility, as partners are unlikely to get directly involved or intervene in our conflicts.

Modi – National Security 3.0

The Armed Forces are engaged in a much-publicised agenda of transformation, technology absorption, and modernisation. While steady progress has been made, the following need to be expedited:

- The finalisation of the **National Security Strategy** (NSS); if required, sensitive portions can be kept classified.
- The operationalisation of **Theatre Commands and taking forward the concept of joint organisations,** structures, training, and doctrines.
- The transition from the current **space and cyber agencies to joint commands.**
- An objective **review of the Agniveer scheme** and the implementation of a modified scheme.

- **The designation of a National Defence University (NDU)**, even if it involves the designation of Rashtriya Raksha University (RRU) for this role.
- **The empowerment of Central Armed Police Forces (CAPFs)** for designated roles.
- **The simplification of the acquisition process to achieve Smart Atma Nirbharta.**

An Uncertain Future

The most important thing is to develop agility and resilience to deal with the geopolitical flux. A few important factors are:

- First, **adjusting to the post-Trump geo-economic and geo-strategic flux.** This could include tariff regime, greater reliance on US technology, and a consequent shift from Russian weapons.
- Second, there is also the talk of **carving out spheres of influences between the US, China, and Russia.** In this eventuality, the US may roll back its Indo-Pacific pivot, creating a severe challenge for us in coping with China.
- Third, and closer to home, there are **worrying developments in Bangladesh, including the possibility of China and Pakistan colluding with an increasingly Islamist Bangladesh**.

Way Forward

China is looking at developing Multi-Domain Warfare (MTDW) and has set up Strategic Support Force (SSF). It is also embarking on a comprehensive civil-military fusion mission. In sum, we can match China in the conventional sphere and are on course to reduce asymmetry. Yet, we need to remain alive to tackle future threats in the cyber and space domains. The three key recommendations are: firstly, expediting formation of theatre commands; secondly, the upgrading of cyber and space agencies; and thirdly, instituting non-lapsable capital fund with enhanced budget allocation. It will be apt to remember that preparation is the best deterrence, and preparation is never complete.

2.6 New Geo-Strategic Reality: A Global Arms Race

The world is increasingly witnessing festering and long drawn conflicts like the Ukraine-Russia war in its third year and Israel's Gaza offensive, now in its seventh month. Even where conflicts are currently capped, like in Syria, and Armenia-Azerbaijan, they are accompanied by uneasy calm and preparation for the next round. As per noted strategic analysts, in most conflicts, while there are no victors or vanquished, the biggest gainer—or the real winner—is the Military Industrial Complex (MIC). These conflicts, even if short and paused, like Operation 'Sindoor' or 'Bunyan-un-Marsoos', have been characterised by the employment of high-tech weaponry like drones, missiles, loitering munitions, AD shields, and surveillance systems.

A Global Perspective

Globally respected think-tank, the Stockholm International Peace Research Institute (SIPRI), in its annual 2025 report, flagged a significant increase in military expenditure, reaching US $2.718 trillion in 2024, approximating to a 9.4% increase from the previous year. In effect, it is the largest year-on-year rise since the end of the geopolitical rivalry during the Cold War in 1991. **The list is topped by five nations—the US, China, Russia, Germany, and India.** These five top spenders accounted for nearly 60% of global military expenditure. The US was right on top, with a 37% share, China was next, with 12%, and these two alone spent nearly half of total expenditure. Translated in GDP metric, expenditure accounted for nearly the 2.5% of global GDP. Analysing regional templates, expenditure increased in all regions, and most notably in Europe and Middle East. Turkey emerged as a significant arms exporter with its advancement in niche, disruptive technologies like the Bayraktar-TB2 drones. South Korea has become another important manufacturer in land, air, and marine systems. A very large part of outlay was on exports and imports, which remained the same over the last two comparative five-year cycles between 2015–2019 and 2024. However, it registered an increase of 18% in comparison with the 2005–2009 five-year cycle. Ukraine emerged as the largest importer due to the ongoing Russia-Ukraine war, followed by India.

Conflicts are not only boosting the order books of armament industries but also providing real-life combat conditions, as sort of test beds for weapons and systems. This has enabled the development of disruptive technologies like drones, loitering munitions, and missile defence systems. **It has also catalysed the adoption of commercial off-the-shelf (COTS) technologies, like Elon Musk's Starlink satellite terminals. As a parallel development, a large number of backyard start-ups have sprung up in Ukraine and Europe to develop low-tech and cost-effective drones/quad-copters.** The indiscriminate destruction evidenced in Aleppo, Gaza, Mariupol, Grozny, and other locations has entailed the use of huge stockpiles of munitions and attrition on delivery systems. Hence, there is an urgent requirement to replenish war reserves before the next round, further adding to the order books.

India – A Status Check

India was ranked as the fifth largest spender and second in imports. In year-on-year comparison, there was a 1.6% increase in expenditure, over the previous year—2023—largely driven by the Chinese threat. Notwithstanding these rankings, India managed to reduce its imports expenditure by 9.3%, powered by a sustained push for Atma Nirbharta (self-reliance). India has also made rapid progress in exports, in the past ten years—defence exports have gone up from ₹686 crores in 2013–14 to ₹21,083 crores in 2023-24, and ₹23,622 crores (approximately US $2.8 billion) in 2024–25, registering a 35% increase from 2022–23. There has been a 31-fold increase in exports over a ten-year period from 2013–14.

Initially, product mix was limited to artillery munitions, bullet-proof jackets, a few interceptor crafts, and Dornier transport aircraft. There was a significant increase in exports due to the Azerbaijan-Armenia conflict and the Russia-Ukraine war. India has added 155 mm artillery guns, Akash surface-to-air missile (SAM) systems, and BrahMos supersonic cruise missile in its export list. The biggest order was for $375 million for three BrahMos Coastal Defence batteries from the Philippines. **It is learnt that Vietnam and Indonesia have expressed interest in acquiring missile systems. It is also heartening that 60% of exports are now coming from the private sector and 40% from public sector enterprises. As many as 100 companies are involved in exports to 90 odd countries.**

The Indian Government is targeting ₹50,000 crores (US $5.9 billion) by 2029–30. India has undertaken major reforms to open up defence manufacturing to private players. The most significant is Tata entering defence aviation sector in partnership with Airbus industries for manufacturing C-295 transportation aircraft. **Even more important is the recent announcement to allow the private sector to participate in building the Advanced Medium Combat Aircraft (AMCA).**

Chinese Shadow

China has emerged as a trendsetter in significantly reducing its imports. Starting with largely Soviet-origin equipment, **it has followed a multi-lateral path of cloning, adaptive cloning, and independent development to become not only largely self-reliant but also a major exporter, especially to developing nations.** Chinese equipment is in service in India's neighbourhood, including Pakistan, Bangladesh, Myanmar, Sri Lanka, Nepal, and the Maldives. This gives the PLA presence through life-cycle support, repairs, and training—particularly in Pakistan..

China North Industries Group Corporation (NORINCO) has set up Heavy Industries Taxila for the licensed production of Haider (VT-4) and joint production of platforms like the Al-Khalid and Al-Zarar tanks. Similarly, Pakistan Aeronautical Complex in Kamra boasts of the joint production of JF-17 variants. **The integration displayed by Pakistan with Chinese systems in the recent Operation Sindoor/ Bunyan-un-Marsoos, particularly the use of PL-15 missiles, needs to be taken note of and factored into our aerial warfare doctrine.**

Operation Sindoor

India fielded a complex mix of French, Russian, Israeli, and American aircraft, AD systems, drones, and munitions, along with indigenous platforms and systems. **It is to the credit of our defence technical experts that they were integrated under the indigenously developed Integrated Air Command and Control System (IACCS), Akash-Teer AD system. BrahMos supersonic cruise missiles, the Akash AD missiles, SkyStriker drones, Netra AWACS system, and Counter-Unmanned Aerial System (CUAS) excelled.** India also customised legacy AD systems like the L-70 and ZU-23 with optoelectronic sights. **Pakistan fielded a mix of Chinese, US, and Turkish equipment.**

Fundamental Rules – Technology Partnerships

- First, **self-reliance is a long-term, tedious process.** It can be aided by genuine technology partnerships, coupled with achieving technology threshold in critical areas.

- Second, **an incremental and collaborative approach is the way forward.** BrahMos, a joint project with Russia, is currently only 76% indigenous and is likely to reach 85%. Hence, sometimes, it is smart to be the lead integrator and not focus on 100% indigenous content.

- Third, in **certain niche areas, disruptive weapons like Bayraktar drones** has given Turkey significant leverage. We need to emulate this approach.

- Fourth, **developing dual-use disruptive technologies, like Elon Musk's Starlink,** can redress technological asymmetry, as evidenced in the Ukrainian conflict.

- Fifth, **technology transfers preclude core and critical source codes. Hence, in Transfer of Technology (ToT), it is largely 'print or produce to design', at best, passing of 'know-how', but rarely the 'know-why'. There are unconfirmed reports of France refusing to share source codes of Rafale aircraft, thereby limiting integration with indigenous weapons/munitions.**

- Sixth, **reverse engineering is abundantly used—notably** by China and Iran—to clone crude versions of advanced weapons. The most important rule is: that there are no free lunches.

Challenges and Opportunities

As per the US Congressional report drawing on reputed sources like SIPRI, **India is the largest importer over the 15-year cycle of armaments in value terms, accounting for approximately 10% of global imports, from 2008 to 2023.** Russian-origin equipment accounts for 62%, declining from 76%. Other top suppliers are France (11%); the US (10%), and Israel (7%). **Our biggest challenge, as flagged by the Air Chief in the recent Confederation of Indian Industry (CII) Conclave, is the inability of Defence Research and Development Oganisation (DRDO) and Defence Public Sector Undertakings (DPSUs) to realise planned deadlines, with Tejas and main battle tank (MBT) Arjuna being striking examples.**

Failure of the Kaveri programme for aero-engines translated to reliance on US F-404/414. The supply of F-404 was delayed, slowing down the Tejas programme. Even the Apache attack helicopter delivery is pending. Similarly, delay in the supply of Ukranian marine gas turbines have caused significant delays in the induction of naval platforms. In case of powerpacks for tanks, Germany's Motoren-und

Turbinen-Union (MTU) failed to supply 800HP engines for the Zorawar, forcing a switch to the American 760HP Cummins. Even the Shakti engine for helicopters is a collaborative effort with Safran. **A national engine mission/challenge is long overdue.**

India deploys the largest fleet of T-90 tanks, even larger than Russia. We also have the largest operational inventory of C-17 Globemaster and P8I Poseidon aircraft outside the US. **The sheer size of Indian inventories provides an opportunity, as no major arms producer wants to be left out in this lucrative market. It is also the most appropriate global/regional hub for Maintenance, Repairs, and Overhaul (MRO) and warehousing.**

The Union of Soviet Socialist Republics (USSR)

India's experience with the Soviet Union has been mixed. The equipment is robust and relatively economical, but a notch below cutting-edge. Russia was benign in the early years, accepting rupees and even commodity (banana) payment. **They also leased strategic platforms like Chakra submarines, enabling the Arihant series. Notwithstanding the foregoing, many ToTs have essentially meant licensed production, often with annual caps on numbers, and the supply of spare parts has been unreliable.**

The US

The US follows the government-to-government route under Foreign Military Sales (FMS). **American equipment is cutting-edge, with reliable support, but it is expensive.** Only limited trials are allowed, offsets are difficult and possible only in peripherals. Source codes are not shared, obviating customisation, and have strict end-user restrictions. The US also has the Countering American Adversaries Through Sanctions Act (CAATSA). India managed a rare waiver for the S-400 AD systems from Russia.

Way Forward

It is time to realistically review the 42 Squadron target and bolster air power with drones and surveillance, transiting to a manned-unmanned mix. The integration of diverse equipment and the upgradation of legacy platforms are key challenges. PM Narendra Modi's national visit rolled out ambitious programmes like Catalysing Opportunities for Military Partnership, Accelerated Commerce, and Technology (COMPACT) and Transforming Relationship Utilizing Strategic Technology (TRUST). **Our challenge is to sidestep the traps like the F-35 offer and seek avenues for indigenous capability building and Smart Atma Nirbharta through meaningful technology transfers.**

2.7 Hamas to Hammer – Trump Unleashes Disruptive Disorder

The world in general and geo-political analysts in particular, are grappling with the disruptive disorder unleashed by President Trump. The new great game playing out in the Middle East really has no rules and very closely approximates the native Indian maxim of '*Jiski laathi uski bhains* (the one who wields the stick will commandeer the buffalo)', essentially implying might is right. In the process, the basic postulates that defined the Westphalian, rule-based order, collegiate consensus, and oversight by international bodies, like the UN, have been consigned to the overflowing Trump garbage bin of bizarre incoherence. In a single fortnight, more has happened to make it a theatre of absurdities than decades of reasoned geo-politics, even if there were aberrations galore, like the invasion of Iraq. The stark reality is that chaos will have long-term consequences till a new template is negotiated.

Unleashing of Chaos

The first nail in this coffin was driven by Russia's Special Military Operation in February 1922, dragging on for more than three years. The next act was a dastardly Hamas raid in Gaza on 7 October

2023. Israel, overcoming the initial setback, has utilised it skillfully to dismantle the dreaded arc of terror crafted by Iran. Resultantly, Hamas, Hezbollah, Hashd-al-Shaabi, and Houthis are in a complete state of disarray. Targeted assassinations have been leveraged to trigger psychological chaos.

Israel, as the new regional hegemon, enjoying US backing, has certainly overplayed its hard-power game. It is indeed sad that there has been no restraining influence, resulting in wanton destruction in Gaza, bordering on genocide. It also highlights rank hypocrisy in the designation of Putin as a war criminal, when Netanyahu is getting a free pass. This is the new normal, expanding from good/bad terror to benign/malevolent genocides and assassinations. Notwithstanding lunch parleys, it was high time and appropriate that Muridke and Bahawalpur were targeted by India. If Israelis are justified in their acts, non-escalatory and carefully curated targeting of terrorist infrastructure in Operation Sindoor is more than kosher. The desire for retribution, after the Baisaran (Pahalgam) massacre, was equally unprecedented. It had reached this tipping point after decades of frustration in combating Pakistan-sponsored proxy war.

Operation Rising Lion and Midnight Hammer

Emboldened Israel unleashed a supposedly knock-out punch, with possible twin objectives of destruction of nuclear facilities and regime change. Initially, Israel did score commendable gains in eliminating the top-brass of Iranian Forces, as well as the nuclear scientist hierarchy. However, it certainly underestimated Iranian resilience and missile arsenal. Iranian response exposed chinks in the Iron Dome, as approximately 35–40% of Iranian missiles managed to breach the famed missile shield. This probably forced a rethink, as IDF and Mossad actions, at best, degraded some nuclear facilities and scientists.

Iran is a civilisational power with a formidable knowledge and resource base. The nation seems to have rallied around the regime. In any case, even if regime change is effected, it may turn out to be just another shade of the same theocratic and autocratic hue, like Khomeini and Khamenei. More importantly, the dominant Shia faith has an inherent, considerable capacity to suffer punishment, and hard power alone may not be enough to subdue it. In the long term, the resolution lies in negotiations, especially when the US National Intelligence Agency (US-NIA) discounted Iran's capability to acquire a nuclear weapon in the short term.

Israeli losses were mounting, its inventory was getting degraded, and there were considerable economic losses. In terms of bearing punishment, Israel has obvious limitations, in demography and geographic dispersion, compared to Iran. It also forced a review, in its aims, as the regime change idea was disowned by both Israel and the US. Interestingly, the fickle-minded Trump regime is also on the verge of disowning Tulsi Gabbard, the much-celebrated head of the US-NIA. It is to the credit of Israel that it managed to do the unthinkable and get the US to launch Operation Midnight Hammer, after a fortnight of increasingly stalemated operations. The bombing raid on the night of 21/22 June targeted Fordow, Natanz, and Isfahan nuclear sites. The US deployed the ultimate vectors, B-52 stealth bombers, and as many as 14 GBU-57A/B MOP (Massive Ordnance Penetrator) bunker buster munitions, along with Tomahawk missiles. Decoy deployments and aerial refuelling were utilised to operationalise the secret plan, which was honed for 15 odd years.

Damage Assessment

President Trump, in his characteristic hyperbolic claim, has asserted that the Iranian nuclear ecosystem is completely obliterated. He immediately declared a ceasefire and diabolically described it as a 'bombing for peace' mission. More pragmatic official briefings have been conservative and, on being repeatedly queried on damage, have stated that assessment is underway. Iran did retaliate, targeting Al-Udeid, a US base in Qatar, on 23 June, but only after 40 fighter jets and a thousand odd troops had been relocated.

The media is abuzz with reports that Iran seems to have relocated 400 odd kg of enriched uranium (60% against the planned 90% for weapon grade) before the bomb run. This Highly Enriched Fuel (HEF), if relocated, could become the key leverage for Iranian resurgence. There are also conspiracy theories of this being a largely choreographed operation. In a world defined by misinformation and cognitive warfare, it is difficult to access reliable information. In all probability, the Iranian nuclear weapon mission is degraded and delayed by one to two years. Yet, its resolve is hardened, and the quest for the bomb will go deeper and more secretive. Iran seems to be isolated with only nominal support. In fact, Saudi Arabia and the Gulf nations would be relieved with the defanging of Iran in nuclear and terror dimensions.

Way Forward

The ongoing operations have shifted focus to a non-contact mode of war-fighting with long-range vectors—missiles, drones, and missile shields. Armament manufacturers are the only winners in losing battles. The desire to acquire nuclear weapons, as an ultimate shield, will only proliferate. Meanwhile, is it time to write an obituary for the UN and nuclear regulatory organisations like the International Atomic Energy Agency (IAEA)? The real casualty of this incoherent, new world order may be the very institutions, once meant to prevent it.

Securing Our Borders

3.1 Understanding the Security of Our Borders (Written in 2017 and updated in July 2024)

Key Takeaways

- Before reading this article, please take a self-quiz. With which country do we have the longest land borders? Most readers answer Pakistan or China, but the correct answer is Bangladesh.
- Despite numerous studies, including the Kargil Review Committee Report, we have been unable to achieve the agreed 'One Border, One Force'. The same complexity prevails even for internal security. In Manipur, we have Assam Rifles (AR), BSF, CRPF, ITBP, SSB, besides the state police.

Introduction

Securing and managing a 15,106 km long and tough land border and a 7,516 km long coastal boundary is a major challenge for the country and also one of the topmost national priorities. The Ministry of Defence (MOD) and Department of Border Management, part of the Ministry of Home Affairs (MHA), are tasked with securing most of India's borders, with some of their key objectives being to prevent infiltrations and drug smuggling as well as facilitate transit, trade, and safe movement of people. While doing so, forces deployed are confronted with challenges of infiltration, transgression, border raids, smuggling of weapons, drugs, goods, human trafficking, counterfeits, and cattle smuggling.

The western borders have witnessed three full-scale wars in 1947, 1965, and 1971, one limited war in Kargil in 1999, and an ongoing proxy war with Pakistan since 1989. On the eastern borders, besides the war in 1971 with erstwhile East Pakistan, China launched an all-out war in 1962, followed by skirmishes in 1967. **The main cause of these ongoing challenges is the unresolved status of our borders with China and Pakistan.**

Preview

The article is laid out in the following parts:

a) Analysis of Borders
b) Responsibilities and Manning Pattern
c) Challenges and Options
d) Recommendations

Scope

The scope of this article is limited to land borders.

An Analysis of Our Borders

Land Borders: India shares land borders with the following six sovereign states:

a) **Afghanistan:** 106 km (66 miles) – **The border is currently included in the illegal part of PoK and is referred to as the Wakhan Corridor; hence, it cannot be manned by India. It is 'de jure' claimed but not de facto under control.**

b) **Bhutan:** 600 km (370 miles) – This is a relatively **open border** manned by the Sashastra Seema Bal (SSB).

c) **Myanmar:** 1,643 km (1,021 miles) – The border has a **Free Movement Regime based on traditional tribal laws permitting transit with head loads to ethnic stock up to 16 km and stay**

up to two weeks without a visa. This border is manned largely by the Assam Rifles with oversight by the Indian Army.

d) **Nepal:** 1,758 km (1,092 miles) – **This is an open border manned by the SSB.**

e) **Pakistan: 3,323 km (2,065 miles) – This is the most complex border with a settled International Border (IB), disputed Maritime Border (MB), LoC, and Actual Ground Position Line (AGPL). The IB and MB stretches of the border are manned by the Border Security Force (BSF) and balanced by the Indian Army, assisted by the BSF.**

f) **China:** 3,380 km (2,100 miles) – **This is an unmarked, disputed border referred to as the LAC and has trilateral dimensions, with certain areas overlapping Bhutan, Nepal, Myanmar, and even Pakistan, if the illegally ceded Shaksgam Valley is included.** This border is manned by the Indian Army and the Indo-Tibetan Border Police.

g) **Bangladesh:** 4,097 km (2,546 miles) – **This border is the longest and is manned by the BSF.** Recently, the complexity on this border was reduced by a mutually agreed exchange of enclaves.

h) **Sri Lanka:** 30 km (19 miles). – This border is on the Ram Setu sand dune, manned by the Indian Coast Guard (ICG).

Maritime Borders

India has maritime borders with seven countries, including Pakistan, the Maldives, Sri Lanka, Thailand, Indonesia, Myanmar, and Bangladesh. Unconventional intrusion by Pakistan-backed terrorists through the Arabian Sea, leading to dastardly 26/11 Mumbai attacks, has indeed opened the possibility of 'Samudri Jihad' (terror from sea) and consequent need for enhanced maritime security. Many states have raised the Coastal Police forces.

Indo-Pak Land Border

Growing Complexity and Disputes: After the Partition in 1947, the border was based on the hurriedly drafted Radcliffe Line, which divides Pakistan and India from each other, traverses a variety of terrains, including inhospitable stretches, viz., swampy Rann, deserts, riverine, hilly, and glaciated areas. Since independence, the border has been contested, has witnessed numerous conflicts and wars, and is one of the most complex, contested, and dangerous borders in the world. The border's total length is 2,900 km (1,800 miles). It can be seen from space at night due to the 1,50,000 floodlights installed by India on about 50 thousand poles. **While the mutually agreed IB is well marked, patrolled, and has joint mechanisms, there are issues connected with illegal infiltration, smuggling, and difficulties associated with the management of agriculture, which extends right up to the very zero line and beyond the boundary fence, which is on the Indian side.**

Disputed Portions: Immediately after Partition, Pakistan launched a war in Kashmir and annexed portions of Indian territory. The redefined status quo was mandated by the Karachi Agreement in 1949, and this temporary arrangement, established under United Nations (UN) supervision, was called the Ceasefire Line (CFL). Despite the 1965 war leading to the Tashkent Agreement, the status quo of the CFL was maintained. India squandered the major leverage of 93,000 prisoners in the 1971 war, and the only concession obtained in the Shimla Agreement was that while the border south of J&K was sanctified as IB, the portion of J&K was accepted as LoC.

The contested portions of this border include the following:

- **Maritime Boundary (MB):** This 96-km tidal estuary of Sir Creek is adjoining the Rann of Kutch and includes the disputed portion of Sir Creek. Please see the accompanying graphic.
- **LoC:** The Indian LoC fencing, Anti-Intrusion Obstacle System (AIOS), is a 550-km (340 miles) barrier along the 740-km (460

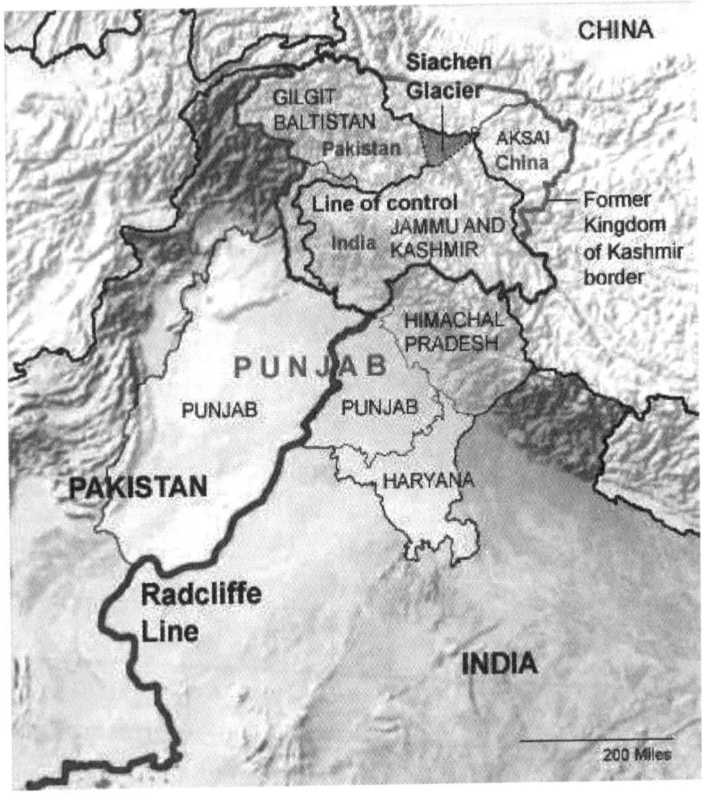

miles) disputed 1972 LoC (or a modified version of the CFL). **The fence, constructed by India, generally remains about 150 yards on the Indian-controlled side. Its stated purpose is to exclude arms smuggling and infiltration by Pakistan-based separatist militants.** The barrier itself consists of a double row of fencing and concertina wire, eight to twelve feet (2.4–3.7 m) in height, that is electrified and connected to a network of motion sensors, thermal imaging devices, lighting systems, and alarms. They act as 'fast alert signals' to the Indian troops, who can be alerted and ambush the infiltrators trying to sneak in. The small stretch of land between the rows of fencing is mined with thousands of landmines. The construction of the barrier began in the 1990s but slowed in the early 2000s as hostilities between India and Pakistan increased.

After the November 2003 ceasefire agreement, building resumed and was completed in late 2004. LoC fencing was completed in the Kashmir Valley and the Jammu region on 30 September 2004. According to Indian military sources, the fence has reduced the number of militants who routinely cross into the Indian side of the disputed state to attack soldiers by 80%.

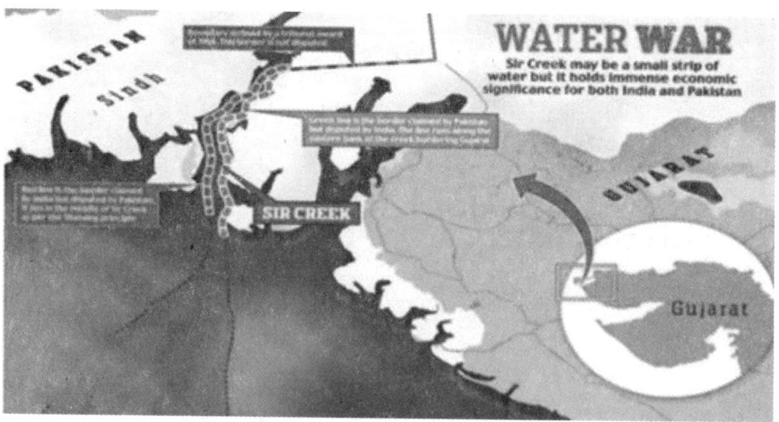

- **Working Boundary (WB):** Despite agreement and proper IB fencing to a point north of Jammu, covering the districts of Jammu, Samba, and Kathua, Pakistan has resurrected the bogey of the whole of J&K being unresolved. Hence, this stretch is called WB by Pakistan. This 198.4 km of border, as per Pakistan, is WB because while on one side Sialkot is settled, on the other side, J&K is still disputed. **From the Indian perspective, we should continue to use IB and avoid using WB, at least in official formal documents.**

- **Actual Ground Position Line (AGPL): The AGPL is the line that divides the current positions of Indian and Pakistani troops in the Siachen Glacier region.** The line extends from the northernmost point of the LoC, also referred to as NJ 9842, to Indira Col. The AGPL is approximately 110 km (68 miles) long and was created to counter the surreptitious efforts of Pakistan to grab this glaciated but strategically vital territory.

Responsibilities and Manning Pattern

Maritime Defence: The primary responsibility of the defence of the maritime border vests with the ICG, assisted by the Indian Navy and Coastal Police under respective state governments. This layered mechanism has coastal radars and a plethora of surveillance mechanisms, many of which are still to be operationalised. The major problem is the creation of an empowered and dedicated maritime security agency. The subject requires a separate and detailed analysis. India now has a dedicated Maritime Security Advisor in the National Security Council.

Land Borders: The manning on land borders is ideally to be governed by 'One Border, One Force'. However, the same is not fully achieved, and currently, responsibilities are divided as follows:

- **Indo-Pak Border:** Currently manned by the **BSF, although in the LoC portion, the primary responsibility is with the Indian Army.** While operational control in such areas is with the army, administrative control is retained by the respective CAPF. It is dealt with in the section on Pakistan.

- **Sino-Indian Border: The designated CAPF is the Indo-Tibetan Border Police (ITBP), but this being an unfenced disputed border, also referred to as LAC, de facto responsibility is with the Indian** Army. This aspect has been covered in greater detail in the section on LAC.

- **Bangladesh: Fencing on the Bangladesh border has been completed for 3,180.65 km out of 4,096.7 km. The main challenge is human and cattle smuggling. Tidal areas are another challenge, and the BSF is creating a marine wing for tidal stretches.** The graphic on this border is included.

- **Other Borders: The SSB has a mandate for Bhutan and Nepal; there is no clarity on Myanmar, where there are reports of a move to transfer responsibility from the Assam Rifles to BSF/ITBP.** A separate article is included on securing the Indo-Myanmar border in this section. Relevant aspects of the border with Bhutan are included in the section on the Sino-Bhutan border. A graphical snapshot of the contested portions of the Indo-Nepal border is included. The dispute with Nepal is rooted in the origin and course of the Kali River. Nepal claims it at Limpiyadhara, whereas India maintains Kalapani as the source.

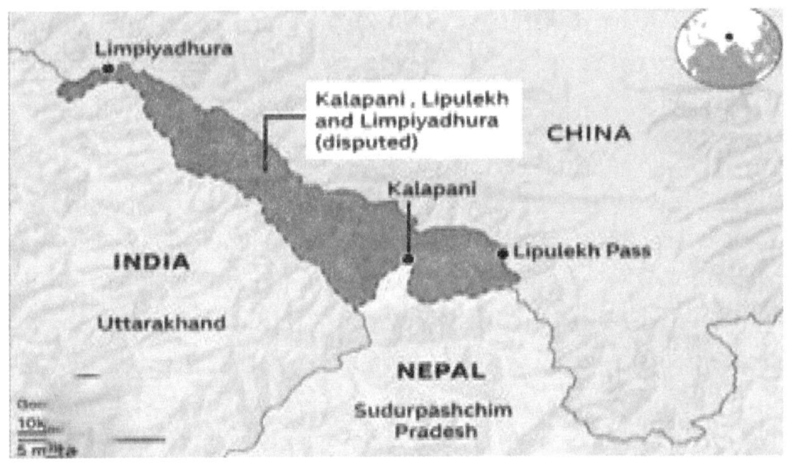

CAPFs – Varying Charters

The Kargil Review Committee (KRC) and other expert groups have highlighted the need for segregation between law and order, internal security (IS), and border management. State police, including the India Reserve Battalions (IRBns), are mandated for law enforcement and IS. The CRPF is responsible for this task, when called for, as well as in areas notified as disturbed areas. **The Border Management function is the charter of BSF, ITBP, SSB, and Assam Rifles. This function can be further divided into Border Guarding (BG) and Border Defence (BD).** BG is for demarcated borders described as IB, which are fenced and have a structured, joint patrolling routine and surveillance/lighting infrastructure. On open and unfenced borders, which are defined and not contested, like those with Nepal and Bhutan, it is again a border guarding responsibility. The Indo-Myanmar border is a sort of hybrid responsibility and is likely to undergo a transition from an open and unfenced to a fenced one.

The maximum complexity is on contested borders like the LoC on parts of the Indo-Pak border and the LAC with China, which is described as BD. On the Indo-Pak LoC, BD is the responsibility of the army, aided by the BSF. The LoC has ad-hoc fencing, described as an AIOS, but is subjected to infiltration due to terrain and abetment by Pakistan. Along the Sino-Indian LAC, the army is aided by the ITBP. The most fiercely contested portion is the AGPL in the Siachen glacier, guarded by specialised army troops.

Although, by and large, there is still a need to bring uniformity in the charters of border management CAPFs to make them interoperable. A careful and detailed reading of charters will bring out variations, which simply cannot be glossed over, even if they are termed as mere semantics.

Table – Tasks of Border Guarding/Defence Forces

S. No.	Assam Rifles	BSF	ITBP	SSB
1.	Safeguard the security of the borders of India and promote a sense of security among the people living in the border areas.	Promote a sense of security among the people living in the border areas.	Safeguard the security of the borders of India and promote a sense of security among the people living in the border areas.	Safeguard the security of the assigned borders of India and promote a sense of security among the people living in the border areas.
2.	Prevent trans-border crimes, smuggling, unauthorised entry or exit from the territory of India, and any other illegal activity.	Prevent trans-border crimes, smuggling, and unauthorised entry or exit from the territory of India.	Prevent trans-border crimes, smuggling, unauthorised entry or exit from the territory of India, and any other illegal activity.	Prevent trans-border crimes, smuggling, and illegal activities.

3.	Provide security to sensitive installations, banks, and persons at security risk.	Prevent smuggling and other illegal activities.	Provide security to sensitive installations, banks, and persons at security risk.	Prevent unauthorised entry into, or exit from, the territory of India.
4.	Restore and preserve order in any area in the event of disturbance therein.		Order in any area in the event of disturbance therein.	Carry out civic action programmes in the area of responsibility.
5.				Performed any assigned duty by central government.

Challenges and Options

Transgressions on the Sino-Indian Border: There are a **large number of areas where PLA troops periodically transgress to keep alive their claim. China has also leveraged ambiguity associated particularly with trijunctions**, like Mt Gipmochi in Doklam with Bhutan; the Lipulekh pass with Nepal, and the Diphu pass near Walong with Myanmar. Please read the chapter on LAC – Unresolved Stand-off for more details.

Limited Infrastructure: There is a lack of infrastructure in border areas **compared to the Chinese state-of-the-art railroad connectivity, which has created a huge asymmetry in response timings.**

Sparse Population: The border belt is dotted with ghost and deserted villages. Even where settlements exist, they are sparse and lack basic amenities and connectivity. **India has started the VVP to develop border villages to combat the Chinese Xiaokangs' border villages.**

Demographics: Many **border areas have seen an influx of certain segments of the population, who are more susceptible to exploitation by elements across.**

Other Options

Technological Solutions : World over, the trend is to seek technological solutions based on **smart fences, intrusion alarms, radar arrays, drones, unattended sensors, etc. India is making somewhat tardy progress in this discipline, which needs to be expedited.**

Manpower: No defence line can be protected merely by technical surveillance alone; hence, deployment of troops is inevitable. However, in our context, the burgeoning strength of the CAPF is being propelled by a turf-centric approach and also justified as a means of an additional employment avenue. However, the need is to right-size CAPFs and invest in quality rather than in quantity. There is an urgent need to have the right mix of technology and human resources. Parliamentary committees have flagged the need to absorb more ex-army personnel in the border management CAPFs. This needs to be achieved by absorbing maximum released Agniveers in CAPFs after reorientation training.

Automated Decision Making: The plethora of agencies on the **ground and technical ones generate a vast volume of data, which needs to be processed on a real-time basis on an automated decision support system.**

Recommendations

Border Resolution: There is a need to expedite border resolution talks with a view to arriving at an early solution, as good fences make good neighbours. In the interim, better confidence-building mechanisms and protocols like lines, border meeting points, and flag meetings should be factored in.

Unified Mandate: In areas where the mandate is border defence, relevant CAPFs should be placed under the army's control, with operational and administrative responsibilities, and mutually agreed career protection measures.

One Border, One Force – Early resolution of the designated force for the Myanmar border should be attempted. The employment of specialised border guarding troops in internal security should be reduced, and this should be entrusted to the CRPF. In Manipur, troops from all CAPFs—Central Reserve Police Force (CRPF), BSF, ITBP, SSB, and Assam Rifles—are deployed, which is indicative of a fire-brigade approach.

CAPF Cadres: The current CAPF cadres are headed at the apex by Indian Police Service (IPS) officers, who lack ground experience and a force culture. It is described as para-dropping by cadres and builds resentment in junior ranks, as they have no vacancies as Director General of Police (DGP) and are very limited in the Assistant Director General of Police (ADGP) ranks. It will be a good idea to have totally home-grown cadres with strong force affiliation, like the Coast Guard, where the navy has yielded control and stopped deputation in the Coast Guard. Another mixed cadre is the Assam Rifles, commanded by army officers on deputation and referred to as the Paramilitary Forces (PMF). This cadre also needs to develop its own integral cadre.

Expediting and Upgrading Fencing: Efforts should be made to complete pending fencing work and upgrade it with smart fences.

Special Administrative Cadre for Border Areas: The old model of the Frontier Areas Administrative Service, duly upgraded to contemporary requirements, should be applied in border areas. This issue was also highlighted by former Governor Mr NN Vohra in his report.

Right-Sizing: Like the Indian Army, CAPFS should also carry out an optimisation study and cut down the increasing flab.

Conclusion

For a country of India's size, terrain complexity, and array of neighbours, border management will remain a major and complex challenge requiring a 'whole-of-nation' dynamic approach. **Newer challenges, like drones and tunnelling to gain access, will manifest and require a dynamic approach.**

3.2 Securing the Indo-Myanmar Border

Update: The National Unity Government asked the Indian Government to suspend fencing work as the border was disputed. This was after a border skirmish accounting for ten armed cadres in the third week of May 2025.

Understanding Our Border

The unfenced, open-border starts in the north, in the vicinity of the Diphu pass, from the un-demarcated tri-point of India, Myanmar, and China. It runs down south and west, to another tri-point of India, Myanmar, and Bangladesh. It passes through Arunachal Pradesh (520 km), Nagaland (215 km), Manipur (398 km), and Mizoram (510 km). A large stretch is hilly, traversing the Mishmi, Patkai, and Chin hills, comprising the Arakan range. In addition, it is covered by thick jungles and is devoid of communication. The challenges are magnified by adverse climate, the presence of wildlife, and the near-total absence of local resources. The writ of the Myanmar state is rather notional, bordering the Kachin, Sagaing, and Chin regions, and even the neighbouring Rakhine state, enabling sanctuary and unbridled access for terrorist groups. The Arakan Army recently gained control of Paletwa, a critical node, on the proposed Kaladan multi-modal project, and now controls a large stretch of territory bordering India (Mizoram) and Bangladesh (Chittagong Hill Tracts).

India's border with Myanmar, remote and largely excluded from public concern, is open and unfenced. It is now in the news, with two important recent announcements. **The government has decided to fence a 1,643-km-long border. The government has also suspended the Free Movement Regime (FMR), which allowed transit up to 16 km on**

either side (with headloads) and a stay for up to 14 days on either side without a visa. This has been done in the wake of unrest in Myanmar, resulting in a large influx of Chin refugees in Mizoram and even Manipur. The implementation of both measures poses tremendous challenges and has evoked widespread opposition. Yet, regulation is required in view of the smuggling of narcotics, arms, timber, wildlife products, and, more importantly, the fear of demographic inversion.

Unlike the old maxim, 'good fences make good neighbours', this imaginary division runs through tribal settlements. **Derived from the Pemberton Line, it is like other boundaries crafted by the British colonial power, which left behind festering complexities. It has illogically divided tribes, like the Konyaks, Khiamniungan, Kukis, and Zomis, in the bordering areas of Nagaland, Manipur, and Mizoram.** The iconic house of the Angh (ruler) of Longwa bears special mention, where the line runs literally through his house. Mercifully, his writ runs over the entire village, spread on both sides of the border. Eastern districts in Nagaland have been demanding the creation of a separate administrative entity, like an autonomous council for the Eastern Naga People's Organisation (ENPO), on the lines of the erstwhile Tuensang Frontier Division.

Challenges and Complexities

The biggest challenge is to overcome resistance and win over tribal society, to build a shared stake for them in regulating access. In any case, land ownership being a collective tribal covenant, their partnership is imperative. Ironically, similar challenges are being faced by Pakistan in fencing the border between Baluchistan and Sistan (Iran). The Pak-Afghan border along the Durand Line, which separates the Afridis and Mehsuds, bound by a common Pashtunwali code, is even more complicated.

Analysis of defence lines, like the Maginot, Siegfried, Bar-Lev, and Berlin Wall, reinforces historical lessons—**no defence line is impregnable and determined intruders (like Fedayeen) will get through.** Defying the trends of globalisation and open borders, the desire to fortify borders has only increased. This is notwithstanding the recent breaching of the formidable Gaza Barrier, the so-called gold standard of defence lines. The requirement is for customised solutions based on an optimal mix of technology (smart fencing), backed up by human vigilance. **It would require considerable effort to get Myanmar on board and set up a joint monitoring mechanism. Equally important is to restore the credibility of our mandated force, the Assam Rifles.**

Way Forward

Securing entails fencing, manning, joint patrolling, and quick reaction. **Barrier systems need to be futuristic and have in-built redundancies, structured in layers, providing depth and reaction time.** While it is important to detect and deny access, the most critical imperative is a quick reaction system to rapidly localise the intrusion and deal with it. Tardy response and failure on this account led to not only high casualties but also Hamas escaping with hostages. It is important to bear in mind that while smartness has no limits, it entails a huge premium in cost. As the physical barrier takes shape, new threats—drones and tunnels—are likely to manifest, as is being witnessed, on the Punjab border. Both ends of the drug combo of Golden Crescent in Af-Pak and Golden Triangle in China-Myanmar are equally deadly, posing formidable challenges.

Currently, barely a stretch of 4 km near Moreh has rudimentary fencing. In addition, two hybrid surveillance-based pilot projects (1 km each) are under execution in Arunachal and Manipur. Fencing is demanded stridently by Meitei groups, but is opposed by the hill tribes. The valley-based population is rooting for a barrier, fearing demographic inversion, citing, somewhat, trumped-up fears of the Zomia tribal homeland. The government has given the go-ahead for the fencing of an additional 20 km in Manipur. Building such systems entails a long gestation period, even in fast-track mode. As per the MHA report of October 2023, fencing on the Bangladesh border has been completed for 3,180.65 km out of 4,096.7 km. The ministry has projected a highly optimistic deadline of March 2024 for the balance of 916 km. The main stumbling block, as stated in the Supreme Court, has been the availability of land, due to the reticence of the West Bengal government.

The project is likely to face multiple challenges, but given the firm resolve, ingenuity, and financial and technological back-up, it is certainly not an impossible objective. Planners will have to devise innovative solutions, like local participation in the erection and maintenance of a fencing system. The VVP can be harnessed to build incentives and imaginative solutions (tried in other borders), like bee farming and cultivation of medicinal plants. The **Act-East policy mandates access and connectivity, but regulated, yet hassle-free, transit can be built into it. It would be pragmatic to initially roll out pilot projects in Arunachal Pradesh and Manipur, concurrently, and get other states on board.**

3.3 Empowering the Central Armed Police Forces (CAPFs) for Designated Roles (Written in March 2025)

The spurt in terrorist incidents in Rajouri-Doda-Kathua last year was blamed on gaps in the security grid caused by pulling out the army division for a more pressing task of beefing up deployment to combat the Chinese build-up. Even after this much belated rebalancing, described as RB-1.0, we have only approximately 30% of our force level deployed against our main adversary, China, on our northern borders. Out of the balance, 70%, at least 30–40% is deployed to combat the proxy war in J&K. Notwithstanding the recent agreement on the restoration of patrolling in Depsang and Demchok, it is imperative to maintain vigil and enhance deployment levels. **The army is reportedly working on RB-2.0. The critical determinant for such rebalancing is whether the designated forces—CAPFs and Police—rise to the challenge and free the army for the primary challenge?**

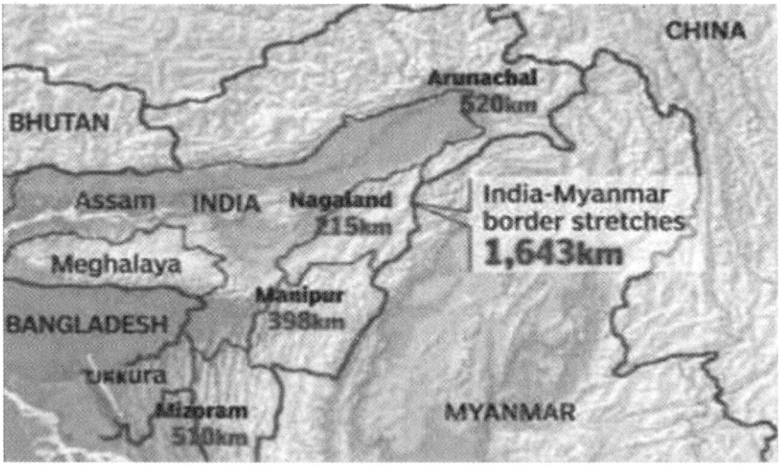

CAPFs, with approximately 10,45,751 personnel, comprises of seven formidable forces for maintaining law and order, IS, counter-insurgency (CI), and protecting borders. They can be broadly grouped as per functions—**first**, the **Central Industrial Security Force (CISF) for industrial and airport security.** It is relevant to reiterate that the Ministry of Railways also has a 75,000-strong Railway Protection Force (RPF). The obvious question is: should the overburdened MHA shed control of the CISF to designated ministries, such as aviation and industry, like the RPF?

Second, the Central Reserve Police Force (CRPF) is mandated to beef up state police forces in maintaining law and order and internal security. As the name suggests, it was created as a reserve for state police forces. Most states, besides the regular constabulary, have 8–10 Armed Police battalions, funded by the Central Government with shared lien on their deployment. These are also referred to as the Rapid Action Force (RAF).

Thirdly, the BSF, ITBP, SSB, and Assam Rifles are for Border Management (BM). The Kargil Review Committee in 1991 had very clearly enunciated the principle of 'One Border, One Force' for BM and dedicated the CRPF for IS. Consequently, rationalisation was attempted with the BSF for Pakistan and Bangladesh, the ITBP for China, the SSB for Nepal and Bhutan, and the AR for Myanmar. Each border has its own challenges, like narcotics delivery by drones in Punjab, cattle/human trafficking on the Bangladesh border, and terrorist intrusions in J&K. The Pakistan border is properly fenced in the IB sector and has modified fencing along the LoC. The Bangladesh border is approximately 80% fenced, but has treacherous riverine and jungle stretches. Borders with Nepal, Bhutan, Tibet (the LAC), and Myanmar (except for 60 odd km out of 1,643 km) are unfenced. BM has two categories, Border Guarding or patrolling on settled borders, and Border Defence on active frontiers (LoC and LAC), where BSF and ITBP work in a supportive role with the army.

Fourthly, AR is dual-tasked for the Myanmar border as well as the CI role in the North-East; it is paramilitary in nature, as the officer cadre is from the army, on a deputation basis. The challenges of managing CI and IS are such that we have battalions of CRPF, BSF, ITBP, SSB, and Assam Rifles deployed in Manipur, reflecting a fire-brigade response of mustering whatever and whoever is available. The force-mix in J&K is similar, though the RR, CRPF, and J&K Police have become the main components. Yet, the recent induction of AR units in J&K is indicative of a fire-fighting approach. The reputation of AR, the original mainstay of the North-East, has been tarnished in Manipur. This is not only unfortunate but also short-sighted. If there are black sheep in a force, fix them by all accounts, but why trash a 189-year-old legacy?

Fifthly, the National Security Guard (NSG) or Black Cat Commandos are on the other end of the spectrum for specialised counter-terrorism, including hostage rescue. It is a mixed force, which should ideally form part of the recently established Special Forces Agency, headed by a two-star officer currently, but could become a separate command like other modern Armed Forces.

Quantitatively, the combined strength of CAPFs and Armed Police battalions matches the army in numbers. They also enjoy similar benefits in pay and perks and wear a similar uniform. They have recently even created similar-sounding headquarters (HQs) like Command HQ, further adding to the confusion. It is time for CAPFs to stop copying the army's uniform and nomenclature for their HQs.

Proposed Reforms

The **first and foremost requirement is to take up the mission to empower CAPFs for their designated roles.** It is predicated on the implementation of the Prakash Singh Committee's police reforms, duly reiterated by the Supreme Court. While it has not been able to get the states to implement them, the Union Government can set the pace for CAPFs and for the police in states with National Democratic Alliance (NDA) governments.

Next, CAPFs have roles requiring specialisation and the development of force ethos. Using CAPFs as a cadre management avenue for senior ranks in the IPS needs to be reviewed. Para dropping in CAPFs at apex ranks and the shifting of DGs degrade cadre cohesion. **They need to have their own integral cadres like the Coast Guard, and even the army should yield control of AR.** CAPFs should absorb released Agniveers after reorientation training.

Third, in the border defence role, the BSF on the LoC and the ITBP on the LAC should operate under undiluted operational control of the army. **In a theatre, all forces and agencies should operate under unified command.**

Fourth, large-scale deployment of CAPFs for elections has impacted their availability for other mandated tasks. The need is to make the electoral process less dependent on CAPFs, with Police/Home Guards shouldering the challenge. The influx of infiltrators as an electoral issue has resulted in counter-accusations that BM is ineffective and porous. The BSF, except for West Bengal, has been allowed to operate up to 50 km in the hinterland along borders, enhancing their effectiveness.

Viksit Bharat can only happen in Surakshit Bharat, for which CAPFs have to take up the challenge and become accountable. **The army is observing 2025 as the Year of Reforms; the CAPFs could consider emulating them with a Year of Empowerment and Accountability.**

3.4 Governing and Securing Vulnerable, Critical, and Strategic Corridor (Written in Nov 2020)

The title of Robert D Kaplan's famous book, *The Revenge of Geography,* readily comes to mind when we take stock of our critical strategic spaces. The challenges have been magnified by our two diabolic neighbours, China, bent upon asserting its coercive dominance, and Pakistan, whose existential raison d'être is to create new criticalities for us. Compounding matters is their much-touted collusion, manifesting in the CPEC.

While every bit on the border has its relevance, the three most critical corridors are—the Siliguri Corridor, the Pathankot-Jammu link, and the Shyok-Daulat Beg Oldi (DBO), touted as 'casus belli' by the Chinese for the current standoff. Critical spaces are characterised by three main factors: firstly, the fragility of communications, secondly, inefficient governance and a lack of development, and thirdly, demographic challenges, especially ethnic balance. These factors generate centrifugal forces, creating ripe conditions for secessionist tendencies.

The Sarpanch (village head) in the remote Pin Valley, while handing over a representation citing a lack of basic facilities to me as Army Commander, cheekily mentioned that if sent across, the Chinese would certainly oblige. Despite 70 years of republic, surface connectivity in bordering states remains tenuous, with misplaced focus on building statues, religious shrines, and spiritual connectivity projects. Many states, like Manipur, are barely beginning to get some semblance of rail connectivity, and it may take another decade for some of them, like Ladakh and Mizoram, to be on the rail map.

The Pathankot-Jammu link, with just 10 odd km of depth (in stretches), has not only witnessed skirmishes in operations, but Pakistan has also made multiple attempts to spread the arc of terrorism from the valley to the Jammu-Kathua-Samba (JKS) region. The riverine terrain along the JKS stretch facilitates infiltration; coupled with this is Pakistan's resort to tunnelling. Terrorists have multiple, highly visible targets within shallow depth. Interdiction of tenuous link to Jammu and Kashmir makes big news and bolsters Pakistan's propaganda. The half-hearted attempts to build redundancy on the alternative Dhar-Udhampur link in depth have not found traction, despite the army pushing it. The pressure of lobbies is such that the proposed Katra Expressway project doesn't mitigate vulnerabilities, as pilgrims will remain easy and high TRP-generating targets. A better option would have been to upgrade the Dhar-Udhampur link and construct a spur to Jammu, like the one linking Amritsar, although it is currently stalled.

It is reassuring to witness some concerted action, though much belated, to ramp up communication in border areas. Besides the Border Roads Organisation (BRO), there is a plethora of agencies constructing and maintaining roads. They are classified as national/ state highways, Public Works Department (PWD), BRO, China Study Group, Border Area Development Project, CAPF, and Pradhan Mantri Gram Sadak Yojna (PMGSY) (rural) roads. The unfortunate part is that there is sub-optimal coordination and near-complete disregard for uniformity in specifications. Funding norms are such that the ITBP can outsource roads to civilian firms, achieving better results, while the BRO is constrained. The BRO excels in projects across Bhutan due to liberal allocations and flexible rules. It is heartening to see the BRO ramping up its procedures and execution.

The disturbing question is the lack of accountability of the PWD, responsible for the deterioration under its charge. There is marked reluctance on the part of states for capacity building. The overall sense is that states want central funding and want to retain the escape clause of passing on the blame to the BRO in the event of road closures. Tunnelling to ensure all-weather connectivity is a welcome new feature, but most projects entail expansive foreign consultancy, banking on imported machinery. The Rohtang tunnel project was stuck due to seepage through the Seri Nullah for nearly four years. Foreign consultants recommended an alternate alignment, entailing massive additional expenditure, but some calculated risk-taking and alleviating 'jugaad' measures enabled completion. It is hoped that designated institutions and Indian Institutes of Technology (IITs) are incorporated to build domain knowledge and competence, including research in tunnelling suited to our terrain.

Demography in border areas remains a challenge characterised by sparse population in ghost villages. In many states, there are serious theological challenges. Moderate strands in the Gurjar society are being radicalised by migrant Wahabi clergy and Deobandi influences. While we can't emulate the Chinese model of Hanisation, allowing the Sufi culture and Kashmiriyat to be completely marginalised amounts to socio-cultural harakiri. Theological filters need to be applied in sensitive areas to protect traditionally moderate communities—the Shias of Kargil, the Gujjars, and the Paharis. Attempts to alter demographic balance by settling outsiders like Rohangiyas need to be guarded against.

Representative local bodies and responsive administration can generate binding centripetal forces to negate aberrant centrifugal ones. Unfortunately, experience suggests that the best in bureaucracy and agencies avoid remote areas. A random check of Deputy Commissioners (DCs) and Superintendents of Police (SPs) in bordering areas after the Pathankot incident revealed that most, like SP Salwinder Singh, were from state services, enjoying a nexus with local political mafias. The recent apprehension of Devinder Singh, who was entrusted with the security of Srinagar Airport, is another such example. **These areas deserve better governance and vigilant monitoring agencies by a committed administration with a unique 'hands-on' skill set.**

Governance has to be anchored by officers like Capt Bob Kathing, to whom the nation owes a deep debt of gratitude for planting the

Tricolour in Tawang. **The suggestion of ex-Governor NN Vohra for a specialised cadre like the Indian Frontier Administrative Service needs to be implemented.**

While it may sound a bit revolutionary, like Ladakh, Siliguri Corridor needs to be reorganised into a Union Territory. It has a complicated demography with just 20 odd km width and is the only terrestrial link to the seven states of North-East, Sikkim, and Bhutan. It borders four countries and has seen Gorkhaland and Kamtapur separatist movements. The elections in Bihar have highlighted a worrying rise of left-wing extremists in the Seemanchal region of Bihar, bordering the Siliguri Corridor. Areas like Kaliachak in Malda have acquired a dubious reputation for crime. The federal structure is fraying, with states like Bengal on the warpath with the Centre. Even within the state, the Gorkhaland council is at loggerheads, holding everyone to ransom by frequent blockades. Chinese intentions post-Doklam appear ominous. Can we allow external forces to exploit our fault lines? **The possible solution, though seemingly radical, lies in examining the option of central rule in this sensitive territory by creating a 'Seemant Union Territory' for the Siliguri Corridor and North Bengal, with Gorkha and Duars councils enjoying limited autonomy within the proposed Union Territory having district councils.** This is discussed in greater detail in the Chapter on the Siliguri Corridor.

LAC – Claim Lines and Unresolved Standoff

4.1 Line of Actual Control, International Boundary, and Claim Lines: Getting a Better Perspective on India's Northern Borders

Key Takeaways

- Chinese claims have been based on selective manipulation of imaginative cartography, aided by lawfare, selective leveraging of favourable treaties, and amnesia on those not supporting Chinese claims. The Ten-Dash Line, an expanded version of the Nine-Dash Line in the South China Sea, exemplifies such revanchist trends.

- China prefers ambiguity as it has not provided any maps indicating its claims. It also wants to put the issue on the back burner and prefers the concept of buffer/no patrolling zones.

- China is altering the geography of borders by setting up model border villages, known as Xiaokangs, to solidify its claim lines.

- The 1959 claim line propounded by Chinese PM Chou Enlai seems to be the current reality in Ladakh. India did miss a great opportunity to partially resolve the issue, as China, till the '70s, was probably aggregable to a swap deal, giving up claims in Arunachal Pradesh in return for Aksai Chin.

- After the standoff, partial disengagement with the designation of buffer zones had initially taken place in Galwan (PP-14), Gogra (PP-17A), and Hot Spring (PP-15). Similarly, in Pangong Tso, the area between Fingers 3 and 8 has become a buffer zone with no patrolling zones or demilitarised area.

- Focus remained on the unresolved standoff in Depsang and Demchok. Access to PP-10, 11, 12, 12A, and 13 in Depsang remained blocked due to PLA deployment. This was resolved in January 2025 with the restoration of patrolling and grazing rights in Depsang and Demchok/Chumar.
- Only the first step—disengagement—has taken place; the next two steps—de-induction and de-escalation—are still being negotiated.

Introduction

India's northern borders with 'aggressively rising' China have remained unresolved despite prolonged and tortuous structured deliberations. The ambiguity on borders has resulted in the articulation of various conflicting claim lines, and the 1962 war, the 1967 skirmish at Nathu La, and other face-offs at Sumdrong Chu in 1986/87, Doklam in 2017, and the recent ongoing Chinese action in Ladakh. This complex situation is falling out of a festering colonial legacy and covenants between Britain, Tibet, Bhutan, Nepal, Sikkim, and China. The current standoff on the LAC has once again raised sensitivities and makes a compelling case for early resolution. **Indian borders range from the settled IB to the LoC and Maritime border (Rann of Kutch) with Pakistan, to the AGPL in Siachen, the Unmanned Border (Shakasgam Valley), and the LAC, unfenced and unmarked, with China.** The complex issue of the Sino-Indian border requires analysis, structured on the following key parameters:

- Basics of the Evolution of Borders
- Geo-Strategic Context
- Chinese Border Policy and Agenda

- Claim Lines
- Way Forward

Basics of the Evolution of Borders

Border, as a term, is commonly understood as the boundary or geographic limits of a country or state. The historic idea of limits or the outer edge of a country included no man's land, buffer states, and frontiers. Buffer states, like Nepal and Bhutan, are relatively smaller and neutral countries that help to keep two major powers geographically apart. They serve to preclude skirmishes and standoffs, while providing time and space to resolve contentious issues. Frontiers like the Federally Administered Tribal Areas (FATA), on the Pakistan-Afghan border, were autonomous areas with limited suzerainty of governing powers. They were an organised form of no man's land, which denoted a lack of institutional control. Tibet, till 1951, was a classic example of a frontier and buffer state. Unfortunately, both Tibet and FATA have been subsumed into China and Pakistan, respectively, thereby altering the geo-strategic template. Ideally, **Tibet should have remained as a buffer between India and China, with its genuine autonomous status.**

In keeping with the old proverb, 'Good fences make good neighbours', the quest is to physically demarcate boundaries. Borders have evolved into international boundaries after a structured process, including the following major stages:

- **Delimitation**
- **Delineation**
- **Demarcation**

Delimitation is the acceptance of broad principles for settling boundaries like watershed, river, or ridgeline. This is followed by translating the delimited concept into an agreed line on the map. Such delineation has resulted in the Radcliffe Line and the Durand Line in the Indian subcontinent, though both were vitiated in finalisation, creating unresolved problems. The most difficult part is the physical demarcation of this line on the ground. In the Sino-Indian context, the McMahon Line is an attempt to resolve the borders based on the concept of a watershed.

Geo-Strategic Context

The unresolved Sino-Indian border has acquired significant strategic heft, in a 'Thucydides' Trap' like situation developing between increasingly aggressive China and aspiring India. China would like to cement its hegemony and limit India to a compliant state. India's quest for strategic autonomy and non-alignment has riled the Dragon. The recent leveraging of alliances, like the Quad by India, is perceived by China as a conspiracy against it. China would like India to join it against the US.

India, on the other hand, has felt threatened by Chinese forays described as a 'string of pearls'. India has also resisted Chinese invitations to join connectivity initiatives, like the Belt and Road Initiative (BRI) and the CPEC. India's stance on the CPEC is linked to the violation of Indian de jure sovereignty due to its alignment through Gilgit-Baltistan (GB). The Sino-Indian border has a complex trilateral dimension with other neighbours, like Pakistan, Nepal, Bhutan, and Myanmar. These areas are described as tri-junctions. They are most contentious and strategically important. The first one is with Pakistan in the Karakoram-Tortuk sector, complicated by Pakistan gifting away the Shaksgam Valley to China in 1963. Similarly, the tri-junction with Nepal in the Lipulekh-Kali River sector is in focus, with Nepal claiming Limpiyadhura-Kalapani. Mount Gipmochi, the tri-junction with Bhutan, became the main issue for the Doklam crisis in 2017. Even the other truncation in the Sakteng Nature Park in the Tashigang district is now being disputed by China to forestall the development of the projected Guwahati-Tawang road. In this trilogy, Pakistan and Nepal have resolved their borders, albeit on Chinese-dictated terms, leaving Bhutan as the only exception.

Chinese Border Policy and Agenda

China has borders with 24 countries, both terrestrial and maritime domains. It has a land border with 14 countries and claims to have settled boundary issues with all except India and Bhutan. However, these claims have to be viewed realistically, in the context that **most disputes have been either put on the back burner or settled on terms laid down by Beijing.** It is also relevant to recount that the People's Republic of China (PRC) launched aggression against India in 1962, a 6-month-long border conflict with the USSR in 1969 and Vietnam in 1979. It is currently engaged in an unresolved standoff with India in Ladakh. Despite Chinese assertions, boundary issues with Nepal and Kazakhstan flare up intermittently. In the maritime domain, China is facing serious issues with all its important neighbouring littorals due to its dynastic claims, which interfere with other nations' exclusive economic zones. It is engaged in serious issues with the Philippines, Taiwan, Vietnam, Brunei, and Malaysia in the South China Sea, and Japan in the East China Sea.

Most experts opine that the Chinese use border disputes to build pressure on smaller neighbours. They have mastered the art of filibustering and endless parleys to tire out the other party. It is also relevant that so-called historical claims based on grazing areas during imperial Chinese dynasties are not sacrosanct and are based on one-sided interpretation. Out of 23 territorial disputes settled since 1949, including 12 in the terrestrial domain, China has substantially retracted claims in 17 of them. China settled a 130-year-old dispute with Tajikistan in January 2011, accepting just 3.5% (approximately 1,000 square kilometres), against the original claim of 28,000 square kilometres. The same trend was evident in settlements with Kazakhstan and Kyrgyzstan, where it accepted just 22% and 32% of the original claims. China is also making use of imaginative cartography by articulating multiple claim lines backed up by a selective use of treaties in what is being termed as 'lawfare'.

Historical Perspective

Claims on Tibet and Ladakh date back to the Dogra regime, as part of the Sikh Empire in 1834. Later, the Chinese defeated the Sikh Army in Ladakh, resulting in the Treaty of 1842, stipulating mutual respect and non-aggression. In 1846, the British took control of the Sikhs. In effect, areas like the Karakoram pass and the Pangong Tso lake were delineated, but the status of Aksai Chin remained vague. In the North-East, the British amalgamated Assam in 1826 and sanctified it by the Treaty of Yandabo. After the Anglo-Burmese wars, Burma (now Myanmar) was incorporated into the British Empire. The trilateral meeting in 1914, with Britain, China, and Tibet at Simla, remained inconclusive as China rescinded after endorsing the initials on the agreement. Britain and Tibet signed the convention, with an appended map depicting the McMahon Line. This agreement conflicted with the Anglo-Chinese Agreement of 1907, which mandated the inclusion of China in all deliberations with Tibet. The Chinese claimed to enjoy suzerainty over Tibet and insisted that the Lhasa regime was a largely temporal authority with a localised writ. They rejected Tibet's Declaration of Independence in 1913.

In the original conception, India and China were to have buffer states of Tibet, Nepal, Sikkim, and Bhutan. The Sino-Indian border has never been officially recognised or demarcated, and is largely a fall-out of the inherited colonial legacy of British rule. The claims are based on traditional control exercised, but not backed up by the agreed-upon maps or documentation. It has been a complex construct based on exchanges between Tibet, Sikkim, Nepal, Imperial China, and British India. Chinese claims date back to the Manchu Dynasty in 1910/11, when the pre-PRC regime staked territorial claims on parts of Tibet and other buffer states. These were reiterated by the Chinese Communist Party (CCP) in 1949, on establishing the PRC. The theoretical construct was outlined in Mao Zedong's diktat and expounded in the party treatise 'The Chinese Revolution and the Communist Party' in 1939, 'the correct boundaries of

China would include Burma, Bhutan, and Nepal'. This implied that Tibet, including Arunachal Pradesh and Sikkim, was part of the Manchu Empire.

Mao emphasised this concept in his expansionist **'Five Fingers of Tibet' policy. Citing Tibet as the palm, the fingers included Ladakh, Nepal, Sikkim, Bhutan, and Arunachal Pradesh**. In the Chinese conception, all these are part of greater Tibet, annexed under unequal treaties. This claim was reinforced with imaginative cartography, including maps as part of the publication, 'A Brief History of China,' published in 1959. Large portions of adjoining areas in territories of other countries were included within the ambit of Chinese claims. **The annexation of Tibet in 1950/51, followed by a 17-point agreement forced on the hapless Tibetan regime, resulted in the withdrawal of Indian and Bhutanese representatives from their missions in Lhasa. This was followed by the rebellion in Tibet in 1959, the flight of the Dalai Lama to India, and a large number of refugees seeking asylum in India and Bhutan.** The PLA occupied several adjoining Bhutanese exclaves in western Tibet in July 1959. These included Darchen, Gartok, and several other villages near Mount Kailas, which had been under Bhutanese control since the seventeenth century for 300 years and had been given to Bhutan by Ngawang Namgyal in the seventeenth century.

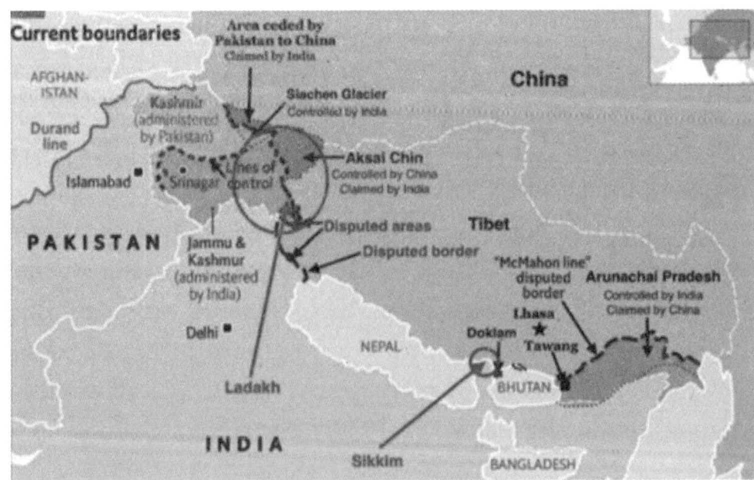

Sectors and Disputed Areas

The Sino-Indian border is based on contested claim lines as follows:

a) **Western (Ladakh) Sector:** Claim lines include colonial-era (British) lines, such as the Johnson Line, the Macartney-Macdonald Line, and the Johnson-Ardagh Line. The Chinese don't recognise them and have their own 1959 claim line, articulated by Zhou Enlai.

b) **Middle Sector:** This sector includes stretches in Himachal Pradesh and Uttarakhand, with areas like Shipki La in Himachal Pradesh and Barahoti in Uttarakhand.

c) **Eastern Sector:** It includes Sikkim and Arunachal Pradesh. China is referring to Arunachal Pradesh as Southern Tibet or Zangnan. The Indian claim line is based on the McMahon Line indexed on the watershed principle.

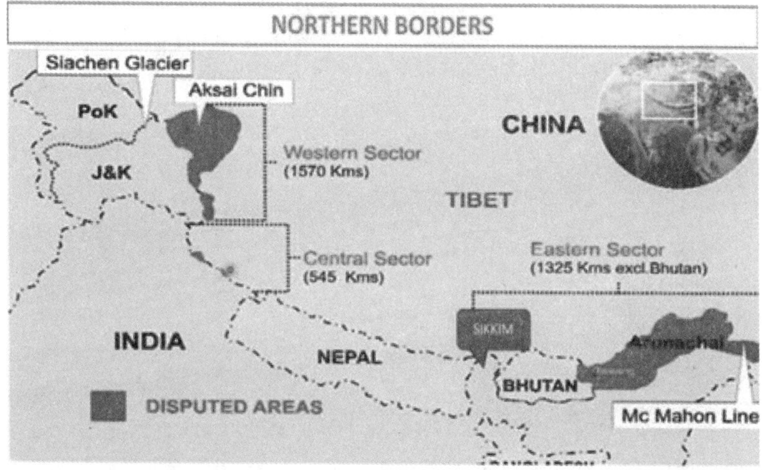

d) **Disputed/Contested Areas:** The main contested areas are Aksai Chin (Depsang, Demchok, Pangong Tso, and Hot Springs), Doklam, and Tawang (Yangtze). China claims that Aksai Chin is part of the Xinjiang Autonomous Region (XAR), and Arunachal Pradesh, according to their claim, belongs to

Southern Tibet. There has been a listing of disputed areas, which is given in Wikipedia and other literature, but it is not official or agreed upon by both parties. To complicate the issue, the PLA has maintained ambiguity and activated new areas in a randomised sequence to basically keep India unsettled.

IDENTIFYING THE AREAS OF DISPUTE

IN JWG TALKS (1990S)

- WESTERN: Trig Heights, Demchok
- MIDDLE: Barahoti
- EASTERN: Namka Chu, Sumdorong Chu, Yangtse, Asaphila, Longju-Bisa

MAP EXCHANGE (2000)

- MIDDLE: Kaurik, Mumri Dogri, Shipki La

MAP COMPARISON (2002)

- WESTERN: North Samar Lungpa, east of Point 6556, north of Kugrang river, area of Kongka La, Spanggur Gap, east of Mount Sajum opposite Dumchele

BY PLA ACTION

- WESTERN: North bank of Pangong Tso, south bank of Pangong Tso, Chumar, Galwan, Hot Springs
- EASTERN: Dichu area, Dibang Valley (Fish Tail I & II), Lamang

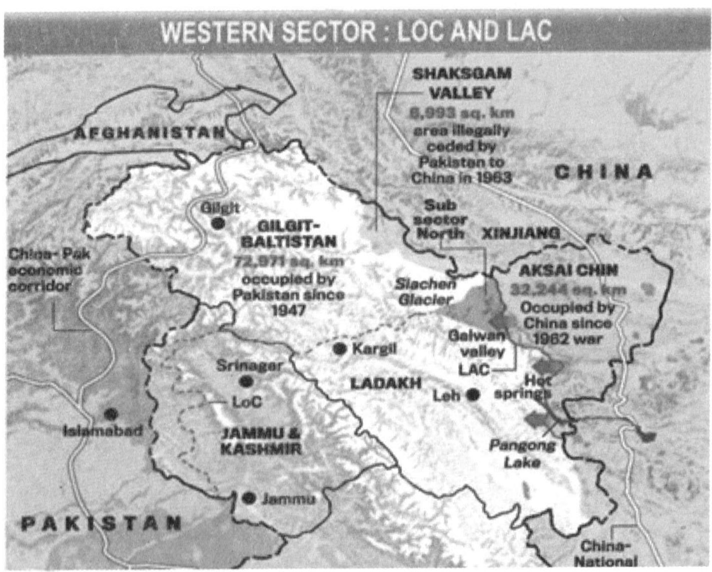

Claim Lines

Line of Actual Control (LAC): It is a notional, unresolved, loosely defined line that separates Indian and Chinese-controlled territories in the Sino-Indian border dispute. The term was first used by the Chinese Premier Zhou Enlai in a letter addressed to the then-Indian Prime Minister, Jawaharlal Nehru. The evolution can be traced to various claim lines.

Johnson Line: The line was proposed in 1865 by a Survey of India (SoI) official. It was a maximal projection, incorporating Aksai Chin in Jammu and Kashmir. The line sought territory up to and even beyond the Kunlun range, including areas of Shahidulla (currently called Xaidulla). While a fortified staging post to monitor caravans was maintained by Dogra rulers in Shahidulla for a period, later, the control of these areas and the Karakoram passed to imperial China in 1892. Accordingly, Sir John Ardagh proposed a more realistic and defendable line, aligned along the crest of the Kunlun range and Yarkund River. This was termed as the Johnson-Ardagh line.

Macartney-MacDonald Line: This line was proposed in 1899 and generally ran along the natural frontier of the Karakoram mountains, south of the Laktsang range. Broadly, it left the Tarim river basin and Aksai Chin for China, retaining the Indus basin for British India. The Foreign Office Line was another correction on the line, ceding control over more area in the Lingzi Tang plain.

McMahon Line: The line was devised by Sir Henry McMahon, Surveyor General, and is based on the concept of watershed. It utilised the Himalayan range to define the watershed, yet contentious areas like Tawang remained unresolved, due to the concept of traditional claims dating back to imperial dynasties like the Qing and Manchus. Chinese claims conform to the watershed in approximately 90% of the border (Map 3).

Chinese Claims: Chinese articulation and designs became clear with the surreptitious construction of the Aksai Chin Road in the 1950s.

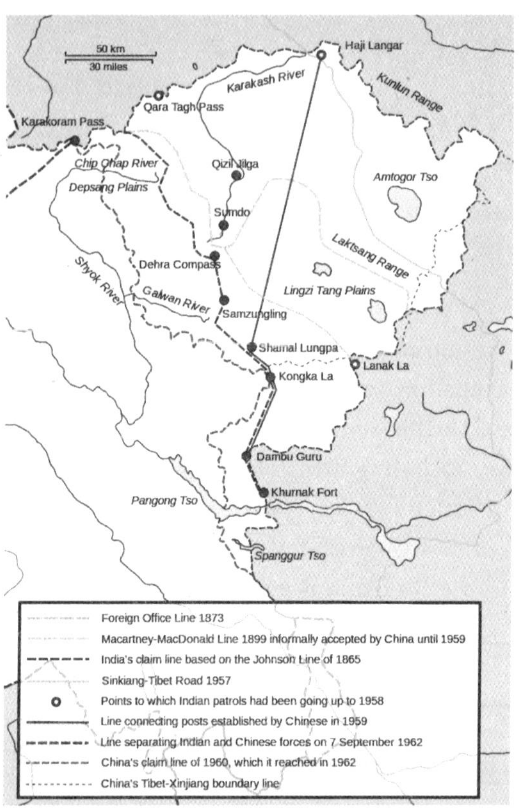

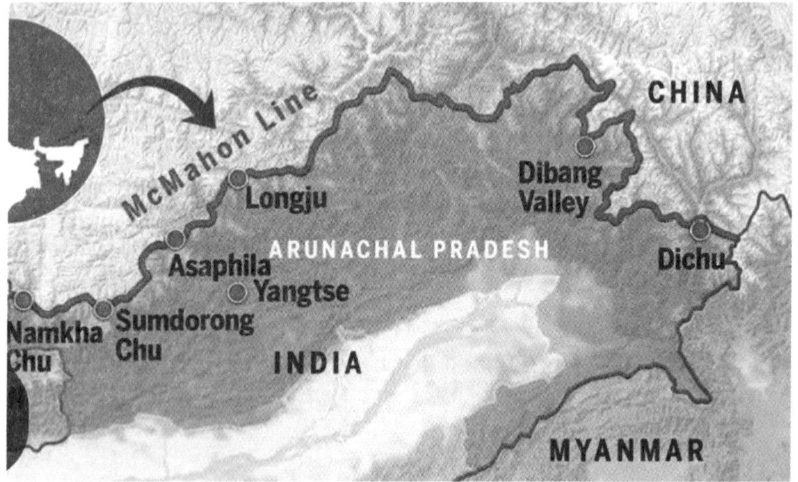

(https://currentaffairs.adda247.com/india-china-troops-clash-along-lac-in-twang-region-arunachal-pradesh/)

This spurred India to adopt the 'Forward Policy', in essence establishing a presence up to the claim line. The Chinese Prime Minister projected the 1959 claim line and reportedly indicated a desire for a package deal. This offer reportedly included giving up a claim in Arunachal Pradesh in exchange for Aksai Chin. This was followed by the 1962 war and unilateral withdrawal by the PLA.

Sikkim Border: China had boundary-related issues with Sikkim, a protectorate of India. This manifested in bloody clashes in Nathu La and Cho La passes in 1967. The standoff at Jalep La pass was averted due to the Indian withdrawal. The merger of Sikkim after a referendum in 1975 was initially rejected by the PRC. However, it was later accepted through a Memorandum of Understanding (MOU), signed in 2003. Notwithstanding the MOU, issues in the Finger area on the Kerang plateau, Naku La, and most importantly, Doklam, flare up occasionally. The most recent happened in 2017, and though supposedly resolved, China continues salami-slicing and building border villages in disputed areas.

Doklam Issue: Strategic heft and the edge are imparted to the Doklam issue due to the relative location of Chumbi Valley, vis-a-vis, the Siliguri Corridor, gateway to the north-eastern states, also called the seven sisters and one brother. The corridor, which is 22 km at its narrowest, is also described as 'chicken's neck' or 'Northeastern jugular'. It can also act as a springboard for forays in Nepal and Bangladesh.

Chumbi Valley: It is a dagger-shaped narrowing wedge between India and Bhutan. The southern narrow portion of the valley, the Dolam plateau with its strategic significance, has the potential to pose a threat to the tenuous Siliguri Corridor, termed as jugular, connecting the North-East with the mainland. The Chinese quest is to widen the extremely narrow base of the valley. The dispute is indexed to the location of Mt Gipmochi and the correct interpretation of the watershed of rivers like Amo Chu. It is a complex bevy of crest lines and heights—Gamochen, Batangla, and Sinchela. The most sought-after is the Zompelri (Jampheri) ridge, providing a launchpad for the reach to the Siliguri Corridor. The balanced view is that while it is indeed a threat, logistics and terrain make it a tortuous and slow exercise, requiring extensive logistics build-up. This is covered in detail in a separate chapter on the Sino-Bhutan border.

Unresolved Status

The trend of standoffs is marked by Sumdrong Chu (1987/88), which festered for nearly a year. Prolonged parleys resulted in multiple agreements in 1993, 1996, 2005, 2006, 2012, and 2013, outlining protocols and Confidence Building Measures (CBMs) to maintain peace and tranquillity on the LAC. The China Study Group devised a concept of a limit of patrolling with designated Patrolling Points (PPs), some of which, like PP 14, 15, 16, and 17, have been in focus during the ongoing Ladakh face-off. **PPs, as cartographic aids, were stipulated by the China Study Group in the 1970s and followed by Indian patrols to stake our claims. In Ladakh, they start from PP-1 in the west near DBO, and there are 65 odd such points stretching to PP-60, towards the east.** Multiple mechanisms like the Joint Working Group, Special Representatives, and the Working Mechanism for Consultation and Coordination have been set up without much headway. In the interim, the frequency of standoffs at Depsang, Chumar, Demchok, and Pangong Tso has increased from 2013 onwards, leading up to the recent Chinese aggression in Ladakh from 2020 onwards.

The current round of resolution involves a three-step process—disengagement, de-escalation, and de-induction. The first step of disengaging was achieved in Pangong Tso, Galwan, Hot Spring, and Gogra. **The PLA has introduced the concept of buffer/no patrolling zones in resolved areas, wherein Indian patrols are not able to go up to claim lines.** After a standoff, disengagement with the designation of buffer zones has taken place in Galwan (PP-14), Hot Spring (PP-

15), and Gogra (PP-17A). Similarly, in Pangong Tso, the area between Fingers 3 and 8 has become a buffer zone with no patrolling zones or demilitarised area. **Prolonged standoff in Depsang was resolved with patrolling access to PP-10, 11, 12, 12A, and 13 in Depsang. Similarly, patrolling and grazing rights were restored in Demchok and Chumar. The next on the agenda are de-escalation and de-induction, which are likely to be a long-drawn affair.**

Disputed Areas – Sikkim and Arunachal Pradesh

There are a number of disputed areas in Sikkim and Arunachal Pradesh. However, the PLA has been activating new areas like the Naku La pass in the Muguthang sector of Sikkim, apart from the agreed list. The patrols on both sides attempt to patrol up to their perceived claim lines. These are mostly temporary to stake claims and are termed in the media as violations/incursions/intrusions/encroachments, but are officially described as transgressions or border incidents.

Way Forward

Unresolved borders between two powerful neighbours, both armed with nuclear weapons and in an aspirational trajectory, have the potential for conflict, given their acrimonious history. It is axiomatic that both settle the boundary dispute on priority. The CBMs and protocols became meaningless due to the unilateral actions of the PLA. It will be pragmatic if interim protocols are worked out, and in the interim, China tones down its 'wolf warrior' approach, respecting the LAC to restore the status quo ante of January 2020.

Notes

1. Mihir Bose, 'Understanding Sino-Indian Border Issues: An Analysis of Incidents Reported', available at https://www.orfonline.org/research/understanding-sino-indian-border-issues-an-analysis-of-incidents-reported-in-the-indian-media/

2. Chervin Reed, 'Cartographic Aggression: Media Politics, Propaganda, and the Sino-Indian Border Dispute', Journal of Cold War Studies, 2020. Jianli Yang, 'Bhutan China Border Negotiations in Context', The Diplomat, 18 November 2021.

3. Harsh V Pant and Aditya Gowdara Shivamurthy, 'Himalaya: The Complexity of Bhutan', available at www.orfonline.org, *The Economic Times.*

4. Manoj Joshi, 'The China Bhutan Deal Should Worry India', available at www.orfonline. *Org, Hindustan Times.*

5. Lt Gen KJ Singh, 'Dynamics of Security of Siliguri Corridor: Way Forward', USI Strategic Year Book, 2018.

6. Lt Gen KJ Singh, 'Siliguri Corridor and Gorkhaland: Generals Jottings', available at https://timesofindia.indiatimes.com/blogs/generals-jottings/siliguri corridor-and-gorkhaland/

7. Lt Gen KJ Singh, 'Threats to Siliguri Corridor Wargamed', *Tribune,* available at https://m.tribuneindia.com/news/archive/features/india-ready-theoreticall%E2%80%98threats%E2%80%99-to-siliguri-corridor-war-gamed-433789

4.2 Debunking Myths of China's Geo-Strategic Moves (After the Galwan Clashes – June 2020)

Remaining focused on time-bound infrastructure development, it will be pragmatic to reduce the hype attached to the construction and inauguration of infrastructure in sensitive areas. A concurrent requirement is to fast-track China-centric, joint theatre commands. To deter the Dragon, we must discard myths, accept new realities, and reduce asymmetries.

A spate of recent border standoffs, at two ends of the unsettled Sino-Indian border in Naku La (Sikkim), followed by multiple incursions in Ladakh's Galwan and Pangong Tso, is another manifestation of coercive salami-slicing by China. For a more informed analysis, the requirement is to debunk prevalent myths and formulate a realistic template.

It is appropriate to start this process with an 'unsettled-settled' border. The then-Chinese Premier Wen Jiabao said in 2005, 'Sikkim is no longer a problem between China and India.' In recent discussions, the Chinese Ambassador alluded to Sikkim as a low-hanging fruit, disregarding the prolonged standoff at Doklam. It is indeed comical that Chinese patrols regularly resort to childish pranks of disassembling cairns (stone heaps) on the Kerang Plateau. The transgression at Naku La, in the desolate and sparsely populated Muguthang Valley, was activated, most surprisingly, the first time in 2017. Galwan, the current flashpoint in Ladakh, is an apt example of 'creeping claim lines' by the Chinese. In contrast, our approach has been fuelled by optimism, conditioned by false notions, which are enumerated.

- **Myth 1**: The Sino-Indian border is largely settled with just a few recorded and identified flashpoints. **The harsh reality is that the PLA activates different areas, in keeping with their grand design, often as diversionary tactics. In this case, Naku La was a distraction prior to Galwan.** Two and a half years after Galwan, the PLA tried an incursion in the Yangtze in Arunachal Pradesh. We draw comfort from nuancing incursions as transgressions, but the unmistakable bottom line is—nothing is settled, till it is delimited, delineated, and demarcated on the ground. We must be prepared for the long haul, with more surprises, as China is in no hurry to resolve issues.

- **Myth 2**: Standoffs are due to overreaction by local commanders. This is another false notion, a convenient excuse to pass the buck. Most standoffs are recorded by PLA patrols, with considerable play-acting, giving the impression that they are vectored by higher HQs. It will be prudent to surmise that the Chinese are masters in centrally planned but locally orchestrated events. In any case, the Chinese Western Command controls the entire Tibet border against four different commands of India, micro-managed by the army HQ, adding to the confusion. **Indian patrols have displayed remarkable restraint and maturity in face-offs. It throws up a disturbing possibility that 'strategic guidance' (agreed to at the summit level) is flouted by the PLA with tacit blessings.**

- **Myth 3**: The Chinese are superior to us. This myth needs to be junked. **Objective comparison proves that our troops are more than a match for their counterparts.** The 1962 syndrome was discarded in a resolute standoff at Nathu La and Cho La in 1967. Unfortunately, we have downplayed this heroic action as a skirmish to avoid embarrassing the PLA. In fact, most Chinese troops are conscripted with questionable domain competence. In Somdrong Chu and other standoffs over the years, as well as in UN operations, China's vulnerability has been exposed repeatedly.
- **Myth 4**: Chinese technological asymmetry will cripple adversaries even before the battle is joined. **The much-hyped technology is yet to be operationalised and is severely degraded by high altitude and weather**. On balance, it is part of psychological warfare and can't be taken as a game changer.
- **Myth 5**: By and large, peace prevails, as no bullet has been fired since 1967. This needs to be moderated with the realisation that **China is already waging unrestricted warfare.** There is considerable evidence of Chinese-engineered cyber disruption in our power grid. Parechu floods, causing severe damage to power plants astride the Sutlej, and the more recent devastating deluge in Assam, coupled with the denial of hydrological data, are a gross misuse of upper riparian leverage. Even in the current standoff, water flow has been blocked in the Galwan River. **Pacifism was rooted in Deng's maxim of economic consolidation, preceding precipitate military action, which has been discarded by Xi's aggressively rising China.**
- **Myth 6: In all situations, China will act responsibly, in accordance with its stature, requires re-visiting. Will any responsible power**

misuse the pandemic for a power play? Conventional wisdom, propagated by experts, is that Pakistan will invariably exploit Sino-Indian hostilities and intervene. China, showing maturity as a global power, will desist from exploiting Indo-Pak hostilities. Chinese reticence in 1971 and Kargil are cited as examples. However, the degree of collusive linkages has strengthened manifold with the CPEC.

- **Myth 7:** China will show reciprocity and respect our sensitivities. 17 Corps, which was initially designated as the Mountain Strike Corps and later played down with the dropping of 'strike' and curtailing of budgetary allocation, has not resulted in any reduction in Chinese intransigence. **China simply doesn't care.**

The coping strategy in dealing with China must factor in existing asymmetry and should be confined within the bounds of realism. We have viable options, though limited, yet we must signal resolve. It may take considerable time, like Doklam, but our sensitivities in terms of security to the new Darbuk-DBO road and unfettered patrolling up to our claim lines, including the Pangong Tso area, should be ensured. In this age of 5G, nail-studded clubs, stoning, and wrestling bouts on the LAC need to be eliminated. While diplomats and commanders are resolving the situation, the electronic media should enable an honourable resolution by avoiding rabble-rousing debates.

Remaining focused on time-bound infrastructure development, it will be pragmatic to reduce the hype attached to the construction and inauguration of infrastructure in sensitive areas. A concurrent requirement is to fast-track China-centric, joint theatre commands. The Mountain Corps needs to be customised as an agile force and, most importantly, funded to generate multiple QPQ options. To deter the Dragon, we must discard myths, accept new realities, and reduce asymmetries.

4.3 Standoff in Ladakh: Defining Reality Checks (Selected extracts from articles from 2021 to 2024)

It will be pragmatic to admit that the Chinese leveraged the pandemic to surprise us. There were enough indicators of build-up and brewing storm, yet we failed to synthesise the complete picture and infer the PLA's intentions. Exploiting the raging pandemic was a classic application of the Chinese proverb, 'loot the house on fire'. In the process, understanding and protocols on border management have been rendered meaningless and replaced with dangerous mistrust.

Chinese affairs expert, Vijay Gokhale, in his recent report, 'A Historical Evaluation of China's India Policy', has outlined a reality check on how Beijing perceives India in zhengzhijunshi-zhang (politico-military war).

- **First, as an unequal and unreliable neighbour, unworthy of any stand-alone status or consideration.**
- **Second, relevant only in hyphenated mode, tagged with great powers in the strategic trinity—US, USSR, and China.**
- **Third, a clear expectation that India should first understand Chinese objectives. To put it bluntly, India should play along.**
- **Fourth, China can afford to deal with India in episodic tactical mode, within its own long-term trajectory. Consequently, a petty 'zero-sum' approach by China to stymie India in the Indian Ocean and neighbourhood continues.**

Key takeaways emerging from the Indian response are as follows:

- **First, at the tactical level, audacious initiative and spontaneous reactions at Galwan and Yangtze would have forced a rethink in the PLA.**
- **Second, at the operational level, pre-emptive and surprise occupation of Kailash Heights and subtle leveraging of the Tibetan (Special Frontier Force (SFF)) card.**

- Third, strategically, rapid induction and sustenance of dissuasive force levels mirrored the PLA build-up. They, in effect, reined the PLA's vaulting ambitions, forcing a stalemate of sorts.

Other Inferences and Recommendations

Unique capabilities of scouts and ITBP should be leveraged as an embedded resource in forward areas rather than deploying them in separate, stand-alone areas. ITBP should be placed under the complete operational control of the army.

It is time that the China Study Group graduates to the China Strategic Response Group (CSRG) with operational orientation.

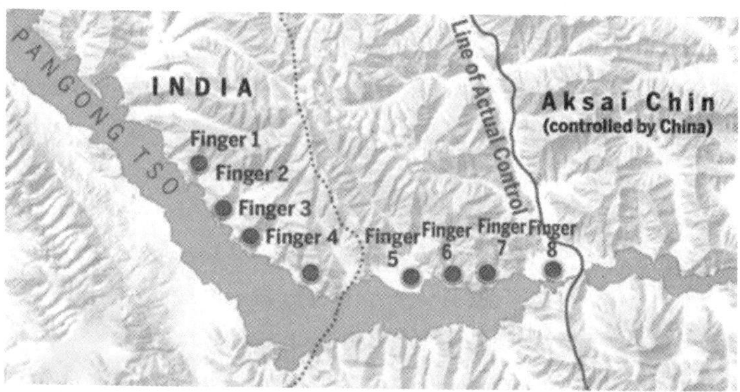

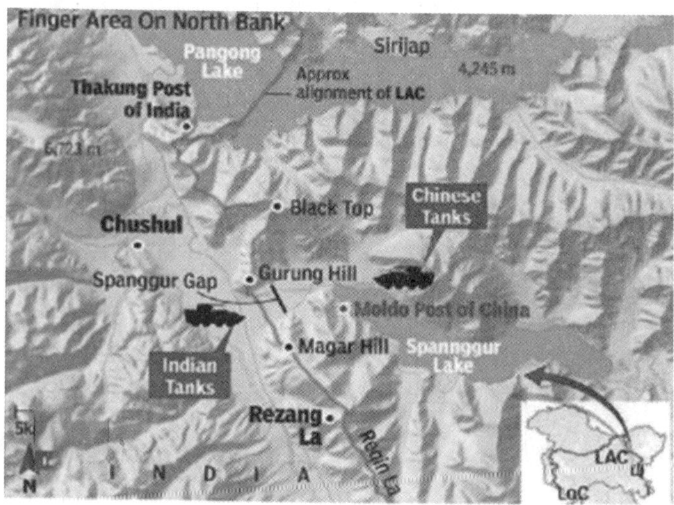

This body should be staffed with professionals to include naysayers, who can flag unlikely scenarios, which often surprise us. With a glut of think-tanks, CSRG should steer clear of mundane issues to focus on measures to hold the Dragon in check.

The Chinese, being past masters in conflict resolution and operating on their own terms, bordering on obduracy, **the possibility of deployment along the Chinese claim line of 1959 being defined as the new normal is very real. There is a likelihood of the LAC acquiring an LoC-type character, entailing the deployment of more formations with attendant penalties in logistics.**

The natural corollary is: **how are we dealing with China? It may sound incredulous, but without a coherent strategy, we are basically responding in reactive mode.** It is a strange mix of optimism and denial amongst decision makers (diplomats and experts) searching for the elusive peace and tranquillity, even when the wolf-warrior remains unrelenting. There have even been instances of conceding the benefit of the doubt and accepting the explanation of the local Commander going rogue. But the same so-called rogue is now in the apex hierarchy in the Central Military Commission (CMC). **Even worse is the sense of bravado seen amongst social media warriors giving clarion calls to liberate Aksai Chin.** As per a reliable opinion poll by an international think-tanks, 60% Indians believe that we can simply put it across to the Chinese.

Belated rebalancing of forces along the northern borders, with additional corps and other formations, is indeed very welcome. It may also be a good idea to conduct a Kargil-type interim review under a group of experts. Maritime and hybrid warfare are viable options to consider for keeping the Dragon in check. The former requires considerable investment, and the latter should be an option if the Chinese force us.

4.4 Rebalancing with China – Can the Elephant and the Dragon Tango? (Written in April 2025)

India and China celebrated the seventy-fifth anniversary of the establishment of diplomatic relations. There has been a flurry of meetings followed by media briefings aimed at rebalancing the ties vitiated by coercive posturing by the PLA on the LAC. Foreign Minister Wang-Yi, during the annual press conference, called for 'cooperative pas de deux, symbolising mutual growth and co-operation'. The hype was accentuated by the use of the metaphor of ballet between Dragon and Elephant, as the 'only right choice for both sides'. Similar sentiment was echoed by PM Narendra Modi's statement of 'preference for dialogue over discord'. The obvious question is: can we achieve mutually rewarding rebalancing after acrimonious exchanges on the LAC?

Mapping the Relationship

The long journey of the Sino-Indian relationship is marked by a heady phase of Hindi-Chini Bhai-Bhai (Sino-Indian brotherhood) and the five postulates of Panchsheel. India even promoted China, replacing Taiwan, as a veto-wielding, permanent member of the security council. Indian support for the 'One China' policy has been out of sync with realpolitik. The only saving grace has been the sanctuary provided to Tibetans and a significant trade relationship with Taiwan.

The Chinese aggression in 1962 was a humiliating wake-up call. Mercifully, this was followed by a redeeming battle action in 1967 at Nathu La, surprisingly still officially described as a skirmish. The resolute deployment in the Somdorong Chu sector in 1986–87, once again reinforced Indian resolve. It resulted in a series of protocols and CBMs, leading to what the PLA described as peace and tranquility, notwithstanding regular transgressions, to keep alive Chinese claims.

China has settled land borders with 12 neighbours, but has tied down India and Bhutan in tortuous negotiations. More importantly, the growing dependency of our economy on Chinese manufacturing/supply chains resulted in overwhelming leverage for the Dragon. The Chinese game plan has been to convince India to relegate border resolution to the back burner and continue to reap the benefits of one-sided trade. This was in keeping with Deng's template of 'hide your shine, bide your time'. The millennial generation, with no recollection of the 1962 treachery, was overwhelmed by the Chinese economic juggernaut. The ascendancy of Xi unveiled an aggressively rising Dragon. It has also revived mistrust and animosity.

This manifested in PLA transgressions acquiring a strident character in Dolam, Depsang, Demchok, Pangong Tso, finally peaking at Galwan in May 2020, and later Tangse in December 2022. The freeze in Sino-Indian relations persisted for more than four years, till a brief meeting between PM Narendra Modi and President Xi on the sidelines of the BRICS summit at Kazan in October 2024. This was followed by a number of high-level meetings, Working Mechanism for Coordination and Consultation (WMCC) and the twenty-third Special Representatives (SR) dialogue between National Security Advisor, Ajit Dobhal and Chinese Foreign Minister, Wang Yi.

The Indian strategy of keeping focus on border resolution has worked to the extent that there is reasonable, negotiated disengagement in place. Patrolling has been resumed in Depsang and Demchok, along with the restoration of traditional grazing rights. A new concept of buffer zones has been instituted in other flashpoints like Pangong Tso (Finger 4–8), Galwan, Hot Springs, and Gogra. This, at best, is a temporary arrangement, and there is an urgent need to put in place more resilient CBMs and expedite the border resolution process. **It will be appropriate to commend the Armed Forces for displaying resilience and audacity through speedy deployment and QPQ action in the pre-emptive occupation of Kailash Heights, as well as their resolute response during the Yangtze standoff.**

Contours of Rebalancing

The realisation that China is indeed the primary threat and a long-term one is the most important catalyst for strategic rebalancing. The Indian Army, as per media reports, has already completed Rebalancing 1.0 with the re-orbating of First Strike Corps and other formations from western (against Pakistan) to northern borders against the PLA. Rebalancing 2.0 is in the pipeline, and clearance for raising another infantry division for Ladakh has been accorded. It will enable the rolling back of Romeo Force to traditional areas to fill the voids created in the Rajouri and Reasi sectors. Notwithstanding the disengagement achieved, both sides continue to have very large deployments of forces on the LAC. Their maintenance is a drain on revenue budget, and even more telling is the impact on human resources in terms of health and stress.

Domestic Twitter-yodhas have described it as a sort of climb-down by China, while the opposition has termed it as a sell-out by us. **There is considerable opacity, but the Army Chief's statement of uneasy stability on the LAC is the most appropriate description. It may seem utopian, but attempting to forge a bipartisan consensus and prepare for a mature acceptance of transition to a 'give-and-take process' from a 'no loss of territory' approach is the pragmatic way forward,** especially for territories under contentious claims and with sparse settled populations. Chinese Xiaokang border villages need to be matched with the creation of vibrant villages by us. Concurrently, the impetus given to the development of infrastructure and connectivity along the northern borders has to be maintained.

The Economic Survey, presented in Parliament on 22 July 2024, was a harsh reality check, exposing the limitations of our economic response. Despite banning TikTok and other apps, the balance of trade has become more adverse. While we are importing goods, Chinese capital, in the form of investments, is heading to Vietnam, Indonesia, Mexico, and other welcoming economies. It is time for fiscal pragmatism—ring-fence strategic sectors but open up other avenues. Trump's tariff-tsunami may provide opportunities for the Indian economy only if we overcome bureaucratic hurdles.

The recent talks and agreements aim to revive the Kailash-Mansarovar Yatra, border trade in Sikkim, and hydrological data sharing of rivers. There is progress in discussions on the resumption of direct flights, the liberalisation of student/business visas, and the exchange of journalists. The basic nature of the relationship, being competitive between two aspirational economies, means that the dance may never get intimate but may remain like a mock-fencing routine, preparing for the real duel. **In sum, the stronger party, China, would like to intimidate and coerce us to follow its diktat as they follow Sun-Tzu's dictum of subduing an adversary without even fighting them.**

PLA Organisation

5.1 Emerging Politico-Military Structure in China

Key Takeaways

- President Xi Jinping has subsumed roles of President, Chairman of the CMC, besides the all-powerful General Secretary of the CCP. In addition, like an emperor, he has waived tenure limitations.
- The PLA has added the Rocket Force (erstwhile Second Artillery) and the SSF as full-fledged verticals, in addition to the army, navy, and air force. SSF has now been reorganised into three separate arms—cyber, space, and aerospace.
- The Western Theatre Command synergises operations across Tibet, combining forces from Chengdu, Lanzhou, and even the Guangzhou region, in some contingencies.
- Update: Notwithstanding reforms and a concerted drive for weeding out corruption, in October 2023, members of the apex decision-making structures, including Defence Minister Li Shangfu and a number of top generals of the Rocket Force, were sacked. The purge continued in 2024.

Introduction

China is at a critical threshold of its rise and ascent in the global power matrix. It has already established its place in the top league, and there is an informed body of opinion within China that feels that institutions that steered China's peaceful rise need to shed their defensive, status-quo orientation to become more proactive, dynamic, and assertive. **This is, indeed, a major departure from Deng Xiaoping's maxim: 'hide your shine, bide your time'. The crux was to have a long stick but hide the capabilities, which was described as the 'peaceful rise of China'.** There was limited knowledge on the structures and organisation to execute this policy, and they all maintained a low profile, staying out of the media glare. Most of it is still shrouded in considerable opacity, with very little known about the nitty-gritty of the functioning and organisation of the politico-military decision-making process and structures.

The shift from a peaceful to an assertive rise was signalled by the recent Chinese aggressive behaviour, especially in the South China Sea, characterised by the conversion of the Fiery Cross Reef into a full-fledged air base, disregarding international opinion and the concerns and sensitivities of the other littoral states. This change has been accompanied by a review of the apex structures and, accordingly, alignment of subordinate organisations to the newly evolved organisation. China is also beginning to showcase its system as a model for others to follow for economic progress. An interesting case study cited in support of the **success of the Chinese model is the lifting of 700 million poor citizens above the poverty line in three decades.** A review of the structure and organisation at the apex of the politico-military decision matrix in China is to enable better comprehension of the changes and their likely implications, along with a brief recapitulation of the history, leading to the evolution of the current structures.

Preview

The subject is analysed in the following parts:

- Evolution of Decision-Making Structures.
- Current Structure and Leadership.
- Major Military Reforms.
- Likely Implications at the Macro Level.

Evolution of Decision-Making Structures

First and Second Generation – Absolutism: The two milestones in the history of Communist China are the formation of the CCP on 1 July 1921 and the PLA in the aftermath of the Nanchang Uprising on 27 August. From the establishment of the PRC in 1949, through the era of the Long March and the Cultural Revolution, till the demise of Deng Xiaoping in 1992—covering the first and second generations of leadership—**the defining characteristics of the Chinese politico-military decision-making were the unparalleled authority of the Supreme Leader and the complete subservience of all decision-making to the CCP. It will be pertinent to recall the statement of Mao at the 9th CPC meeting in 1929, 'The role of the military is chiefly to serve the political ends.'** The two doyens of this period were Mao Zedong (1949–76) and Deng Xiaoping (1978–92). While this facilitated rapid decision-making and unity of purpose, this arrangement was probably inevitable due to a lack of mature leadership. Hence, key strategic articulations, like joining the Korean War and exporting Communism abroad, had the unmistakable stamp of the so-called Great Helmsman, Mao. Many of these decisions, in hindsight, proved to be hurried, and some even turned out to be catastrophic, as evidenced by the unprecedented casualties in the Cultural Revolution. Mao had the unique distinction of being the father of the Chinese Communist movement and enjoyed a life tenure.

Break from the Mao Era and Deng's Reforms: A subtle and gradual transition to the maxim of 'Collective Leadership' was approved in 1978, after the Mao era, at the Third Plenary Session of the much-heralded 11th Party Congress or CPC. 'Absolutism' or unquestioned authority was diluted, and more collective leadership was gradually introduced; yet, key strategic decisions regarding Taiwan, Hong Kong, and the island territories in the East and South China Seas continued to have the influence of Deng right till his demise. This was also facilitated by the fact that the new generation of leaders lacked the prestige and legitimacy that was enjoyed by the generation of Mao and Deng. **Deng also instituted a two-term limit and age criteria; the latter, though not clearly specified, has been understood to be 68 years.** The aim of these reforms was to essentially weed out the dead wood and the staunch loyalists of Mao. **Deng Xiaoping ushered in a series of reforms under the 'Four Modernisations', even opening up the economy in line with his famous remark, 'It doesn't matter whether a cat is black or white, as long as it catches mice.'**

Third and Fourth Generation – A Shift to Collectivism: The reinforcement of collective leadership was more notable during the reign of the third and fourth generations of leadership, with Jiang Zemin (1993–2002) and Hu Jintao (2002–2012). This transition, in its application, may seem well short of the Western norms, yet it was significant, with the initiation of 'democratic centralism'. **The overall opacity of the Chinese system hides a complex, nuanced, and subtle interplay of factions and interest groups—like the core elitists or princelings, also referred to** as **'*taizidang*', and the populists known as 'tuanpai'**. Besides these well-known groupings, there have been formulations like the Gang of Four, the Shanghai Group, etc.

Current Structure and Leadership

Apex Structure: The basic structures of the CPC include the National People's Congress (NPC), which comprises delegates representing all the regions. The NPC, being a very large body, with currently 2,970 deputies, elects a politburo, which is the de facto decision-making body, as the NPC remains largely a rubber-stamping body. In this matrix, the most powerful appointments are of the General Secretary of the CPC and the President of the CMC. The CMC is the apex military decision-making structure, which is staffed predominantly by military officers. The process of control over the PLA by the party in the earlier era was facilitated by Mao and Deng having their roots in the PLA itself.

Fifth Generation Under Xi: Xi Jinping heralded the ushering in of the fifth generation of leadership in the 18th Party Congress in

November 2012 by taking over as President with a five-year term lasting till 2017. **Xi engineered a major constitutional amendment on 11 March 2017, duly ratified by the NPC, wherein the two-term limit introduced by Deng Xiaoping in the 1990s was dropped. Resultantly, when Xi got elected for a second term on 17 March, it really implied an indefinite lifelong term, a rare privilege, which was the exclusive preserve of Chairman Mao. Without this amendment, which makes 64-year-old President Xi virtually an emperor, he would have ruled till 2023 only.** This move did generate its usual share of controversy; yet, informed analysts opined that the earlier two-year term had its own complications, like the exit of Jiang Zemin after two terms despite being groomed as Deng's successor. Resultantly, Hu came to the fore, but his term did cause certain imbalances and latent crises, which manifested during the Xi era.

Along with Xi, his trusted loyalist and close aide, 69-year-old, Wang Quishan was also elected as Vice President for a lifelong stint. Here again, the age criterion of 68 years, in vogue for nearly three decades, was waived. Wang is the most dreaded official, as he steered the anti-corruption purge in the first five-year term of Xi, which saw the sacking of 1.5 million bureaucrats and party functionaries, including nearly 100 ministers and top generals in the biggest crackdown in the history of China. While working under the overall direction of Xi, he is likely to steer the global outreach, including relations with the US, vitiated by Trumpism.

Premier Li Keqiang, who was appointed to a second five-year term, is virtually No. 2 in the hierarchy and handles economic affairs, but he has been reduced to a truncated role as Xi has taken over some of the key economic charters under his direct control. Xi intends to continue with his anti-corruption agenda through a newly instituted National Supervisory Commission (NSC), headed by Yang Xiadu. This body will also serve to enforce the party's control over a burgeoning bureaucracy and society. It has been given draconian powers to detain suspects for up to six months without a court order. Yang has some sort of India connect as he was China's special representative for the

Sino-Indian boundary talks in his capacity as State Councillor, the top diplomatic post. Wang Yi, erstwhile Foreign Minister, steps into this job and will now handle boundary negotiations with India.

Wang Fenghe, a former Commander of the Second Artillery, and a noted missile expert, was appointed as the new Defence Minister; he was later sacked as part of the anti-corruption purge. It is an astute choice as he is likely to bring his experience to mentor separation of the Missile Force into the recently reconfigured Rocket Force and SSF besides overseeing the infusion of cutting-edge technologies in surveillance, drones, AI, radars, submarines, aircraft carriers, and the whole range of weapon systems. Xi has entrusted the NPC to his erstwhile Chief of Staff, Li Zhanshu. Chen Wenquing has been retained to manage internal security, which includes the troubled and insurgency-affected region of Xinjiang. Other functions of Chen would include counter-terrorism, internal security, espionage, and counter-espionage. While many top-ranking appointments are retained, the system is likely to induct many new faces when lower-level appointments are finalised in what are officially described as elections, but are really guided by the top hierarchy.

Major Military Reforms

While Mao was a legendary leader, objective analysis suggests that his approach was 'attrition oriented', which is borne out by the over half a million casualties in the Korean War between 1950 and 1953. The PLA also suffered a considerable loss of face in the Vietnam War in 1979.

The process of reforms in the PLA was triggered off as part of Deng's 'Four Modernisations', which included reforms in the Armed Forces. However, the process remained diffused. Learning from the Revolution in Military Affairs (RMA) initiated by the US in the Gulf War in 1992, President Jiang decided to orient the PLA to prepare for its own version of RMA in what was dubbed as winning 'local wars under modern conditions'. The process crystallised into

'*Linaggezhuanbian*', which in essence was 'twin transformation', encompassing a shift from 'Quantity to Quality' and 'winning local wars under high-tech conditions'. President Flu Jintiao gave enhanced clarity and refined the mission to 'win local wars under informationalised conditions', thereby highlighting the overarching importance of information operations. Hu's vision contained in the famous White Paper titled, 'New Historic Missions' was promulgated in 2004. The process of reforms in China, starting with the Deng era, is well thought out, deep-rooted, and reflects long-term commitment, though it is tweaked to keep it in sync with contemporary realities.

The installation of Xi and the fifth-generation leadership initially focused on two key issues: firstly, preparing the PLA for emerging global and enhanced roles; and secondly, getting the PLA under the party apparatus firmly under party control. As a follow-up to the 18th Party Congress, it was decided in 2013 to set up an NSC headed by the President. To reiterate the party's hold over the PLA, President Xi Jinping addressed a conference of party workers at Gutian, where Mao had outlined the philosophy in 1929, stating that the PLA is the party's army. Xi's remarks were: 'The PLA still remains the party's army and must maintain absolute loyalty to the political masters.' President Xi has also given additional impetus to the ongoing reforms, like a reduction in strength by three lakh troops to downsize the overall PLA strength to two million from the earlier 2.3 million. As has been outlined earlier, right-sizing has been part of a trend: the PLA was 4.5 million till 1980, resized to three million in 1985, and now to two million. The optimisation also includes cutting down the army and enhancing the strength, equipment, capabilities, and role of the maritime forces. The prime example is the induction of aircraft carriers and the deployment of a naval task force for counter-piracy in the Gulf of Aden from 2009 onwards. China has also acquired a number of bases and operating/surveillance facilities in ports like Djibouti, Gwadar, Hambantota, Maldives, Coco Island, and Fiery Cross Reef, in what is described as the 'string of pearls' or, more benignly, as the Maritime Silk Corridor.

Xi has also chosen to address the issue of corruption and other malpractices in the PLA head-on. In a somewhat risky and bold move, as many as 3,000 personnel, including over 50 top generals, were removed, and some were meted out serious punishment. This has also served to build a loyal stream of the PLA, duly vetted by him. Despite his non-PLA background, he has established a firm grip over the Armed Forces and is also seen donning combat gear to identify with them. Notwithstanding reforms and concerted drive for weeding out corruption, in October 2023, members of apex decision-making structures like Defence Minister Li Shangfu, his predecessor, Wei Fenghe, and Foreign Minister Qin Gang were sacked. Besides, nine PLA generals, including five top generals of the Rocket Force, the former Air Force Chief, and the Fleet Commander of the South China Sea, were removed from the NPC. More importantly, the Chairmen of China Aerospace Science and Technology Corporation and the major manufacturing entity, the NORINCO Group, were also sacked. **It raises very serious concerns about, firstly, the scale and degree of corruption; secondly, the process of selection and appointment, and most importantly, the very quality of products made in such a compromised system. It has also raised questions on the competence of Xi as all top appointments are cleared by him.**

Structurally, the PLA has been reorganised as the Ground Force Command (erstwhile army), PLA Navy (PLAN), PLA Air Force (PLAAF), with two new service HQs: Rocket Force and SSF. The Rocket Force is essentially an upgradation of the Second Artillery, which will operate strategic and conventional missiles. The SSF is tasked with the emerging disciplines of cyber, space, and political (psy-ops). These reforms reflect an enhanced role for the maritime forces, missiles, cyber, space, and technology, at some cost to the army. However, in April 2024, SSF was reorganised into three separate arms—Aerospace Force, Cyberspace Force, and Information Support Force. In effect, the PLA will have four theatre-grade arms—army, navy, air force, and Rocket Force, along

with four sub-theatre level arms reporting directly to the CMC. These are aerospace, cyberspace, information support, and joint logistics forces.

These reforms have been followed through at the operational level with the **reorganisation of 17 unwieldy commands into just five Theatre Commands. The net result is that the Tibet border is now managed by one Theatre Command, the Western Command, instead of the forces of the Chengdu and Lanzhou Military Regions, with some reserves from Guangzhou, in certain contingencies.** All resources, including ground, air, maritime, missile, cyber, space, and logistics, are now seamlessly integrated at the command level, ensuring synergy. These reforms have been followed through at the operational level with the creation of 84 corps-level organisations, including 13 operational ones. A matching review of training, repair, and logistics structures has also been carried out.

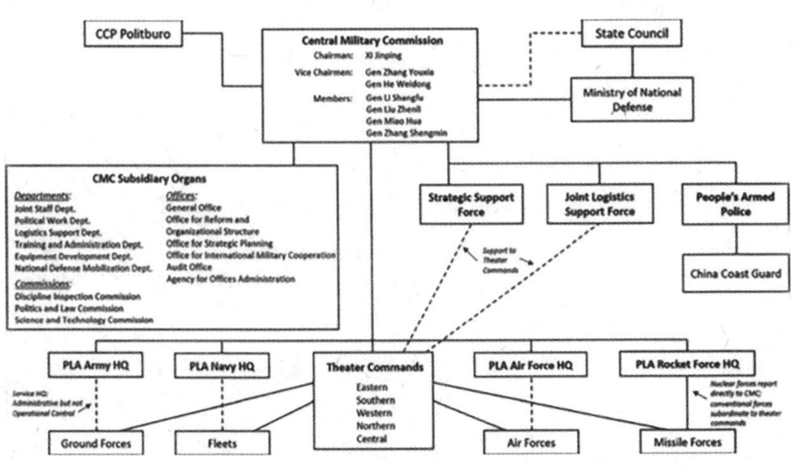

(Graphic – Courtesy Wikipedia)

The outline organisation of Theatre Commands with their responsibilities is as follows:

- **Eastern Theatre Command:** HQ at Nanjing with responsibilities for Taiwan and the East China Sea, comprising 71, 72, and 73 Corps.

- **Southern Theatre Command:** HQ at Guangzhou, with the charter of Vietnam and the South China Sea, and including 74 and 75 Corps.
- **Western Theatre Command:** HQ at Chengdu, with responsibilities of Tibet and internal security, primarily Xinjiang, including 76 and 77 Corps.
- **Northern Theatre Command:** Shenyang as HQ, with charge of the Russian border and Korean peninsula, with 78, 79, and 80 Corps.
- **Central Theatre Command:** HQ at Beijing, with responsibilities of internal security and reserves with 81, 82, and 83 Corps.

Likely Implications at the Macro Level

The changes have functional as well as political ramifications, which are of special relevance to us. An assured life term does give the system great stability, ensuring continuity, yet it also leads to absolutism and sycophancy. It can lead to a vacuum and even a power struggle in the event of the untimely demise or removal of the President. It also removes all pretensions of democracy and collectivism, which the Chinese emphasise very stridently. It will endow Xi with an enhanced international stature and a larger-than-life image, as such unparalleled authority has been enjoyed only by a very few like Mao, Fidel Castro, Saddam, and Gaddafi. However, unfortunately, all of them earned considerable notoriety for being autocratic and despotic. Functionally, changes, especially in the PLA, notably of right-sizing reorganisation, like the Theatre Commands, an enhanced role for the maritime forces, reliance on technology, and the eradication of corruption, are all path-breaking, commendable, and will set the stage for continued transformation. China's modernisation of the PLA is reflected in the increasing footprint of the Chinese in the South China Sea, Indo-Pacific, and even Africa. China has also enhanced its participation and funding in UN peacekeeping missions. It has also engaged the African countries in a concerted drive and pledged $100 million for a Standby Force for the African Union, as well as resources for a disaster management force. The PLA has achieved considerable capability to produce armaments and munitions and has emerged as the largest exporter of small arms and light weapons, as per the latest SIPRI projections.

Conclusion

China, under its fifth-generation leadership and the PLA, after its transformation, has started muscle flexing, causing considerable discomfort and concern amongst the neighbours. While China continues to downplay these concerns, it will be in order if China walks the talk and settles the maritime and other border disputes. For India, all these changes have a direct implication, and it is axiomatic that these are analysed and carefully watched.

References

1. CPC Report to the 18th CPC.
2. CPC Report to the 19th CPC.
3. Nalin Surie, ' Past 19th Party Congress: China's Strategic Direction and Behaviour', *USI Strategic Yearbook, 2018.*
4. Maj Gen GG Dwivedi, 'China's Revolutionary Military Reforms; Salient Imperatives: Strategic Implications', *USI Strategic Yearbook, 2018.*
5. Maj Genl Deepak K Mehta, 'Xi Set to Rule For Life', IMR, April 2018

5.2 Coping with Chinese Techno-Psy War (Written in January 2021, updated post Operation Sindoor)

Key Takeaways

- **Drones have emerged as a potent weapon system and a sort of game-changer.**

- **Chinese hype on decisive tech asymmetry over India needs to be debunked.**
- **Update: The myth of Chinese technical asymmetry being decisive is largely debunked. Indian forces have been able to execute their missions effectively. However, complacency on this account cannot be allowed in the future, and efforts must remain focused on technical modernisation.**
- **Update: Operation Sindoor: Pakistan extensively utilised Chinese equipment, including aircraft—J-10C, JF-17; PL-15 missiles, HQ-9B and HQ-16 AD systems, and SH-15 artillery guns. As per international opinion, Pakistan integrated PLA systems well, yet suffered losses in radars. Indian strikes and significant degradation of Pakistan Air Force assets debunk hype on Chinese tech asymmetry, yet we have to learn appropriate lessons.**

Notable examples of PLA's hype have been stories of the positioning of microwave oven-type devices to literally vaporise troops on the Kailash range. Another fable has been swarms of drones, flying noodles to PLA troops with the capability to deliver munitions. The more recent one is the supply of 50 Wing Loong II armed drones to Pakistan. These may have been provided with conditions to enhance the security envelope of the CPEC installations. However, attacks on Chinese assets and personnel engaged in the CPEC and other projects have continued. The accompanying hype in Chinese media predicts that Indian troops will be sitting ducks. It will be prudent to debunk such attempts, aimed at cognitive manipulation as part of the three-warfare strategy. The aim is to trigger another psychological collapse, like the one witnessed in Armenia.

Chinese technology, especially in aerial weapons, though cheap and widely proliferated, has its share of serious hiccups. In 2011, China unleashed a kind of 'supply shock', selling drones to a large number of countries. Michael Horowitz of the University of Pennsylvania described this proliferation as 'pursuit of status: synonymous with tech innovation'. Algeria has had a series of accidents in the last six years with CH-4 unmanned combat aerial vehicles (UCAVs). Jordan had to put on sale Chinese-supplied unmanned aerial vehicles (UAVs) after they failed on all parameters. In the recent war in Nagorno-Karabakh (NGK), the only Chinese equipment was a WM-80 multiple launch rocket system (MLRS) on the losing side. Chinese UAVs are yet to prove their efficacy and reliability in contested environments. There are growing concerns about Chinese-supplied platforms like aircraft and tanks in Pakistan, Nigeria, and Myanmar. This appraisal notwithstanding, we should prepare for this inevitably promising weapon of the future, as both our adversaries are building potent capabilities. Preparations must be in both offensive and defensive domains.

We have a functional AD control and reporting system, which should be tweaked. Indigenous initiatives on Radio Frequency (RF) guns to distract incoming drones and an anti-drone radar system developed by Bharat Electronics Limited (BEL) need fast tracking. In the offensive domain, our limited stock of Israeli Harop (Harpy-2) requires an urgent boost with the induction of munitions, currently under order. The project of arming Heron UAVs needs to be expedited. After the conclusion of the Basic Exchange and Cooperation Agreement (BECA), negotiations for armed MQ-9 drones from the US should find greater traction. **With the induction of drones, forces need a technological upgrade, along with a review of inventories of aircraft and costly platforms. Drones should be the key focus for the Atma Nirbhar initiative. The biggest takeaway is that frontline entities require better and organic air defence envelopes.**

Sino-Bhutan Border, Siliguri Corridor, and Dolam (Doklam)

6.1 Bhutan-China Border Problems and Boundary Talks: Implications for India

Key Takeaways

- The annexation of the buffer state of Tibet by China in 1950 jolted Bhutan into a strategic shock of China as a neighbour.
- China has deliberately kept its land borders with India and Bhutan unresolved.
- The issue has a trilateral dimension with strategic implications for India due to Chinese forays in Dolam (Doklam), posing a threat to the Siliguri Corridor.
- Bhutan seems to be showing signs of altering its long-standing policy of conducting external affairs through India, yet it has reassured that it will keep India's interests in mind.
- Regime change in Bangladesh has resulted in anti-India sentiment gaining ground. Hobnobbing with China and Pakistan, these elements have added to the threat to the Siliguri Corridor.

Introduction

China has unresolved land borders with just two countries, India and Bhutan, out of a total of 14 bordering nations. The Sino-Bhutan border in the western (Doklam) and eastern (Sakteng) sectors has strategic significance for India, as it not only includes a tri-junction but also has far-reaching operational implications. Bilateral talks between Bhutan and China, which had stalled since the Doklam crisis in 2017, notwithstanding the signing of an MOU incorporating a three-point framework, were revived with the 25th round on 23 and 24 October at Beijing. In a move that has ominous portents for India, both sides signed another cooperation agreement. It appears that Bhutan is willing to settle its boundaries, notwithstanding Indian reservations, although Bhutan has assured that it will consult India and keep its interests in mind.

Aim

The basic aim of this paper is to map various dimensions connected with the Sino-Bhutan border and analyse the issue in a trilateral format, factoring in implications for India.

Preview

This paper is laid out in the following parts:

a) Chinese Border Disputes – Major Inferences.

b) Geo-Strategic Significance.

c) Historical Context.

d) Disputed Territories.

e) Border/Boundary Resolution Process.

f) Indian Concerns.

g) Way Forward.

Chinese Border Disputes – Major Inferences

China has borders with as many as 24 countries, including terrestrial (land) and maritime domains. It has land borders with 14 countries and claims to have settled boundaries with all its neighbours, except India and Bhutan. However, these claims must be viewed

realistically, in the context that most disputes have been resolved on terms stipulated by China. There are contentious claims in some sectors in countries like Kazakhstan and Nepal. The PLA has a belligerent history, marked by aggression against India in 1962; a six-month-long border conflict with the USSR in 1969, and a brief armed conflict with Vietnam in 1979. It is currently engaged in an unresolved standoff with India in Ladakh since 5 May 2020. Apart from this, there have been unilateral Chinese attempts at salami-slicing in the eastern sector in Arunachal Pradesh and Sikkim. The recent instances include the 72-day-long standoff in Doklam in June 2017 and in Yangtse on 9 December 2022.

In the maritime domain, China has serious issues with all its neighbouring littoral states. It is engaged in serious skirmishes/standoffs with the Philippines, Taiwan, Vietnam, Brunei, and Malaysia in the South China Sea and Japan in the East China Sea. China has unilaterally proclaimed its own claims in terms of the ambiguous Nine-Dash and even Eleven-Dash lines. The layout of these has varied over the years, and claim lines are contested by other affected states. These have been misused to take control of tiny, uninhabited reefs and shoals and convert them into artificial islands for naval facilities. An arbitral tribunal in 2016 declared the Chinese claim to be a violation of the United Nations Convention on the Laws of the Sea (UNCLOS). **International strategic experts opine that China uses border disputes to build pressure on smaller neighbours by bullying them. It has mastered the art of filibustering and endless parleys to tire out the other party. It is also described as the application of Mao Zedong's dictum, 'Tan, tan, da, da'—talking, talking (but) preparing for war. Settlement, if any, has to be within the Chinese template, with time being of no consequence.** It is also making use of imaginative cartography by articulating multiple claim lines backed up by the selective use of favourable treaties, in what is increasingly being termed as lawfare. These have acquired a dangerous overtone with China in 'wolf-warrior' mode, being referred to as the Dragon, on the hegemonic overdrive.

Geo-Strategic Significance

Bhutan and China, as two neighbours, are a very apt manifestation of the biblical analogy of David and Goliath. Bhutan was envisaged as a buffer state between India and Tibet and had no border with China. The region was confronted with geo-strategic shock when Tibet was annexed and amalgamated with China in 1951. Coupled with this is the unresolved border between India and China, further vitiating the imbroglio. It has acquired a strategic dimension in the 'Thucydides trap' type of situation, developing between the rising powers of China and India. With China's proclivity to dominate India's immediate neighbourhood, it also affords opportunities to smaller states like Nepal, Maldives, and Bhutan to play the balancing game between two contestants, India and China. Bhutan, with an area of 38,000 square kilometres, is a very sparsely populated, hilly, and landlocked state with just 7,50,000 people. For ease of comprehension, it is even smaller than Denmark in area but with one-seventh of its population. Its capacity to police and manage its disputed borders is very limited. Bhutan follows an insular and gateway approach to preserve its ecology. Even tourism is regulated through numbers under the 'minimum impact with maximum revenue' paradigm. Bhutan shot into prominence by topping the Gross National Happiness (GNH) rankings.

Bhutan's border with China is bounded by two tri-junctions with China and India, and extends 477 km or 295 miles. In the east, the border starts from Mt Gipmochi (the location of which is contested) and was highlighted during the Doklam crisis in 2017. The border starting from the western sector, extends northwards, over the partially-disputed Jomolhari (also known as Chomolhari) range, turning eastward near Mt Masang Gang, including a large unresolved stretch in the northern sector and turning south-eastward, in proximity of Singye Dzong, the provincial capital, ending at a tri-junction point. The eastern stretch, including the Sakteng Wildlife Sanctuary, was traditionally considered settled but has now been claimed by China, thereby expanding the scope of the dispute. Access from Bhutan to China is regulated through the road trail at the Tremo La pass, which connects Tsento Gewog and Phari.

Bhutan-India Border: India has a border of 699 km, spanning four Indian states (Sikkim, West Bengal, Assam, and Andhra Pradesh). Most of the Indo-Bhutan border is open, and transit is channelised through Phuensholing/Jaigaon, Gelephu, and Samdrup Jongkhar border towns. **The geo-strategic edge and sensitivity are imparted to the Sino-Bhutan-India border issue due to the relative location of the Chumbi Valley in the western sector vis-a-vis the Siliguri Corridor. The corridor, which is just 22 km at its narrowest, is also described as 'chicken's neck' or 'north-eastern jugular'.** It is literally a gateway from the mainland to the north-eastern states, also known as the 'seven sisters and one brother'. It can also act as a springboard for forays in neighbouring Nepal, Bhutan, and Bangladesh. Please refer to Map-1.

Historical Context

Bhutan's border with Tibet has never been officially recognised or demarcated, and is largely, a fallout of the inherited, ambiguous colonial legacy of British rule. It has been a complex construct based on exchanges between Tibet, Sikkim, Nepal, and British India. Chinese claims date back to the pre-PRC regime of the Manchu Dynasty in 1910–11, when Zhao Erfeng staked a territorial claim on parts of Bhutan and Tibet. These were reiterated by the CCP in 1949, on establishing the PRC. The theoretical construct was outlined in Mao Zedong's diktat expounded in the Communist Party treatise 'The Chinese Revolution and the Communist Party', in 1939, 'the correct boundaries of China would include Burma, Bhutan, and Nepal'.

Mao also emphasised this in his expansionist 'Five Fingers of Tibet' policy. Citing Tibet as the palm, the fingers include Ladakh, Nepal, Sikkim, Bhutan, and Arunachal Pradesh (referred to as South Tibet). In the Chinese conception, all these are part of greater Tibet, annexed under unequal treaties by the erstwhile colonial powers. This claim was reinforced with imaginative cartography, including maps that formed part of the publication, 'A Brief History of China', published in 1959. Large portions of Bhutan, as well as territories of other countries, were included within the ambit of Chinese claims. The annexation of Tibet in 1950–51, followed by a 17-point agreement forced on the hapless Tibetan regime, resulted in the withdrawal of Indian and Bhutanese representatives from their missions in Lhasa. This was followed by a rebellion in Tibet in 1959, the flight of the Dalai Lama to India, and approximately 6,000 refugees seeking asylum in Bhutan and many more in India. Consequently, Bhutan, fearing being swamped by migrants and refugees, closed its borders. The PLA occupied several adjoining Bhutanese exclaves in Western Tibet in July 1959. These included Darchen, Gartok, and several other villages near Mt Kailash, under Bhutanese control for 300 years since the seventeenth century. These had been given to Bhutan by Ngawang Namgyal in the seventeenth century.

Diplomatic Ties with India: Indo-Bhutanese ties are based on the Treaty of Perpetual Friendship signed in 1949 and renewed in 2007. Fearing Chinese expansionist forays, including repeated incursions and denial of traditional grazing rights, Bhutan established military relations with India. These included Indian Military Training Team (IMTRAT), joint check posts for access, and joint defence contingencies. **In this situation of inequality with China, instead of 'Balance of Power', for Bhutan, it is realistically 'Balance of Terror' due to aggressive salami-slicing by the PLA. Bhutan, officially, still maintains a neutral stance in order to retain an uneasy balance in the triangular matrix.** India represented and negotiated Bhutan's concerns in talks with China during the Sino-Indian border conflicts resolution parleys till 1970. India has been the largest export market for Bhutan, accounting for 93% of its total exports, and is also the largest aid provider. Bhutan also plays a vital, synergistic role in India's Neighbourhood First and Act East Policies.

Bhutan – External Affairs: Bhutan has been dealing with the outside world through a reliable ally, India, and has allowed just three embassies in Thimphu to India, Bangladesh, and Kuwait, despite having diplomatic ties with 53 countries. Bhutan joined the UNO in 1971. Like India, Bhutan has followed the 'One China' policy. China is actively pushing for opening a mission in Thimphu. India has discouraged unregulated diplomatic forays in Bhutan to shield the tiny state from avoidable great power game and manipulation. China has made huge inroads into the economy of Bhutan, replacing India as Bhutan's largest trading partner, albeit in one-way traffic with mounting dependencies. Chinese footprints have proliferated in infrastructure projects, including connectivity, power generation, and communications. All these are building up to tremendous economic coercive leverage.

Disputed Territories

Bhutan's perception of disputed areas was outlined in official statements in the National Assembly. These have listed four disputed areas between Bhutan and China—please see maps. In the west, it includes approximately 89 square kilometres in the Dolam (increasingly referred to as Doklam) plateau—please see map. Sinchumlumpa and Giu (approximately 180 square kilometres) make it 269 km of unresolved stretch, bordering the Chumbi Valley in the western sector. The Chumbi Valley is a dagger-shaped narrowing wedge between India and Bhutan. The southern narrow portion of the valley, the Dolam (Doklam) plateau, with its strategic significance, has the potential to pose a threat to the tenuous Siliguri Corridor, termed as jugular, connecting the North-East with the mainland. **The Chinese quest is to widen the extremely narrow base of the valley. The dispute is indexed to the location of Mt Gipmochi and the correct interpretation of the watershed of rivers like Amo Chu. It is a complex bevy of crest lines and heights—Gamochen, Batang La, and Sinche La**—please see Map. The most sought-after is the Zompelri (Jampheri) ridge, providing a launch pad for reaching the Siliguri Corridor. A balanced view is that while it is indeed a threat, logistics and terrain make it a tortuous and slow exercise, requiring extensive logistics build-up. However, it remains a very potent threat in the future.

Unresolved areas in the northern region are in two pockets of Jakarlung and Pasamlung, spanning approximately 495 square kilometres. In June 2020, China sprung a surprise by bringing in unspecified areas in the eastern region of the Sakteng Wildlife Sanctuary in the Tashigang district. This was surprisingly articulated in virtual meeting of the Global Environment Facility (GEF) discussing a grant for Sakteng, wherein China termed it as a disputed region. It is opined that the claim may only be to increase leverage as a bargaining chip in a swap deal, and also to preclude the development of joint infrastructure by Bhutan with India.

Border/Boundary Resolution Process

The first outreach to China by Bhutan was an invitation to the Chinese envoy in New Delhi for the coronation of K-5, King Jimmy Singhe Wangchuk. The steering role of the present king's father, K-4, is that of an elder statesman based on his domain knowledge. He remains the key enabler for Bhutan in boundary dispute resolution. Two Foreign Ministers, Wu Xueqian and Dawa Tsering, held parleys in New York for formulating a mechanism for bilateral ties. Some reports state that these talks happened without taking India into confidence, taking it by surprise. This resulted in annual direct boundary talks starting from 1984. Both countries signed a bilateral agreement for maintaining peace on the border, broadly based on the five principles of Panchsheel. Peaceful co-existence is to be based on mutual respect for sovereignty and territorial integrity. After 14 years, both sides signed a memorandum on the Guiding Principles on the Settlement of Boundary Issues in 1988.

China proposed a 'package proposal' in 1990 in the seventh round of talks. It proposed to concede its northern claims (495 square kilometres) in exchange for Bhutan agreeing to China's western claims, including 89 square kilometres of Doklam. China has already renounced its claim on 154 square mile area in Kula Khari in the north, explaining it as a cartographic error.

This is in line with the Chinese quest for strategic reach through the Chumbi Valley. Bhutan in the 10th round (1995), appeared willing to accept the package deal. However, Bhutan retracted in 1996, allegedly under Indian influence. China and Bhutan signed the Agreement on Maintenance of Peace and Tranquillity along the border areas. However, China's building of roads on the Bhutanese territory, allegedly in violation of an informal 1998 standstill agreement, provoked tensions again. In the 2002 round of parleys, China presented purported 'evidence', asserting the ownership of disputed tracts of land; after negotiations, an interim agreement was reached. Foreign Minister Damochi Dorji visited Beijing in August 2016 for the 24th round of boundary talks with Chinese Vice President Li Yuanchao. Both sides indicated a willingness to settle the boundary issues. The entire process hit a major roadblock with the Doklam standoff in 2017, when India objected to the PLA attempting to build a road to the Zompelri (Jompheri) ridge, passing through contested Bhutanese territory in close proximity to Indian deployment on the unresolved LAC. The issue got resolved after a 72-day-long standoff between Indian and Chinese troops.

The Bhutan-China MOU of October 2021, signed in a video conference, is based on a three-step roadmap for a settlement. The stages are likely to be, firstly, establishing a framework; secondly, confirming and focusing on identified disputes, including the exchange of maps and finally, the resolution stage. Ironically, disputed territory, especially in the western region, is already under PLA control, making it a 'fait accompli' situation. **Bhutanese Foreign Minister Tandi Dorji held the 25th delegation-level talks on 23 and 24 October 2023 with his Chinese counterpart during his maiden official visit to Beijing. They signed a cooperation agreement—Responsibilities and Functions of the Joint Technical Team (JTT) on the Delimitation and Demarcation of the Bhutan-China Boundary.** These talks came after the first joint delimitation meeting, earlier in August 2023, held as part of the 13th Experts Group Meeting. Both sides exuded confidence for the early conclusion of talks. The Chinese side also expressed hopes for setting up a diplomatic mission in Thimphu. While Bhutan has not commented on Chinese optimism, it has not ruled out this possibility.

Indian Concerns

The Bhutanese side has assured that no agreement would be made 'against India's interests' and clarified that any talks about the 'tri-junction' at Doklam would only be held trilaterally between India, Bhutan, and China. Major concessions by China, especially in the western sector of the Chumbi Valley, are unlikely. China, when asked to be considerate to the smaller neighbour, reportedly responded that China has two dozen bordering states and cannot give such concessions. In this context, China, with its aim to establish its hegemony by keeping India in check, wants to expand its hold on the Chumbi Valley to pose a threat to the Siliguri Corridor. Physical salami-slicing combined with economic dependencies is eventually building coercive leverage on Bhutan. It appears that the Chinese strategy is to finally force Bhutan to accept terms being set by the Dragon.

Soon after the resolution of the Doklam crisis, China intensified efforts to build Xiaokang, dual-purpose, so-called model (moderately prosperous) villages on the Mochu River with military and logistics infrastructure, including habitation, helipads, ammunition dumps, and communications. Robert Barnett and his team of China experts claim that, since 2015, the PLA has been building military infrastructure, habitation, and communications in disputed areas of Northern Bhutan as well. Satellite imagery experts have mapped Gyalaphug as one of the five established villages. They have deciphered approximately 105 km (66 miles) of new roads/tracks, small hydropower generating station, two CCP administrative complexes, a communications centre, a disaster relief storage, five military/police outposts, and suspected major installations like a communications tower, satellite receiving station, military base, and potentially up to six security sites and satellite outposts. China claims that these constructions are in parts of Lhodrak in the Tibet Autonomous Region (TAR), but in reality, they are located in Northern Bhutan. This infrastructure with a distinct military character can be utilised to build up threats and operations against the Siliguri Corridor and India.

Update

The recent elections in January 2024 resulted in the voting out of Lotay Tshering, seen to be pushing for the resolution of the Sino-Bhutan border dispute. **The new Prime Minister, Tshering Tobgay, and his party, the People's Democratic Party (PDP), is more sensitive to Indian concerns. The Bhutanese king visited India and discussed the biggest connectivity and megacity project anchored in Gelephu Mindfulness City.**

Regime change in Bangladesh and the establishment of a new government under Muhammad Yunus has resulted in anti-India sentiment gaining ground. These elements are hobnobbing with China and Pakistan. This has added to the collusive threat to the Siliguri Corridor. There are reports of China being roped in to upgrade Lalmonirhat airbase, just 20 km from the Siliguri Corridor.

Way Forward

Bhutan is faced with the challenge of walking a tight rope between increasingly aggressive China in 'wolf-warrior' diplomacy mode, and its time-tested ally, India. While India would like to safeguard its interests, Bhutan may, at some stage, yield to the Chinese package deal offer. India needs to balance its core interests with Bhutan's compulsions. It will be appropriate to guide Bhutan to seek the best deal, especially in limiting Chinese ambitions in the Doklam plateau. India should also remain invested in capacity building in Bhutan, especially in the security domain, to limit Chinese footprint in the economy and communications. It will be ideal if India is able to maintain joint defence capabilities and joint border check posts, even enlarging their scope. However, scaling down of these after border resolution is a very distinct possibility.

Autonomy and balancing are sensitive issues and can be built by long-term trust and healthy respect for mutual interests, eschewing a 'big brother' attitude. In this context, it bears reiteration that the ill-advised embargo on Liquid Petroleum Gas (LPG) and Kerosene in 2013 is still quoted and lamented by the Bhutanese populace. **India should cater for the contingency of Bhutan yielding to Chinese pressure and strengthen its hedging strategy. This would entail reinforcing the security grid and response matrix to safeguard the Siliguri Corridor. It is axiomatic that India's endeavour to build alternative connectivity in the North-East and resilience through strategic stocking is given enhanced impetus to cope with the growing Chinese threat.**

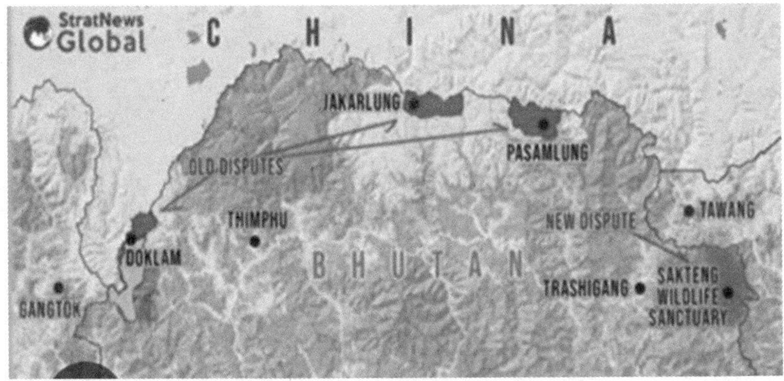

Google Maps

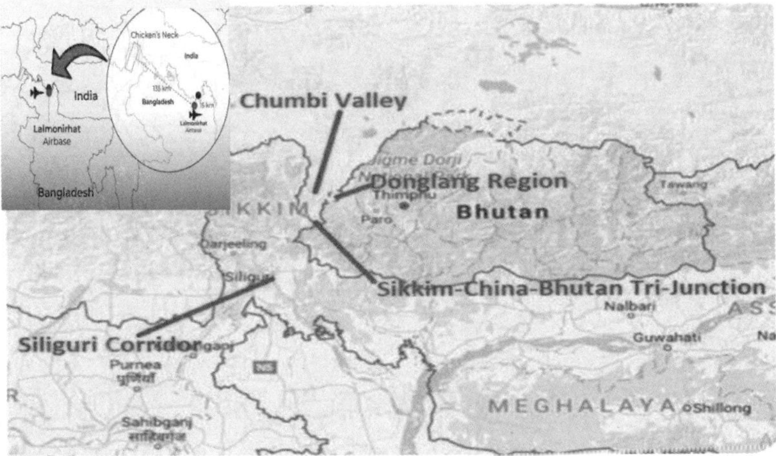

Wikki Maps – Wikipedia

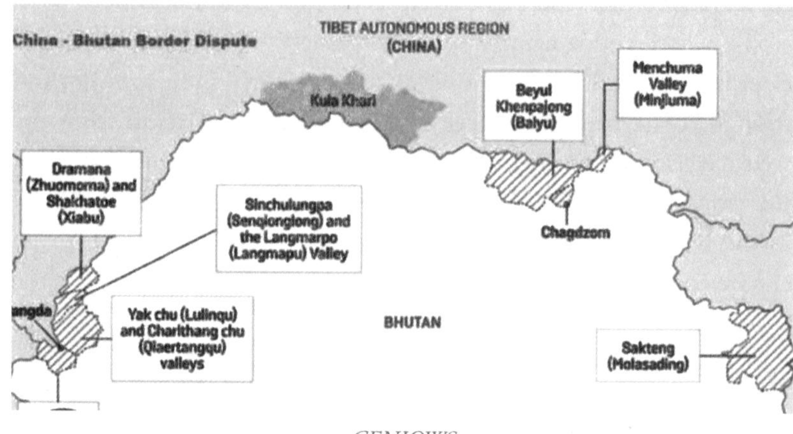

CENJOWS

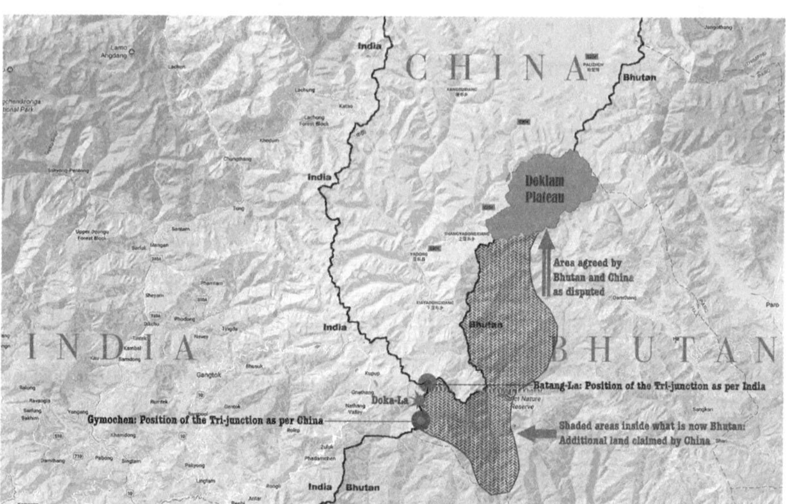

StratNews Global

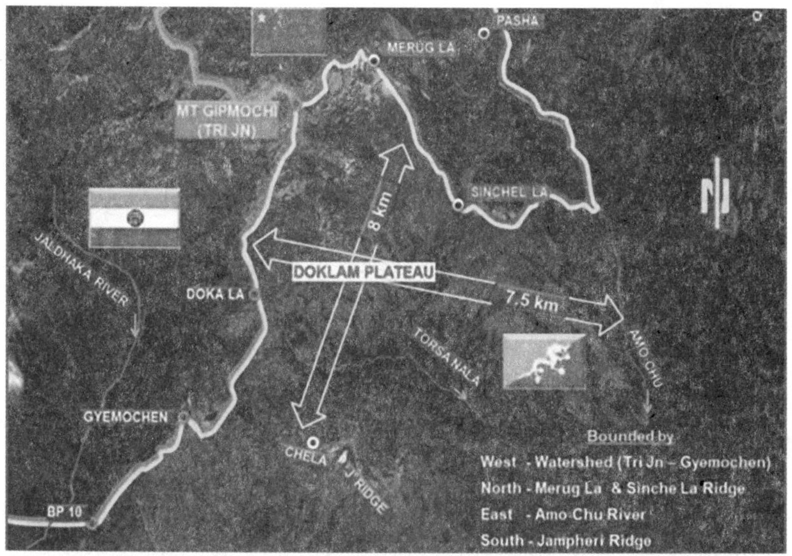

6.2 Dynamics of Security of Siliguri Corridor – Way Forward

Key Takeaways

- The Siliguri Corridor has borders with four countries and is a gateway to the North-East—the seven sisters and one brother.
- Multiple fault lines include the Gorkhaland and Kamatapur movements.
- Mitigating measures in surveillance, strategic reserves, and alternative connectivities need to be accorded priority.
- Regime change in Bangladesh and the new government under Muhammad Yunus has resulted in anti-India sentiment gaining ground. These elements are hobnobbing with China and Pakistan. This has added to the collusive threat to the Siliguri Corridor. There are reports of China being roped in to upgrade Lalmonirhat airbase, just 20 km from the Siliguri Corridor.

Introduction

Geography in terms of neighbours and boundaries throws up a myriad of challenges, which are classified as cartographic anxieties. These concerns and challenges, if not managed well, magnify into strategic vulnerabilities. The Siliguri Corridor, a tenuous link with the eight North-East states and a gateway for more than 50 million Northeasterners, is indeed a critical national vulnerability. This situation can be attributed to many geo-strategic and geo-economic factors, accentuated in the recent past by the aggressive activities of the Chinese in the Doklam or Dolam plateau. Apart from this, centrifugal forces manifesting in unresolved insurgencies and separatist movements in the North-East further accentuate these concerns.

Besides the external drivers, sensitivity is exacerbated by the mismanagement of lines, most notably the Gorkhaland problems, combined with other problems like the Kamtapur and Rajbongshi movements, which, though currently subdued, can spin out of control. This issue provides an opportunity for external elements to fish in troubled waters, keeping the region on boil. The corridor has a multitude of external and internal challenges, like illegal migration, counterfeits, narcotics, and cross-border smuggling of animals and wildlife products.

Dynamics of the Siliguri Corridor

The Siliguri Corridor is approximately a 200-km stretch with a width varying from 17 to 60 km. It is also aptly referred to as 'chicken's neck' and measures approximately 12,203 square kilometres. The eastern part of the corridor is wider and borders Bhutan and Bangladesh. The Chumbi Valley, tapering into the Dolam/Dokalam plateau, is barely 50 to 100 km away, depending on the contrasting boundary claims. While it is approximately 50 km as the crow flies, in such hilly and wooded terrain, large-scale movement is restricted and is confined along beaten paths/tracks. Mapping the corridor is a challenge as its limits are a matter of interpretation. The corridor is criss-crossed by streams like the Teesta, Rangeet, Mahananda, and Torsa, and a large number of nullahs and rivulets. Please refer to the maps at the end of this article. The corridor has a large number of reserve forests and wildlife, including elephants, in plenty, and also serves as a migration corridor for them. The corridor is defined by low hills, jungles, and broken ground, dotted with numerous rivers, streams, and nullahs, thereby posing multiple obstacles and formidable defence lines.

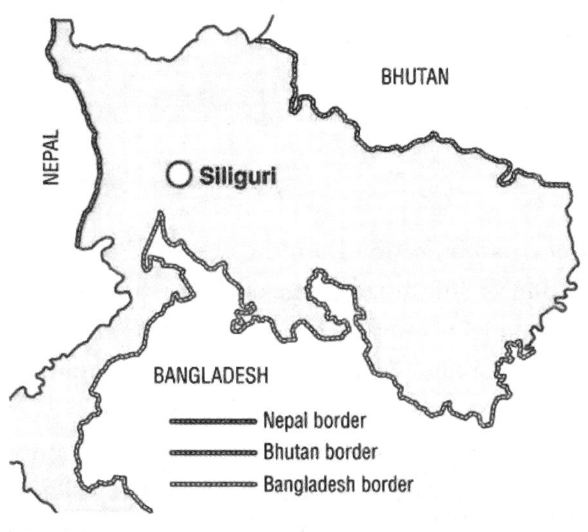

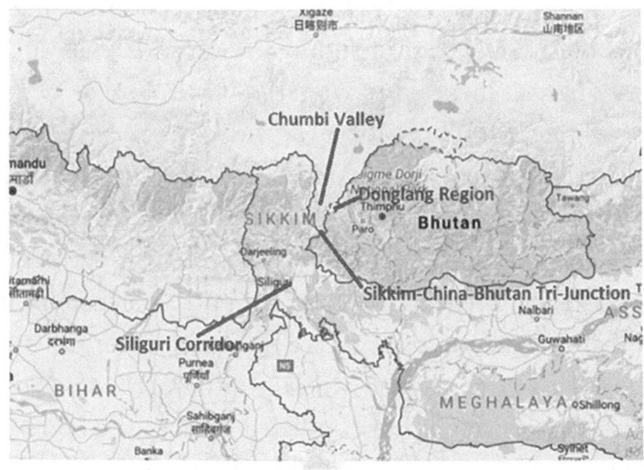

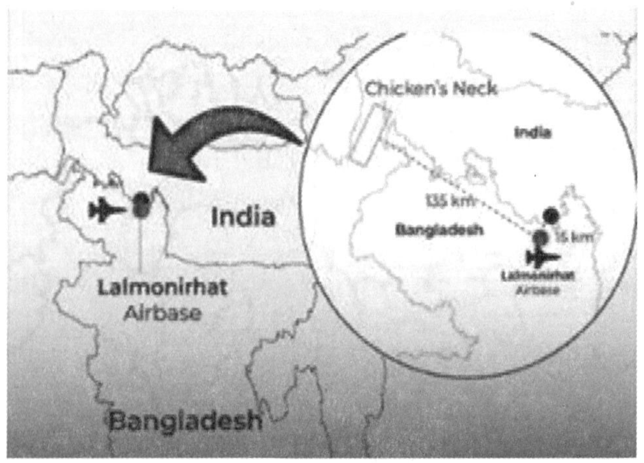

Map Credits – Wiki Maps and The Telegraph, Kolkata

Terrestrial communication from the mainland to the North-East is based on a double-line broad-gauge rail link. That is complemented by two national highways, which also provide a gateway to Bhutan through the twin townships of Jalgaon and Phuntsholing. In addition, vital hydrocarbon pipelines pass through this stretch along with communication links based on Optical Fibre Communication (OFC) systems. The corridor has two major airbases, Bagdogra and Hashimara. In addition, the army aviation base at Shaugaon is also planned to be operationalised. A large number of army and CAPF installations and their HQs, including a Corps HQ, are located in this narrow stretch. In keeping with the 'One Border, One Force' policy, the responsibility of borders is divided between the army and ITBP for China; SSB for Nepal and Bhutan; and BSF for Bangladesh. The multiplicity of forces and agencies requires an effective and tailor-made coordination mechanism. Most of the border, except for Bangladesh, is unfenced and porous, with treacherous riverine stretches. Tea, timber, and tourism are the main drivers of economic activity, controlled from Siliguri, which is the de facto capital of North Bengal, with regional HQs and associated offices. The booming city is also becoming a trading and medical tourism hub for neighbouring countries, besides being a skill provider based on education centres located in hill towns in the vicinity.

Kaliachak in Malda, in proximity to the corridor notorious for criminal activities, is the hub of counterfeit trafficking, narco-terrorism, and bomb-making. Uncontrolled migration from Bangladesh has complicated demographics, and Islamist radical groups and Madrasas have proliferated with the tacit support of the government agencies. Adding to the complexity are non-indigenous Meitei and Bodo settlements, which provide shelter to cadres, in addition to the United Liberation Front of Assam (ULFA) and Kamtapur Liberation Organisation (KLO), utilising it for transit, as was highlighted in Operation 'All Clear' in South Bhutan in December 2003. The simmering Gorkhaland problem, coupled with the Kamtapur insurgency, has made this region a potential target for hybrid warfare. Insurgency in Cooch Bihar is of a low order and follows twin tracks of demand for Kamtapur and Rajbongshi causes. These movements are sustained due to the support of other groups, who often seek shelter in parts of Southern Bhutan in collusion with KLO and other such splinter groups. These groups have also maintained linkages with Bhupalese (Nepali origin) elements settled in Southern Bhutan. However, Gorkhaland is a much more serious issue. The obvious question is, why should we allow it to become an Achilles' heel in our geo-strategic calculus and in this critical space? More of the Gorkhaland problem is discussed in the next part.

Parameters of the Gorkhaland Problem

The Gorkhas, early settlers from Nepal, migrated in the seventeenth century as part of the expansion of the Nepali kingdom and made the hills their homeland. In 1777, Nepal appropriated Sikkim, including the Darjeeling district. Settlers leveraged their entrepreneurial skills and took over Sikkim and the adjoining Darjeeling, marginalising native Lepchas and Bhutias. The Treaty of Sugauli in 1816 brought these areas under British rule.

The Gorkhas first articulated the demand for a separate administrative unit in 1907 through the Hillmen Association; however, it didn't find critical traction. The Gorkha National Liberation Front (GNLF), under ex-soldier Subash Ghising, gave the movement a new lease in the '80s. This led to the establishment of the Darjeeling Gorkha Hill Council (DGHC) in 1988 after a violent phase from 1986 to 1988, which claimed 1,200 lives. The GNLF ruled for 20 years, with a say in economic development, tourism, and culture. Following in the mould of militant-turned-failed leaders like Laldengs, Ghising was virtually booted out in 2008 and remained a non-entity till his demise. His legacy was appropriated by Bimal Gurung and Roshan Giri under the Gorkha Janmukti Morcha (GJM), surprisingly riding the popularity wave for Indian Idol candidate, Prakash Tamang. After the second wave of agitation lasting three years, the modified council, the Gorkha Territorial Administration (GTA), was established in August 2012 with an enhanced mandate and an additional five mouzas (revenue units corresponding to villages), thereby notionally enlarging its geographical scope into the Dooars. Gorkhaland, demanded by the protagonists, combines the hill tracts of Darjeeling, Kalimpong, Mirik, and the Dooars, which is a relatively plain area and low-rolling hills.

Dilution from the original demand of 398 mouzas to just five, and the non-inclusion of tea revenue, indicated that the problem is likely to fester. Notwithstanding the fact that departments under the GTA have been increased from 19 to 59, real delegation never happened. The ruling party in Bengal decided to utilise the British trick of divide and rule by instituting councils and boards for Lepchas, Shrepas, Bhutias, Tamangs, and other communities. Buoyed by the recent success of the Trinamool Congress (TMC) in the Mirik municipal elections and on the verge of the GTA elections due in July, Chief Minister Mamta made the ill-advised move of declaring Bangla as an additional language in the hills. The motive behind this move was revealed in the immediate rescinding of the decision, but it gave the GJM an escape route, as it was starting at a possible Ghising moment due to its failure on all fronts. However, a large share of the blame lies with the state government. Currently, there is an uneasy truce with Bimal Gurung going into hiding, consequent to being declared a proclaimed offender. The dissenting faction is running an interim arrangement till elections, which have been delayed indefinitely.

The Gorkhas deserve our gratitude and understanding for their loyalty, as they have made unparalleled sacrifices in many wars, starting from the legendary Maharaja Ranjit Singh, but more importantly, they need committed leaders. The state that they want is hardly economically viable, but it can find negative resonance and cause economic disruption in neighbouring states like Sikkim and even Bhutan, where the Bhupalese (Nepalese settled in Bhutan) issue has caused its own share of problems. **The governance and development of such a sensitive strip is a national responsibility and obligation. However, it has been conspicuous by its near-total absence. It is high time the state government, aided by the Centre, calms down frayed tempers in the hills and establishes a genuine and functional autonomous administration, as they have made unparalleled sacrifices in various campaigns.**

North Bengal

There is an emergence of a demand for the division of West Bengal into North Bengal and South Bengal provinces. **This demand, though politically motivated, has the potential for better security management if a Union Territory is carved out around the Siliguri Corridor and its borders. It needs to be taken into cognisance for the possibility of consideration in the future.** A Union Territory would be easy for governance and the operation of central agencies, but it would require a great deal of sensitivity in dealing with Bengali sentiment. It would also require the accommodation of the aspirations of the Gorkhas, which can be done through an autonomous district council. Similarly, for political reasons again, the Lepcha and Bhutia councils were recommended within the ambit of the GTA to dilute the Gorkhaland movement. **Any new measure needs to be carefully deliberated and executed after due consensus-building.**

The Chumbi Valley

Chumbi is a dagger-shaped valley, broad at the top and narrowing down to barely 15 to 20 km at the southern tip in the TAR, China. The valley is on the south side of the Himalayan drainage divide, near the Chinese border, sandwiched between Sikkim (India) and Bhutan. The Chumbi Valley is connected to Sikkim to the southwest via the mountain passes of Cho La, Nathu La, Jelep La, Batang La, and Doka La from north to south. While Jelep La is controlled by the Chinese, Nathu La is managed jointly by both countries. The three passes of Cho La, Batang La, and Doka La are controlled exclusively by India. The valley is at an altitude of 3,000 m (9,800 ft) and, being on the south side of the Himalayas, it enjoys a wetter and more temperate climate than most of Tibet. It is on one of the primary routes between India and Tibet; hence, the Chumbi Valley has been at the forefront of several military expeditions, like the Young Husband expedition. The British military expedition of 1904 occupied the Chumbi Valley for about three years after the hostilities to secure Tibetan payment of an indemnity. Contemporary documents show that the British continued the occupation of the Chumbi Valley until February 1908, after having received payment from China. Since the valley is dominated on both flanks, the Chinese endeavour has been to increase its width with unilateral claims, as the narrow valley restricts manoeuvre and deployment. China has already unilaterally extended its control in the east, up to its claim line. Towards the south, the Chinese quest is being mounted through Doklam, the tri-junction, to gain a foothold on the Jampheri ridge as a launch pad.

Doklam

Doklam or Dolam, as referred to by India and Bhutan, is called Donglang by the Chinese and Zhoglam in Standard Tibetan. It is an area with a plateau and a valley, sandwiched between Tibet's Chumbi Valley to the north, Bhutan's Ha Valley to the east, and India's Sikkim state to the west. While traditionally it has been depicted as part of Bhutan in the Bhutanese and other maps since 1961, it is also claimed by China. To date, the dispute has not been resolved despite several rounds of border negotiations between Bhutan and China. The area is of strategic importance to all three countries due to its proximity to the Siliguri Corridor, as well as providing launch pads into Sikkim and Bhutan.

Humphrey Hawksley's Dragon Fire and *The Assassin's Mac*e by Brig Gen Bob Butalia outline a scenario of the Dragon using the Chumbi Valley through Doklam and Jaldhaka to cut off the corridor. The recent 73-day standoff at the Doklam (also referred to as Dolam) plateau was a stark projection of the Chinese desire to build a road from the Chumbi Valley across the Torsa Nullah to the Bhutanese Chela post to gain a foothold on the Jampheri ridge with a view to threaten the Siliguri Corridor. Please refer to the maps in the previous article on the Sino-Bhutan border dispute.

Way Forward: Reducing the Vulnerability of the Siliguri Corridor

Defence of the Corridor: The Siliguri Corridor, with its low hills, jungles, and broken ground dotted with numerous rivers, provides multiple formidable defence lines. **Various possible scenarios with associated forms of threats, like airborne raids, have been war-gamed many times, with devil given more than its due, but in every such exercise and simulation, the Dragon is not only stymied short of the corridor, but the stage is set for QPQ options. While India certainly does not want war, yet for such an eventuality, troops, including mechanised forces, are not only earmarked but are regularly rehearsed.**

Managing Internal Fault Lines: It is absolutely important to deal with internal fault lines, most notably Gorkhaland and, to some extent,

Kamtapur and Rajabongshi in the corridor, on priority, and not allow them to be exploited by external players and intelligence agencies. It is also important to follow a zero-tolerance policy towards narcotics, counterfeits, and other illegal activities. State governments should rise above narrow interests, as in the case of sharing Teesta water during the lean season through the Farrakka Barrage, to accommodate the interests of Bangladesh to forge better ties, which can open possibilities for a transit corridor.

Inter-Agency and Force Coordination: There is a need to have a clear-cut division of responsibilities between security, intelligence agencies, and Border Guarding Forces to set up efficient coordination mechanisms. Problems of illegal migration, cattle smuggling, narco-terrorism, and trafficking counterfeit/wildlife products need to be managed efficiently.

Theatre Dynamics: In the eastern theatre, India is likely to engage in three separate sub-theatre battles in respective corps zones due to terrain configuration. The primary defensive architecture with inbuilt reserves is already in place. Newly raised Mountain Corps can be applied to further stabilise and even create limited QPQ options. Strategic airlift capability can be utilised to induct additional reserves. Even with attrition on communication links, at worst, there can be partial degradation, but certainly not disruption, for lots has been changing since 1962 in terms of building of infrastructure and force levels by India, as well as a will to stand up to bullying China, which was displayed in ample measure at Doklam. The requirement is to boost this dissuasive capability with additional surveillance, mechanised forces, air defence, and surveillance resources. There is also a requirement to have a separate designated HQ for the defence of the corridor with multi-agency coordination.

Building Redundancies: Risk mitigation dictates focused investment in strategic storage for critical commodities like hydrocarbons and munitions to boost the sustenance capability of the eastern theatre to reduce dependence on the corridor. The overall thrust should be to reduce the salience of the corridor.

Alternative Connectivities: There is a need to invest in the 'Act East' policy to link the North-East to the ASEAN, thereby reducing dependence on the mainland. The success of this policy is predicated on maintaining amiable relations with neighbours, especially Bhutan, Bangladesh, and Myanmar. There is also a need to invest in alternative connectivities, such as the Sittwe-Kaladan multi-modal project, which has been inordinately delayed, like the much-touted tri-lateral friendship highway connecting India, Myanmar, and Thailand.

The Bangladesh Corridor: A very viable project is a transit corridor through Bangladesh, as sustenance on an aerial bridge, even in an emergency, has limited potential. **Contagious to the corridor is the long-pending project of the Tetuliya link (4 km) through Bangladesh, which has the potential to reduce vulnerability and transit distance.** The security of the region is linked to partnerships with neighbours, particularly Bangladesh, for which the early resolution of the Farakka/Teesta dispute is mandatory. All these factors, cumulatively applied, have the potential to reduce the salience of the corridor.

Operationalising the 'Act East' Policy: India is showing increasing focus and interest in regional groupings oriented towards the east, like BBIN (Bangladesh, Bhutan, India, and Nepal), BIMSTEC, and now ASEAN. India needs to build on the diplomatic coup of getting ten ASEAN Heads of State as chief guests for Republic Day by graduating from symbolism to concrete measures, like the swift conclusion of the Regional Comprehensive Economic Partnership (RCEP).

The Indo-Pacific Switch: India needs to partner with Pacific countries by joining the Asia-Pacific Economic Cooperation (APEC) and further strengthening the Quad grouping, forged with the US, Japan, Australia, and India.

Conclusion

The Siliguri Corridor is an important strategic space—in fact, critical—yet, if handled well and leveraged with our resilience and capabilities, it can ensure that it does not become our Achilles' heel or a critical vulnerability. Since aggressively rising China is showing interest in this space and region, we need to apply a range of measures to build up our strategic deterrence from persuasive to credible deterrence. It is axiomatic that we build our capabilities and infrastructure, as well as forge regional linkages to reduce dependence on the corridor.

Relevance of Mechanised Warfare – Countering Drones and Chinese Tanks in High Altitude

7.1 Armoured Warfare: Relevant or Outdated?

Abstract

Tanks and armoured platforms have suffered very high attrition in the recent conflicts in Ukraine, Azerbaijan, and Syria, which has been amplified in the media. Consequently, this has triggered a serious debate on the very relevance of armoured warfare. **Tanks have traditionally been described and viewed as a sort of silver bullet; however, their limitations have been exposed by low-cost, armed drones, attacking in 'top-attack' mode, and their invincibility has been questioned.** On the other hand, countering the sceptics, Israel has recently fielded Merkava-Mk 4-Barak, duly fortified, against drone attacks. Hence, it may be premature to write the obituary of tanks and armoured warfare itself. It is imperative to carry out an objective appraisal of the efficacy of Armoured Fighting Vehicles (AFVs) as a fighting platform and examine the continued relevance of armoured warfare. Concurrently, relevant improvements in operational philosophy, employment, training, and design to prosecute armoured warfare more effectively in the contemporary battlefield environment need to be identified. It is also imperative to examine the relevance and applicability of these in our environment. **It may not be a zero-sum game, but it's better to rework the mix of weapon systems and platforms with drones, tanks, and other armoured platforms.**

Introduction

Hybrid warfare, with its growing relevance and largely being contested in the urban environment, has exposed the limited efficacy of AFVs in this genre of warfare. It has even prompted a few experts to opine that tanks, like the Walkman (discarded audio device of yore), have become obsolete. This concern has been amplified due to statistics of inordinately high tank casualties in recent conflicts like Ukraine, Nagorno-Karabakh (Azerbaijan), Syria, and Libya. **The success of armed drones has exposed the vulnerability of tanks against munitions in top-attack mode. The relative cost differential of tanks compared to considerably cheaper drones, and even anti-tank missiles, has magnified concerns amongst the strategic community.** It has become possible to saturate battle spaces, especially the restricted urban ones, with drones and portable anti-tank weapons. Various conflicts have witnessed the fielding of disruptive technologies in the form of anti-tank missiles, remotely delivered mines, attack helicopters, and armed drones, as well as loitering munitions, which seek to challenge the conventional hierarchy and invincibility of established weapon platforms in the new paradigm of asymmetric warfare. **A large number of anti-drone measures, both passive and active, like mock-up platforms, electronic soft-kill options, and hard-kill measures, are being fielded.**

It will be pragmatic to carry out an empirical analysis of the relevance of armoured warfare and AFVs, as premature sounding of the death knell will put ongoing research and development on hold. In our context, we have large armoured formations deployed on the western borders. In addition, recently, a large number of tanks were deployed in Ladakh and Sikkim at high altitudes. They were even applied in the vanguard of the pre-emptive occupation of the Kailash ranges. India and its potential adversaries (China and Pakistan) have a very large fleet of AFVs and have shown no inclination to discard them. India has also recently launched a project to develop a light tank, Zorawar, in response to the fielding of a light tank, ZTQ-15, by the PLA, opposite us in Ladakh, a high-altitude environment, indicating our continued commitment to armoured warfare.

Preview

The subject is discussed in the following parts:

a) Armoured Warfare – Early Trends.
b) Anti-Tank – Emergence of Challenges.
c) Performance Appraisal in Recent Conflicts.
d) Specific Issues Relevant in Our Environment.
e) Recommended Way Forward.

Armoured Warfare – Early Trends

Quest for the Silver Bullet: Starting with spears, shields, bow-and-arrows, gun-powder, and chariots, the quest for super weapons has been shaped by movement (manoeuvre), firepower for lethality, and protection for survivability as the three key determinants for designing and development of weapons. Armed Forces propelled by innovations, industrial revolutions, and the military-industrial complex tend to strive for the magical 'silver bullet' to secure decisive results on the battlefield. In the terrestrial domain, the quest started with elephants, horses, and chariots, progressing to mechanical locomotion, coupled with protected, armoured platforms. The tank was described as the game changer on its appearance on the battlefield of the Somme in 1916. Armoured warfare in the great world wars was introduced as the answer to static, trench warfare designed around the Maginot and Siegfried lines. Armoured battles have often been hyped up in war movies in Rambo-type imagery, of a tank being the ultimate terminator.

Design Parameters: Tanks combine three key elements of mobility (agility), firepower (lethality), and protection (survivability) in varying proportions, reflecting the war-fighting and design philosophy of stakeholders. While the stress is to design a lighter (more agile) platform, it must also carry a large-caliber gun and missiles, with all-around protection. **Yet, it finally turns out to be an optimised, compromise product that balances conflicting macro determinants**

and even adjustments within each key designing attribute. This explains the current vulnerability of tanks against top-attack munitions, which results from an emphasis on protecting the frontal arc, leaving the top portion of the platform (turret) relatively vulnerable. Different countries accord varying importance to design parameters. Germans advocate for agile platforms, citing mobility (agility), which aids survivability, as the governing paradigm. In contrast, Israel, with a premium on human resources, gives protection overriding importance, fielding much heavier tanks, and even placing the engine in front for additional protection.

Russian Tank – Design Philosophy: The Russians follow the **evolutionary design** concept with incremental improvements. The Chinese have cloned this approach. These tanks have a lower and rounded silhouette. In order to curtail weight, they have opted for an auto-loader and ammunition stowage in the crew compartment. This has caused horrific incidents of turrets getting yanked off and ammunition infernos in fighting compartments. In contrast, Western nations have ammunition stored in special compartments/pods, equipped with blow-off panels that shield crews.

Combined Arms and Joint Operations Concept: Tanks were designed to be utilised as part of an integrated war-fighting matrix, referred to as a combined arms team or integrated battle groups (IBGs), in a joint operations regime. Combined arms, as a term, is all-inclusive and incorporates combat support and logistics elements. They are certainly not stand-alone weapon platforms. Hence, it is more appropriate to use 'AFV' instead of 'tank' as a term. Even where the term 'tank' is used in this paper, it includes relevant implications to the connected AFV family. Over the years, driven by combat experience, the family of AFVs has grown with the spawning of newer complementary variants like infantry fighting vehicles (IFVs), reconnaissance/amphibious variants, combat support (firepower, AD, combat engineering, and network management) platforms, duly supported by logistics carriers. The bottom line and defining paradigm for armoured warfare has been fighting as part of a well-integrated matrix in a combined arms and joint operations template, duly supported by timely and responsive logistics. Matching mobility, complementary firepower, and shared protection have been key drivers, reflected in variants like Self-Propelled (SP) tracked guns, mounted AD carriers, half-tracked, and even high mobility wheeled vehicles like Stryker's, currently on offer by the US. Unlike India, many modern armies invariably have a complement of AFVs with infantry, especially those deployed in plains and deserts. The Israeli Merkava can carry up to eight infantry soldiers, making it a unique combo-platform.

Operating Paradigms: In armoured warfare, emphasis is on manoeuvre, to **generate surprise and shock action.** It is ideally prosecuted in open terrain to leverage attributes of mobility and long ranges. Combined arms teams, dispersion, and inexorable manoeuvre have been the overriding parameters. The complexity of multiple platforms, over a large dispersed battle space, has resulted in the incorporation of battlefield management and situational awareness systems. These are based on optronics (optics and electronic sensors), making it the fourth key design ingredient. Despite multiple lethal and long-range vectors, **AFVs have the unique capability to manoeuvre and close in on the target, projecting protected, vectored firepower to directly deliver shock and awe, triggering psychological dislocation.** Over the years, the large fleet of AFVs, Russia (12,000), the US (6,300), China (5,900), Pakistan (2,500), and India (4,300), provides ample proof of the proliferation of this concept. Even Bangladesh recently acquired the Chinese VT5 medium tanks. This large global inventory is backed by a proven combat track record and performance, albeit peppered with some recent reverses.

Anti-Tank – Emergence of Challenges

The Yom Kippur War – 1973: The Sinai war of 1973 was one of the largest deployments of mechanised formations after World War II. The

IDF fielded approximately 1,000 Israeli armoured vehicles against 2,400 AFVs of the Arab forces. **This war witnessed the introduction of wire-guided, first-generation, Russian Malyutka (AT-3 Sagger) missiles as a cost-effective anti-tank weapon system.** It also highlighted the Israeli crew's proficiency, enabling them to hold off superior Russian T-62s and T-55s with their older Centurions and M-48 tanks in the Golan Heights. **Israelis also displayed commendable skills in retrofitting and recovery during combat, to resuscitate damaged tanks, sometimes fielding 60–70% repaired AFVs in a 24-hour cycle.** This was based on classifying AFVs as, firstly, M-kills (only locomotion impaired but utilised as pill-boxes); secondly, F-kills (armament non-functional but capable of movement), and very few K (complete)-kills. Even K-kills were scrounged for sourcing functional components for cannibalisation. Conflict also highlighted the efficacy of the integration of weapons as part of combined arms and joint operations, including aircraft, AD, tanks, missiles, and artillery. The relative dominance of AFVs was challenged by the decisive reiteration of relatively economical 'anti-tank' weapons, in the form of anti-tank missiles, munitions, and mines.

The Gulf War I – 1991: Coalition forces, in 1991, during Gulf War I (Operation Desert Storm), a multinational offensive, anchored by the US, employed as many as 3,000 tanks, including 1,772 Abrams (594 with heavy armour). This fleet also included 180 Challengers, M-60, AMX-30, and lighter Sheridan tanks, clad with aluminium. Asymmetry created by multiple force multipliers like the Patriot AD system and bypassing manoeuvres in desert terrain, rendered Iraqi defences completely ineffective. **Defining manoeuvres enabled columns to advance 350 km in 97 hours.** As per reliable accounts, Iraq lost 3,300 AFVs against just 31 of the coalition forces. This war highlighted the relevance of IBGs, led by mechanised forces, especially in open desert terrain.

Gulf War II – 2003 to 2011: In stark contrast, Gulf War II in 2003, **after the initial success catalysed by technical asymmetry with force multipliers including AFVs, degenerated into a slogging hybrid**

war that lasted for eight years, till 2011. It underscored the limited efficacy of AFVs in counter-insurgency and urban fighting. Skilful use of anti-tank weapons contributed to negating asymmetry and conflict degenerating into a prolonged unresolved stalemate, where multinational forces and Americans were forced to seek face-saving exit. Success in Gulf War I and the initial phase of Gulf War II spurred a debate on the RMA; however, it was eroded to a considerable extent in Gulf War II, particularly due to forces getting bogged down in a quagmire of slogging hybrid war.

The Lebanon Conflict – 2006: Anti-tank tactics were successfully employed by Hezbollah against the mighty Merkava 4M tanks in 2006 in Southern Lebanon. **Fifty-two such platforms, each costing $2.5 million, were hit and disabled by Kornet missiles and even basic rockets, costing just $900 per piece.** This was despite Israel adopting the revolutionary concept of putting the engine in front to bolster protection. Out of this array, missiles and rockets made it difficult for tanks to operate in an urban milieu, where tanks lost their standoff leverage due to restricted fields of fire. Consequently, the ill-fated Operation Change of Direction was called off midway due to heavy casualties and a dent in the famed invincibility of the IDF, particularly its signature platform, Merkava 4M. Over-reliance on Merkava tanks proved suicidal for the IDF. The lessons of this conflict were reinforced in the concurrent, unresolved Gulf War II due to the similarity of terrain, weapons, and tactics.

Tank and Anti-Tank: Anti-tank warfare array has seen the introduction of 'top-attack' by long-range vectors, like artillery-delivered Krasnopol, guided bomb-lets, and remotely delivered mines. Attack helicopters and armed drones have boosted this capability. A modern tank costs ₹75–80 crores, whereas drones cost around ₹40 lakhs, and missiles, just a fraction. This also gives a bit of David vs. Goliath characterisation to this contestation. **Low-cost and versatile anti-tank weapons can be used to saturate the confined urban battle space. In an urban milieu, tanks lose their advantages of manoeuvre and long**

ranges. AFVs have sought to boost their protection by improvising the Tank Urban Survival Kit (TUSK) and Bradley Urban Survival Kit (BUSK). Kits incorporate cage-like structures, comprising spaced, slat claddings, and flails. The Indian Army recently ordered mock-up tanks to confidence drones. AFVs also incorporated Explosive Reactive Armour (ERA) panels and grenade launchers, which disrupt penetrative jets of High Explosive Anti-Tank (HEAT) attack. Automated Active Protection Systems (APS) like Arena, Shtora, and Trophy, though expensive, are also being incorporated to detect and degrade threats to AFVs. It would be seen that, like a cat-and-mouse game, every new disruptive effect or weapon triggers an antidote. At best, an asymmetrical advantage like the current one, in favour of armed drones, is only temporary until it is offset by an effective antidote.

Performance Appraisal in Recent Conflicts

Nagorno-Karabakh – 2021: Inordinately heavy casualties suffered by Armenian tanks fuelled concerns about the vulnerability of Russian tanks, particularly against Byraktar (TB-2), Turkish-supplied drones. It was reported that Armenia lost as many as 255 tanks. One hundred forty-six (approximately 57%) were completely destroyed, as K-kills. Of these 146 K-kill tanks, 83 (nearly 57%) were destroyed by Bayraktar-TB2, operated by Azerbaijan forces. Others were partially damaged (F or M-kills) by a combination of TB2 strikes, artillery shelling, and anti-tank guided missiles. It bears reiteration that most targets were located by aerial and drone surveillance. Some other Armenian tanks were also destroyed by loitering munitions. The stage for unprecedented destruction was set by the creation of asymmetry in the opening gambit by Azerbaijan, in the very first hour, destroying approximately 60% of AD and 40% of artillery. **The resultant air superiority gave armed drones a virtually free run against tank columns, which were bunched up, ignoring basic tactics of dispersion, camouflage, and concealment.** While acknowledging the efficacy of armed drones, it is pragmatic to place on record that Armenia's AD system was inadequate to defend its AFVs and artillery guns from Azerbaijan's airpower, including drones.

Important Trends – The Ukrainian Conflict: While it may be a bit premature to draw conclusive inferences/lessons from the ongoing and unresolved Ukrainian imbroglio, a few indicative trends need to be examined. The mandatory caution is also necessitated due to the absence of impartial, objective reporting and information warfare, characterised by narrative shaping. Inferences applicable to armoured warfare are as follows:

a) **The operation, described as a special operation by Russia, was planned in utmost secrecy and lacked consultative planning.** In mechanised operations, instructions in the form of a briefing have to be disseminated down to junior leaders.

b) **The objectives of the operation were not only highly optimistic but also rigid, lacking any fallback options.**

c) The Russian offensive defied the key terrain parameter of the **bogging effect of 'Rasputista', also described as General Mud or Marshal Mud.** The thawing snow, combined with mud, prevented manoeuvres and forced movement on linear road axes.

d) **The Russian movement was designed along too many linear axes, widely separated and without mutual support.** These long linear columns had no dispersion, providing easy bunched-up targets, much like those in Nagorno-Karabakh.

e) **Russian crews lacked motivation and abandoned their platforms.** Even senior leadership was found wanting, leading to the sacking of many senior commanders.

f) The Russian offensive relied too heavily on mechanised columns, **ignoring the seminal reality of the combined arms concept.** Most notable was the lack of infantry to secure and clear areas.

g) The Russian offensive had **inadequate logistics back-up,** as it was based on the hope of capitulation by the Ukrainians. An apt example was the abandonment of a large number of functional T-80 tanks with gas turbine engines, due to a temporary shortfall in special fuel replenishment.

h) In sum, it appears that large platforms, fighter aircraft, tanks, and ships didn't deliver, leading to these being described even as obsolescent. **In the domain of mechanised operations, drones, anti-tank missiles (Javelins), and artillery barrages emerged as an effective anti-tank shield.**

Objective Evaluation of High Russian Tank Losses: An objective comparative analysis of losses has to wait, but an indicative (preliminary) one reveals a few trends. As per the estimates of Mossad and the Oryx blog, Russia suffered 994 tank losses. These included 334 AFVs (approximately 34%), simply abandoned. It implies that abandoned AFVs were partially functional and only M or F-kills, not K-kills. In the first month of the offensive itself, 53% of the losses were abandoned platforms by demotivated crews. Many platforms were first abandoned and later destroyed by Ukrainians, and often by the civil populace. It would be fair to surmise that approximately 50% of Russian tank losses can be ascribed to crews abandoning them, much unlike Israeli crews, who fought with partially damaged tanks and carried out amazing repairs and resuscitation during operations. In Chechnya in 1999–2000, the Russian Army lost 122 out of 146 tanks and IFVs due to a similar lack of motivation and ignoring basic tactics. Concurrently, it is estimated that Ukraine may have lost approximately 6,320 AFVs again due to confusion, capitulation, and Russian fire assaults. **Notwithstanding losses, the continued relevance of AFVs is being reiterated on both sides by seeking and fielding more platforms, like Leopard tanks and T-90s.**

Specific Issues Relevant in Our Context

The large stretch of open terrain in the form of desert, plains, and plateaus at high altitudes provides an ideal template for the employment of AFVs. Unlike many other countries, India doesn't routinely employ tanks in counter-insurgency warfare. Starting with 1947 operations, Stuart tanks were hauled across the Zojila pass by intrepid crews after stripping and reassembling turrets, across the formidable pass. They proved to be game changers, exploiting legendary 'jugaad' (improvisation), resourcefulness, and dedication of Indian crews to their weapons and platforms. In the 1965 war, Pakistan based its plan on the stratagem of fielding otherwise hidden second armoured division (6 Armoured Division), which had been raised in secrecy and utilised the latest American M-48 (Patton) tanks against the old Indian tanks—Centurions, Shermans, and AMXs. Once again, our crews devised a simple yet effective three-round technique to create a graveyard of Patton tanks, appropriately christened as 'Patton Nagar'. While Indian crews improvised, Pakistanis fumbled with optical, coincidence range finders. In 1971, during operations on both fronts, mechanised columns were in vanguard, duly supported by all-arms columns. Indian crews overcame boggy terrain and optimised even medium tanks, like the T-55s. In the final push, the audacious utilisation of amphibious PT-76 tanks across the Meghna River and heli-lift of troops, coupled with para-drops, enabled the capture of Dacca.

The Indian subcontinent boasts of approximately 13,000 AFVs, with the PLA leading with 5,900 and in collusion with 2,500 of Pakistan against 4,300 Indian AFVs. Pakistan, Bangladesh, Myanmar, and Sri Lanka have Chinese-supplied equipment. This provides China a base for life-cycle support and modernisation in India's neighbourhood. Pakistan's heavy industry plant, Taxila, and ordnance factory, Wah, have a very large Chinese presence. China plays a significant role in the production and modernisation of Al-Zarar and Al-Khalid tanks and other Pakistani AFVs. Notwithstanding the disquiet and erosion of confidence in AFVs, their relevance in the Indian subcontinent is likely to endure due to large inventories and ongoing modernisation programmes. **It bears reiteration that life spans and efficacy of AFVs need to be enhanced by following the Israeli model of retrofitting and upgradation.**

India has also made a switch from large mechanised columns aiming for deep thrusts to IBGs with shallow objectives. These objectives are below the nuclear threshold. The PLA has recently fielded its version of light tank, ZTQ-15, optimised for high altitude operations, thereby triggering the Indian light tank programme for Zorawar. In the recent operation of the pre-emptive securing of the Kailash ranges, medium tanks were in the vanguard, with our skilled crews, even defying the conventional power-to-weight ratio ceiling, in audacious, QPQ operations. It is also important to take into account the fact that the performance of drones is degraded due to environmental challenges at high altitudes. APSs are being incorporated in modernisation programmes to minimise the top-attack threat from drones. Hence, AFVs, albeit modernised (to combat contemporary challenges), are likely to remain relevant in our battle space.

Recommended Way Forward

Armoured warfare is already witnessing an introspective churning in organisations, employment, and the design of platforms. The US has already opted for lighter Stryker brigades. The Marine Corps has deactivated tank battalions and transferred assets to the army. The UK Army has rolled back the Chieftain modernisation programme. Major shortcomings of Russian tanks, including ammunition fires and turrets getting detached, are being addressed. **Russian Armata tanks have drawn from the Swedish design of turret-less S-tanks by putting the crew in protected armoured capsules (pods) and incorporating unmanned turrets.** This design is also being refined in the US development prorammes such as the Next Generation Combat Vehicle (NGCV) program and the Decisive Lethality Platform (DLP). AbramX is experimenting with a much more agile tank, powered by hybrid-electric diesel power plants, incorporating AI technologies besides the crew in a safe pod, in the hull. Indicative trends identified in recent conflicts are already being incorporated into the design philosophy of AFV development. The same is also finding resonance in organisations, employment, and training. Even objectives are being limited to shallow, attainable, and realistic ones.

Drones are a potent and low-cost threat. Hence, it will be axiomatic to field tanks as part of all-arms systems with integrated AD systems. The defensive envelope includes camouflage, mock-ups, dispersion, and the efficient use of terrain. At the same time, platforms should incorporate protective measures—both soft-kill and hard-kill, and even rudimentary cage-like structures—to ward off drones and missiles.

Conclusion

AFVs in general and tanks in particular have been utilised as a main platform in major battles and have witnessed periodic improvements and design changes. The recent conflicts have thrown up interesting trends, which should be validated and applied in our environment. These need to be utilised to refine our organisation, armoured warfare operational philosophy, and as inputs in AFV development programmes. **In sum, armoured warfare and tanks may lose their salience but are likely to remain important platforms, more so if applied as part of combined arms teams and in a joint operations format. The seminal paradigm is that all asymmetry is temporary and can be countered with resilience and countermeasures.** Armoured warfare is redefining itself with the incorporation of better surveillance and protection systems, as part of battlefield management systems. It is also likely to see the introduction of autonomous platforms incorporating AI.

References

1. Sébastien Roblin, 'in 1973, the Yom Kippur War Gave the World a Horrifying Glimpse of What a Modern Mechanized Warfare Would Look Like', *The National Interest,* https://nationalinterest.org

2. Dave Roos, *History*, 'How Tanks Played a Critical Role in Persian Gulf War', July 11, 2022. https://www.history.com/news/tanks-abrams-persian-gulf

3. Rob Lee, *War on the Rocks,* 'The Tank is not Obsolete and Other Observations About the Future of Combat', 6 September, 2022. https://www.warontherocks.com

4. Lt Gen AB Shivane, *CLAWS* Journal, April 2022, 'Eleven Big Lessons for the Employment of Tanks in Future Battlespace: The Russia-Ukraine Conflict'.

5. Lt Gen KJ Singh, General's Jottings, 'Have Light Tanks Become Irrelevant Like Walkman?', TOI Chandigarh, https://timesofindia.indiatimes.com/blogs/generals-jottings/have-light-tanks-become-irrelevant-like-walkmans/

6. Lt Gen KJ Singh, 'Relevance of Mechanised Forces and Tanks in Future Battle Space', Scholar Warrior-Autumn 2023, *CLAWS* New Delhi.

7. Lt Gen KJ Singh, 'Drone's Edge over Tanks only Temporary', *Tribune* Chandigarh, https://www.tribuneindia.com/news/features/drones-edge-over-tanks-only-temporary- 568010

8. Lt Gen KJ Singh, 'PLA Armour Offensive in Himalayas', https://chanakyaforum.com/pla-armour-offensive-in-himalayas/

7.2 PLA Armour Offensive in Himalayas

Background

The PLA executed its 'Three Warfares' strategy, spearheaded by an array of armoured formations in Ladakh. PLA exercises in the last few years have **included mechanised manoeuvres and the heavy drop of armoured vehicles, as well as the assimilated capture of passes and lightly held areas at high altitude.** It is widely reported that the 6 Highland Mechanised Infantry Division and 4 Highland Motorised

Infantry Division have deployed assorted AFVs—medium, light tanks, and heavy support equipment—across the LAC in Ladakh to project their coercive messaging potential as part of psychological warfare.

At the very outset, it can be categorically stated that India not only stalemated the situation but also caused a criticality for PLA by the pre-emptive occupation of dominating features on the Kailash range. **The operation on the Kailash range had mechanised elements in the vanguard and was in the face of massed PLA armour across the Spanggur gap.** According to informed experts, the stalemate, for the initiator claiming global hegemony, amounts to a loss.

Theme Setting

The PLA has injected more versatility in its armoured fleet with the **introduction of the light tank, ZTQ, first fielded during the Dolam (Doklam) crisis.** Our BMP-2s, ICVs, which are duly integrated with medium tanks, have been adapted for some of the relevant tasks at high altitudes. The Chinese threat, though stemmed currently, could manifest again, and more such forays can't be ruled out. Hence, it was axiomatic that a review of the mechanised fleet is carried out to meet emerging challenges in the Himalayan sector. Consequently, a Request for Information (RFI) for 350 light tanks has been issued. Concurrently, customised modernisation of the existing fleet of medium tanks, especially uprating the engine to 1000 HP, is also being fast-tracked.

PLA's Mechanised Profile in Tibet

6 Highland Mechanised Infantry Division and 4 Highland Motorised Infantry Division are equipped with two Mechanised Infantry Regiments (Brigades) supported by an armoured regiment. Each Mechanised Infantry Regiment has four mechanised battalions. It has combat support elements—artillery, air defence regiments supported by engineers, electronic warfare (EW), and CBRN defence battalions. **The division has a reconnaissance**

battalion equipped with eighteen ZBD-04A IFVs armed with anti-tank guided missiles (ATGMs). Artillery, air defence, and most other combat support equipment are tracked. Other associated equipment, like helicopters, drones, and rocket artillery, are grouped as per envisaged tasking.

Comparative Evaluation – Medium Tanks

PLA medium tank battalions are equipped with **thirty-five ZTZ-99A (Type 99)** tanks or earlier versions, like Type 96. Chinese tanks follow an evolutionary approach and are **reverse-engineered** from original Russian models and cloned by NORINCO. **Their numbering has a typical psychological hype attached. The T-54 clone is referred to as the Type 59, and the T-90 equivalent as the Type 99. The current lot of PLA medium tanks weighs around 55 tonnes, features 125 mm smooth-bore guns, and is equipped with 1000 to 1200 HP engines.**

Our medium tanks, the T-90s and T-72, in the right combination, are more than a match for these tanks. It is pertinent to highlight that numerically, four of our regiments can match five Chinese regiments, as our regiments have nearly 50 'A' vehicles. However, our mainstay, the T-72, needs to be equipped with an upgraded engine. **Additional power is required to compensate for the de-rating of engines by approximately 25% in high-altitude areas.** Russian tanks are customised to operate in extreme cold climates, but customised value additions, like Auxiliary Power Units (APUs), have been identified as part of the ongoing modernisation, including creating an ecosystem of heated garages and repair bays, which needs to be fast-tracked.

Comparative Evaluation – Mechanised Infantry

PLA's mechanised infantry **is a mix of old tracked Type 86 ICVs, wheeled WZ-551 APCs (6×6), and a limited number of more contemporary VN-1 (8×8) ATGM carriers with Red Arrow missiles.** Our BMP-2s are more than a match to PLA ICVs. **It is seen that the PLA infantry has got used to being transported and operates**

largely in motorised mode. Although we enjoy a marginal edge in our ICVs, modernisation in terms of the **upgradation of the power pack** is a critical requirement for operation in high-altitude terrain to offset losses in engine power. While India follows the traditional philosophy of employment of infantry, largely without vehicles, the need is to give them some **protection and mobility in the form of mechanised/ motorised infantry.** It is indeed commendable that much-needed though belated correctives are underway with the induction of the Kalyani M4, Mahindra ALSV, and TATA LAMV variants.

Appraisal – PLA Light Tank

China added considerable versatility to its mechanised fleet by fielding a light tank, the **ZTQ-15, also referred to as the Type 15 or Xinquingtan.** It is essentially a lighter medium tank, with a weight of around 34 tonnes, amounting to a sort of hybrid between medium and light tanks. Classically, light tanks are generally in the sub-30 tonne class, ideally 25 tonnes, with a power-to-weight ratio (PWR) between 30 and 35. The Type-15 has been fitted with extra-wide tracks to offset additional weight and reduce Nominal Ground Pressure (NGP). PWR and NGP are key enablers for agility and trafficability in marginal terrain. To that extent, it is a sort of compromise solution, especially in terms of protection, firepower, and mobility.

Type 15 has been utilised in heavy droppings, giving it as an edge for utilisation in quick reaction forces. This tank was introduced in 2017, and 40 tanks have been supplied to Bangladesh, with 140 more in the pipeline. **The main features of this tank are 105 mm rifled guns and a 1000 HP engine. Type 15, though hyped as a game changer, is neither really light nor a replacement for medium tanks, certainly not a panacea.** In keeping with Chinese reliance on incremental or evolutionary designs, this tank is a follow-up and replacement for the antiquated Type-62 tanks.

History – Indian Light Tanks

As is well known, we currently don't have a light tank in our inventory. Historically, light tanks had a defining and iconic role in 1947 operations, when **Stuart tanks** were inducted across Zojila to stem raiders. AMX-13 was again utilised in Chusul during 1962. **We had Stuarts, Shermans, AMX-13, and assorted armoured cars in 1965 and earlier operations till the '70s. Russian PT-76 tanks, a replacement for older light tanks, proved their mettle in 1971 operations.** Light tanks have their utility in reconnaissance, scouting, and out-of-area contingencies, including peacekeeping operations. They can also be utilised in riverine, creeks/marshy backwaters, island territories, and coastal areas, as well as high-altitude terrain. **Light tanks, if applied audaciously and with imagination for reconnaissance in force, can open up possibilities for QPQ operations.**

Quest for the Replacement of the Light Tank

After the deinduction of PT-76 tanks in 1989, which I was privileged to crew, half-hearted attempts to find replacements were made, including the trials of the Brazilian Uruthu, British Scorpion, and French light tank in the late '80s. Formalised RFI for 200 wheeled and 100 tracked light tanks was promulgated again in 2009 as part of the build-up for the Mountain Strike Corps. Major specifications were 22 tons with gun calibre between 105 and 120 mm. The wheeled variant was to be in an 8×8 or 6×6 configuration. However, this RFI was retracted. Concurrently, the DRDO has experimented with certain variants, utilising BMP chassis with a 105 mm gun as well as the French GIAT TS-90 chassis. Even certain private manufacturers like TATA, Mahindra, Bharat Forge, and DPSUs/ordnance factories have produced prototypes in both wheeled and tracked versions of protected platforms, finding limited but belated traction, like the fielding of Bharat Forge M-4 and Mahindra LBPV.

Options and Current RFI

A scan of global inventory generated a few options, ranging from eight-wheeled Stryker variants, which were tried out in the Yudh Abhyas series of joint exercises. These were pushed rather persistently by the US, for acquisition through the FMS route, but were not found suitable. Russia has the 2S25 Sprut-SD light tank, weighing 18 tonnes, with a 125 mm SB (low pressure) gun and a PWR of 28.3 HP/ton. These tanks have also been air-dropped in exercises; however, Russia has hesitated in fielding them in the ongoing Ukrainian conflict. Thc Israeli Sabrah tank is in keeping with its protection-oriented philosophy and weighs 55 tonnes, and is only suited for the desert terrain. The most viable line of development is to utilise expertise gained in the production of the K-9 Vajra SP gun. This is aligned with the South Korean K21-105 Hanwaha tank. This tank is a joint production endeavour with the Belgian John Cockerill Defence. Prima facie, it can be tweaked to meet most of the RFI parameters, thereby adhering to the stipulated time deadline.

India has a projected requirement for 364 light tanks on a fast-track basis. This would translate to six to seven regiments, depending on equipping norms. The DRDO is slated to manufacture 59 tanks. The rest 295 will be manufactured under the Make-I category. The selection of a development partner will be after a competition, where Zorawar will also participate. It will have a crew of three, implying the fitment of an auto-loader. Besides the main gun, the platform will have machine guns to combat terrestrial and aerial threats. There is also a stipulation for a third-generation ATGM, preferably fired from a gun tube. The tank must be equipped with an APS, ERA, offensive and defensive electronic countermeasures (ECM), a missile warning system, nuclear, biological, chemical (NBC) protection, 360° day-and-night cameras, a battle management system (BMS), and a hybrid navigation system. The user is even looking for a captive drone launching and counter-drone capability. The tank, reportedly, will have special tracks to minimise damage to fragile communication arteries, which are at a premium in such terrain.

Zorawar – India's Light Tank

India has rolled out Zorawar, described as an Armoured Fighting Vehicle-Indian Light Tank (AFV-ILT) for trials and evaluation. The tank has been developed in fast-track mode in three odd years, after the PLA fielded light tanks and deployed them in Doklam in 2017 and in the ongoing unresolved imbroglio in Ladakh in 2020. The tank is named after the legendary, Dogra General, Zorawar Singh, renowned for extending the Sikh empire to Ladakh in the nineteenth century. Implied in the name is the reiteration of India's resolve as well as confidence in the growing defence manufacturing ecosystem. The project has been mentored by DRDO and has utilised facilities and assembly line, developed by L&T for K-9 Vajra SP gun system at Hazira (Gujarat). Vajra has been developed in collaboration with the South Korean Hanwaha-Techwin. Zorawar (1.0) integrates available indigenous systems with a Belgian Cockerill turret with Cummins (750 HP) power plants, sourced from the US. The original plan was for MTU engines (1,000 HP) from Germany, which are not available due to the closure of the German assembly line. The plan should be to graduate to various variants in series like 1.1, 1.2, and so on, to make it both local (in content) and more potent with product improvement, to face the ever-growing contemporary challenges.

Zorawar – Is It Enough?

The most important paradigm of mechanised warfare emphasised in recent conflicts is that the tank is just a part, albeit an important one, in a combined arms and logistics system. It certainly is not the silver bullet; its vulnerability against top-attack delivered by drones, loitering munitions, and ATGMs has even prompted many to question its continued utility. Hence, it is important to reiterate that we need an optimised mix of medium and light tanks supported by other platforms like ICVs, guns, AD for mitigating drone and aerial threats, combat support, and logistics with matching mobility. The light tank will have to fight as part of a combined arms matrix.

Concurrently, there is imperative criticality to upgrade the existing power packs in T-72s and BMPs to compensate for the de-rating of engine output due to rarefied atmosphere. It is relevant to state that, based on articles and projections by the author and a few others in 2020–21, the K9 SP gun has been fielded in Ladakh after undergoing high-altitude hardening and has proven effective.

Inevitably, in our development, there is a worrying quest by the user to pitch for more features, leading to cascading delays, cost overruns, and design rebalancing. It will be prudent if the user scales down aspirations and scales them to an appropriate scale. **Can the drone launching capability be limited to one AFV per squadron and structured on the support platform of an Armoured Recovery Vehicle? Similarly, missile launchers can be scaled and optimised at a suitable level.** It is also recommended that developers should develop a basic variant, with the flexibility to strap-on customised add-ons. One such contraption could be a cage-like contraption with slat and spaced armour. Modernisation, in terms of APS, anti-drone measures, and rubberised tracks, could be incorporated later. The key challenges are developing an indigenous engine of 1,000 HP and a turret system. Most importantly, the overriding parameter is the ownership of not only TOT from foreign partners but also 'know-how' and 'know-why' through co-development under the Atma Nirbhar route. Another challenge is to boost the protection level, as a light tank has only basic protection and relies on agility, low signature, and support from other accompanying platforms, like medium tanks. One suggested line could be to develop composite armour with low-density ceramics and metals/alloys for optimising the protection suite.

Way Forward

- **First and foremost, the requirement is to build a versatile family of 'A' vehicles with an optimum mix of medium and light tanks with customised support equipment. Consequently, there is an**

urgent need to fast-track the development process for light tanks in a time-bound manner.

- **Secondly, we need to find partners and achieve indigenisation and joint production.**
- **Thirdly, the existing fleet of medium tanks in high-altitude areas needs to be modernised, most importantly by upgrading their power packs.**
- **Fourthly, ageing ICVs should be given a much-needed upgradation package, including a power pack and a better protection system.**
- **Fifthly, an ecosystem for garages, training, and sustenance should be set up in these areas.**
- **Sixthly, infantry should be provided with protected high-mobility vehicles.**
- **Seventhly, the commonality of the platform should be attempted to reduce logistical challenges.**

Update: There are reliable reports of India buying a few hundred Stryker Wheeled ICVs, fitted with Javelin missiles from the US through FMS. There could even be a possibility of their co-production in India. However, there are reports of equipment having failed in trials.

Two Front or Single Front Reinforced Threat

8.1 India's Strategic Gameplan Vis-a-Vis China-Pakistan Collusive Linkages

- Update: Operation Sindoor – Pakistan fielded a large inventory of Chinese equipment in Operation Sindoor. This includes aircraft—J-10C and JF-17, PL-15 missiles, HQ-9B and HQ-16 AD systems, and SH-15 artillery guns. As per international opinion, Pakistan integrated the PLA systems well, yet suffered losses in radars. Indian strikes and significant degradation of the Pakistan Air Force assets debunk the hype on Chinese tech asymmetry. Notwithstanding India's success, near-seamless collusive sharing of satellite data, targeting parameters, and interoperability are ominous developments. This is also being referred to as 'One Front Reinforced'. It has also been described as 'Single Border-Three Adversaries' alluding to Pakistan assisted by China and Turkiye.
- Bangladesh is an added and emerging collusive threat.

> *'For China, Pakistan is a low-cost secondary deterrent to India, while for Pakistan, China is a high value guarantor of security against India.'*
>
> —Husain Haqqani

Introduction

The ongoing Chinese aggressive deployment and prolonged face-off in Ladakh has rekindled the debate on collusive threat posed by two of our neighbours, China and Pakistan. The latter has maintained an aggressive and hostile posture with calibrated proxy war in J&K, fire assaults on the unsettled LoC, and hostile presence on the AGPL. It is heartening that the ceasefire on the LoC inked in February 2021 has been holding for the last fourteen months. China has delayed the resolution of the border, coupled with the orchestration of transgressions and 'salami-slicing' at periodic intervals, to stake its claim on shifting claim lines on the LAC. **India and Bhutan are the only two neighbours having the dubious distinction of unsettled land borders with China, due to stonewalling and obduracy by Beijing.** These coercive orchestrations are primarily designed to keep India in check and unsettled, thereby denying her development, progress, and stability.

The recent strategic situation on the northern borders, coupled with the ongoing proxy war in J&K, has once again stoked concerns about the challenges of a two-and-a-half-front threat. It has thrown up a number of issues, relating to the scope of collusion, likely manifestation scenarios, designation of primary and secondary threats, and above all, the need for an effective response strategy. **The scope of collusion between Pakistan and China transcends from geo-strategic to geo-economic and other domains like defence manufacturing, transportation, power generation, nuclear weapons, and space.** The most notable multi-dimensional, collaborative project is the ongoing CPEC, which is described as a signature project for the BRI and sets a new benchmark in collusive collaboration.

Approach and Scope

The basic approach of this article is to **discuss an outline of an optimum strategy or broad gameplan to tackle collusive Sino-Pak threats.** The detailed strategy and specific action plan are beyond the scope of this article. However, deliberations and inferences drawn in this article can help refine/validate the template for such formulation. It will be appropriate to reiterate that clarity on threat parameters is an essential pre-requisite for planning levels of preparedness, force structures, equipment profiles, modernisation, and budgetary allocations; hence, these are discussed briefly. Reasonable assumptions have been factored in, where necessary, as detailed national security policies are yet to be promulgated.

Preview

The subject is analysed with focus on the following major parameters:

a) Collusive Linkages – Definitions, Scope, and Manifestation.
b) Historical Context.
c) The CPEC – A New Collusive Paradigm.
d) Constructs and Catalysts for Collusion.
e) Strategic Options to Counter Collusion.
f) Summary of Recommendations.

Collusive Linkages – Definitions, Scope, and Manifestation

Definitions: 'Collusion' and its derivatives, like 'collusive', are terms increasingly used in geo-strategic dialogue and have spawned another more commonly used, non-dictionary but colloquially popular variant, 'collusivity'. The word may soon get included in the dictionary, considering its extensive usage. Webster's dictionary defines 'collusive' as 'secret agreement or cooperation especially for an illegal or deceitful purpose'. A more appropriate formulation in our context is outlined in the Collins Dictionary as an adjective: '**Collusive behaviour involves secret or illegal cooperation between countries or organisations**'. There are many other definitions, but a common strand in almost all is threefold: **cooperation characterised by secrecy and deceit.** Collusion requires collaboration or working together, albeit in covert or secret mode, combined with deceit. China and North Korea provide an apt example of such comprehensive collusive linkages. The Sino-Pak relationship is another such case study. With China acting as the nucleus, relationships with North Korea and Pakistan are a complex web of concentric, collusive networks, including nuclear proliferation. As a concept, it is natural that alliances, especially in the security domain, facilitate or promote some degree and form of collusion. Most security pacts invariably have classified/secret clauses and even classified annexures. An apt example was the leasing of the Shamsi airbase by Pakistan to the United Arab Emirates (UAE) for hunting, and, in turn, the base being sublet to the US forces for drone and missile operations against the Taliban. Tri-lateral collusion was essentially a clever ploy for bypassing regulations and pressure from domestic lobbies. However, the presence of American personnel on airbases like Shamsi and Jacobabad accorded Pakistan some degree of immunity during Operation Parakram in 2001–02. In all probability, India would have been constrained to omit these bases from possible target lists in the event of hostilities.

Scope: The scope of collusion is defined by geo-political and geo-strategic templates, but increasingly transcends into geo-economic domains. Recently, Chinese President Xi Jinping, in a telephonic chat with Imran Khan, hailed their ties as between 'iron brothers'. A commentary in state-run Xinhua news agency in 2013 during the visit of Chinese Prime Minister to Pakistan, stated, 'China and Pakistan have shaped a paradigm of neighbour-to-neighbour relations. Their time-tested friendship, described by some as "**higher than the mountains and deeper than the oceans**", is not just a bunch of empty words.' The important and relevant details of Sino-Pak collusion are mapped later in this paper, in the section on historical context. It will be appropriate to emphasise the growing scope in collaborative linkages, which is now being referred to and alleged in secret bio-weapon labs in China and, more recently, in Ukraine, reportedly funded by the US and Western pharmaceutical lobbies. The CPEC also has plans for vaccination projects.

Manifestation of Collusion: Collusive ties, as per conventional understanding, are described as secretive, like the nuclear exchange between China and North Korea and Pakistan. They even incorporate deniability, as was attempted by AQ Khan and his clique, in the proliferation of nuclear designs to Iran and Libya. Notwithstanding the emphasis on secrecy in the basic definition, there are methods to project positive aspects and hide spin-offs with security payoffs. It is axiomatic that in the age of enhanced transparency through satellite imagery and remote sensing techniques, collusion will be **couched and designated, invariably for benign purposes, like communications, connectivity, and economic development. The CPEC, which is discussed later, is the most relevant example in this context.** In an era where wars are described as 'special operations', **collusion rather than declared collaboration is likely to become the new normal, accompanied by deniability.**

Forms of Collusion: Collusion may adapt various forms, like synchronised or sequential/deferred in timing. It may be planned or even impromptu, to take advantage of a situation/opportunity or to redress a reverse/criticality. Deployment of the Seventh Fleet by the US in the Bay of Bengal during the 1971 operations was a case of deferred collusion to bail out East Pakistan in dire straits (criticality), though it failed to have the desired effect. In application, collusion may be in the same theatre, in proximity, or even in different theatres. Gulf operations witnessed the application of multiple national forces in the same theatre and in synchronised mode. Collusion and collaboration may have a **deterrent effect, even when not actually applied, as a threat.** Fear of Chinese posturing in 1971 forced the deferring of operations to December during the pass-closure period to preclude two-front scenarios. Collusion can be short-term or even episodic, **essentially a** tactical, long-term, or strategic collaboration/collusion. Sino-Pak collusion meets the criterion of a long-term and strategic one, having completed nearly 50 years. On the other hand, US-Iran collusion in the CENTO era was broken off with the advent of the Ayatollah regime in Iran, making it a short-term engagement.

Historical Context

Setting the Stage: Pakistan was among the first to accord diplomatic recognition to the PRC in 1950. The **first signs of China-Pakistan collusion manifested as early as the '50s, when East Pakistan became a sanctuary for Naga rebels.** Phizo escaped to London via East Pakistan in December 1956. Mowu Angami and others trekked to China for training. Similarly, Naga rebels were ferried from the eastern wing to the western one for specialised commando training in the late '50s.

Pakistan gifted vast tracts of strategic territory of the Shaksgam Valley, measuring 5,180 square kilometres in 1963, enabling it to settle boundary issues with China. The treaty incorporates Section 6, which mandates that after the settlement of the Kashmir dispute, there will be another round between China and the treaty-designated sovereign state for final settlement. It actually was an abject surrender of territory, which de jure belonged to Kashmir and India. It was also a flagrant violation of the standstill arrangements mandated in the UN resolution. Pakistan planned the 1965 operation to take advantage of the situation in India after Chinese aggression in 1962. It was based on an assessment of Indian forces being demoralised and unprepared. As per some media reports, a US-based think tank had reportedly recommended 1965 as a now-or-never opportunity to put it across India. In the interim, the US, as a reward for membership in military pacts, had armed Pakistan with modern weapons like Sabre jets and M-48 Patton tanks, emboldening it to undertake the 1965 aggression on India. Beijing, having warmed up to Pakistan in the early '60s, issued an ultimatum to India during the Indo-Pak war of 1965. This was followed by the formalisation of military assistance in 1966, leading to the provision of assorted weapons worth $60 million. In the economic domain, there was the inking of trade pacts in 1979, triggering growing economic cooperation.

Pakistan's Propensity for Alliances: Unlike the Indian policy of non-alignment and stress on near-equal partnerships, rather than alliances, **Pakistan has displayed commendable diplomatic manipulation and**

dexterity. Pakistan has managed to leverage her geo-strategic location, at the crossroads of civilisations, to the hilt by forging concurrent, collusive linkages across a divergent spectrum. It first became part of the Southeast Asia Treaty Organization (SEATO) in 1954, the Baghdad Pact in 1955, and the CENTO in 1956. This, in effect, made it an outpost for the US in Central Asia. Surprisingly, it was also cosying up to China in the '60s, as well as concurrently keeping alive the Organisation of Islamic Cooperation (OIC) connections. **Pakistan became a surprising enabler, 'midwifing' relations between the US and China.** Henry Kissinger's visit to China in July 1971 was shrouded in secrecy and concealed as a diversion during his Pakistan visit. After Bangladesh operations and losing the eastern wing, it established a strategic alliance with China in 1972, concurrently retaining active membership of US-led military alliances like CENTO. **Pakistan has shown compliance and even agreed to become a client state in unequal tie-ups.**

Indian Response and 1971 Operations: Trilateral linkages between Pakistan, China, and the US **forced India to sign the Indo-Soviet friendship treaty in 1971, which acted as a restraining check on Chinese designs to provide aid to Pakistan during the Bangladesh Liberation War.** However, China extended flying rights and passage to Pakistan for operations in the eastern wing. Pakistan's linkages with China impacted India's plans in responding to the refugee crisis in 1971 and deferring planned operations to December to preclude Chinese intervention. In the intervening period of six months, India had to cope with an unprecedented humanitarian crisis, caused by a massive influx of refugees. Both in the 1965 and 1971 wars, despite choosing an appropriate period to preclude Chinese intervention, minimum forces and readiness posture had to be maintained on the Sino-Indian border, thereby restricting the availability of forces to be applied against Pakistan.

Proxy War and Insurgency: The sordid chapter of collusion between China and East Pakistan, and later Bangladesh, although documented, is rarely discussed. Ironically, **the Inter-Services Intelligence (ISI) and the Chinese managed to keep camps and sanctuaries active till the Sheikh Hasina regime.** It was only the Awami League government that handed over fugitives like Anup Chetia and threw out others like Anthony Shimray after cracking down on insurgent camps. Ruili in the Yunnan province, reportedly, still acts as a hub for procuring weapons and a sanctuary for fugitive insurgents of the North-East rebel groups. Pakistan employed the Kabayali narrative in the 1947–48 conflict and later infiltration task forces in the 1965 war. Having suffered humiliation in 1971, **it adopted the 'bleeding by a thousand cuts' strategy.** It fomented terrorism by funding and aiding Khalistanis in the '80s and the '90s (1984–1995). Later, it initiated a proxy war in Kashmir in 1988, which is still simmering. Kargil raiders in 1999 were also described as Mujahideen despite clear evidence to the contrary. The challenges for India in terms of narco-terrorism, counterfeit smuggling, and arms trafficking remain. The ISI has also been toying with the idea of K2 (Khalistan and Kashmir) after the opening of the Kartarpur Corridor.

Mujahideen and Taliban: Pakistan has the dubious distinction of setting up Mujahideen and jihadi militias at the behest of the US in the '90s. Pakistan managed to calibrate its duplicity and perfidious behaviour to remain America's main interlocutor in Afghanistan. The first venture was training, arming, and aiding Mujahideen militias for overthrowing the Russian-backed regime, from 1979 to 1989. Since then, it has remained a frontline state till the US withdrawal in September 2021. It still retains some degree of control and is now engaged in carving a role for China in Afghanistan. This turnaround comes at considerable cost to Indian interests, including investments of $3 billion in development projects. **China and Pakistan are colluding to deny India a legitimate role in Afghan talks.**

Calibrated Chinese Collusion: China has taken a carefully calculated approach in supporting Pakistan. There has been undiluted support in international bodies like the UNO and the Financial Action Task

Force (FATF). It put up the facade of responsible power during the Kargil operations in 1999, when it chose to maintain a restrained posture despite appeals by Pakistan. This has even spawned a strong belief that in a conflict initiated by Pakistan against India, China may not intervene. Indian strategic thinkers opined that historically, China had not made decisive interventions in the 1965, 1971, and Kargil conflicts and limited support in providing arms, issuing ultimatums, and tying down troops deployed on the Sino-Indian border. Any intervention by Chinese troops is likely to generate signals of opportunism, fear, and awe among smaller neighbours. There was also a feeling that even in conflicts initiated by China, she might not want to be seen colluding and taking help from Pakistan. However, there are unverified reports of intelligence sharing and posturing in the recent Ladakh standoff, but physical participation has not yet been proven. There is also a belief that **Pakistan will invariably try to take advantage in any conflict initiated by China against India.** It will be appropriate to place on record that Pakistan has acted in a restrained manner in the current standoff with China in Ladakh, in all likelihood at the behest of its controlling partner, China.

The CPEC – A New Collusive Paradigm

Defining Treaty: A special bilateral China-Pakistan Treaty of Friendship, Cooperation, and Good-Neighbourly Relations, ratified by both sides in 2005–06, is the most significant milestone in China-Pakistan collusion. It mandates the two nations to desist from '**joining any alliance or bloc which infringes upon the sovereignty, security, and territorial integrity of the other side**'. It also forbids both countries from concluding a similar treaty with a third country, thereby closing avenues for a strategic pact with the US. It really set the stage for the CPEC. **It has been pitched as a show-piece for the BRI, adding geo-economic heft to the collusion.** The project, with a projected investment of $62 billion, is also being dubbed as the colonisation of Pakistan economically by China, thus adding an ironic twist to the acronym itself. Dependencies and debt traps are likely to lead to China getting ownership of Gwadar and chunks of the transportation corridor on a long-term lease basis. Pakistan also figures prominently in maritime, digital, and health silk routes, also described as 'string of pearls.

Strategic Drivers: The CPEC is showcased as a benign, economic collaboration in the open domain; yet, behind this cloak of development, it conceals and downplays collusive strategic drivers like warm-water port (Gwadar) connectivity for China to the Makran coast. The collateral benefits of enhanced interoperability between the two Armed Forces, including two additional divisions for the protection of the corridor, maritime cooperation, logistics, and optical fibre connectivity, are all downplayed. The very alignment and execution of projects in GB and PoK, like Kohala and Daimer-Basha dams, are altering the very status quo mandated in UN resolutions. **These projects challenge the de jure sovereignty of India and extend the legitimacy of Pakistani claims.** Pakistan has allowed access and deployment of the Chinese workforce along with security personnel in GB and PoK. This amounts to challenging the de jure sovereignty of India and negating its territorial claims. **The Chinese presence, in operational terms, constrains targeting options to avoid escalation, consequent to the collateral damage to Chinese personnel and assets.**

Constructs and Catalysts for Collusion

Pakistan's Objectives: Pakistan as a state is defined by the **self-professed raison d'être for its creation, the need to be a separate theological state and anti-India in its orientation.** This urge and mindset acquired a fanatic flavour when **Pakistan added ideological frontiers** as an add-on to its physical boundaries. Pakistan chose to name its capital as Islamabad and even describes its nuclear bomb as 'Islamic bomb'. Most of its strategic missiles have been named after invaders like Babur, Ghaznavi, and Shaheen. Even the infiltration task force in 1965 was named similarly—Saladin, Khilji, etc. Kargil raiders were described as Ghazis and Mujahideen. This has **spurred a craving for 'parity fixation in strategic domain'**, a tendency of constant comparison with India, articulated recently by former Pakistani Prime Minister Imran Khan's recent comparisons of Pakistan's foreign policy with Indian neutrality, strategic autonomy, and heft in the international community. In blunt terms, it amounts to Pakistan's desire to punch much above its weight classification. The quest for parity has degenerated into multiple aggressions, proxy wars, and a constant affliction to foment anti-India narratives. Pakistan, while aspiring to be the leader of the Islamic ummah, has displayed rank hypocrisy by maintaining stoic silence on Chinese atrocities on the Uyghur community in Xinjiang.

Chinese Aspirations: China, on the other hand, wants to establish its hegemony and keep India hyphenated with Pakistan. It is a **diabolic 'push-pull' formulation of pushing down India to keep it embroiled in the sub-continent, denying it rightful place on the global stage.** This is concurrently accompanied by pulling up to artificially hoist Pakistan to drum up the notion of parity. The only glue in this collusive relationship is to deny India strategic salience. Chinese actions in denying India membership in the Security Council and NSG are reflective of this trend. Ironically, Beijing links Indian admission with Pakistan, being concurrently given membership of the NSG, notwithstanding its dodgy record in nuclear proliferation. Double pincer collusion drives multi-spectral linkages, like helping Pakistan acquire nuclear weapons. China has aided and colluded with Pakistan to bypass the Missile Technology Control Regime (MTCR) and Nuclear Proliferation Treaty (NPT). Collusion between these two nations was predicted by **Samuel Huntington** in his famous book, *Clash of Civilizations*, **wherein he had flagged congruence between Sinic and Islamic civilisations.**

Multi-Spectral Collusion: China has emerged as the largest arms supplier to Pakistan, replacing America. Pakistan has allowed

Chinese cloning experts to reverse-engineer US-supplied equipment, in flagrant violation of proprietary end-user clauses. China and Pakistan are also engaged in regular training exercises, manoeuvres, and exchange visits. All these weapons and expertise are likely to be focused against India, and some of it is being used in the proxy war. China allows Pakistan to piggyback on strategic projects like missiles, defence production, and space collaboration. NORINCO and other Chinese arms manufacturers have upgraded Heavy Industries Taxilla (HIT), Ordnance Factories in Wah, the Aviation Complex at Kamra, and the missile plant at Tarwanah near Rawalpindi. It has enabled Pakistan to execute joint production of JF-17 aircraft, Al-Khalid Main Battle Tanks, howitzers, missiles, and a variety of munitions. China has announced joint projects in submarines and underwater vehicles. **The proliferation of Chinese-origin weapons in neighbouring countries enables Pakistan's presence for servicing and repairs, besides export orders.** Pakistan's reliance on Chinese equipment has its own glitches due to relative technological and serviceability levels. There have been reports on problems in Chinese-supplied equipment and its comparison with modern American platforms like Huey Cobras, Strykers, Chinooks, drones, and Javelin missiles.

Strategic Options to Counter Collusion

Strategic Baggage: Till the recent course correction on the designation of primary threat, Indian policymakers believed that China could be managed diplomatically. There was marked reluctance to discuss 'two-and-a-half-front' scenarios, with half denoting internal security threats like Left Wing Extremism (LWE). It was coupled with a **primary focus bordering on the Pakistani threat as a sort of strategic affliction or even strategic historical baggage.** There is an over-reliance on Dual Task Formations (DTFs) and inter-theatre switching of forces. This belief was based on three premises: firstly, the Chinese focus on internal economic consolidation and development. It was inferred that China would avoid distractions. Secondly, reliance on border treaties and protocols, especially on agreed CBMs. India rightly expected maturity on the part of China in keeping with its rising stature. This was bolstered by historical reticence on the part of China to decisively intervene in Indo-Pak conflicts. Thirdly, global coupling of supply chains and trade linkages, especially with the huge Indian market, will discourage such adventures. However, China seems to have leveraged Indian dependencies in critical sectors in a smart and coercive format.

Recalibration: However, the recent trend of '**aggressively rising China**' and '**wolf-warrior diplomacy**' as well as flagrant violation of agreed CBMs, treaties, and protocols during the Ladakh face-off have forced a complete rethink and recalibration of strategy. Discarding a sort of self-generated denial syndrome, there is a clear designation of China as the primary threat. Collusion has been accepted as a corollary and reality. Collusion in many facets like intelligence, info operations, cyber, surveillance, manufacturing, preparation, and many more disciplines has **acquired abiding permanency and seamless fusion between the two nations.** The two-front challenge refers to a simultaneous or synergised armed conflict (aggression) with both China and Pakistan engaging India. China and Pakistan could follow either a collaborative or a collusive approach; the difference in these two terms has become a mere semantic distinction, as collusion is permanent. Collaboration is declaratory and becoming rare; it implies one country openly aiding the other militarily, whereas collusion involves covert cooperation between the two. **In this case, we are confronted with collusive collaboration.**

Response Matrix: Indian preparation levels against **Pakistan are reportedly pegged on parameters of 'credible deterrence' to be upgraded to 'punitive deterrence'. Against China, it has been indexed as 'dissuasive deterrence' and is being upgraded to 'credible deterrence'.** Punitive deterrence entails building up asymmetrical capabilities in niche domains to deliver sharp and surgical responses. These, like the Balakot air strike, can be pre-emptive, provided targets are carefully selected with due justification for international opinion. Execution has to be surgical, with minimum collateral damage and backed up by information operations to amplify the message. As a corollary, the initiator has to be prepared for a retaliatory response and retain control of the escalatory ladder. Against this, China's mandate is to graduate from defensive dissuasion to credible deterrence, which should at least ensure a stalemate; as for an aggressor, an unresolved stalemate amounts to a loss of face. This would require building and executing QPQ options, like pre-emptive deployment on the Kailash Heights, South of Pangong Tso. **Such QPQ responses predicate meticulousness and, more importantly, willpower to act.** The application of riposte or counter-offensive in other theatres facilitates horizontal escalation. This can be applied in vertical mode by enlarging the conflict to maritime or nuclear/space domains. India is opposed to both as it believes in the peaceful use of space and also that there is adequate space below the nuclear threshold for conventional conflicts.

Rebalancing: There has been a **rebalancing of force levels and resources across frontiers in keeping with the reappraisal of threats.** The most notable change is the reorientation of One Strike Corps from the western to northern borders, primarily for the Ladakh theatre, and its reconfiguration from a mechanised to a mountain-based force. It enables two mountain strike corps to focus on their respective theatres. **The scope of rebalancing is holistic and extends to mechanised, firepower, surveillance, air power, cyber, and communications domains.** There is also enhanced focus on the development of infrastructure, logistics, and connectivity in border areas. This reorganisation has consequences for reduced force levels on the Western Front. It can impact the notion of 'decisive victory', and emphasis has shifted to focused surgical capabilities and synergised IBGs with limited objectives. It will be appropriate if integrated theatres are formed, on priority, to synergise and orchestrate a more coherent response. There have been concerns about ammunition stocking for a two-front war, especially with the earlier decision to prune stocking levels to cater for a short war scenario. The ongoing Ukrainian war has brought into question this premise; it is axiomatic that stocking policy and levels are reviewed. It is imperative to maintain enhanced focus on internal security and expedite conflict resolution to tackle the ubiquitous half-front threat and internal fault lines. India is also evaluating its 'No First Use and Massive Retaliation' nuclear policy to inject a certain degree of ambiguity for better deterrence vis-a-vis China. **In a scenario where all three players are** armed with nuclear weapons, the need is to build genuine CBMs, more transparency, and reduce collusion.

Partnerships and Maritime Domain: India is forging strategic partnerships like the Quad to create external leverage to ensure a rule-based order and adherence to the laws of the commons. Notwithstanding the ramping up of deliberations, interoperability exercises, and other connected initiatives, **alliances/partnerships are not silver bullets or panaceas and have their inherent limitations.** It is unlikely that alliance partners will commit troops on the ground, especially as India is the only Quad nation to have land borders with China. It is relevant that currently, the primary challenges against Pakistan are in the hybrid domain, and the threat from China is confined to high-altitude terrain. **However, terrestrial threats can be countered by acquiring dominance in maritime theatres, at least in critically important seaboards.** Concurrently, India has to maintain a strong dissuasive presence in the Indo-Pacific, especially to accentuate the Malacca dilemma in the Andaman Sea. The challenge is in balancing focus on terrestrial threat, which is current and relevant in the near/mid term, with the maritime domain, as the latter requires massive investment and has a long gestation period. Chinese web of the BRI connectivity and string of pearls needs to be matched/outflanked with alternate corridors like the 'necklace of diamonds' and the North-South corridor. Chabahar can be an effective counter to Gwadar, and similar strategic salience is possible through maritime presence in Àgalega in Mauritius; Duqm in Oman; Sittwe in Myanmar; and Trincomalee in Sri Lanka. They need to be developed as shared and collaborative endeavours, downplaying the hubris of terming them as bases. India is conscious of the Mandala theory, the wisdom of realpolitik of engaging with the neighbours of our potential adversaries like Mongolia, Taiwan, South Korea, Vietnam, the Philippines, and Central Asian nations like Uzbekistan. Our diplomatic engagement matrix, of course has to retain **primary focus on regional initiatives, like Neighbourhood First, Act East, and Security And Growth for All in the Region (SAGAR), among others.**

Strategic Autonomy: Countering collusive linkages requires strategic autonomy, which can be achieved by **Smart Atma Nirbharta.. The thrust should be on minimising dependence in strategic and critical technologies.** Some examples include power plants for aircraft and naval crafts, as well as cyber, guidance, surveillance, and communications systems, autonomous and remote systems, rare earths, and API for the pharmaceutical industry and many more sectors. It bears reiterating that self-reliance is not self-isolation. Smart edge can be acquired by transitioning to the role of lead integrator. It will be axiomatic to gain autonomy in strategic sectors, coupled with acquiring leverage in niche areas. **This is a long-term agenda and predicates sustained focus backed up with budgetary allocations to acquire 'know how' besides 'know why'.** This will entail expenditure on R&D and building up domain competence.

Summary of Recommendations

In conclusion, the following need to be emphasised:

a) Collusive collaboration by China and Pakistan is an abiding strategic reality. Bangladesh could accentuate the collusive challenge.

b) Aggressively rising China has emerged as the primary challenge, yet Pakistan remains a permanent irritant.

c) Internal fault lines need to be addressed and conflict resolution expedited to reduce scope for collusive interference.

d) Alliances/strategic partnerships are certainly not enough, and reliance has to be on building our own capabilities.

e) A 'whole-of-nation' approach to boost Comprehensive National Power can make Pakistan irrelevant due to decisive asymmetry and reduce the gap with China.

f) Force rebalancing and theatrisation need to be expedited to synergise integrated responses.

g) Modernisation, capability building, and infrastructure require a sustained focus, backed up by an adequate budget.

h) The terrestrial and maritime domains need to be concurrently developed.

i) Smart Atma Nirbharta is the recommended way forward to gain salience in niche and disruptive technologies.

j) Realistic scenario-based war-gaming and simulations, backed up by net assessment, should be carried out to improve responses and preparation levels.

k) Notwithstanding Chinese obduracy, India should continue efforts to resolve the boundary dispute and also build credible CBMs to avoid border flashpoints.

A collusive two-and-a-half-front scenario is the ultimate challenge and requires synergy at all levels and a 'whole-of-nation' approach. It will be appropriate to quote Clausewitz: 'War is the continuation of policy with other means.' Deft diplomacy is required to prevent and mitigate this threat. Intelligence and surveillance agencies should remain vigilant to generate appropriate warnings. Security agencies have to rebalance and reorganise optimum force levels to generate appropriate responses. **Preparation in itself is the best deterrent.**

References

1. Shura Nawaz, *Crossed Swords* (Karachi: Oxford University Press, 2008).
2. Ayaz Babur, *What's Wrong with Pakistan?* (Faridabad: Fay House, India, 2003).
3. Hussain Haqqani, *Pakistan Between Mosque and Military* (New Delhi: Penguin Viking, 2005).
4. Christophe Jefferson, *Pakistan At the Crossroads: Domestic Dynamics and External Pressures* (Gurgaon: Random House India, 2016).
5. Kamal Davar, *Tryst with Prefidy: The Deep State of Pakistan* (Mumbai: Rupa, 2017).
6. Lt Gen KJ Singh, *Evolution of Pakistan Army's Character and Ethos* (New Delhi: CLAWS, Scholar Warrior, Autumn 2019).
7. Lt Gen KJ Singh, *Leveraging of Religious Diplomacy by Pakistan* (New Delhi: CLAWS, Scholar Warrior, Spring 2020).
8. Pradip Baijal, *Containing the Chinese Onslaught* (Gurugram: Quadrant, 2019).
9. Henry M Paulson, *Dealing with China* (London: Headline Publishing Group, 2015).
10. Lt Gen AK Singh & Lt Gen BS Nagal, Ed, *Military Strategy for India in the 21st Century*
11. Lt Gen Prakash Katoch, Gp Capt Sharad Tewari, *China Pakistan Military Nexus: Implications for India* (New Delhi: Om Publications, 2019).

Pakistan Army – Ethos and Hierarchy

9.1 Evolution of Pakistan Army's Character and Ethos (Updated May 2025)

> *'There are armies that guard their nation's borders, there are those concerned with protecting their own position in society and there are those that defend a cause or an idea. The Pakistan Army does all three.'*
>
> —Stephen Cohen, a Renowned Strategic Expert

Key Takeaways

- The Pakistan Army has usurped a dominant role in governance and created a 'deep state' to retain control.
- Khaki generals are driving the nation on an anti-India trajectory and are afflicted with parity syndrome.
- Gen Zia has put the army on the Islamist (jihadi) path.
- The army has also created an empire with tentacles in all profit-making ventures, wherein larger national interests have been relegated.
- There have been reports of a growing divide between senior and junior officers, with the latter rooting for Imran Khan.
- Gen Munir has resurrected the 'two-nation' theory and has termed Kashmir as the jugular (Shah rug) for Pakistan.

- **After Operation Bunyan-un-Marsoos (Wall of Unity) in response to Operation Sindoor, despite reverses, the army has succeeded in rallying the country behind it, overcoming a sharp decline in its credibility. Gen Munir has been promoted as Field Marshal.**
- **Please do read Sections 2.1 and 2.2 on Operation Sindoor in the chapter: 'Opening Perspectives'.**

Introduction

The Indian and Pakistani armies were carved out of the British Indian Army consequent to the Partition and were like identical twins for the first few years, but both have charted different trajectories in the 72 years since independence. In the case of Pakistan, a major slant came in 1956, with the Americans deputing the Military Assistance Advisory Group (MAAG) to shape Pakistan's integration into the CENTO and SEATO. The collapse of the Soviet regime in Afghanistan in the 1990s gave Pakistan an opportunity to emerge as America's proxy. The evolution of both armies has also been shaped by two contrasting systems of governance: **in Pakistan, especially, military rule has given the army a pivotal and all-pervasive role. Apart from this, theological drivers have also conditioned the ideological dimension. Gen Zia-ul-Haq has the dubious distinction of giving the Pakistan Army Islamist overtones, with the open espousing of the 'Quranic concept of warfare'**. The Pakistan Army, unlike most other armies, has added the defence of ideological frontiers, besides geographic borders, in its revised mandate. This slant was further cemented with Pakistan running the *fasaadi* (mistakenly also referred to as jihadi) assembly line at the Western powers' and America's behest, for employment in Afghanistan.

Moving from the colonial British legacy to the American slant, lurching onwards to the sinister *fasaadi* makeover and now the collusive Chinese embrace are indeed major milestones in the evolution of the Pakistan Army. **Generals in khaki have shown amazing politico-diplomatic dexterity in balancing the Americans**

with the Chinese and Russians, to a limited extent, and Sunni Saudis with Shia Iranians, to leverage their geo-strategic relevance due to the location at the confluence of cultures. It is, indeed, ironical that despite the crushing defeat of 1971, leading to the loss of the larger wing of East Pakistan, the reverse in 1947, and the stalemate in 1965, major setbacks in Siachin and Kargil, the army continues to enjoy the patronage of the populace, sustained on the narrative of vilification and marginalisation of other legitimate instruments of the state, that are painted as corrupt and lackadaisical.

Scope

Despite a shared heritage, currently, the two armies of India and Pakistan, while retaining some commonalities, are poles apart, meriting a comparative analysis. The thrust of this article is to flag the macro trends in the evolution of the current character and ethos of the Pakistan Army. The scope of the analysis has been confined to the army, with only an outline discussion on connected issues relating to the army. The Pakistan Army has an overriding and dominant role, which was officially promulgated in March 1956, with Pakistan jettisoning the traditional order derived from colonial powers of Navy-Army-Air Force to Army-Navy-Air Force.

Politicisation of the Pakistan Army

Pakistan veered toward the concept of 'guided democracy', leading to military rule, just a decade after independence, in October 1958, with Ayub Khan seizing power and promoting himself to the rank of Field Marshal. An interesting fact is that **Ayub was not even in the panel of three seniormost officers considered for appointment as the first chief, and, after his appointment, engineered multiple extensions and two promotions. This trend has continued through Zia, Musharaff, Raheel, and Bajwa, and even Asim Munir, wherein the appointing authority disregarded seniority to pick suitable and apparently pliable nominees. But, invariably, each of these**

incumbents outgrew their stature to assert their independence and even upstage those appointing them. The unluckiest was the former Prime Minister Zulfikar Bhutto, who was hanged by his protégée, Gen Zia. Close on his heels is Nawaz Sharif, who was upstaged by all four chiefs appointed by him. Ayub's rule for more than a decade was followed by Yahya Khan, till the defeat in 1971. The initial spell of military rule stretched to 13 years. After a break of seven years of civilian rule, there was another spell of military rule and a dubious Islamic decade under Gen Zia-ul-Haq from September 1978 to August 1988. The third spell of military rule lasted seven years under Gen Pervez Musharraf from June 2001 to August 2008. In effect, Pakistan has been ruled by army generals either openly (through martial rule) or by proxy by having pliant puppet regimes. This is in sharp contrast to India, where the mere whiff of an unusual move of troops towards Delhi spooks the entire ruling elite on Raisina Hill, as it happened in 2014. **Another interesting indication is that soon after independence, the Governor General's residence in Delhi was taken over and converted into the Prime Minister's residence, and is now a museum. In contrast, all four *fauji* Presidents in Islamabad retained the Chief of Army Staff's appointment and continued to run the country from Army House in Rawalpindi**. The status of character of governments till 2024 was as tabulated below. This excludes the proxy rule, which has been a constant factor.

In essence, the army enjoys an overriding say in defence (including the budget), sensitive issues of foreign policy like Kashmir, Afghanistan, and nuclear weapons (including their development and employment). In addition, intelligence organisations like the ISI and Inter-Services Public Relations (ISPR) continue to operate under the army, with no civilian oversight. The army retains firm control over traditional homeland security subjects, including internal security, frontier areas, and border management. The current Minister for Internal Security, Brig Ijaz Shah (Retd), like many of his predecessors, has an army and ISI background. The list of subjects and concerns is only indicative, as subjects can be added or deleted at the whims and fancies of the Pindi generals. **The sheer range and scope of interference has resulted in independent analysts pointing out, 'While nations have armies, the Pakistan Army has the nation at its disposal.'** The installation of Imran Khan in what is dubbed as 'managed elections' and the army and ISI chiefs accompanying Imran during his recent US visit are clear indicators of the control exercised by the army. The trend has continued with Imran being eased out and an interim regime being installed in place, and with controlled elections being planned.

Civilian Govt	Military Regime	Total
40 yrs	36 yrs	76 yrs

Types of Governments

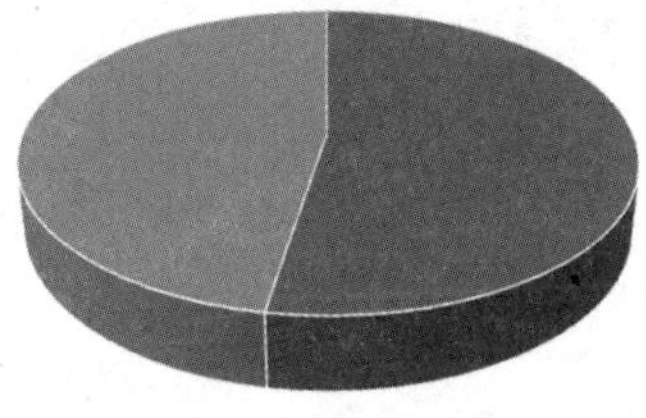

Anti-India Bias

The Pakistan Army, in pursuance of the two-nation theory, chose to make the anti-India bias its *raison d'être*. This has manifested in multiple attempts to destabilise and even mount aggression on India. Immediately after Partition, Kashmir was taken up as an unfinished agenda, leading to raids in October 1947 by plundering tribal *lashkars* (militias), notably Mehsuds and Kabayalis, aided by the Pakistan Army's Chitra Scouts and regulars. This war lasted for 15 months till the one-sided ceasefire, applied by India, despite its ascendancy at that juncture. Hein G Kiessling has pointed out in his book *Faith, Unity,*

Discipline: The ISI of Pakistan that **Pakistan started aiding and training Naga rebels in the 1950s. After the 1962 war, Pakistan forged links with China despite being in American formal alliances like CENTO and SEATO, primarily in pursuit of its quest to marginalise India.** Sensing this opportunity, Pakistan again launched an attack in the Rann in April 1965, followed by full-scale operations in September 1965. It is also interesting that India mounted the Siachen operations in April 1984 to stymie Pakistan's plans to occupy the glacier. Pakistan aided Khalistani extremism in the 1980s and later the ongoing proxy war in J&K. The failed Kargil operation was another manifestation of this deviant tendency. An interesting explanation has been provided by Khalid Ahmed, a leading Pakistani columnist, 'Pakistani nationalism comprises 95% India hatred. They call it Islam because that is how we learn to differentiate between ourselves and India.' This bias has fuelled tendencies like the parity syndrome despite the very basis of the two-nation theory becoming shaky with the liberation of Bangladesh. Gen (now FM) Aseem Munir, in a speech in March 2025, reiterated the 'two-nation' theory and described Kashmir as the jugular (Shah rug) for Pakistan.

Parity Syndrome

The Pakistan Army has always suffered from the parity syndrome, wherein it seeks to match its Indian counterpart. This has been sustained on false narratives, unfortunately dressed up with religious metaphors, alluding that a single Pakistani soldier (*momin*) can defeat five Indians (*kafirs*) merely due to religious beliefs. It will be pertinent to quote ZA Bhutto, 'If India builds the bomb, we will eat grass and for a thousand years, even go hungry, but we will get one of our own.' Despite clear reverses, Pakistan has continued to pursue ambitious policies of 'bleeding by a thousand cuts' and proxy war forays, first in the North-East, then in Punjab, and currently in J&K. This is combined with a tendency of provocation and nuanced irrationality, which will be discussed later. It will be relevant to recount the seminal wisdom of C Christine Fair, in her landmark book, *Fighting to The End: The Pakistan Army's Way of War,* Pakistan has to recognise that it simply cannot match India through whatever stratagem it chooses; it is bound to fail. **The sensible thing, then, is for Pakistan to reach the best possible accommodation with India now, while it still can, and shift gears toward a grand strategy cantered on economic integration in South Asia—one that would help Pakistan climb out of its morass and allow the army to maintain some modicum of privileges, at least for a while. The alternative is to preside over an increasingly hollow state.**

Theological Template

The Pakistan Army, like the rest of the nation, jettisoned the secular ethos of the British Army and the vision of Jinnah to embark on the Quranic concept of war, as outlined by Brig SK Malik. This trend was fuelled by Zia, who made it a compulsory text in military courses. The book legitimises instruments of terror and gives a mischievous twist to the concepts of *jihad, fedayeen,* and *ghazi*. **Zia also discarded the original secular motto, '*Ittehad, Yaqeen, aur Tanzeem*' implying 'Unity, Faith, and Discipline'. The new motto was '*Imaan, Taqwa, Jihad-fi-Sabilillah*', meaning 'Faith, Piety, Holy war in the path of Allah'.** This has resulted in Pakistan describing its quest for a nuclear device as one for an Islamic bomb. It is ironic that if Iran makes a separate 'Shia bomb', Pakistan's lofty idea may get stymied into just a 'Sunni bomb'. Pakistan has also given provocative names of invaders to its task forces and missiles, like Ghauri, Ghazni, Babur, etc. It is most ironic that due to this dangerous dalliance with terrorists, the Pakistan Army, espousing *jihad* in its very motto, named its anti-terror operation 'Raad-ul-Fasaad', terming *jihadis* as *fasaadis*. It will be once again appropriate to quote C Christine Fair, 'Pakistan's military journals frequently take as their subjects famous Quranic battles, such as the Battle of Badr. Ironically, the varied Quranic battles are discussed in more analytical detail in Pakistan's journals than are

Pakistan's own wars with India.' This dangerous trend has proliferated in the air force, as seen in the assassination attempt on Musharraf, and even in the navy, as evidenced during the raid on the PNS *Mehran* in 2011. Gen Aseem Munir, in a recent speech in Mar 2025, pointed out that only two republics were created on a 'Kalma' (theological invocation) basis, Riyasat-e-Madina and Riyasat-e-Pakistan.

Notwithstanding its struggling economy, Pakistan has taken over the mantle of protecting the larger Islamic brotherhood (*ummah*), which led to the development of the so-called Islamic bomb. Former Army Chief General Raheel Sharif commands the Islamic Military Alliance, also referred to as the 'Sunni Force'. Pakistan Army troops and pilots operate, as well as run, training teams and maintenance facilities in many Sunni countries like Saudi Arabia, Jordan, and other Gulf countries like the UAE, Qatar, and Bahrain. It will be pertinent to recount that a Pakistani pilot flying a Syrian Air Force plane was shot down during the Yom Kippur War in 1973. However, none of these countries has allowed its equipment, like aircraft (even when flown by Pakistani pilots), to be used in wars against India. **Pakistan has made a substantial contribution to various UN peace-keeping missions and has earned an enviable reputation.**

Deceit and Denial

The Pakistan Army has utilised theological narratives to incorporate infiltration as an instrument in its operations. Infiltration task forces were utilised in both the 1947 and 1965 operations and named after Muslim raiders. Pakistan banked on these tribal militias, aided by the Chitral Scouts and regulars, but kept denying their presence till caught by the UN-mandated Dixon Commission. The 1965 operations were timed with the missing *Moi-e-Muqqadas* (holy hair of the Prophet) controversy, which was probably engineered to foment trouble. In addition, despite the aggression by Pakistan and the stalemate weighted in India's favour, Pakistan continued to celebrate the 1965 operations as a victory and ironically called it *Yom-e-Difa* (celebration of defence). The genocide and plunder in erstwhile East Pakistan were denied by the generals despite evidence presented by international observers and the media. Pakistan used the Northern Light Infantry (NLI) troops in the Kargil operations, building a deniability clause, and even refused to accept the dead bodies of its soldiers.

Cultivated Nuanced Irrationality

Pakistan has tried to offset its asymmetry by cultivating a nuanced irrationality wherein it threatens to transition from hybrid war to the tactical nuclear domain with a declaratory policy. As described by C Christine Fair, 'Pakistan's nuclear weapons are India-specific.' **The nuclear threat is accentuated by vague red lines and tactical delivery means.** However, the Balakot strike and the American warning during the Kargil crisis seem to have resulted in the carving out of some discreet space below the nuclear threshold.

Quest for Strategic Depth

Pakistan's policy on its western borders is conditioned by a lack of strategic depth and realisation of the informality of the 2,600-km Afghan border, termed as the Durand Line. While Pakistan considers it a settled border, the Afghans demand a greater Pashtunistan. This border is neither demarcated nor properly fenced. In effect, the Pashtun population, steeped in the frontier culture, spills over onto both sides. Pakistan is now embarking on a project to fence selected stretches and demarcate crossing points after clashes with Afghan forces and reports of rampant narco-arms trafficking. Similarly, the Iranian border, between Balochistan and Sistan, spanning 959 km, has only a tattered fence, which is being replaced by a concrete wall fortified with steel by Iran, due to its concern about Sunni insurgency in the Sistan province. The fear of being swamped by India has spurred the Pakistani quest for strategic depth and nurturing of the Taliban. Noted author Ahmed Rashid describes the Pakistani policy in Afghanistan as: '**Islamabad views its Afghan policy through the**

prism of denying India any advantage in Kabul.' C Christine Fair has debunked the popular fallacy that Pakistan is caught up in the Afghan conflict due to its role in aiding the Western powers in the fight against the Soviets. She has reiterated that Bhutto set up the Afghan cell in the ISI much before this operation.

Tentacles of MILBUS

The Pakistani Armed Forces have created a labyrinthine foundation comprising the Fauji Army Welfare Trust, the Shaheen for the Air Force, and the Baharia for the Navy, to extend their tentacles into the Military-Business (MILBUS). Apart from this, they have a controlling stake in major public sector corporations, like the National Logistics Cell (NLC), Frontier Works Organisation (FWO), and Special Communications Organisation (SCO). Also, a critical utility provider, the Water and Power Development Authority (WAPDA) has been placed under the Armed Forces. This logistics framework has dual-use capability and is leveraged by the army and the other two services. Ayesha Siddiqa, in her book, *Military Inc: Inside Pakistan's Military Economy,* has observed that 'Milbus is military capital that perpetuates the military's predatory style.' This mega financial empire, worth approximately $40 billion, gives the army fiscal autonomy and assured pre-eminence. It is both a manifestation of the feudalistic character of the Pakistani society and a perpetuation of non-democratic forces. **Army-affiliated entities (SCO and FWO) also cornered a number of ancillary projects of the CPEC, especially when Gen Aseem Bajwa headed it in a rather controversial tenure. The latest ill-advised foray is the army taking over large tracts of land for contractual farming as part of the CPEC.**

Alliances and Collusion

Pakistan has shown amazing flexibility and dexterity in balancing alliances with America and China. The first alliance was with the US through SEATO and CENTO in the 1950s. It resulted in the induction of frontline equipment like Sabre jets, Patton tanks, and guns, which, unfortunately, emboldened Pakistan to attack India in 1965, resulting in the Americans cooling off in the 1960s and 1970s. The Americans returned in the 1980s to use Pakistan as a firm base for their Afghanistan operations for two decades and then lost interest, only to return again. The US has essentially used Pakistan intermittently, yet Pakistan got considerable largesse in funds and equipment like the F-16s. **Pakistan also opened a channel to China after the 1962 operations and even acted as a facilitator to set up Kissinger's forays to Beijing.** The Pakistan-China friendship is described metaphorically as 'stronger than steel and deeper than oceans', but China has been discreet enough to only posture this and not get embroiled physically in the 1965, 1971, and Kargil operations. China has helped Pakistan to build nuclear weapons and missiles, flouting the proliferation regime. It has also got a significant footprint in armament complexes at the HIT, the ordnance factories in Wah, and aviation complexes, with the latest being the joint production of the JF-17. This collusion with China is getting further cemented through the CPEC, notably the development of the Gwadar port.

Conclusion

Notwithstanding these peculiar biases in the ethos of the Pakistan Army, specifically at the higher echelons, it is not a pushover but has a considerable professional framework. At the unit level, the army is cohesive and remains efficient; hence, it will be pragmatic not to underestimate it. Independent and competent experts feel that in the long-term interest, it will be in order if the army yields the mandated space to other legitimate agencies of the state. **The recent domestic chaos unleashed after the dismissal of Imran Khan, with the storming of the Corps Commander's residence in Lahore by angry crowds in May 2023, is indicative of developing angst, yet it may be premature to underestimate the Pakistan Army's capability to regain control.** Though it may appear highly optimistic and unlikely, it is hoped that the army will embark on correctives to become a functional and professional army.

Selected Bibliography

1. Syed Nur Ahmed, in Craig Baxter, ed., From *Martial Law to Martial Law* (Lahore: Vanguard, 1985).
2. Shuja Nawaz, *Crossed Swords* (Karachi: Oxford University Press, 2008).
3. Ayaz Babar, *What's Wrong with Pakistan?* (Faridabad: Hay House India, 2013).
4. Hussain Haqqani, *Pakistan Between Mosque and Military* (New Delhi: Penguin Viking, 2005).
5. C Christine Fair, *Fighting to The End. The Pakistan Army's Way of War* (Oxford: Oxford University Press, 2014).
6. Christophe Jafferlot, *Pakistan at The Crossroads: Domestic Dynamics and External Pressures* (Gurgaon: Random House India, 2016).
7. Kamal Davar, *Tryst with Perfidy: The Deep State of Pakistan* (Mumbai: Rupa, 2017).

9.2 Pakistan Army Chiefs: Interesting Facts and Facets (Also read Section 2.3 in the chapter – Opening Perspectives)

The Commander-in-Chief Era

Both Indian and Pakistani armies started with a Commander-in-Chief (C-in-C) at the apex, with British generals as the first two chiefs. After Gen Lockhart and Gen Bucher, India appointed Gen Cariappa as the first Indian Chief of Army Staff (COAS) on 15 January 1949, realising British complicity in the Kashmir conflict. India had only four Cs-in-C and transitioned in April 1955 (in less than eight years) to the COAS appointment, with Gen Maharaj Rajendrasinhji Jadeja being re-designated from C-in-C to COAS.

Pakistan continued with British Cs-in-C (Frank Messervy and Douglas Gracey) till January 1951. It also persisted with the Cs-in-C system till Mar 1972 (for nearly 25 years), but had only six incumbents. Leaving out the first two British incumbents and Gen Gul Hasan Khan (the last one), the other three—Gen Ayub Khan, Gen Muhammad Musa, and Gen Yahya Khan—enjoyed five to seven years' tenures.

Extension of Tenures Common, Truncating a Rarity

Pakistan chiefs grant themselves or organise extensions, some of which are multiple, like Gen Zia. Amongst recent incumbents, cases of extension for Gen Pervez Kayani and Gen Qamar Javed Bajwa were even contested in court. On the other hand, extensions for the Indian Army COAS are very rare. **The current Army Chief, Gen Aseem Munir, has already secured the first extension, making his tenure till November 2027, making it five years. Even Air Chief Marshal Zaheer Ahmed Babur Sidhu got a second extension.**

Gen Raheel Sharif, though denied extension, fixed a tenure for himself as the chief of Saudi Arabia's anchored International Task Force for the conflict in Yemen. Gen Gul Hassan was removed with less than three months (74 days) in the appointment. Gen Zia-ul-Haq and Gen Asif Nawaz Janjua died in harness; both deaths remain a matter of speculation regarding being engineered accident and poisoning, respectively, by an external intelligence agency. Gen Jehangir Karamat was eased out and forced to resign by Prime Minister Nawaz Sharif after the nuclear tests.

Martial Law Proponents

Three Pakistan Army COASs (Ayub Khan, Zia-ul-Haq, and Pervez Musharraf) applied martial law, taking over the reins. Gen Ayub promoted himself as Field Marshal. Gen Yahya Khan replaced Ayub Khan, becoming the fourth one to rule under martial law, concurrently with being COAS for two years and nine months.

Pakistan chiefs, who took over as Martial Law rulers (except Ayub), like Yahya, Zia, and Musharraf, carried on as army chiefs. Concurrently, Gen Ayub had two surrogate chiefs—Musa and Yahya. At the same time, Zia didn't risk anyone as chief for the entire ten-year span as Martial Law Administrator. Gen Musharraf appointed Pervez Kayani, only after six years as concurrent COAS and in his contrived political avatar as President, which lasted less than one year.

Army House More Attractive than the Presidential Palace

Double-hatters like Zia-ul-Haq and Musharraf continued to occupy the Army House in Rawalpindi rather than the Aiwan-e-Sadar, the Presidential Palace. The eviction of Pervez Musharraf by Gen Kayani from Pindi House in May 2009 (nine months after he ceased to be President) became an ugly spat and was covered in the media also.

Field Marshals

After Ayub Khan, Aseem Munir was conferred with the rank of Field Marshal in May 2025, becoming the second Marshal.

Civilian Govt	Military Regime	Total
40 yrs	36 yrs	76 yrs

Types of Governments

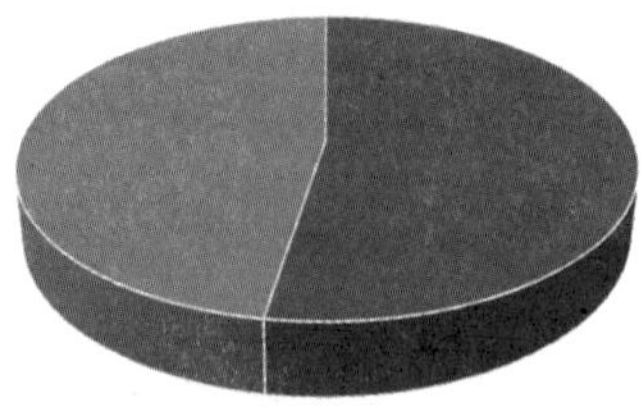

▪ Civilian Regime ▪ Military Rule

Lengths of Tenures

The longest tenure was of Gen Zia-ul-Haq (12 years), and the shortest was Gen Khawaja Ziauddin, less than six hours. Even Gen Gul Hassan had less than three months' tenure, becoming a casualty of the post-Bangladesh shake-up. In the Indian Army, Gen Thimmaya had the longest tenure of 4 years.

Civil and Military Confrontations

After the Kargil fiasco, Nawaz Sharif tried to sack Gen Musharraf, returning from an overseas trip, and appoint Ziauddin as chief. In a counter coup, Musharraf took over the reins, and Prime Minister Nawaz Sharif was packed off to exile.

Supersession has been the norm to build personal loyalty; however, loyalty, ironically, has been transient.

Nawaz Sharif had a role in the appointment of six COAS, including Waheed Kakkar, Musharraf, Ziauddin, Raheel Sharif, Qamar Jawed Bajwa, and Munir. With shifting loyalties, they contributed to his removal, too. Gen Kakkar, in a somewhat even-handed approach, got both the President (main supporter) and Prime Minister Nawaz to resign after a constitutional face-off. Musharraf not only executed a coup but also forced Nawaz into exile in Saudi Arabia. Gen Bajwa

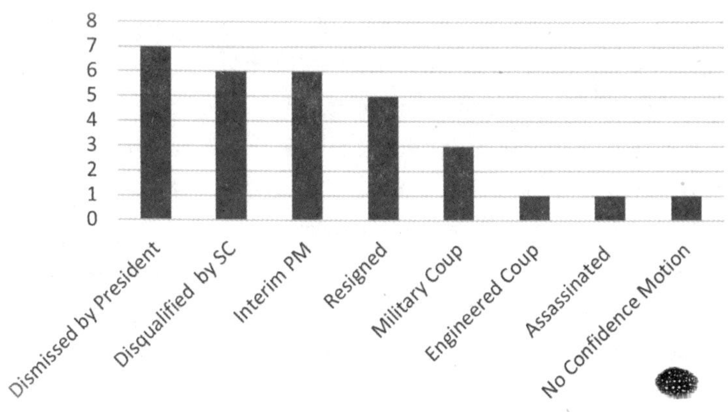

acquiesced in the court-dictated resignation of Nawaz and subsequent exile to London. Bajwa hoisted Nawaz's bete-noir, Imran Khan, as Prime Minister in a doctored election, only to get him unseated.

Pre-Eminence of Infantry Officers as Top Guns

Most chiefs have been from the Infantry, though the armoured corps had three—Gen Gul Hassan, Gen Ziq-ul-Haq, and Gen Jehangir Karamat. Coincidentally, all three had their tenures truncated; two were eased out, while Zia-ul-Haq not only became the military ruler but also carried on till his death in an air crash. Artillery had two incumbents, Tikka Khan and Pervez Musharraf, both of whom became Martial Law Administrators.

The Baloch Regiment has the maximum—five on the coveted list—Gen Yahya, Gen Aslam Beg, Gen Kayani, Gen Bajwa, and Gen Aseem Munir.

Demographic Count of Army Chiefs

Punjabis (56% population) account for only eight out of 17 chiefs, with a combined tenure of 36 out of 77 years (47% till 2024). Gen Tikka Khan, in 1972, was the first Punjabi chief (25 years after independence). Three chiefs, Tikka Khan, Asif Nawaz, and Raheel Sharif, are Rajputs from Pothwar in Punjab. Zia-ul-Haq (though Punjabi-speaking but part Mohajir) was the chief for 12 years. The current one, Aseem Munir, is also of the same category; the families of both Zia and Munir migrated from Jullundur.

Five chiefs (Ayub, Yahya, Gul Hasan, Waheed Kakkar, Jehangir Karamat) with combined tenures of 16 years (21%) have been Pashtuns (16% population).

Muhajirs (6% population) have contributed two—Musharraf and Aslam Beg, both Urdu-speaking, who accounted for 12 years (15%). In essence, Pashtuns and Muhajirs have punched above their weight class. Trends may be changing as the last three and the current one (Aseem Munir) are all Punjabis.

No Sindhi (17% population) or Baluchi (3%) has made it to be COAS, though Gen Muhammad Musa Khan was born in and a resident of Baluchistan. Gen Mohammed Musa, a Hazara (from the minuscule population of Shias of Afghan descent), was C-in-C for eight years (10% tenure share).

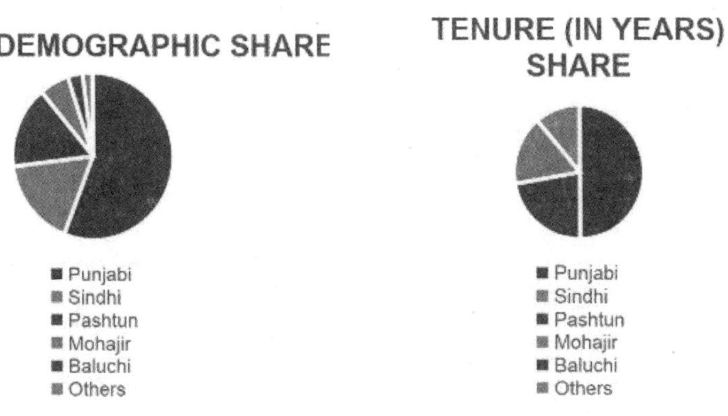

Besides, Musa, Yahya Khan also belonged to the Shia community, which makes 17% of the population in a predominantly Sunni (90%) country with unending Sunni-Shia strife. Shias have been at the apex for 12 years (16% tenure share). Musa led the Pakistan Army in the 1965 operations, and Yahya in the ill-fated 1971 war. Gen Bajwa, as per some reports, was alleged to have distant familial links with the Ahmediya community, now declared heretics. There were even some rumours about Gen Aseem Munir having some Shia relatives on his wife's side.

Ayub and Yahya were both Pushtuns and ruled the country for 14 years. Non-Punjabis (Ayub, Yahya, and Musharraf) were at the helm for 25 out of 34 years of military rule. Zia-ul-Haq, part-Punjabi, accounted for the remaining nine years.

The Indian Connection

Three chiefs—Zia-ul-Haq (Jullundur born, St Stephen's educated, IMA commissioned); Mirza Aslam Beg (Azamgarh born and Shibli College graduate), and Pervez Musharraf (born in Neharwali Haveli, Old Delhi)—had Indian connections. Zia put Pakistan on the radical path; Aslam Beg initiated the proxy war in Kashmir, and Musharraf launched the failed Kargil operations. The current Chief Aseem Munir's family has Indian roots and has resurrected the 'two-nation' theory.

Miscellaneous

Pervez Musharraf lived and died in exile in Dubai. His successor, Pervez Kayani, lives abroad in Australia. Almost all former chiefs have interests and assets abroad.

9.3 Leveraging of Religious Diplomacy by the Pakistan Army

Key Takeaways

- **Pakistan has ascribed to itself the role of the guardian of Islam.**
- **Islam within Pakistan has acquired extremist overtones, with the radicalised Pakistan Army driving the narrative.**
- **Islamic society in Pakistan is witnessing contestation and violence between Sunnis and Shias and even between various strands within Sunnis.**
- **Radicalisation triggers competitive radicalisation in non-radicalised societies and faiths.**
- **There is a need for inter-faith dialogue and forging a more moderate form of Islam.**

Introduction

Three terms—religion, faith, and theology—are used interchangeably but are seldom analysed for their nuances and subtle variations. The first two—religion (*dharma*) and faith—are used frequently as synonyms and relate to the practice of a particular religious order and cover outward expression and rituals. On the other hand, theology (*dharma shastra)* encompasses analytics and detailed reasoning. **Religion and faith have always been potent drivers in national politics and increasingly even in international diplomacy and power politics.** Despite articulations and pretensions of secularism and assertions of keeping politics insulated from religion, propelled by a wave of nationalism, religion has become a potent instrument in international diplomacy. The tendency is more apparent in monotheistic or theocratic states like our neighbour Pakistan, which is an early proponent of this, and of late, has tried to leverage it for sinister purposes.

American and International Context

This trend further gained traction after the 9/11 terrorist attack. However, the US had created a special office with a designated ambassador-at-large for 'International Religious Freedom' in 1999, consequent to the proliferation of Islamist extremism. Out of five incumbents, only one has been a non-Christian, Jewish rabbi. The current ambassador, Senator Sam Brownback, was appointed after the casting of a vote by the Vice President, reflecting the ironic polarisation for an appointment mandated to promote consensus. He recently visited Dharamshala for parleys with the Dalai Lama. **The biggest current theological challenge is to evolve a more moderate form of Islam, containing the designs of caliphates and groups like Al-Qaeda and ISIS. The king of Jordan and Saudi royalty are also engaged in this effort, without much success.** It appears that the outsourcing of the Wahabism and Salafi strains to the extended neighbourhood, especially the Indian sub-continent, has run its course, and radicalism is already back in the Middle East. Hence, it is more of a compulsion to roll back radicalisation or at least keep it within manageable limits.

The American prodded initiative for moderate Islam is not free from internal contradictions and has naturally led to the coalescing of radical states. Malaysia recently led an initiative outside the traditional body, the OIC, as an alternative platform with Indonesia, Turkey, and Qatar as prominent participants in the meeting. The platform has been seen as an alternative and a challenge to the traditional Saudi-led theological Islamic bloc. Pakistan pulled out at the very last minute, forced by the relentless pressure of the Saudis and the Gulf nations. Imran's move to play a key role in forging the proposed alliance has annoyed Saudi Arabia, the UAE, and other Gulf nations. **The reticence of Gulf nations during the Pakistani fiscal emergency and refusal to get drawn in Indo-Pak issues has raised pertinent questions about the '*ummah*' (Islamic Brotherhood) and its efficacy.**

It is also pertinent to take note of the fact that radicalisation promotes competitive radicalisation in other societies and, consequently, it has spawned neo-conservative movements and hardening tendencies in other religions like Buddhism and now even Hinduism and Sikhism. All these malevolent strands are dangerous and need to be curbed.

Manifestations in Pakistan

India has been at the receiving end of the malevolent forays of Pakistan's religious diplomacy, which has acquired *fasaadi* overtones. **The use of the term *fasaad* in preference to the incorrectly used *jihad* is theologically validated. The Pakistan Army chose to call its anti-terror operations Raad-ul-Fasaad. Even the American cultural education discourages the misuse of the term *jihad*.** It is hardly logical to have different terms for the indigenous and exported versions of *fasaad*. The Pakistan Army's hypocrisy was first exhibited in the early 1950s, when it colluded with Naga militant groups, despite these groups openly striving for a Christian regime and Nagaland for Christ. The army under Tikka Khan indulged in the rape and massacre of fellow Bengali Muslims, disregarding the concept of *ummah* (Islamic brotherhood), leading to East Pakistan breaking away. This, in effect, negated the very *raison d'être* for the two-nation theory and the rationale for a separate Islamic nation. Giving primacy to religion, it disregarded other equally relevant factors, like the lack of geographical connectivity, and cultural and linguistic disparities between the two wings of Pakistan. Hypocrisy is currently seen in the silence of Pakistan and the *ummah* on the rampant persecution of the Uyghurs in Xinjiang by the Han Chinese. Hence, Pakistan and other Islamic nations have misused theocracy as per their convenience and in conjunction with other drivers and interests.

Pakistan, created as a homeland for Muslims, got the initial thumbs down when 35 million Muslims chose to cast their lot with secular India despite the Partition riots. Compared to this, Hindus and Sikhs deserted Pakistan in droves, despite Jinnah's assurance that the new nation would be inclusive, allowing minorities their fair share. Soon after Jinnah's death, the Islamic nation, which had Karachi as the capital, chose to make Islamabad, a suburb of Rawalpindi, the new seat of power. With this naming, it also chose to carry the cross or (crescent) of Islam. Manifestations were seen in the K*abayali lashkars* in Kashmir under Col Akbar (anointed as Gen Tariq) and R*azakars* in Hyderabad, albeit the religious aspect was subdued. More sinister was the contrived misplacement of the *Moi-e-Muqqadas* (holy hair relic of the Prophet) to whip up emotions in the Kashmir Valley in 1963. Despite failure to achieve its diabolic designs, Pakistan launched Operation Gibraltar in 1965. Infiltration by Mujahideen task forces, named after mostly infamous Muslim raiders, Salahuddin, Ghaznavi, Tariq, Babur, Qasim, Khalid, Nusrat, and Khilji, was organised under Gen Musa. The provocative tendency of using Islamic symbolism, particularly for the raiders, continues in the naming of missiles as Ghaznavi, Babur, and Ghauri.

In this dangerous lurch from sub-continental Sufi/Barelvi to Deobandi, Wahabi, and Salafi forms of Islam, *Khuda Hafiz* has become *Allah Hafiz*, and *Ramazan* has been replaced by the Arabic *Ramadan*. Pakistan seems to have linked its socio-cultural and theological moorings westwards, choosing Arabic influences over traditional linkages. Another major milestone was Bhutto's articulation of resolve to manufacture the Islamic bomb. Sadly, competitive radicalism under Zia-ul-Haq and later the Taliban accounted for the death of both Zulifkar, his daughter Benazir, and probably even Zia. The very dream of an Islamic bomb is getting reduced to a Sunni bomb because Shia Iran doesn't trust the Sunnis. In Talibanised Pakistan, Jinnah's Shias and Nobel Physicist Abdus Salaam's Ahmediyas are being targeted and eliminated. Former Army Chief Gen Raheel is now leading a coalition of Sunni forces against the Shia Houthi rebels. Pakistan also provides troops to guard sheikhdoms and royalty in many Gulf countries like Saudi Arabia. It has also been training pilots and other specialists, including veterans engaged in the maintenance of equipment. **Within Pakistan, various strands of Islamic faith are at loggerheads, overtaken by competitive extremism. The first manifestation is to apply the label of blasphemy on other faiths like Hindus, Sikhs, and Christians, though in the minority. The next are Ahmediyas, dubbed as non-Islamic. The dominant Sunnis often target Shias, Bohoras, and even Sufis, questioning their practices and beliefs. Sunni society has contestation amongst Barelvis, Deobandis, Ahle-Hadith, Salafis, and Wahabi sects.**

The mainstreaming of Islamist activists in electoral politics, and the army's utilisation of radical groups like Qadri's Tehreek-e-Labbaik Pakistan (TLP) to build pressure on governments, are worrying trends. These groups have not only gained legitimacy but are also wielding blasphemy as a weapon to target others. The lynching of a Sri Lankan manager is a dangerous manifestation of such tendencies. Even the highest courts have utilised ambiguous Shariat criteria, like non-compliance to 'Sadiq and Ameen' (truthful and honest) norms, to disqualify and unseat Prime Minister Nawaz Sharif.

Zia's Decade and the Rise of ISI

This dangerous course had been defined by Zia's decade of 1978 to 1988, which catalysed the Pakistan Army's Shariasation, committing itself to *Nizam-e-Mustafa* (rule of the Prophet) and taking upon itself the guardianship of the ideological frontiers. The traditional motto of '*Ittehad, Yaqeen, aur Tanzeem*' (Unity, Faith, and Discipline) was changed to 'I*maan, Taqwa, Jihad-fi-Sablillah*' (Faith, Righteousness, and Holy war in the path of Allah). How do minorities reconcile to such exhortation? Zia also made *The Quranic Concept of War* by Brig SK Malik, which legitimises the use of terror, a mandatory text for the forces. An interesting quote from the Pakistan Army's official website (reading like the objective of extremist groups) states, 'The mission and aim of a *Momin* is martyrdom'. American compulsions of tackling the Afghan imbroglio gave Pakistan an opportunity to emerge as the vanguard in this misplaced campaign, which was legitimised as a theological necessity. Since then, turmoil in the Middle East and plans of a caliphate with Khorasan, which includes India, have enabled Pakistan's terror assembly line to remain active. **A radicalised army in control of the nation and its foreign and security policies, including nuclear weapons, is, indeed, a dangerous warning for the neighbourhood. ISI and ISPR remain two key catalysts in this diabolic game.**

Kartarpur Challenge

The ISI, having probably realised that Kashmir is proving to be a case of diminishing marginal returns, has come up with the diabolic K2 plan to exploit the latent sub-nationalism of the Sikhs. The timing of the Kartarpur Corridor, and the initial offer by Gen Bajwa are indicative of the Pakistan Army's ownership of this move. Apart from this, the anchoring of the construction by the FWO and the timing with SFJ 2020 are all ominous indicators of the shape of things to come. While nobody doubts the loyalty of the Sikhs, fringe groups can be potential prey. It is also pertinent that the Punjabis defeated extremism and are cognisant of the state being put back by a couple of decades. Nobody is even remotely suggesting that the Sikhs are so naive that they will be brainwashed by a couple of posters and the display of remains of a bombshell with a provocative placard blaming India for attacking a gurudwara. Yet, it does open up possibilities for profiling and long-drawn psychological warfare. Combating the Pakistan-aided Druggistan designs remains a major challenge for the Punjabis. While the proxy war in Kashmir may be on a lower level, there are attempts by the ISI to fish for trouble spots and establish linkages with splinter groups in the hinterland to foment trouble. This has been coupled with attempts to raise the Kashmir issue at various international bodies, notably the UN, including the Security Council. While these efforts have not found much traction, the efforts continue and are likely to intensify basically to discredit India, especially on the handling of Kashmir. China, as a declared ally, has been anchoring these efforts. Indian diplomacy has to remain vigilant to counter these efforts.

The Two-Nation Theory and the Kashmir Bogey

Gen Aseem Munir, in a reprehensible speech, resurrected the 'two-nation' theory and described Kashmir as the jugular (Shah rug) for Pakistan, just before the dastardly Pahalgam terrorist attack on 22 April 2025, wherein 26 innocent people, including one local Muslim guide, were killed. The massacre was launched after identifying the victims as non-Muslims.

Conclusion

The near-complete disregard of the Kashmir rhetoric by the *ummah* has resulted in Pakistan blaming fellow international bodies, especially the Islamic nations, for giving market-driven compulsions preference over the *ummah* and religious issues. **The crying need of interfaith diplomacy is a collective endeavour for theological correction to evolve a moderate religion. Concurrently, Pakistan needs to demonstrate sincerity by dismantling export-oriented, *fasaadi* assembly lines and detoxifying its army.** India has no choice but to keep its guard up against Pakistan's designs. As the nation with the second-largest Muslim population, India also needs to promote Sufi and moderate Islam to preserve its diversity and secular traditions.

Pakistan – Descent into Chaos

10.1 Pakistan – Withering State (Written in September 2023, updated May 2025)

Introduction

Pakistan is witnessing probably the most dangerous implosion of institutions triggered by Imran Khan and his followers. Citadels and symbols of army supremacy, residences of corps commanders, HQs, and even the Mianwali airbase were plundered by crowds. Social media posts of mobs marauding through the residence of the corps commander (4 Corps) in Lahore and reported torching of the iconic F-16 throw up serious apprehensions about the security of the nuclear arsenal. The constitutional crisis comes at a time when the country is facing a grave economic crisis after defaulting on its fiscal obligations. The obvious conclusions are being drawn on Pakistan being a failing and withering state. The issues and criteria that merit discussion are as follows:

- **Constitutional and Institutional Crisis.**
- **Fiscal Emergency and Economic Distress.**
- **Internal Security and Ethnic Fault Lines.**
- **Unresolved Borders.**

The scope of this discussion is focused on the current evolving situation largely on the institutional crisis. The other issues are flagged very briefly.

Constitutional and Institutional Crisis

Pakistan, impacted by frequent martial law regimes and the Partition of East Pakistan, currently has the third variant of the constitution, which was adopted in 1973. Even this version has witnessed fundamental flip-flop changes with the adoption of the Presidential system and later shifting back to the Parliamentary one. **Political parties, the judiciary, and the army are the main players in this troika, with the army seeking to retain supremacy and override control.** The other instruments, bureaucracy, and media are marginalised as insignificant elements. The country has witnessed the assassination of the first Prime Minister Liaqat Ali Khan, the hanging of Prime Minister Zulfikar Ali Bhutto, another assassination of Benazir Bhutto, and the mysterious death of Gen Zia-ul-Haq. Apart from this, Pervez Musharraf and Nawaz Sharif had to seek exile.

Political Parties

Imran Khan and Pakistan Tehreek-e-Insaaf (PTI): Imran Khan, the propped-up creation of Khaki generals, was installed as Prime Minister in August 2018, after getting rid of Nawaz Sharif by questionable judicial disqualification. **He was essentially a leader with no real grassroots support or organisation, and was hoisted by the army in the form of PTI. The elections, as per the Sharif brothers, were hijacked by Khalai Mukhlooq (unseen ghosts), in an apparent reference to a hidden Khaki hand.** In less than four years, on April 2022, the army got rid of Imran, who had taken the ultimate risk of trying to break free of the army's stranglehold. Imran has also tried to drive an internal wedge and cultivate a younger lot of officers. He even recently named an ISI general, labelling him 'Dirty Harry'. He has skilfully leveraged social media to build the narrative of being the only honest leader, capable of ushering the much-touted, ***Riyasat-e-Madina***. Imran has mastered the art of serving theological chimera and playing the victimisation card by releasing videos, including pre-recorded ones. **His partner, Bushara Begum ('Pirni'), is reported to**

enjoy mystical powers, being part of a makeover from playboy to Taliban Khan.

Track Record: In his tenure, Imran has a dubious track record of destroying ties with traditional allies like Saudi Arabia, the Gulf countries, and the US. He even launched an ill-advised foray to create an alternate Islamic axis with Türkiye and Malaysia, annoying Saudi Arabia. Iron brothers, China and Iran, are wary of his grandstanding. He did nothing significant to stem or redress the financial mess, leading to Pakistan becoming a basket case for an IMF bailout. **Notwithstanding his being equally guilty of having contributed to the chaos and fiscal distress, the stark reality is that currently, he is the most popular leader.** He defiantly won six out of seven by-elections to the National Assembly, and mobs are out on a rampage, following his call. President Arif Alvi, Imran's appointee, has been accused of seeking directions from his party.

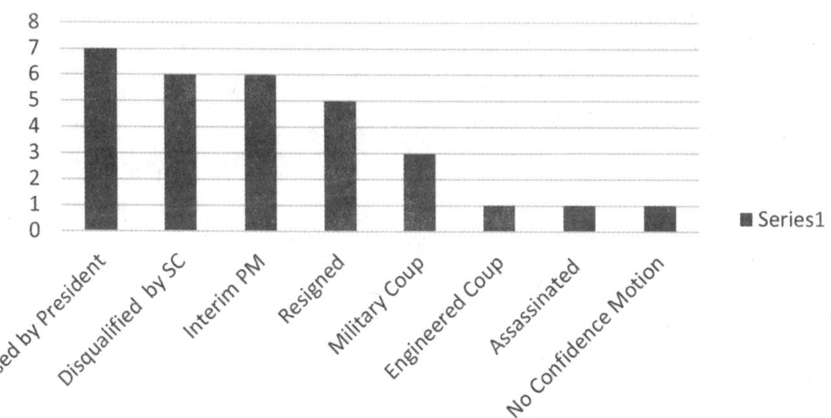

Sharif Brothers and Ruling Coalition: The ruling rag-tag coalition, Pakistan Democratic Movement (PDM), cobbled up by the army has Pakistan Muslim League (Nawaz) (PML-N), Pakistan People's Party (PPP), and Jammat-e-Islami Pakistan (JIP). Sharif's faction had been branded corrupt, at the army's behest by the National Accountability

Bureau (NAB) and the Supreme Court. Consequently, PML has Nawaz, ex-Prime Minister, exiled in London, remotely controlling the government with Shahbaz, the current Prime Minister, and Mariyam, his daughter, frequently rushing to London. Zardari-Bhutto dominates the other coalition partner, PPP. Asif Zardari, notorious for corruption, is again in remote control mode, and the 'immature' Bilawal Bhutto is in the cabinet. In effect, the entire political class is being discredited, and Pakistan has no real credible options. The main demand of Imran Khan is for early elections, to tap his popularity. **The ruling party wants to delay elections till October 2023, when the President and the Chief Justice would have retired.**

Judiciary

In this crumbling edifice of institutions, the judiciary has increasingly taken a conflicting and blatantly partisan stance. Chief Justice of Pakistan (CJP), Umar Ata Bandial, has been accused of displaying a pro-Imran tilt, pushing for early elections, and granting him bail. The judiciary had used questionable theological criteria of 'Sadiq and Ameen' (truthful and trustworthy), to impose a lifelong disqualification on Nawaz Sharif in April 2018, citing the Panama-gate papers. Yet, the same stringent parameters have not been applied to Imran and others. The anti-corruption watchdog and quasi-judicial body NAB is currently headed by Lt Gen Nazir Ahmed Butt. **After fixing Nawaz Sharif during Imran's regime, the body has now turned against Imran and is out to arrest him. The apparent agenda is to book Imran in Al-Qadir, Toshakhana, and other cases, including treason, to disqualify him from fighting elections.**

Army

The Pakistan Army, despite serious blunders and unchecked plunder through Fauji Welfare, Shaheen, and Baharia foundations, has retained a pivotal position in the power matrix. The army has a pervading presence in major projects, with Gen Aseem Bajwa, who headed the CPEC Authority, until his removal. Both COAS Gen Qamar Bajwa and Aseem Bajwa have been accused of large-scale corruption. Mobocracy has been promoted as an instrument of coercion by the ISI and ISPR through the dubious TLP during the siege of Rawalpindi in October 2021. It is now like the proverbial rogue genie, refusing to get capped. **Pakistani populace has always had suppressed angst against the luxurious lifestyle and draconian measures adopted by the army. The present situation is unprecedented in the scope and audacity of mobs.**

Types of Governments

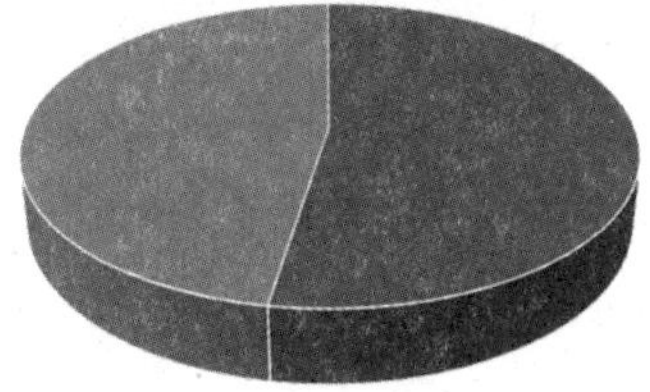

▪ Civilian Regime ▪ Military Rule

The former COAS had promulgated his Bajwa Doctrine, stipulating that the army stay out of politics. Notwithstanding this, Gen Bajwa had a major role in the sacking of Nawaz Sharif and later Imran, as well as the installation of Imran in 2018 and Shahbaz recently. The tenure of the current chief (Bajwa protégé) was truncated on Imran's insistence.. The senior hierarchy is divided and retains contact with political lobbies. Imran's favourite general was the retired Lt Gen Faiz Hameed, whose tenure was cut short by Gen Bajwa. There are credible reports of three corps commanders not being on the same page as the COAS. There is also increasing talk of Gen Shamshad Mirza, Chairman Joint Chiefs of Staff Committee (CJCSC), replacing COAS Gen Aseem Munir. **The air is thick with conspiracy theories, and the use of rangers in arresting Imran was essentially an immature ploy to circumvent the Bajwa Doctrine.**

Fiscal Emergency and Economic Distress

Pakistan is witnessing another spring or colour revolution triggered by corrupt governments and desperate, ill-informed awaam (populace), provoked by Imran. A sinking economy, natural disasters (devastating floods), and uncontrolled inflation, accentuated by a reticent IMF, have added to the desperation. As per some reports, **Pakistan has external liabilities amounting to approximately US$80 billion and needs emergency relief of US$8 billion.** The much-promised game changer, CPEC, seems to be floundering. The government has been forced to apply strict fiscal correctives, like the withdrawal of subsidies, further multiplying its unpopularity. Does Imran realise that the anti-establishment wave is easy to unleash but difficult to harness? Will it devour him next, for he has no magic wand to rebuild the economy?

The basic problems of Pakistan are food, energy (electricity), water, employment, and education (skill development). **A demographic dividend is threatening to turn into a demographic disaster. Cities like Karachi are becoming urban nightmares with ghettoisation into ethnic pockets like Muhajirs, Pashtuns, Sindhis, and Punjabis, with gang lords and mafia.** It may be worthwhile to create an economic revival task force under a proven economist like Mehboob-ul-Haq and empower him.

Internal Security and Ethnic Fault Lines

The chaos has the potential to **accentuate problems of unresolved ethnic fault lines like Baloch, Pashtun, Sindh, Muhajir, Kashmir, Shia, Ahmediyya, and Baltis.** Coupled with this is the incessant threat posed by resurgent Tehreek-e-Taliban Pakistan (TTP) and Islamic State-Khorasan Province (ISIS-KP). The subject requires separate and detailed analysis, but the way forward is genuine devolution of power and the grant of autonomy. It is axiomatic that Punjabi domination is reduced for inclusive development.

Unresolved Borders

Pakistan's dream of strategic depth is eroding with the Taliban refusing to accept the Durand Line. Pakistan has been forced to start fencing and strengthening border posts, like Torkham. However, cross-border raids have increased. The border with Iran also has serious issues relating to a Sunni insurgency in the Sistan province of Shia-dominated Iran. Mercifully, the ceasefire on the LoC, signed with India in 2021, is still holding, but the Pak-engineered proxy war continues, raising the possibility of surgical raids and even strikes like Balakot.

Way Forward

Indian strategic thinkers have unsuccessfully tried to discredit the military establishment, attempting to trigger psychological collapse and implosion. Imran seems to have unwittingly grabbed the baton on his own and is engaged in destroying the image of the army. **After Gen Zia-ul-Haq, who had put the Pakistan Army on a dangerous Islamist course, destroyed its professional ethos, Imran will go down in history for destroying internal cohesion, and also the external invincibility of the army. The Pakistan Army will have to work overtime to regain its internal cohesion and repair its image.**

As Pakistan lurches towards chaos, initially, one can exult, but the task is cut out for the strategic community, as **Pakistan has displayed resilience in the past. Its geo-strategic location keeps it relevant for the major powers, and they are likely to bail it out for their own great game.**

- **First, keep up the vigil, as disparate elements often resort to irrational and suicidal recourse.**
- **Second, ensure the ceasefire holds, as opening another front with China in a belligerent mode is avoidable.**
- **Third, any significant dialogue is unlikely until elections in both countries are over.**

- **Fourth, engage with the international community to build better safeguards for Pakistan's nuclear arsenal, to rule out the spectre of *fasaadi* (jihadi) and dirty bombs.**
- **Fifth, the humiliated Pakistan Army, after 1971, devised a 'thousand-cuts' strategy; hence, in the long term, our challenges are likely to remain formidable. China, in a collusive mode, seeks to revive the CPEC and the BRI by roping in Afghanistan and even Iran.**
- **Most importantly, the army and the deep state, though temporarily down, are unlikely to be permanently out and are likely to regroup.**

10.2 Resetting Templates in Pakistan (Written in November 2023, updated May 2025)

The return of Nawaz Sharif, after a four-year exile in London, adds yet another twist to the tragicomedy charade of proxy democracy in Pakistan. **Nawaz, in his three non-consecutive tenures, has been unseated four times. He has logged nine years, starting from November 1990, the maximum among the neighbouring country's Prime Ministers.** The moot question is: will Nawaz, an avid cricket aficionado, play another innings by beating Imran? More importantly, will the ultimate survivor rescue the nation and its economy, which faces an impending disaster, just like its cricket team in the ongoing World Cup?

Sharif: The Comeback Artist

Nawaz's first removal in April 1993 was orchestrated by his mentor (during Zia-ul-Haq's dictatorship), President Ghulam Ishaq Khan. This was Khan's second such high-handed action of removing an elected Prime Minister. The first to be dismissed was Benazir Bhutto, paving the way for Nawaz to be elected in November 1990. Nawaz was reinstated by Pakistan's Supreme Court after five weeks, but the reprieve was brief. He was forced to resign, ironically by his own COAS,

Gen Abdul Waheed Kakar, in July 1993, barely six months into his tenure. In Nawaz's second innings, Pakistan tested a nuclear bomb in May 1998, which Nawaz continues to tout as his major achievement. Buoyed by the nuclear euphoria, Nawaz sacked Gen Jehangir Karamat, a Benazir appointee, in October 1998. **Gen Karamat was the kind of army chief Pakistan really needs—erudite and apolitical.** After the Kargil fiasco, on 12 October 1999, Gen Khwaja Ziauddin was sworn in as the chief during Gen Pervez Musharraf's foreign visit, and orders were passed to deny landing to the returning aircraft. In a parallel coup, Gen Ziauddin was bundled off in less than six hours by Musharraf loyalists. Musharraf not only removed Nawaz but forced him into a seven-year-long exile in Saudi Arabia. Musharraf, ironically, had been preferred by Nawaz, superseding two seniors.

Nawaz's third tenure started in June 2013, after an orchestrated victory in elections, forced by the assassination of Benazir Bhutto, allegedly at the ISI's behest. Once again, in July 2017, he was forced to resign after the famous Supreme Court verdict in the Panama Papers case, declaring him to have failed the specious criteria of 'Sadiq and Ameen' (faithful and trustworthy). **Nawaz was eased out and Imran Khan was hoisted as Prime Minister by the mysterious Khaki 'Khalai Mukhlooq' (unseen ghosts of the ISI and ISPR) through manipulated elections.** Indicted in multiple cases, Nawaz was banned from political office for life. The sordid drama was masterminded by a Sharif appointee, Gen Qamar Javed Bajwa, who, like Musharraf, was made chief by superseding seniors and overlooking his alleged familial links to the Ahmediyya sect of Islam. It is now being rumoured that Gen Bajwa did help Nawaz with falsified medical reports to proceed to London, purportedly for treatment, which Nawaz converted into an exile by refusing to return.

Deep State Keeps Control

In this unending tale, Nawaz has been given a legal breather by the new CJP, Qazi Faiz Isa, who is known to harbour a grudge against Imran for ordering investigations against him and stalling his appointment. The clock of favouritism and reprisals seems to have come full circle, as the previous incumbent, Umar Ata Bandial, was not only an Imran appointee but also a known Sharif family baiter. The current kingmaker, Gen Asim Munir, has many scores to settle with Imran, most notably his unceremonious removal as DG-ISI and his declaration of opposition to his elevation.

The adage 'the more things change, the more they stay the same' applies, at least, in Pakistan.

Three key inferences are as follows:

- **Deep state (mil-establishment) is bent upon carrying on with proxy rule by its appointees.**
- **The Pakistan Army is manipulating the Presidents and even the judiciary to further its agenda.**
- **Those who exhibit defiance, like the father-daughter duo of Zulfikar Ali Bhutto and Benazir, were eliminated. Others have been banished either into exile, like Nawaz, or lodged in Adila jail, like Imran, notwithstanding their immense popularity. Chief Justice Isa's tenure could be leveraged to sound the judicial death knell for Imran by barring him from contesting elections.**

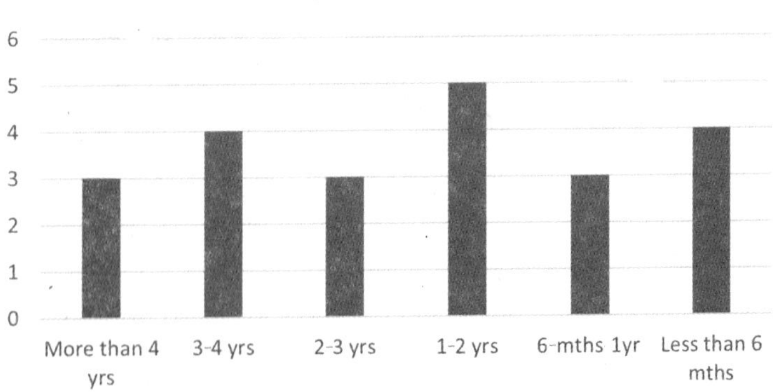

Resetting Templates

Pakistan is grappling with resetting its economic and socio-political templates. The army cleverly manipulated Amerika (sic) and misused religion (packaged as jihad) to create a dubious model of an extractive, rentier economy. **The American exit from Afghanistan and the failure of the so-called game-changing CPEC have reduced Pakistan, literally, to an 'on ventilator' status.** Usual reasons, like corruption and misgovernance by politicians, are being cited. Imran did play his part by burning bridges with the US, with his populist, anti-American rants and ill-timed visit to Moscow. To make matters worse, he riled Saudi Arabia and the UAE by attempting to forge an alternative Islamic grouping of Turkey, Malaysia, and Pakistan.

Gen Bajwa's rear-guard action in supplying munitions to Ukraine was a desperate action to reverse the situation. Both Nawaz and Gen Munir enjoy a much better relationship with the Gulf nations. The return of Nawaz may be part of an attempted re-opening of the *ummah* (Islamic brotherhood) pipeline. However, like the International Monetary Fund (IMF) aid, assistance is likely to come with conditions and strings attached. China has also become reticent about further funding the CPEC. With impending elections in both countries, Indo-Pak relations are unlikely to see any improvement till next year, notwithstanding Nawaz's professed inclination to restore trade ties.

The most obvious question is: why not hold the military accountable, which rules by proxy and has intertwined its entities, like the Fauji Foundation, in all key economic activities. Lt Gen Aseem Bajwa's two years with the CPEC were mired in corruption.

It is time Pakistan and its supporters, especially the Gulf countries, realise that the Triple-As should be awaam (genuine democracy), aman (zero terrorism), and araam (retreat to barracks for khaki), and not Amerika, Allah, and Army, which has been the norm.

Elections in January – February 2024 threw up interesting trends. The major ones are enumerated:

- **The stage was set for the exclusion of Imran by getting him convicted and jailed. His party, PTI, was also denied its symbol of cricket bat; resultantly, candidates were forced to contest as Independents.**

- **The public defied the army by voting for proxy candidates of Imran's PTI, contesting as Independents. However, the army managed to roll back the verdict and install Shehbaz Sharif as Prime Minister, Maryam Sharif as Chief Minister Punjab, and Asif Ali Zardari as President.** Except for Khyber Pakhtunkhwa (KPK), where Imran's PTI captured power, in all other provinces, ruling alliances installed their governments by cobbling up alliances.

Update (2024–25)

- **2024 turned out to be the deadliest year in the decade, a nine-year** high, with 685 security personnel losing their lives in 444 terror attacks, besides more than 1,000 civilians. As per the Centre for Research and Security Studies (CRSS), there was a 66% increase in casualties from 2023.

- **KPK and SW Baluchistan accounted for the maximum number of attacks, with TTP and Baluchistan Liberation Army (BLA) being responsible for them.** Pakistan also blamed India and Afghanistan for financing and assisting them. **Pakistan carried out air raids in Afghanistan, targeting TTP bases.**

- **Sunni-Shia clashes in the Kurram region of KPK** over land rights resulted in 150 deaths.

- **Shehbaz Sharif led a coalition with Nawaz, providing political guidance, and the army, providing solid support, hobbled along.** Increasingly draconian and strong-arm methods like Internet shutdown and censorship were applied to control pro-Imran forces, media, and other groups.

- The only silver lining was the **gold medal won by Javelin thrower Arshad Nadeem in the Paris Olympics.**

- **Pakistan also orchestrated the capture of Mohammad Sharifullah of ISIS-K, responsible for the killing of 13 US soldiers at Baghram during evacuation.** This was aimed at regaining relevance in the US.

- **Another positive development for Pakistan has been its increasing proximity with the new Bangladesh regime under Muhammad Yunus.** It has resulted in the restoration of direct talks, exchange of visits by military delegations, joint exercises, and the restoration of direct flights and shipments.

- **A spate of attacks on CPEC projects and Chinese personnel** working on other projects has soured ties with China, with China wanting to deploy security personnel.

- There are **signs of recovery in FY-2024,** with inflation recorded at a 44-month low of 5%, dropping from 38%. The deficit was reduced marginally, while foreign currency reserves increased from $3 billion in 2023 to $12 billion. **The GDP recovered from a -0.2% contraction in 2023 to 2.5% growth in 2024–25. In sum, the IMF has managed to anchor an immediate partial recovery to ward off a fiscal emergency. Pakistan managed to get another emergency bailout of $1 billion in May 2025.**

- As per figures released by DG-ISPR in April 2025, Pakistan had 3,700 terrorist incidents in a 17-month period. In these incidents, 3,896 people—2,582 civilians and 1,314 security personnel—lost their lives.

- The most significant terrorist incident was the **hijacking of the 2025 Jaffer Express running from Quetta to Peshawar on 11 March 2025 by the BLA with 380 passengers on board.** After a four-day long operation, the Pakistan Army claimed killing 33 BLA insurgents but losing 31 people, including 18 soldiers.

- Pakistan vectored a dastardly terrorist strike in Pahalgam on 22 April 2025, resulting in India launching Operation Sindoor. Notwithstanding significant losses, Pakistan responded with its own **Operation Bunyan-un-Marsoos and managed to regroup and rally the nation behind the discredited army by whipping up war hysteria.**

10.3 Implications of Institutional Implosion in Pakistan (Written in June 2023)

Pakistan is witnessing probably the most dangerous implosion of institutions triggered by a new maverick, Imran Khan. Notwithstanding his being equally guilty of having contributed to the chaos and fiscal distress, the stark reality is that currently, he is the most popular leader. He defiantly won five out of seven by-elections to the National Assembly, and mobs are out on a rampage, following his call.

Mobocracy, promoted as an instrument of coercion by the ISI and ISPR through TLP during the October 2021 Rawalpindi siege, is now like the proverbial rogue genie, refusing to be capped. Social media posts of marauding mobs at the corps commander's residence in Lahore and the reported torching of an iconic F-16 throw up serious apprehensions on the security of the nuclear arsenal. Are we witnessing another spring or colour revolution triggered by the ill-informed awaam (populace)? A sinking economy, natural disasters (devastating floods), and uncontrolled inflation, accentuated by the reticent IMF, have added to the desperation.

The government has been forced to apply strict fiscal correctives, like the withdrawal of subsidies, multiplying their unpopularity. Does Imran realise that the anti-establishment wave is easy to unleash but difficult to harness? Will it devour him next, for he has no magical wand to rebuild the economy? Imran, the propped-up creation of Khaki generals, was installed as Prime Minister in August 2018, after getting rid of Nawaz Sharif by judicial disqualification. The elections, as per the Sharif brothers, were hijacked by Khalai Mukhlooq (unseen ghosts), in an apparent reference to a hidden khaki hand. In less than four years, in April 2022, the army got rid of Imran, who had taken the ultimate risk of breaking free of their stranglehold. He also tried to drive an internal wedge and cultivate a younger lot of officers.

Imran even named an ISI general, labelling him 'Dirty Harry'. He has skilfully leveraged social media to build the narrative of being the only honest leader, capable of ushering in the much-touted Riyasat-e-Madina. **He has mastered the art of serving theological chimera and playing the victimisation card by releasing videos, including pre-recorded ones. His partner, Bushara Begum ('Pirni'), is reported to enjoy mystical powers, being part of a makeover from playboy to Taliban Khan.** A leader with no real grassroots support or organisation was hoisted by the army, in the form of PTI. In his tenure, Imran has the dubious track record of destroying ties with traditional allies like Saudi Arabia, the Gulf countries, and the US. He even launched an ill-advised foray to create an alternate Islamic axis with Turkiye and Malaysia, annoying Saudi Arabia. China and Iran are wary of his grandstanding. He did nothing significant to stem or redress the financial mess, leading to Pakistan becoming a basket case for an IMF bailout.

The ruling rag-tag coalition cobbled up by the army has PML-N, PPP, and JIP. The Sharif faction had been branded corrupt, at the army's behest, by NAB and the Supreme Court.

Consequently, PML has ex-Prime Minister Nawaz, remotely controlling the government with the current Prime Minister Shehbaz Sharif and his daughter Maryam, frequently rushing to London. Zardari-Bhutto dominates the other coalition partner, PPP. Asif Zardari, notorious for corruption, is again in remote control mode, and immature Bilawal Bhutto is in the cabinet. **In effect, the entire political class being discredited, Pakistan has no real credible options.**

President Arif Alvi, an Imran appointee, has been accused of seeking directions from his party. In this crumbling edifice of institutions, the judiciary has increasingly taken a conflicting and blatantly partisan stance. CJP Umar Ata Bandial has been accused of displaying a pro-Imran tilt, pushing for early elections, and granting him bail. **The**

judiciary had used questionable theological criteria of 'Sadiq and Ameen' (truthful and trustworthy) to impose lifelong disqualification on Nawaz in April 2018, citing the Panama gate scandal. Yet, the same stringent parameters have not been applied to Imran and others. The anti-corruption watchdog and quasi-judicial body, NAB, is currently headed by Lt Gen Nazir Ahmed Butt. After fixing Nawaz during the Imran regime, it has now turned against Imran and is out to arrest him. The apparent agenda is to book Imran in Al-Qadir, Toshakhana, and other cases, including treason, to disqualify him from fighting elections.

As Pakistan lurches towards chaos, one can exult, but the task is cut out for the strategic community.

- **First, keep up the vigil as desperate elements often resort to irrational and suicidal recourse.**
- **Second, engage with the international community to build better safeguards for Pakistan's nuclear arsenal, to rule out the spectre of *fasaadi* (jihadi) and dirty bombs.**
- **Third, the humiliated Pakistan Army after 1971 devised a 'thousand-cuts' strategy. In the long term, our challenges remain formidable. China in collusive mode seeks to revive CPEC, roping in Afghanistan.**
- **Most importantly, the army and the deep state, though temporarily down, are unlikely to be permanently out.**

10.4 Fiscal Implosion in Pakistan Economy and Impact on Defence Spending (Written in May 2023)

Key Takeaways

- While the dollar pipeline is shut, the ill effects of profligate expenditure induced by rentier mindset have crippled the economy.

- **The IMF and even traditional allies, like the Gulf countries, are insisting on deep-rooted fiscal reforms.**
- **Defence spending may only witness a cosmetic and nominal reduction.**
- **Update: Pakistan, even during escalating tensions in the run-up to Operation Sindoor, managed to secure a $1 billion emergency bailout from the IMF, albeit with stringent implementation guidelines. Pakistan is likely to get $20 billion package in June 2025. President Trump, while freezing aid, made an important exception of $400 million in aid to Pakistan. In all probability, it is to ensure the serviceability of the F-16 fleet and US-origin equipment. Earlier, Trump had thanked Pakistan in apprehension of the ISIS commander responsible for the Bargham base attack.**
- **Meanwhile, a close confidante of the Trump family anchored a mega deal to set up a cryptocurrency hub in Pakistan. Despite a modest trade balance, President Trump alluded to the possibility of greater trade as part of his ceasefire nudge to Pakistan.**

Pakistan has landed itself in a fiscal maelstrom due to its profligate rentier mindset. The country's economy is on a ventilator and is literally gasping for external bailouts. The talks with the IMF remain inconclusive, and the only lifeline has been China announcing a $700 million loan to redress the immediate forex emergency. The country's foreign currency reserves had dipped to an all-time low of $3.2 billion, barely enough to cover three weeks of imports. Chinese loans will boost forex reserves by 20%. Pakistan's forex funds are derived from foreign loans and the inflow of remittances, as the country's exports are rather insignificant. Manufacturing is dependent in most cases on imported raw materials, creating a vicious cycle of dependency on forex.

Pakistan, lulled by its geo-strategic location, had forged alliances with CENTO/SEATO and iron-brother format ties with China. It has also ascribed to herself a larger-than-life role of guardian of faith, trying to be the leader of OIC. **It will be appropriate to recall the quest for the Islamic bomb, where ZA Bhutto stated, 'We shall eat grass but make a nuclear bomb.'** The ISI also set up terrorist assembly lines to further the US agenda in Afghanistan. Pakistan blatantly milked security funding and managed to double-time the US by concurrently playing along with the Taliban. The dollar pipeline got shut off with the withdrawal of the US troops from Afghanistan. **A rentier and extractive, manipulative mindset has led to profligate expenditure and failure to build the economy. The belief that the *ummah* (brotherhood) will ultimately bail out the awaam (populace) lies in tatters as Saudi Arabia and the UAE want the IMF process to be concluded first to obviate profligate spending.**

The major share of the contracts and benefits was cornered by the military establishment through their foundations like Fauji, Shaheen, Baharia, FWO, and SCO. The details of this mega empire are chronicled by noted Pakistani expert Ayesha Siddiqa in her book *Crossed Swords*. **Nawaz Sharif's plan of adding geo-economic heft by the so-called game changer, CPEC, has met a similar fate due to inefficiency and corruption. Lt Gen Asim Bajwa and army-affiliated entities, once again cornered their share in the CPEC, making it a failing project.** An oligarchic mindset transcends beyond the khaki into the civilian domain. As per Ishrat Hussain, in his widely acclaimed book, *Pakistan: The Economy of an Elitist State*, 1% population constitutes the elitist oligarchy. The resultant inequality has reduced very large segments to abject poverty and penury. The recent floods in 2022 and the widespread destruction in their wake have added to fiscal distress.

China accounts for the largest share, i.e., 30% of total debt, which is more than twice the combined borrowings from the World Bank and the Asian Development Bank. It is approximately three times larger than loans advanced by the IMF. **The total debt had reached 77.8% of GDP in 2022. Pakistan, as per Topline Securities in a report in the Wall Street Journal, is required to repay $73 billion by**

2025. The IMF has been negotiating a rescue package amounting to $6.5 billion with an initial tranche of $1.1 billion. The significance of these rather tough negotiations by the IMF is that they will trigger the unlocking of other promised packages, like $7 billion from Saudi Arabia and the UAE. Iran has also promised to boost bilateral trade from $2 billion to $5 billion by revamping border markets. Uzbekistan has also promised a similar boost in border trade.

IMF negotiations have remained inconclusive, as the IMF would like to ensure that its funds do not get diverted to pay the largest creditor, China, but are instead invested in economic revival. The IMF diktat stipulates paring down subsidies and limiting them to only the needy sections of the populace. They also want higher taxation on the ultra-rich and to bring the privileged sections into the taxation net. Pakistan tops the chart with 25 projects under IMF scrutiny. Murtaza Syed, former deputy governor of the State Bank of Pakistan, laconically confessed, 'In fact, we are the IMF's most loyal customer.' Desperation is such that radicals are making outlandish suggestions of monetising nuclear know-how.

While Pakistan looks for external largesse, it has to revisit the age-old wisdom of 'charity begins at home'. Objective advice to Pakistanis is, make no mistake, that it is an implosion, triggered by internal catalysts like predatory corruption, bordering on organised plunder and a populist freebie culture, breeding a sense of entitlement to subsidies, particularly in petroleum prices and electricity tariffs. **Imran Khan, who currently tops the popularity charts, would have to take a large part of the blame for mismanagement, besides burning bridges with traditional allies like the US, Saudi Arabia, and the UAE.** Unlike India, Pakistan blew up its chances of cheap petrochemical imports from Russia by supplying munitions to Ukraine. This was a self-serving initiative anchored by Gen Qamar Bajwa to garner US support.

Pakistan's Defence Minister Khawaja Asif, in an event in Sialkot, confessed that the country has already defaulted on financial commitments and is bankrupt. He blamed the establishment, bureaucracy, and politicians for this mess. The desperation is such that rabid elements have been touting outlandish ideas like selling nuclear know-how. The runway inflation has touched nearly 40%, with riot-like conditions for basic commodities like wheat flour (atta). Pushed by the IMF, the Shahbaz Sharif government has launched a major austerity drive. A slew of new taxes, being dubbed a mini-budget, have been announced to raise PKR 170 billion.

He also opined that the IMF or any other external agency cannot redress the situation. He unequivocally stated that the solution lies within. He made a startling revelation that one-fourth of the debt can be paid off if only two golf clubs built on government land are sold off. Former Army Chief Gen Bajwa and now Gen Asim Munir have taken the mantle of loan negotiation without much traction. **The Pakistan Army budget has traditionally been pegged at 2.8% of GDP in 2000, which was pared down to 2.2%. In contrast, India has been limiting its spending to around 2%, and in the current budget, it is projected at 1.87% of GDP. Pakistan has earmarked 17.5% of total government expenditure, which is an increase of 11.16% from last year. Comparatively, Indian spending is only 13.18%. Most countries spend 10–14% on defence.** There has been considerable opacity in defence spending, particularly with regard to allocations made to the ISI and ISPR. Pakistan has treated terrorists as strategic assets and has been funding them through counterfeit and drug economy. Both have come under increasing scrutiny, including international agencies like the FATF.

The moot question is how this will impact defence spending and the deep state. Few demonstrative cuts, like disposing of diplomatic properties, are taking place. However, the deep state is unlikely to jettison its dalliance with terrorism. It may temporarily pause, but Pakistan is likely to remain invested in core projects, like the K2 cell of the ISI. The deep state is already voicing its demands for additional funds and has stated that funds are not even adequate to feed troops. It will be pragmatic to remain vigilant with regard to desperate measures that may be adopted by Pakistan. While it may give us some temporary comfort due to fiscal distress but, in the long run, it will be pragmatic if nuclear-armed Pakistan is put on a leashed IMF-monitored economic recovery.

Update (2024–25)

- Pakistan has managed to put in place an **IMF-monitored programme of $7 billion over 37 months with stringent guidelines** on fiscal reforms and time-bound revival of the economy.
- **Key challenges** include high inflation, weak rupee, high debt to GDP ratio, balance of payment deficit, political uncertainty, climate change, and disasters.
- There are **signs of recovery in FY-2024, with** inflation recorded at a 44-month low of 5%, dropping from 38%. The deficit has been reduced marginally, and foreign currency reserves have increased from $3 billion in 2023 to $12 billion. **GDP has recovered from a -0.2% contraction in 2023 to 2.5% growth in 2024–25.**
- **In sum, the IMF has managed to anchor an immediate partial recovery to ward off a fiscal emergency.**
- **Defence Budget:** Approximately $7.6 billion, despite a fiscal emergency; **allocations have registered a 17.6% increase.** In GDP terms, it is around 1.7%.

10.5 Pakistan – Clashes on the Western Border and the Terrorism Inferno Within

Pakistan, already battling a grave and debilitating fiscal emergency, is now getting mired in internal chaos and escalating tension on its western border. The military establishment has been utilising the eastern border with India to prosecute its diabolic K2 agenda, coupled with a deadly drug and drone combo. It has been leveraged as a tool to mislead and rally the awaam (populace), ensuring liberal funding and unbridled control in the management of security policy. The deep state has touted the 'strategic depth' dream, with Afghanistan as a surrogate/puppet state. It has also claimed peace and tranquility with *ummah* (Islamic brotherhood) states on the eastern border, in contrast to the western one, with India. The much-cherished dreams are in tatters with repeated skirmishes, aerial attacks, and artillery duels with both Afghanistan and Iran. Most importantly, Pakistan is known for terrorist breeding Madrasas and treating them as 'strategic assets', primed to be vectored against others. Hillary Clinton, in her famous warning to Khaki generals, had warned them that 'Snakes in your backyard will not just bite the neighbours'. Ironically, it is now battling them within. Coupled with border clashes are the escalating Baluchi and Pashtun secessionist movements and a raging inferno of terrorist attacks.

The Afghanistan-Pakistan Border

The Durand Line, negotiated in 1893, after the Second Anglo-Afghan War, defines the border. It was negotiated between Mortimer Durand, a British bureaucrat, and the Afghan Emir, Abdur Rehman Khan. The border traverses treacherous, mountainous terrain and unilaterally divides the tribal homeland of Pashtun tribes like Mehsuds, Afridis, and others. This line has never been recognised by tribal bodies (Shuras) or the government in Kabul. Hamid Karzai asserted that Afghans will never recognise it. Aimal Faizi, spokesman for the President, stated in October 2012 that the Durand Line is 'an issue of historical importance for Afghanistan. The Afghan people, not the government, can take a final decision on it.' Pakistani attempts of fencing it have met with fierce opposition. Notwithstanding resistance, Pakistan claims to have completed it with just 50 odd km remaining. It is also seeking to reinforce it with ditches and berms as well as create 338 crossing points. Notwithstanding these endeavours, its efficacy is highly suspect. This border has witnessed uneasy peace disrupted by artillery duels, aerial strikes, and cross-border raids. After negotiations, there have been no aerial strikes for two years, since April 2022.

The recent heightened tension was triggered by a massive truck bomb attack on 16 March on Mir Ali border post in North Waziristan by six fedayeen. It accounted for lieutenant colonel (probably commanding officer), captain, and five Frontier Corps (FC) soldiers. Relatively obscure group, Jaish Fursan-e-Muhammad, with links to TTP, claimed responsibility. Pakistani authorities blamed the Hafiz Gul-Bahadur faction and retaliated on 18 March, with aerial strikes in two adjoining provinces of Paktika and Khost. Afghan authorities severely criticised the violation of territorial sovereignty and the killing of eight women and children. However, ISPR claimed that the perpetrator of the attack, Sehra alias Janan, was eliminated. The Afghan Government responded with retaliatory mortar strikes on the Pakistani border posts, killing and injuring more civilians. On 23 March, a troop convoy in Dera Ismail Khan was subjected to another fedayeen attack, killing two and injuring 22 soldiers.

Pakistan blames the Afghan Government for providing sanctuary and freedom to TTP, ISIS-K to target Pakistani targets. As per security analysts, last year (2023), there were as many as 789 attacks, accounting for 1,524 casualties with the security forces, bearing the major share of the brunt. Pakistan has sought to deal with terrorism through a multi-pronged approach. This includes ruthless counter-terrorism operations like Raad-ul-Fasaad, characterised by disproportionate use of force and heavy-calibre weapons like gunships, tanks, and artillery. Fencing of the Durand Line, border closure, and pressure on the Afghan Government are other measures applied. The most unpopular measure has been the directive on 1 November 2023 to expel Afghan refugees, numbering approximately 1.7 million. They were identified as undocumented refugees after a preliminary screening of the 3.8 million population of Afghan origin. Sanitisation drive in Karachi and around security establishment pockets like Malir Cantt and Mehran air base revealed collaboration by refugees in terrorist attacks. Approximately four lakhs have already been driven out, including 80% women and children. This ongoing exercise portends to drive a permanent wedge between the two ethnicities.

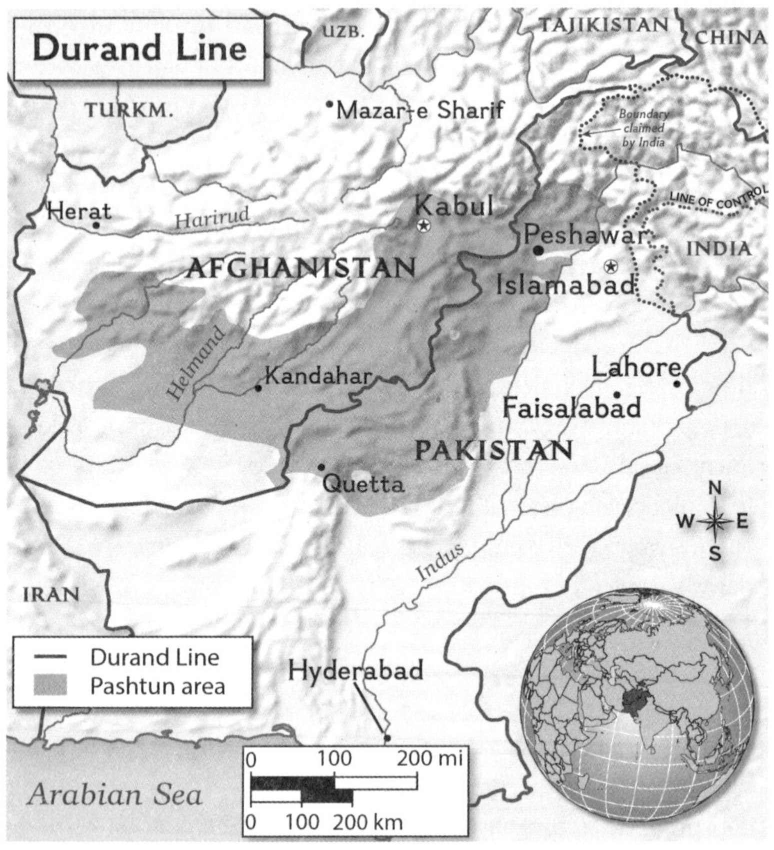

(Map Credit – National Geographic Maps)

Pakistan-Iran Border

Pakistan has a 909 km long border with Iran, decided in the colonial era, spanning hilly and rugged terrain and sparsely populated areas from Taftan to Mand. Iran is building an elaborate barrier system with a 3 ft (91.4 cm) thick and 10 ft (3.05 m) high concrete wall, fortified with steel rods, reinforced with ditches and embankments. Concurrently, Pakistan has also fenced 80% of the border on its side. This border divides the Baluchi (Sunni) tribal population, on both sides—Sistan in Shia-dominated Iran and Baluchistan, traditionally neglected by Punjabi-dominated Pakistan. Both provinces have festering secessionist movements demanding a unified, Baluchi homeland. The uneasy peace on the border was broken when Iran launched missile and drone strikes on 16 January in the Koh-e-Sabz area. It targeted the Jaish-al-Adl group (repackaged version of Jundallah), holding it responsible for the killing of 11 Iranian Police personnel in the Sistan province in December 2023. Pakistan retaliated two days later, with multiple drone strikes in Sistan. Unfortunately, both attacks accounted for a dozen odd civilian casualties, including women and children. Eleven days later, nine Pakistani workers perished in another terrorist attack in a bordering town in Sistan. Attacks were part of Iranian attacks on targets in the Kurdish areas and Syria. Viewed in the context of the ongoing Gaza imbroglio and Houthi raids, the spectre of a widening arc of conflict in the Middle East was very real. The attacks were fueled by mutual suspicion and Iranian apprehensions of the US using Pakistan to unsettle her. It required a flurry of visits by diplomats, supplemented by brokering by the Chinese minister, to restore uneasy and fragile sanity on the border. Stakes for China for de-escalation are indeed high, with Chinese companies engaged in the Gwadar and Saindak Copper and Gold mining projects in northwestern Baluchistan.

Ramzan and Mayhem Cycle

Sanctity and traditional peace of the holy month of Ramzan in Pakistan have been bloodied by relentless terrorist attacks. Recently, elected President Asif Zardari and Army Chief Gen Aseem Munir attended the funeral of the Frontier Corps lieutenant colonel, killed in a terrorist attack, and vowed revenge. The new government, formed after the February election and considerable manipulation, is under intense pressure to show results.

A mayhem cycle stretching for ten days (from 16 to 26 March), included five different attacks, three in the KP province and two in Baluchistan, resulting in the deaths of at least 18 people. All five attacks were fedayeen (suicide) bombings. Twelve military personnel, five Chinese nationals, and a few Afghans and Pakistani civilians were collateral casualties. The BLA claimed responsibility for attacks in Baluchistan. Some obscure splinter groups claimed orchestration of two attacks in KP. Nobody has owned up to the attack on Chinese engineers.

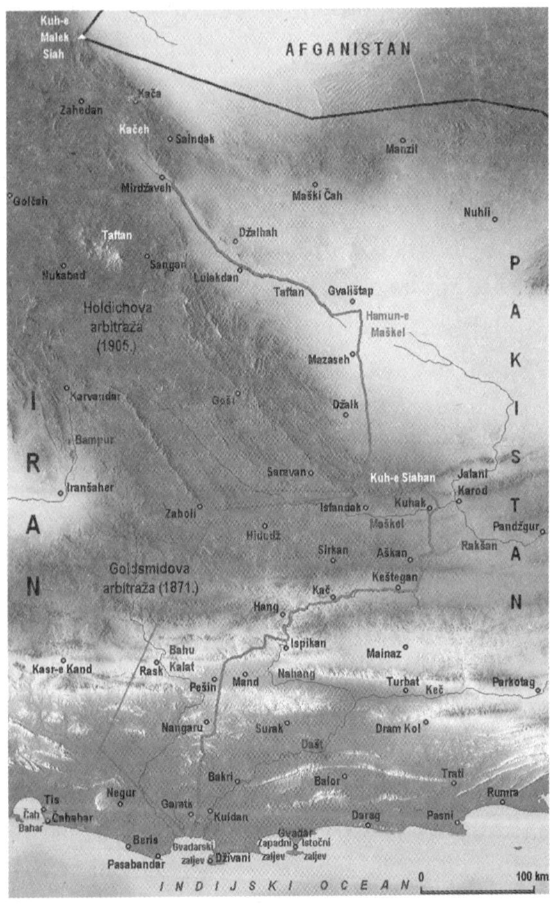

(Map Credit – Wikipedia Maps)

China-Pakistan Economic Corridor (CPEC) – A New Fault Line

On 24 March, eight fedayeen of the BLA tried to storm the Gwadar port complex. While the attack was thwarted, there were conflicting claims on casualties and damages. Pakistan acknowledged losing two security personnel and eliminating all attackers. In the vicinity and two days later, four fedayeen of the Majeed Brigade targeted the second-largest naval aviation base, Pakistan Navy Ship (PNS) Siddique at Turbat on 26 March. Amongst conflicting claims, authorities claimed the elimination of all fedayeen and the loss of only one Frontier Corps personnel. The Turbat base is strategically located 150 odd km north of Gwadar and also supports the Pakistani naval bases of Jiwani and Pasni, both in close proximity (100 km on either side of Gwadar).

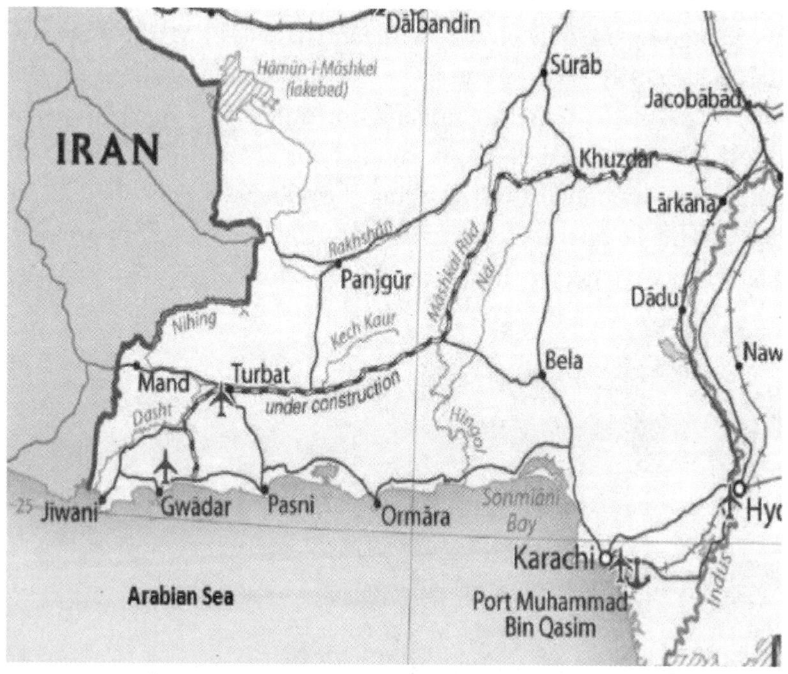

(Map Credit – Research Gate)

The most significant attack happened on 25th at Besham, near the upcoming Dasu dam, on the Indus River in Kohistan, killing five Chinese engineers and a Pakistani civilian bus driver. The attack served as a reminder of the July 2021 incident, wherein nine Chinese engineers were killed in a similar attack. TTP has denied any role in the attack, and there is much speculation on the possibility of involvement of ISIS-K, Tehrik-e-Jihad Pakistan (TJP), East Turkmenistan Independence Movement (ETIM), or unidentified groups. Chinese assets on the CPEC have literally opened a new array of high-profile targets and internal fault lines for terrorist tanzeems. The Karachi Stock Exchange, the Chinese Consulate, and the Confucius Centre have all been targeted. After recent attacks, Chinese companies (with approximately 2,000 Chinese workforce) have suspended work on not only Dasu (4,320 MW) but also Dimer-Basha (4,800 MW) and Tarbela extension (1,400 MW) projects. Work is going on, only on the Mohmand dam (740 MW). Work was stalled for nearly two years after the last attack and could be resumed only on payment of a hefty compensation of $30 million. Pakistan has raised two specialised divisions, funded out of the CPEC funds, yet attacks continue unabated, exposing the vulnerability of the CPEC, due to a fragile internal security environment and, more importantly, a lack of acceptance by the awaam (local populace).

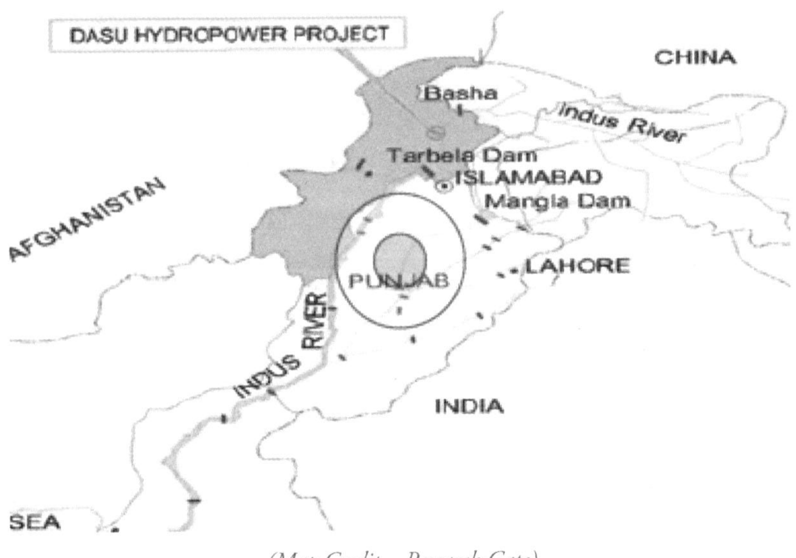

(Map Credit – Research Gate)

Uneasy and Bleak Future

Despite the desire to designate Pakistan as a failed or failing state, its geo-strategic location and large young population still help it to retain relevance. The recent communication and assurances by US President Joe Biden to Prime Minister Shahbaz Sharif reinforce this inference. The challenge for Pakistani policymakers and their international facilitators is to undertake meaningful and holistic reforms instead of cosmetic, quick-fix measures. Genuine reforms like dismantling the military establishment, terrorist infrastructure, and accommodation of genuine Baluchi and Pashtun regional aspirations are long overdue. For the Pakistani awaam (populace), Robert Frost's poem is most relevant, albeit rephrased (with due apologies), as 'Woods infested with tanzeems, are indeed dark and deep, And miles to march, Khaki back to barracks, before we sleep.'

Western Front – Countering Pakistan

11.1 Review of Challenges on the Western Front (Please also read Sections 2.1, 2.2 and 2.3 in the chapter – Opening Perspectives)

Key Takeaways

- Chinese aggressive forays have forced India to undertake a review and strategic rebalancing.
- Despite the Northern Front being designated as the primary one, challenges on the Western Front remain in both proxy war and conventional domains.
- India, with the Balakot strike, after the Pulwama attack in 2019 and surgical raids after the Uri attack in 2017, has crafted space for conventional strikes/war below the dreaded nuclear threshold. Conflict resolution in J&K and the creation of integrated theatre commands, coupled with modernisation, are recommended.
- India delivered a calibrated response in Operation Sindoor from 7 to 10 May after the terrorist attack in Pahalgam. Please read the details in the Introduction chapter.

Western Command, the pivotal command on the Western Front, celebrated its platinum jubilee on 15 September 2022. It is an opportune time to look beyond nostalgia and ceremonials, to take stock of operational dynamics and emerging challenges on the Western Front. The review is also warranted because we have belatedly chosen to discard our obsessive affliction with the Western Front. **Jolted by**

Chinese actions in Doklam and Ladakh, the Northern Front has been belatedly designated as the primary front. Consequently, there has been a shift of forces from the western to the northern borders, as part of rebalancing.

It is presumed that we intend to upgrade from a dissuasive to a credible deterrence posture against China. Concurrently, we have also planned to graduate from credible to punitive deterrence against Pakistan. **The obvious questions are – will we be able to maintain a punitive or decisive deterrence on the Western Front, or is there a recalibration in the deterrence ladder?** Most importantly, it is imperative to avoid getting trapped in a collusive two-and-a-half-front imbroglio. **This review is structured on four key parameters, i.e., border determination, topography, strategy, and operational strategy.**

Scope: This **paper focuses on conventional operations**. Some key aspects of non-contact, kinetic operation are covered in two articles on Operation Sindoor in the Introduction chapter.

Border Determination

The border is based on the hurriedly crafted Radcliffe Line (approximately 3,323 km). Its sanctity was challenged by Pakistan in October 1947. After UN mediation, a ceasefire (CF) was enforced in January 1948, and the Karachi Agreement was signed in July 1949. It redesignated the 830-km border in erstwhile J&K as the CFL. In April 1965, Pakistan launched an offensive in the Rann of Kutch, resulting in another round of British and UN mediation. The Sir Creek dispute covers 93 km of an unresolved maritime border. The Shimla agreement in 1972 converted the CFL to a more defined LoC, measuring 740 km, starting from Sangam (near Akhnur), extending towards the north. Pakistan continues to dispute the settled portion, **covering Jammu, Samba, and Kathua districts (193 km), terming it as a working boundary to keep alive the bogey of the entire state**

being disputed. To this end, there is a constant attempt to extend the arc of proxy war up to Samba-Kathua. Northern stretch, beyond NJ 9842, spanning the Siachen Glacier (approximately 110 km), became the AGPL in 1984, after pre-emptive Indian deployment.

Approximately 2000 km of IB has been properly fenced as part of a phased programme, starting from the '80s. The system, besides tiered fencing, has surveillance towers, patrolling tracks, and a lighting system. In addition, after the CF agreement on the LoC in 2003, the LoC was also fenced with an ad-hoc system. Notwithstanding fencing, riverine and hilly terrain provide ample avenues for infiltration. In addition, Pakistan has been utilising tunnels and increasingly using drones for fomenting narco-terrorism. The legitimacy of the LAC was enhanced by India choosing to confine operations in Kargil (1999) in the LoC sector. More recently, the CF agreement on the LAC was again reiterated by both sides on 24 February 2021. **However, the right to respond and target terrorist infrastructure was reiterated during coordinated cross-border raids, post the Uri attack. More importantly, Balakot surgical strikes reinforced this assertion, as the target was beyond even the disputed PoK, in KPK.**

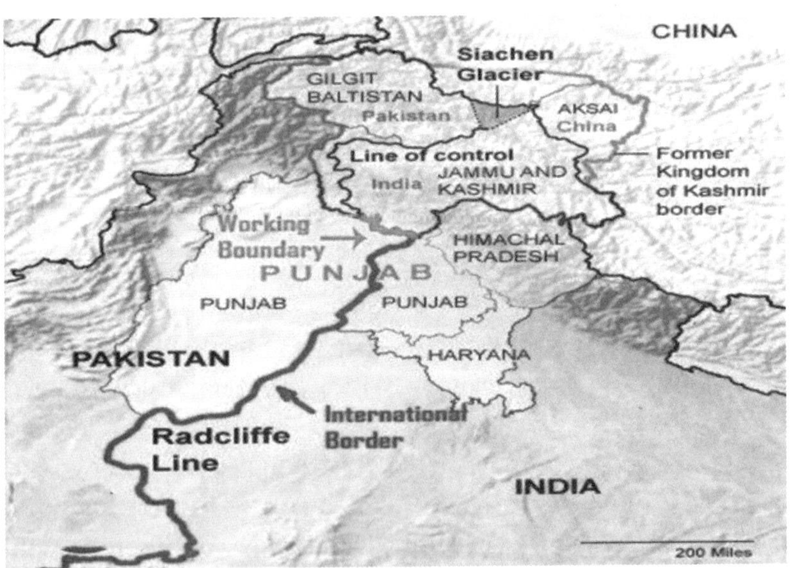

Topography

The next parameter is topography, which has undergone significant changes. Pakistan utilised the IWT award to build new irrigation channels. Canals, salinity, and flood control projects were designed to boost the defensive layout. Similarly, canals on the Indian side, like the Indira Gandhi Canal, have enhanced obstacle potential. After the 1965 war, both sides added an array of Ditch-cum-Bundh (DCB) systems to bolster their defence potential further. The net result is that space for manoeuvre and application of large formations in heartland Punjab has been restricted. The flank of the decision has been pushed to the desert. Conflicts in the developed sector are likely to be like slug fests with shallow objectives, akin to the current unresolved imbroglio in Ukraine, stretching beyond six months, with no end in sight. In our context, Kargil stretched to only 11 weeks, while the rest ranged from two to seven weeks.

Operational Strategy

Pakistan has been driven by a relentless revanchist approach. It has been matched by a reactionary but more resilient response by India. Pakistan's recklessness is fuelled by 'parity-fixation' and self-ascribed role of guardian of ideological frontiers of the Islamic world. It manifested in the Kabayali raiders in 1947 and the failed Operation Gibraltar infiltration, as a prelude to the 1965 operations. Defeat in Bangladesh and the initial success of US-funded Mujahideen assembly lines in the '80s resulted in Pakistan opting for proxy war as the preferred tool. Kargil was a repeat episode of a failed infiltration plot.

Pakistan projects a facade of cultivated irrationality, posing a threat of nuclear war to preclude conventional one and yet keeps bleeding India with a thousand cuts. India seeks to apply agile IBGs as a refinement of its cold-war strategy. **A decisive victory with the destruction of strategic reserves seems unlikely, given current force levels, and punitive deterrence is more pragmatic for India. Objectives will have to be shallow and limited, with built-in exit**

options, in case of a stalemate. It bears reiteration that with the Balakot strike and surgical raids, India has partially debunked the much-touted Pakistani nuclear bluff and carved out a nuanced space for conventional war/strike, below the nuclear threshold. In the long run, coercive leverage as an upper riparian state needs to be developed. The endeavour to build disruptive capabilities in cyber and other emerging domains is warranted as a counter to proxy war.

Force Levels

Finally, a brief analysis of force levels and organisational structures. **India didn't really anticipate a serious threat from Pakistan and opted for an ad-hoc and temporary Delhi and East Punjab (DEP) Command after Partition.** The DEP Command was designated as Western Command after the unprovoked J&K conflict. The operational responsibility was from J&K to Bikaner (Rajasthan). Operations in 1947–48, 1965, 1971, and even the Ladakh sector in 1962, were primarily orchestrated by the Western Command. The Southern Command was in a supporting role. The 1971 war highlighted the complexities of span of control, setting the stage for the raising of the Northern Command. Later, the South West Command was carved out in 2005, five years after the air force had raised theirs. Proxy war in Kashmir, raging since the '90s, the Siachen, Kargil, and Ladakh conflicts have validated this pragmatic step. In fact, the arc of terrorism in the Western Command is limited to the Samba-Pathankot-Gurdaspur belt.

The primary instruments of operational articulation are corps, especially the Strike Corps. 1 Corps was raised in April 1965 and saw action within months. 2 Corps was raised for the Bangladesh operations. However, after the war, it was retained and shifted to the west. 21 Corps came up in 1990. New pivot Corps—12 (1987), 14 (after Kargil in 1999), and 9 (2005)—added to force levels. Pakistan has managed to maintain force parity to match force levels. It is now reported that 1 Corps and a few other formations have been affiliated with the Northern Front; however, all three armoured divisions remain on the Western Front. **The focus should be shifting from quantitative to qualitative asymmetry as Pakistan manages to juggle numbers with Mujahids and rangers. The thrust has to be on agile IBGs.**

The proxy war has created two distinct response paradigms against Pakistan. The Northern Command is engaged in tackling the challenges of terrorism, while the other forces on the Western Front and even the Northern Command, to an extent, are geared up for conventional warfare. In the proxy war-impacted region, the objective is to work towards conflict termination and, in the interim, maintain a secure environment to run functionally elected governments. It is supplemented by the capability to execute punitive surgical strikes. The latter requires intelligence, political willpower, backed by differentiated and specialised capabilities.

Way Forward

The natural corollary is, do we require a huge investment in conventional war capabilities? The notion that hybrid wars will spell the death knell for conventional ones is being discarded after the Ukrainian war. It bears reiteration that the opening of the Punjab front in the 1965 war helped India upset Pakistan's plan to localise the conflict in J&K. We need to retain options in the conventional domain. Both India and Pakistan use tanks as a primary platform and have a large fleet. The challenge lies in retrofitting and imaginative dispersed employment to reduce vulnerability against a top attack by drones. Answers lie in agile platforms and disruptive technologies, as well as leveraging drones and cyber warfare.

The way forward is speedy conflict termination in J&K, backed by an effective punitive surgical strike capability. In the conventional domain, an integrated theatre command, subsuming the Western, South-Western, and Southern Commands of the army and Western and South-Western of the air force to generate synergy and create

options, is overdue. The revamping of surveillance, modernisation, disruptive technologies, and cognitive warfare remain key challenges in this transformation.

11.2 Pulwama: Our Response and Retribution Need to Be Served Cold (Written after Pulwama Terrorist Attack in February 2019)

The nation is in a state of deep outrage and anger, consequent to the martyrdom of more than 40 CRPF soldiers, in a dastardly attack on an administrative convoy at Pulwama. Pakistan-based JeM brazenly claimed responsibility and even released a video announcing the details of the fedayeen (suicide) bomber. This portends ominous trends, return of home-grown fedayeen, and explosive-laden vehicle bombs after two decades, coupled with the unabated radicalisation of local youth becoming *'fasaadis'*. **I choose not to name such cowards masquerading as fedayeen and refuse to conspire in the misuse of 'jihad' for reprehensible acts; *'fasaad'* has to be called out as such.**

Many well-meaning and angry people want revenge. Social media is abuzz with demands ranging from naval blockade to the employment of IBGs and, of course, 'surgical strikes'. **One is reminded of the famous quote of Desiderius Erasmus, 'War is delightful to those who have had no experience of it.'** Many a Twitter yodha, fresh after seeing Uri, feels that it is as simple as rustling up two-minute noodles. They even outline the attack plan: take a briefing from babus in South Block, get the magical Garuda to vector commandos to the JeM hideout of Masood Azhar, and after bang-bang, have dinner on the Raisina Hill. Our well-meaning public deserves to be educated better. **Concurrently, overexposure to the Armed Forces on a daily basis and 'josh' without 'hosh' are counterproductive.**

Options like the withdrawal of the Most Favoured Nation (MFN) status, revoking the IWT, declaring Pakistan a terrorist state, and breaking diplomatic ties are mentioned as add-ons. Each of these has complications and, of course, limitations, especially in payoffs.

Our response and retribution need to be served cold and at a place and time of our own choosing. Leo Tolstoy has summed it up most appropriately: 'The two most powerful warriors are patience and time.' Let operational commanders look at contingencies and apply them after detailed analyses. The hype on revenge induces needless hurry and recklessness. The government seems to be following the sane path by giving the Armed Forces a free hand.

It is time for politicians to display statesmanship; all parties should affirm solidarity with the government and forces. A distant hope, but nations strive on optimism and well-intentioned initiatives. Can a few statesmen (though they are a dying breed), like Pranab Da, Manmohan ji, and Advani Sahib, step forward and articulate national will and formulate guidelines on the politicisation of security matters? These ombudsmen can indeed deliver a message of national consensus to Pindi generals, infusing some sense.

The government has already withdrawn the unilateral MFN status accorded to Pakistan, but it has only limited signalling value because bilateral trade is already at its lowest ebb. Isolation of Pakistan is a long haul, as geography, combined with the CPEC and a new role as China's proxy, has bestowed it with enviable advantages. Short of war, leverages are indeed limited; revoking IWT without having reservoirs and dams to absorb additional water is pointless. We require nearly a decade to construct a planned infrastructure. It will also give China upper riparian status on the Brahmaputra and Sutlej, an avoidable precedent. The obvious lesson is within treaty norms, to build on recent welcome initiatives on the Ravi and Chenab, with a time-bound, task force orientation, and expand the scope to the Jhelum and Indus.

Pragmatically considering our current state of equipment and ammunition inventory, we seem to lack the decisive edge and requisite force asymmetry for a full-scale conventional war. Localised grab action is possible, but the resultant stalemate is not worth the effort. The biggest challenge is keeping it below the much-touted threshold for tactical nuclear weapons. This government seems to have the political will to call off the nuclear bluff, but the Armed Forces need time to prepare and augment their conventional arsenal. India, aspiring to become a net security provider, should maintain more than one option, including a conventional domain with a decisive edge. This requires sustained investment backed up with a vibrant defence manufacturing ecosystem and functional procurement policies, none of which seem to have been a priority agenda.

The foremost requirements are objective investigation and follow-up. Despite the much-acclaimed National Investigation Agency (NIA), we have not been able to nail local collaborators to achieve full closure in earlier incidents. Such an operation would have required preparation and an extensive support network, but, once again, there was a lack of specific intelligence. The reported usage of approximately 300 kg of explosives indicates a porous monitoring mechanism. The movement of such a large convoy with 80 odd vehicles and more than 2,000 personnel defies logic. **The relevant standard operating procedures (SOPs) need to be updated, and safeguards against the emerging threat of vehicle bombs need to be factored in.**

The only viable option seems to be trans-border surgical raids, but they have already become subject to the law of diminishing marginal returns. The need is to invest in more lethal and precise delivery means, like drones and standoff missiles. This, coupled with surveillance and gunships, will make them surgical and lethal to the extent that they have a deterrence effect. Currently, aerial and standoff attacks seem to be the most discussed options, but they require deliberate planning with careful selection of targets, based on accurate intelligence. **Targeting proven terrorist hubs should be justifiable, provided there is minimal collateral civilian damage and international opinion is sensitised, Americans are already nodding approval.**

While the need is for kinetic retribution, a full-spectrum response should include internal dialogue, socio-political measures, and theological correctives, including counter-radicalisation entailing smart soft power. Anger and anguish are understandable, but arson amounts to furthering the agenda of '*fasaadis*' to exploit fault lines in society.

11.3 When Threshold of Tolerance Is Breached: Balakot (Written after the Balakot Air Strike in March 2019)

India and Pakistan, the nuclear-armed nations, are in a state of undeclared war. The whole world, with powerful nations leading from the front, is trying to broker de-escalation. The worrying questions are: Where do we go from here? What happens in the proxy war in Kashmir? **The Balakot aerial strike is indeed a historic and defining milestone on India's strategic calculus and escalation matrix. It qualifies to be classified as a 'real surgical strike', meeting the criteria of targeting in depth and the application of aerial/standoff means.** The strike, spearheaded by Mirages, took Pakistan by complete surprise. It also exposed the chinks in the famed formidable AD umbrella. The emphasis on 'real' is intentional because surgical strikes after Uri, though bold, were technically, 'synergised shallow trans-border raids'.

The aerial capability has existed and been considered, but unfortunately, it has never been exercised. It is to the credit of the government that they displayed political will, with attendant risks, political and operational. In this hour of national crisis, warranting consensus, the situation has been vitiated due to the impending elections and misplaced politicisation. Surgical strikes are likely to become the new normal in the quiver of options and strategic calculus. It will now be difficult for successive governments to ignore this option.

Bahawalpur, a hub of JeM, the obvious choice, was vacated and risky to engage. On the other hand, the Taleem-ul-Quran seminary at Balakot, managed by Azhar Yousuf, brother-in-law of Masood Azhar, is situated beyond PoK, where strikes can't be explained away as within Indian (de jure) or disputed territory. It was a bold and apt messaging choice, with a historic connection to the early manifestation of fasaad (mischievously referred to as jihad) during Maharaja Ranjit Singh's period. These theological linkages have been misused to brainwash recruits with eighteenth-century exploits of Syed Ahmed Barelvi and Shah Ismail (ironically, natives of Rae Bareli). It is in Pakistan Prime

Minister Imran's native Khyber-Pakhtunkhwa province, which hosts a large number of terrorist training camps.

India's focus was on strategic messaging to convey that the Pulwama terrorist attack had indeed breached the threshold of tolerance. More importantly, we have capacity, skill, and, above all, political will to strike. Anger and desire for retribution (bordering on revenge) define the angry and impatient 'Naya Bharat'. **It would also be pragmatic to note that, notwithstanding public pressure and media hype, the government carefully selected a terrorist facility, away from the population centre, for targeting.** The clamour by some 'doubting Thomases' for proof of dead bodies and Pakistan's ploy to describe it as eco-terrorism is literally missing the wood (message) for a few pine trees. The implied message is, if you don't act, we will be forced to.

India nuanced its articulation by initially utilising civilian spokespersons and describing it as a non-military target. An elaborate rationale for explaining it as a pre-emptive action for self-defence against elements being trained for proxy war in Kashmir was spelt out. Overall, India offered a viable window for de-escalation, provided the proxy war was rolled back. Imran Khan, despite shouting about 'Naya Pakistan', failed to decipher strategic signalling. Driven by public pressure, military establishment, and parity syndrome, it decided to take the dangerous escalation course, that too, the very next day, by targeting military installations. It was a double whammy, firstly, missing the targets, and then losing an F-16 to a MiG-21. This engagement proved fortuitous for Pakistan; they suddenly had an Indian pilot in their custody. In a comedy of errors, Pakistan refused to accept its casualties and even the use of F-16, amounting to a violation of contractual obligations. Imran and voluble DG-ISPR kept on trotting conflicting claims, starting with two MiGs and three pilots. International pressure forced Pakistan to hand over the Indian pilot, but after considerable drama. Till the very last moment, attempts were made to leverage it for de-escalation and resumption of dialogue.

Wg Cdr Abhinandan has emerged as the real hero, who refused to let go of the 'missile lock', risked his life, and created a record of shooting down an F-16 with a MiG-21. His conduct as a prisoner was commendable, and he will remain a role model for generations. Gnats outsmarting Sabres, Centurions outgunning Pattons, MiGs downing F-16s; mercifully, we have redoubtable crews despite a deja vu freeze. Indian strikes and counters by Pakistan have debunked the nuclear bluff, and the nuclear bogey seems hollow. Two aerial engagements have reinforced considerable space below the much-touted yet ambiguous nuclear red lines. The logical corollary is, how much more leeway can be crafted, and can there be more aerial strikes/exchanges?

Pakistan's desire is to settle for a temporary pause on the proxy war with cosmetic actions. Our dilemma is that a stalemate amounts to a victory of sorts for Pakistan. Escalation is 'heady' but must be carefully calibrated, and after giving Imran a chance to act on his assurances. Pakistan's actions must be verified and are time-bound. The war on terrorism is likely to be lonely, as the isolation of Pakistan can only be transient. **It will be a long haul, requiring a range of measures, both internal and external. The ongoing crisis is just punctuation, and certainly not a period.**

Security stabilisation is an essential prerequisite, yet it has to be complemented with internal healing and de-radicalisation. We need to rein in warmongering media and educate the public, as losses are an occupational hazard. **There is a need to forge a national Kashmir policy after the elections. It is also axiomatic to build a range of options, including conventional domains besides cyber and surgical ones. There is an urgent need to address the hollowness, especially in AD and ammunition, through an empowered mechanism with fast-track, liberalised procurement procedures.**

11.4 Belling the Cat: Diplomatic Engagements with Pakistan (Written in May 2019)

India and Pakistan, two nuclear 'frenemies', are locked in a series of senseless confrontations, distracting them from a more relevant and pressing war on the socio-economic front. Surgical strikes, Balakot, and the proxy war in Kashmir drain the exchequer and prevent the optimisation of traction and trajectories of economies. The debilitating effect on the sinking economy of Pakistan, currently seeking doles and bailout packages, is more serious. **It is for the first time that the Pindi top brass has decided to take voluntary budgetary cuts. In all likelihood, it may turn out to be just an exercise in tokenism with no effect on force ratios, yet it highlights the magnitude of the crisis and a reluctant acceptance that the Pakistan Army is being overfunded.**

The clinching issue in the recent Indian parliamentary elections was national security, which really implies dealing with Pakistan. There are a few major derivatives—firstly, the government has publicly committed to a hard line, which means that terror and talks can't mix. Consequently, it will be well-nigh impossible for the ruling dispensation to backtrack in a hurry and without commensurate payoffs. Impending assembly elections will further postpone any such possibility. Hopefully, establishment across would have picked up the sense of national muscular resolve. Analysts in the deep state should also link it with the real message of Balakot that terrorists will be targeted without self-imposed limitation of the LoC and with the most effective means of delivery. Some more nuanced space has been discovered below the nuclear threshold, and Pakistan may be less inclined to flaunt tactical nukes. They would have also read the writing on the wall: it is 'Naya Bharat'—a five-year mandate with a stable, hardline government.

On the other side, Imran Khan has four odd years; unfortunately, his mandate is a fabricated one, and the real control of 'Naya Pakistan' rests with the generals. With the economy in shambles and the additional challenge of managing the western frontier, the only silver lining is a lap dance with China. The Dragon's indulgence comes with riders, and the security of the CPEC is the foremost. The moot question is, will China realise the strategic reality and coerce Pakistan to tackle the terror assembly line within? **Pakistan has tried to generate positive signals on the Kartarpur Corridor and by restricting the activities of Muhammad Saeed of LeT during the recent Eid prayers.**

There is also a flurry of invitations and offers to revive dialogue on all issues.

Under immense international pressure, Pakistan sees the commencement of diplomatic engagement with India as its immediate objective. Notwithstanding positive signals, it is indeed very difficult to trust Pakistan, and the bottom line in all engagements should be proceeded with abundant caution and after verification. From Zulfikar Ali Bhutto to Muhammad Zia-ul-Haq, extending to Pervez Musharraf and Gen Qamar Javed Bajwa, it has been an uninterrupted nightmare of doublespeak and treachery, punctuated by a spate of terrorist attacks. Expectations must be pegged down and conditioned on meaningful progress on issues of proxy war, peace on the LoC, and circumscribing terror dons like Hafiz Saeed, Masood Azhar, and Dawood Ibrahim. The new Lok Sabha should consider adopting a unanimous resolution on national security to strengthen the hands of the government and reinforce messaging for elements across.

While official diplomatic channels can maintain contacts through National Security Agencies (hopefully, Pakistan will appoint one) and casual meetings on the sidelines of multilateral exchanges, in the interim, we should explore the utility of back-channel and track-two dialogues. We have had some success with envoys like RK Mishra in the Vajpayee era and Satinder Lambah for the United Progressive Alliance. Even informal contacts, like Sajjan Jindal leveraging links with the Sharif family, had limited utility. **The government could nominate a seasoned domain expert to act as a designated back-channel interlocutor. It will serve to fend off mounting pressure to start diplomatic engagement, as a concern in the global community, about heightened tension between two nuclear nations is natural.**

International pressure to resume negotiations should be managed with the Chinese strategy implying, 'hurry but slowly and only when it suits you'. The recommended approach is to keep engaging informally till the other party yields on our core national interests. Concrete measures to improve atmospherics, like an overland transit corridor to Afghanistan, MFN status, and liberalisation of trade, can be considered, but only when reciprocated with commensurate benefits. **Being large-hearted and sentimental must be replaced with a business-like transactional approach accompanied by verification.** Resumption of trade must be preceded by a multi-spectrum solution backed by technological aids like full-body scanners to stymie Pakistan's propensity to misuse it for smuggling of drugs, explosives, and counterfeit currency.

There is limited space for track two, which got a fillip with the revival of the Neemrana dialogue, the oldest in this genre. Anchored by seasoned diplomats, Vivek Katju and Rakesh Sood, it has informal official acceptance. It will be a good idea to continue to vector such dialogue with official briefings, especially on red lines, and debriefing after every round. Expectations from such parleys must be realistic, and they should remain discreet. **The proliferation of these exchanges without official concurrence should be discouraged, as they build avoidable pressure on the government. A relevant case in point is Navjot Sidhu's** foray on the Kartarpur Corridor, where Gen Bajwa seems to have outsmarted him.

It is learnt that the Pakistan Army has expressed the desire to engage with its Indian counterparts. Traditionally, our diplomats have discouraged this, probably wanting to reinforce democratic forces across and imaginary fears of contracting a coup virus. **They are wrong on both counts, as the Pakistan Army is not yielding ground in a hurry, and the democratic DNA of our *faujis* is made of teflon. It is time veterans play a rightful role on this front.**

11.5 Vacation of PoK: The New Dimension in the Strategic Matrix (Written in 2020)

The resurgence of demand for vacation in PoK is the new milestone in Indo-Pakistan strategic exchange. Though earlier rubbished as mere rhetoric, it is now being discussed as a likely possibility. Bilawal Bhutto, heir apparent of the PPP, has been asking Prime Minister Imran Khan to stop fretting about Article 370 and focus on saving

PoK. It is indeed like forcing a reckless batsman onto the backfoot. Pakistan, since Partition, has taken a revanchist line, aiming to gain control of the entire state of J&K. A malevolent line of thinking was fuelled primarily by parity (getting more than even with India) fixation, self-appointed guardianship of faith (ideological frontiers) syndrome, and, above all, gross under estimation of Indian capabilities, notably a belief that India lacks the willpower and intent to take on Pakistan.

Khakhi generals have been repeatedly leveraging a first-mover advantage, combined with a nuanced and cultivated facade of irrationality, to gain control of the escalation matrix in strategic exchanges and retain initiative. **The narrative of Kabayali Lashkars in 1947, infiltrator task forces with provocative names like Babur, Khilji, and Ghaznavi in 1965, Razakars in East Pakistan, Mujahids in Kargil, and the ongoing proxy war in J&K, has continued unabated.** The horror story has been punctuated with the incitement and support of rebels in the North-East and Khalistan terrorists. In keeping with our forgiving nature, the new generation of Indians, obsessed with the present situation in the valley, has little idea of now-forgotten links between erstwhile Pakistan and militant groups in the north-eastern states dating back to 1952. Utilising East Pakistan as a staging post, sanctuary, weapons, and training, including Chinese assistance, were funnelled to Naga militants. This misadventure continued till the '90s with the scope extended under complicit military rulers of Bangladesh to include many other groups, notably the United Liberation Front of Assam. The entire story has been documented by Hein G Kiessling in the highly acclaimed book *Faith, Unity, Discipline: The Inter-Services Intelligence (ISI) of Pakistan*.

India, in contrast, has been tentative, reactive, and defensive and was able to grab control of strategic interplay only temporarily, for brief periods during the liberation of Bangladesh and Operation Meghdoot in Siachen. **This appears to be changing now with the Balakot surgical strikes and the revocation of Article 370. India seems to have called off its nuclear bluff, discovered a new strategic space below nuclear sabre-rattling, and even injected a sense of shock**

and awe into the Rawalpindi General Headquarters. It is indeed heartening to note that, for once, we are in control of the escalation matrix and are living up to the name of 'fox land', used by Pakistan to describe us in their war games.

The call for re-integration of PoK is not all about being wily or clever, but fits in with our concept of 'Dharma Yudh' or struggling for the right cause. The vast stretches of occupied territory originally included GB, the Shaksgam Valley, and even Aksai Chin.

Even if Pakistan is given the benefit of the doubt on Aksai Chin, illegally seized by China in the '50s while India slept, it cannot be absolved of the criminal act of gifting away 6,993 square kilometres of strategically important Shaksgam to the Chinese in 1963. Even worse was the diabolical plot of engineering a secret Karachi pact on 29 April 1949, with forged signatures of the founder president of PoK, Sardar Ibrahim Khan, and the chief of J&K Muslim Conference, Ghulam Abbas. The pseudo agreement separated and legitimised the forcible occupation of 72,971 square kilometres of GB to some extent, notwithstanding reservations by India. The entire occupied territory was technically in 'stand-still' mode and actions were executed without consultation with the local populace, India, and not even reported in the media. By this act, Pakistan took direct control of GB. The sordid plot was kept secret for 59 long years, till it was revealed in the court proceedings of the High Court of PoK in the 1990s and later included in the so-called Constitution of PoK in 2008.

Shia soldiers of the NLI were misused as cannon fodder in Kargil, and their sacrifices and mortal remains were not even acknowledged by the ungrateful Pakistan Army. With their leaders in exile, 18 lakh Shias in GB face increasing persecution. **The entire region is being subjected to demographic and cultural inversion, along the lines of Hanisation of Xinjiang. Their natural resources, like gold mines, have been handed over to Chinese companies.**

The vast hydrographic potential of this region is planned to be tapped as part of the CPEC. It is ironic that GB is being subjected to ecological plundering with the submergence of large tracts of territory. In one case, the reservoir is planned to be situated in GB and the powerhouse in Khyber Pakhtunkhwa, thereby giving royalty benefits to the latter. **Residual PoK, which is only 13,297 square kilometres and one-sixth of GB, with a population of 40 lakh, is facing increasing marginalisation of local Kashmiris and Mirpuris by Punjabi Pothoharis and Pashtuns.** The province has a sham democracy with no voice in Parliament, and parties demanding freedom are not even allowed to contest in local elections. All dissent in GB and PoK is suppressed brutally under Schedule IV of the notorious Control of Terrorism Act. On the other hand, the earthquake of 2005 was utilised by Hafiz Saeed and Jamaat-ud-Dawah-affiliated NGO Falah-e-Insaniyat to proliferate Madrasas and radicalism, creating terror launch pads.

The liberation of PoK, or at least strategic stretches vital for our security, is likely to be a long, tedious, and tough struggle, entailing the building up of required niche capabilities and asymmetries besides a tacit nod or at least an acquiescing stance of relevant powers. In the interim, it is good bargaining leverage to retain initiative on the strategic matrix.

11.6 Pakistan's First National Security Policy Doesn't Spell Out a Cogent Road Map (Written in January 2022)

Pakistan has announced its first-ever and much-touted National Security Policy (NSP). The document spells out a national security vision with vague guidelines for goals. It has been projected as a citizen-centric initiative, and the document is liberally peppered with phraseology like 'whole-of-nation,' inclusive national dialogue, unity in diversity, normalisation, pluralistic anti-terror strategy, etc. One typical statement is 'Pakistan safeguards its sovereignty by ensuring national cohesion and harmony, preserving territorial integrity, enhancing economic independence, and ensuring the writ of the state.'

The document is laid out in eight sections, spanning 110 pages. However, the public version has 48 pages, hiding more than it reveals, even in quantitative terms. NSP has been prepared after a seven-year-long, supposedly consultative effort, reportedly with inputs from 600 odd security analysts and research scholars, toiling under the National Security Division (NSD). The document has a five-year currency from 2022 to 2027, subject to revisions/updates. It was approved by the cabinet on 28 December 2021, and the public version was released on 14 January. The endeavour was initiated by the erstwhile NSA, Sartaj Aziz, in the Nawaz Sharif regime and finished by the Moeed Yusuf and Imran Khan duo. The operating environment (both geo-strategic and geo-economic) for Pakistan has changed drastically in the interim. America has been replaced by China, the iron brother, and the US barely finds mention in the document. The policy is skewed in focus, towards China, India, and Afghanistan. In sum, critical catalysts of **three As (Allah, Army, and Amerika (sic)) have been replaced by ABC (Allah, Bajwa, and China)**. The general is already in his sixth year of tenure, and clamour for another extension after November 2022 is again growing. The document carries the stamp of the Bajwa Doctrine mandating a shift towards geo-economics and avoiding hostilities for 100 years. Of course, the proxy war is an unstated, yet acceptable variant!

Pakistan has been subjected to ignominy of being placed in grey list, just short of being blacklisted, thanks to Chinese veto. Its economy is in doldrums, and ironically, on the day of release, the State Bank of Pakistan, under the IMF diktat, was placed under restricted autonomy, limiting profligate tendencies. The moot question is: will it impact the defence budget, and by how much? Pakistan's fiscal crisis is accentuated by a marked loss of support from traditional bailout benefactors—Saudi Arabia and the UAE. The only constant has been the unrelenting Modi regime.

Economic security is projected as a core objective, seeking to raise the populace to a middle-income status. It makes lofty claims—a desire to make economic bases and not military ones. This fits in with yearnings for Imran's 'Naya Pakistan'. The problem is modelling on the ideal of 'Riyasat-e-Madina'. The most serious challenge and inherent contradictions of reining in *fasaadi*, extremist elements, anti-blasphemy warriors like TLP, and avoiding the repetition of Sialkot-type lynching incidents are not even addressed.

The nub and relevant part of the policy from our perspective is the fifth section, dealing with conventional military threats, maritime competition, deterrence in the South Asian region, space, and cybersecurity issues. **India appears 14 times in the document, and the Indian Ocean thrice. Barring a single expression of desire to improve relations with India, all other mentions are negative.** It perceives the expansion of India's nuclear triad and investment in modern technologies as triggers for disturbing the regional balance. It pointedly refers to India seeking to join the Nuclear Suppliers Group without signing the Nuclear Non-Proliferation Treaty.

The policy also highlights growing asymmetry in conventional forces. **Interestingly, it states that 'the possibility of use of force by the adversary, as a deliberate policy choice, cannot be ruled out'. This seems to be driven by the continued hangover effect of surgical strikes.** NSP prescribes a focus to be maintained on the LoC and the working boundary. Kashmir remains central to its security matrix, and Pakistan blames India for unilateral alterations in the constitutional framework. India is projected to harbour 'hegemonic designs' and is held responsible for frozen bilateral ties.

NSP outlines three major challenges, i.e., external imbalance, vertical inequalities among classes, and horizontal inequalities between regions. It seeks to prioritise national security objectives by mapping traditional as well as non-conventional threats. **Surprisingly, it introduces the concept of irreconcilable challenges, alluding to the Baluchi insurgency.** NSP remains in denial mode on Pashtun separatism and problems of managing the Durand Line region. Afghanistan is projected as a strategic gateway. However, strategic depth compulsion and proxy warriors as strategic assets are probably hidden in the classified version.

The CPEC and connectivity are projected as sort of silver bullets, yet zero access to India remains the dominant narrative. The document gives undue weightage to the central geographical location and its potential. NSP reinforces Pakistan as an insecure state, seeking parity with India. Anti-Indian culture seems to be the raison d'être for its existence. It has compounded its problems by including protection of faith as a self-imposed additional frontier, forcing it to punch above its weight.

In sum, NSP is a compilation of rhetorical wishlist and reminds one of NDC dissertation days. The document does not spell out a cogent road map. Most importantly, it fails to indicate a commitment to transformational changes to achieve lofty objectives. Notwithstanding contradictions and unrealistic projections, it indicates a sobering realisation of economic problems. It is also evident that clamour for sanity is gathering traction. It will be somewhat reassuring if Pakistan applies itself to NSP and geo-economics, giving India space to tackle wolf-warrior on the northern borders.

It is recommended that India should also finalise its NSP. The current reliance on ambiguity makes defence planning difficult. Without clear-cut goals, we deny ourselves the benefits of accountability and net assessment, which contribute to strategic deterrence.

Afghanistan-Pakistan and Taliban

12.1 A Virus Incubating Across the Durand Line (Written in April 2020)

India seems poised to manage the current pandemic triggered by the Wuhan Virus, but another equally deadly pathogen of religious extremism is being incubated across the Durand Line in Afghanistan. This has ominous implications for India, as evidenced in the **recent ISIS-K attack on 25 March 2020 on 200-strong religious congregation in the historical Gurdwara Hari Rai Sahib in Kabul. Twenti-five Sikhs, including an infant, were brutally killed in the ghastly attack,** lasting six hours.

Sikhs, approximating two lakhs in the '80s (in the pre-Mujahideen era), were tolerated due to their belief in the holy book, rather than idol worship. Sikhs and other minorities, as well as their religious places, have come under increasing attacks, with current numbers dwindling to barely 700. Last July, prominent Sikh leader Awtar Singh Khalsa, the only non-Muslim voice in Loya Jirgah (Afghan parliament), was killed with 20 others, in a suicide attack at Jalalabad. In yet another attack in March this year, 32 Shias were brutally killed. The attack in Kabul was followed up, the very next day, with a remotely activated blast, in the vicinity of funeral rites, as cremations are abhorred by Islamists and crematoriums are being forcibly shut.

In the aftermath of attacks, the minuscule Sikh and Hindu population of Afghanistan has been trying to migrate to other countries, even temporarily coalesce in Jalalabad or across Khyber. US Congressman Jim Costa has asked his government to give refuge to persecuted communities. The overwhelming desire is to get back to India. It has thrown up a tricky dilemma, as evacuation will be tantamount to a vote of no-confidence in the current regime of Ashraf Ghani. **Will it ultimately result in the destruction of the Afghan connection with Guru Nanak's legacy after the senseless plundering of the Bamiyan Buddhas? These obviously fit into the ISIS and Taliban monotheistic template of Khorasan Wilayat.**

The mastermind of the Kabul attack, Abdullah Orakzai, a Pakistan national known as Aslam Farooqi, has been nabbed by the National Directorate of Security (NDS). He has a dubious background, having operated with TTP and other groups. Having been recently anointed as leader, he was involved in petty intra-group rivalry. **The attack has a sinister implied message for India, as ISIS claimed that the terror squad included Abu Khalid al-Hindi, originally Muhammad Muhsin (28), a resident of Kasargod in Kerala. If verified, this would make him the second ISIS suicide bomber, after Abu Yusuf al-Hindi or Shafi Amar, who was eliminated in August 2015.** Doubts have arisen, as some reports point out, that Muhsin was killed in a drone strike in June 2019. It may be an attempt to utilise Indian connect, as another diabolic, divisive propaganda ploy.

Prima facie, it is difficult to believe that the attack in Kabul could have been orchestrated without ISI facilitation and complicity. It

appears to be part of Pakistan's design to prop up acceptable Taliban and use ISIS for dirty tricks. The NIA has joined investigations, and it is hoped that the plot will be unravelled, with the NDS showing initial determination. As per intelligence analysts—Satellite Instructional Television Experiment (SITE) and other researchers, nearly 40% of IS-K leaders in Afghanistan and Pakistan have cross affiliations with other groups. The recent discovery of three joint Mustaquils (camps) of Taliban and JeM in the Nangarhar province, where Indian ISIS recruits were also operating, points to sterner challenges for us. As per an alarm raised by Castelium.AI, an American technology regulatory agency, Pakistan has utilised the COVID-19 crisis to halve its terror watch list from 7,600 to 3,800, omitting even dreaded Zaki-ur-Rehman Lakhwi.

Afghanistan is hurtling towards catastrophic disaster, as the US has decided to abandon the Afghan government. The problem has been outsourced to Pakistan and the Taliban. The vague agreement with the Taliban of 29 February seeks to abandon the legally constituted government and the much-needed endeavour of building a democratic and tolerant society. The most ironic element is—concessions amounting to abdication, without the government even being made party to deliberations. **There are no verifiable parameters and obligations expected from the Taliban except a reduction in violence, duly sweetened by the release of prisoners.**

Bluntly, a new American policy is—'Afghans, you are on your own, and we are off!' **This, after sinking more than $3 trillion, and most importantly, losing more than 4,000 lives, including civilian contractors.** During my interaction with passing out Afghan cadets at IMA in December 2014, despite repeated attempts to establish their regional ethnicities, the resounding reply was—'We are Afghans'. The much-cherished dream of evolving a more moderate theological model and society, backed by unified security forces utilising collaborative Western influences with Saudi and Jordanian royalties, lies in tatters.

The Taliban is gaining increased ascendancy against some resistance by the Afghan National Defence and Security Force, with dwindling assistance by remnants of NATO and Resolute Support Mission, it is a new extremist great game unleashed. Al-Qaeda, Taliban, ISIS, TTP, Islamic Movement of Uzbekistan (IMU), and multiple competing Shuras, like Quetta and Miran Shah, are vying to scale newer heights of Salafism. The game has multifarious ethnic indigenous players, Pashtuns, Tajiks, Uzbeks, and Hazaras, as well as international performers—Uyghurs, Turks, Kazakhs, and other nationalities.

The old proverb that Afghan warlords can agree on only one thing—to continue quarrelling,—has added another sinister dimension, competitively demonstrated extremism. A bleak future awaits future generations of Afghans, particularly women.

As the world combats the COVID-19 pandemic, it will be apt to recall that Henry Kissinger's secret trip to China was routed through and facilitated by Pakistan. The ongoing, ill-advised midwifing foray, in Afghanistan is likely to sprout deadlier contagions. **George Santana famously remarked: 'Those who cannot remember the past are condemned to repeat it.' Will we ever learn from history?**

12.2 Retaining Relevance in the Afghan Imbroglio (Written in August 2020)

Afghanistan is in turmoil. The Taliban, combined with assorted desperate factions, is battling Afghan National Security Forces (ANSF) in a violent struggle to take over coveted and pivotal geo-strategic space. **The salience is drawn from its 'buffer state' location on the confluence of Han, Persian, Turkish (Xinjiang and Turkmenistan), Arabic, Central Asian (connected to Russian), and Indian civilisations.**

The British, after unsuccessful forays, were forced to endure this unruly territory as an autonomous bulwark against the Soviets. In the great game in the '80s, Western-backed Mujahideen were pitted against the Soviets, in a proxy war, finally driving the Russians out. Yet another edition of a great game, witnessed Americans edging out the Taliban, in the Global War on Terror (GWOT), targeting Al-Qaeda and later ISIS, after the 9/11 attack in 2001.

The turbulent frontier has always defied conventional governance parameters and norms, with an assortment of autonomous tribal ethnicities. The Afghanistan-Pakistan region, astride the Durand Line, has been traditionally administered through seven autonomous agencies, like Waziristan, Bajaur, and tribal assemblies or Shuras of tribes like the Mehsuds. These Shuras hold 'Loya-Jirgahs', grand assemblies entailing tortuous and lengthy confabulations, ending with a 'khap' type of diktats. **The codified traditions and edicts, like 'Pashtunwali', override all other laws, including Sharia and Hadith.**

Outwardly, seeming united, the Taliban is, in effect, a complex conglomeration of disparate groups, like the TTP. Many are described with appendages of Shura that they owe allegiance to, like Quetta, Peshawar, Jalalabad, etc. **The fractious nature of Afghan society is best summed up in the famous words of noted scholar Ahmed Rashid, after a Loya Jirga, 'Afghans have only agreed to disagree amongst themselves.'**

In the current context, Taliban factions have a consensus on getting rid of Americans and Western forces, as well as the recently anointed President Ashraf Ghani. The atmosphere after the recent American exit from the Bagram base is accompanied by a sense of euphoria, of once again forcing out another external power. The tally now includes the UK, USSR, and US, with a pertinent question: will China be the next one, provided it decides to intervene with the PLA?

The US forces are finally pulling out from Afghanistan after two decades. **Many describe it as a sort of abandonment, after having sunk more than $2.26 trillion and losing 2,442 bravehearts and 800 private security contractors. In addition, the toll includes 1,144 soldiers of the 36-nation International Security Assistance Force (ISAF) (NATO) coalition, 72 journalists, and 444 aid workers of non-governmental organisations (NGOs).** Ironically, the British, with an enviable tradition of the Commonwealth War Graves Commission, are unable to give appropriate honour to their 450 bravehearts in Afghanistan.

The Soviet Union lost 14,400 soldiers in the decade of 1979–89, in American-organised, Saudi allies-funded, Pakistan-orchestrated, fasaadi (packaged and justified as jihadi), Taliban-executed mayhem. Afghan casualties at the most conservative scale were approximately 70,000 odd combatants of various militias, 47,000 civilians, and ten million refugees, including the internally displaced populace.

Americans had some justification for initial intervention. It could be termed overreach, but it lost the plot in execution. **Gen Dave Miller, former head of Army Training and Doctrine Command, most aptly remarked: 'Believe me, it's a lot easier to invade a country than to leave it in an ordinary manner.'** The Taliban was created through contrived midwifery, wherein Mujahideen (religious fighters) were given a semblance of respectability. Mujahideen, having acquired considerable notoriety in the Civil War, the ISI chose to fix it by inducting Madrasa graduates, with a more acceptable name of Talibs (students in Pashto).

Taliban 1.0 was a bunch of compliant, self-obsessed fighters led by the late Muhammad 'Mullah' Omar, willing to dance to the ISI's tunes. He chose to usurp Mehdi-like powers for himself by wearing the Prophet's spiritual cloak of Khirqa-e-Mubarak, at Kandahar. This act, borrowed from Sufi mystical practices, doesn't meet Wahabi or Salafi criteria. They rose like a phoenix in 1994, and after consolidation in 1996, ruled till 2001. The ISI's puppetry often drew lighthearted comment that the Taliban were functioning in effect, more like Shagirdan (followers).

Taliban 2.0, in comparison, comprises more politically aware and confident leaders. They are likely to be more autonomous. Pakistan has been most surprisingly trusted once again to exercise its influence on the Taliban, to salvage some sort of face-saving exit for the US. Having assessed altered dynamics, Pakistan has already reiterated that it is only a facilitator and not the guarantor in the peace process. Is Pakistan looking for risk mitigation before another spell of civil war?

The proposed solution seeks to avoid a unilateral, 'winner takes it all' solution, in favour of the Taliban. It promotes an inclusive solution, giving due representation to all segments of society. The Western world wants a fair share for women in education and employment. It also hopes that the new regime will not allow the resurgence of Al-Qaeda and ISIS. In essence, it doesn't want the re-establishment of the Emirate of the Taliban.

It is important to remember that Pashtuns constitute a roughly 40% share, followed by Tajiks at 25%, Hazaras at 10%, and many other smaller tribes, such as Uzbeks, Nuristanis, etc. A north-south fault line exists from the times of late Ahmad Shah Massoud (Lion of Panjshir) and Rashid Dostum. Apart from this, the Herat province, bordering Iran, under Ismail Khan, is also arrayed against Pashtuns. The Taliban has taken care to induct non-Pashtuns and Haji Furqan, and Uyghur key commander, who led the recent offensive in the north. It is learnt that China wants its role to be circumscribed. In this age of hypocrisy, it is likely that the Taliban will follow Pakistan and jettison Uyghurs and the *ummah* (Islamic brotherhood).

The Taliban in a psy-war offensive, aided by Pakistan, has been proclaiming that it has gained control of 85% territory, key border crossings, and major districts. **Reliable demographic experts opine that 75% of the population is currently huddled in cities, with 25% in the Kabul capital region alone.** It will be more appropriate to accept that the Taliban retains contested and shifting control, in a 45–50% area, over 25–30% population and one-third of the 421 districts. Key districts remain under government authority.

The real control on Afghanistan is through its population centres—Kabul, Herat, Jalalabad, Kandahar, Mazar-e-Sharif, Kunduz, strategic communications, and border check posts. The US, despite reservations, has agreed to allow Turkey, a part of the NATO mission, to guard Kabul airport, providing an airhead for diplomatic presence, vital for the peace process. Turkish Forces have the wherewithal and expertise to execute this mission. It is very likely that Turkey may develop leverage and stake in the peace process, though currently, the Taliban doesn't approve of their presence.

The Pakistan-aided Taliban propaganda has triggered waves of migration and exodus. It is important to remember that conflicts in Afghanistan are characterised less by fair play and more by shifting loyalties, treachery, and Bakshish (bribery) combined with propaganda. The ANSF, with approximately 3.5 lakh strength, has been limited to a counter-insurgency force format. Its officer cadre and junior leadership trained by India have shown remarkable resilience and are currently contesting the complete Taliban takeover.

Update: Most surprisingly, the entire Afghan National Army capitulated and did not show any cohesion or resilience.

Pakistan's insistence and India's reticence have resulted in the ANSF being devoid of air power, guns, and tanks. India has provided only eight refurbished MI-35 gunships, but could have done much more. America's promised 'over-the-horizon' air support remains critical for the ANSF, as evidenced in the recent Kandahar raid and in Balkh, where the Taliban suffered considerable casualties.

The challenge for the US is to generate actionable intelligence and find a suitable base, preferably in proximity, for such operations. The option of the Shamsi base in Baluchistan (on lease with the UAE for hunting) is no longer feasible, as the lease has expired. Apart from this, the Chinese presence in Gwadar and hostile public sentiment preclude it. The US is looking at options for bases in Uzbekistan and Tajikistan, though the latter, with its pro-Soviet tilt, is less likely. Russia has scheduled exercises with Tajik and Uzbek forces as part of the Collective Security Treaty Organization (CSTO) at the Harb-Maidon training ground, close to the Afghan border, from 5 to 10 August 2020. **The underlying message is that everyone wants a stake in the great game.**

The Doha peace process is making slow progress. Concurrently, Russia, with the US and China, has activated the troika, which has been extended by inviting Pakistan. Some analysts, including Soviet FM Sergey Lavrov, have mooted the idea of the inclusion of Iran and India in the extended troika. Surprisingly, Zamir Kabulov, designated representative, countered this with his dampener, 'India can't join because it has no real influence with the Taliban.' This is strange, for the Taliban barely represents 45%. Pakistan and the Ghani regime are constantly sniping at each other, and Islamabad enjoys very little trust amongst non-Pashtun ethnicities.

Mullah Abdul Ghani Baradar, leading the Doha delegation, is assiduously creating a facade to garner better acceptance. The Taliban realise that to manage Afghanistan, they need external funding and support for the economy, employment, and reconstruction. Once again, Pakistan has facilitated a connection for China. In the early '70s, it was Kissinger and Nixon who were the conduits to Beijing. This time, it was Mullah Baradar travelling to Timjin. Ready assurances have been given to China regarding the curtailing of activities of ETIM, security for Chinese economic activities, like Aynak copper mines, and peace in Xinjiang. Sources indicate that the Taliban is willing to give similar guarantees to India for Kashmir.

Objectively analysing, assurances on security, women empowerment, and an inclusive solution are like manifesto promises. Once a new regime is installed, it may become a game of competitive Salafism, leading to the revival of Khorasan, ISIS, and even ETIM. These trends were seen in attacks on Sikhs and their shrines. The Taliban denied their role, leaving ISIS as the most likely culprit. China needs to learn appropriate lessons from the recent casualties of nine engineers at Dasu despite funding two light special security divisions (34 and 44), tasked with the protection of CPEC assets and workforce.

Analysts are waiting to unravel the Chinese enigma and riddles. Firstly, will China show real commitment and put boots on the ground? The second option is whether Beijing will utilise a combination of outsourcing to Pakistan and buy its way out through funding. Most countries want China to get bogged down in Afghanistan, as a logical sequel to its aggressive rising-China policy. **However, China is likely to prefer the second option of relying on Pakistan and leveraging its deep pockets. Like all historical misadventures, these, in all probability, are likely to backfire in the unscrupulous killing fields of Afghanistan. The question is, how soon?**

Indian prime concerns are the protection of infrastructure assets created, safeguarding the interests of our traditional allies (Northern Alliance), and retaining goodwill generated through education, assistance in health, and equipment serviceability. India has twin macro challenges of maintaining discreet channels with the Taliban, yet building capability to provide aid to friends. India needs to retain its traditional domain awareness through intelligence networks in the region.

Concurrently, India should seek to convince Central Asian Republic (CAR) nations to allow India to join their efforts in providing regional security. Uzbekistan and Tajikistan, where medical and other assistance teams were stationed at Ayani, are most relevant. Revival or partnership in such endeavours can be major enablers for us. India also needs to work with both the Soviet Union and the US to seek participation in their regional initiatives. One such recently announced endeavour is the US-promoted 'Afghan Quad' with Pakistan, Uzbekistan, and Afghanistan.

While India shouldn't put boots on the ground, it should build its relevance through astute diplomacy and networking with all players. It will be in India's interests to contribute wholeheartedly towards an inclusive and tolerant regime in Kabul.

Relevant details from another article on the same subject, written in July 2020 titled '**Indian Role in Afghan Peace Process**' have been included.

12.3 Seeking Clarity on Taliban 2.0 and the Afghan-Pakistan Situation (Written in September 2021)

Great game in Afghanistan is an addictive affliction, having engineered the ignominious defeat of most external forces, except Maharaja Ranjit Singh. In Higher Command (2001–02), my dissertation was 'Containment of Jihadi Fundamentalism in Afghanistan'. Prescriptive initiatives included forging strategic linkages with Iran and CAR, backed up with connectivity. Chabahar, rail/road links, air bases in CAR, and connecting with ethnic groups, especially the Pashtuns, were other main recommendations. They remain relevant.

The driving factor was needed to outflank the Turkmenistan-Afghanistan-Pakistan-India (TAPI) pipeline, with Taliban 1.0 clamouring to act as pipeline police. With the ascendancy of Taliban 2.0, the CPEC becoming 'Afghan-Pakistan'-EC is an ominous possibility. The next great game could be the colonisation of 'Afghan-Pakistan' economically by China.

In 2008, I studied the same subject at a macro level at the National Defence College (NDC), with initial assigned topic, 'Combating jihadi fundamentalism with soft power'. During the course of a one-year-long study, I forced four refinements in objective, settling on: managing Islamist extremism with smart power. Another column can be written on refinements, but only relevant aspects are enumerated.

- Firstly, **the most important prerequisite is defining the correct end state. Americans obviously chose and stuck to the wrong one, finally abandoning it.**

- Secondly, the **Afghan situation mandated inclusive regional management. The US failed to exhibit flexibility and, notwithstanding a dubious record, outsourced it to Pakistan.**

- Thirdly, **smart power dictates customising localised solutions. The US, on the contrary, tried imposing its own models of governance and security on tribal society.**

- Fourthly, **management requires long-term commitment. The least President Biden could have done is to time the US exit in the winter, when the tempo of the Taliban operations would have been slower.** It should have fulfilled commitment on 'over-the-horizon' (OTH) air and drone cover to the Afghan National Defense and Security Forces (ANDSF).

- Finally, in a lighter vein, my initial guide was Maj Gen GD Bakshi, and our academic attrition resulted in research, getting the top honour.

Answers to the sudden collapse of ANSDF lie in a 120-page, US Congress-mandated report from 2015 by the Special Inspector General for Afghanistan (SIGAR). This report gives enough clues on the ghost army and police, propped up on bloated payrolls, cornering $300 million in salaries. It highlights many dubious deals, like the junking of 20 G222 Italian cargo aircraft, costing $549 million for merely $40,257, with no real flying, indicating a vicious stranglehold by contractor lobbies. Most commentators underestimated the potential of bribery (Bakshish) and deal-making, overriding instruments, in the Afghan model of war fighting.

The emerging situation has triggered the following two sensitive issues meriting deliberation.

12.4 Regaining a Sense of Relevance in Afghanistan Maelstrom (Written in December 2021)

Afghanistan is reeling under an ever-worsening humanitarian maelstrom with harsh winter, pandemic, and famine. The disaster is compounded by an inept Taliban government, struggling to find even basic international acceptance. The stark reality festers in the form of the plight of a significant number of refugees in the Western and Gulf countries. It has also triggered in Europe a feeling of being let down by the unilateral US pullout, as well as guilt pangs on the current plight of the Afghan populace, particularly refugees, minorities, women, and children.

Growing difference in perceptions is a diplomatic opportunity that Pakistan and China seek to exploit by giving the humanitarian crisis overriding importance and relegating other critical issues to the background. **There is a concerted orchestration by Pakistan to magnify projections of crisis, to secure the release of frozen funds amounting to approximately $9.5 billion, thereby whittling down minimal leverage still retained by the Western nations.** Pakistan organised an international seminar to coincide with the Troika plus meeting to hype up its pro-Taliban agenda.

It will be worthwhile to reiterate red lines—inclusivity and pluralism; zero tolerance on terrorism, including proliferation of narcotics and arms; ensuring basic human rights, especially for women, children, and minorities. Humanitarian relief under the regime, where minorities like Shias and Sikhs are being targeted and women terrorised, mandates the incorporation of safeguards to enable just coverage to include marginalised sections. India, as a likely major donor of wheat, needs to ensure international monitoring. **Chinks in collective resolve to link diplomatic recognition with compliance with red lines is already manifesting. Taliban appointees have taken over embassies and consulates in Pakistan. The same may happen in China and later in Russia. The need is for collective action to retain leverage and incentivise compliance with internationally agreed objectives.**

The collapse of the Doha process has sprouted alternative mechanisms like the Troika plus (Russia initiated with the USA, China, plu—currently, Pakistan and Iran), the Moscow format (enlarged regional formulation, including India), and the recent Delhi dialogue, amongst others. India is literally at the margins, struggling to regain relevance. We are paying a heavy price for supporting a duly elected regime and not opening parallel channels with the Taliban. The US, on its part, has tried to initiate regional dialogue, concurrently aimed at countering China, through Quad variants. The Central Asian one, announced before the Taliban takeover, is unlikely to take off. The US, Afghanistan, Uzbekistan, and Pakistan are members of this one. The Middle Eastern variant includes the US, Israel, the UAE, and India. Ironically, Israel and the UAE have long-standing security cooperation arrangements with China, including technology exchanges.

In these confusing times of plurilateralism, India's initiative with Russia, Iran, and all five Central Asian countries is a very timely endeavour. Unfortunately, Pakistan stayed away and even influenced China to do likewise. India has very difficult and complicated choices, starting with the need to accept fait accompli and 'realpolitick' of dealing with the Taliban. Between inactivity dubbed as strategic patience and smart engagement, the latter is a pragmatic option. **The harsh reality is that transition has been outsourced to Pakistan; yet, India must forge a consensus to preclude Pindi from hijacking the plot completely.**

The challenge can be outlined as regaining relevance, cementing consensus to nudge the Taliban towards responsible governance, in effect, retaining leverage till compliance, more importantly, exploring shared concerns and safeguarding them. In the Delhi dialogue, notwithstanding the Russian participation, some backtracking by Moscow on the Delhi consensus has been reported. The need is to be wary of the stance of Zamir Kabulov, Russian interlocutor in the Troika plus dialogue and his alleged pro-Pindi leaning. Is Russia utilising Nikolai Patrushev and Kabulov to remain engaged with two differing approaches?

Indian opportunities lie with Iran and its ire at the continuing marginalisation of Shias, Hazaras, and Ismailis. Insurgency in Sistan and a growing number of refugees from Afghanistan have heightened concerns in Tehran. **It is an opportunity to re-energise connectivity projects like Chabahar, Zaranj-Delaram, as part of the North-South Corridor.** Side-stepping US antagonism towards Iran and sanctions is the key challenge. Though seemingly tough, India needs to keep chipping at the possibilities of reviving its stake in the Ayani air base in Tajikistan. **This is especially critical as China has reportedly secured the go-ahead for a policing and surveillance facility, essentially a benign euphemism for a military base.** Our forays and efforts should include the Ferghana Valley in Uzbekistan, which is supposedly more autonomous.

It may seem non-Kosher, but it will be worthwhile to tie up with Americans, including utilisation of an operating base, for over-the-horizon surveillance of possible areas of operation of ISIS and variants. It can have spin-offs in capability building, technology exchanges, and messaging to ward off Chinese designs in GB. It is time the US woke up to the mess created due to over-dependence on Pakistan and built redundancies through India. **Euphoria in Pakistan over the Taliban victory is having a blowback effect. The government there caved in to the self-appointed, anti-blasphemy warriors of TLP by accepting its unreasonable demands.** It has resulted in main-streaming and virtual carte blanche to the extremist party, whose cadres fired at and killed security personnel. In another incident, Pakistan's Prime Minister **Imran Khan had to appear before the Supreme Court to explain amnesty to TTP, perpetrators of the massacre of APS Peshawar. The growing perception is that the military has virtually capitulated in the Sirajuddin Haqqani brokered agreement.**

Repeated assurances on ISIS and TTP being under control are not even worth the value of rapidly sinking Afghan currency. It is time the world woke up to the triggering of the domino effect of competitive extremism by legitimisation of TLP and TTP. The malevolence needs to be capped before we confront new variants of ISIS, IMU,

ETIM, and more radical offshoots of the Taliban. **The answer lies in keeping focus on red lines and ensuring zero tolerance on terrorism, especially its proliferation in the neighbourhood.**

12.5 Re-Engaging with the Taliban (Written in June 2022)

The dastardly attack on Gurdwara Karte Parwan in Kabul on 25 May 2022 virtually sounded the death knell for the multi-cultural character of Afghanistan. Another historic shrine, Gurdwara Har Rai Sahib, was targeted in an even more ghastly attack, exactly two years back, accounting for 25 deaths. While the recent attack had only one Sikh casualty, structural damage to the only functional shrine was extensive. The same gurdwara has been subjected to periodic encroachments under the pretext of road widening. In 2018, an attack on historic Gurdwara Nanak Sahib in Jalalabad left 18 dead.

Sikhs, numbering 2–5 lakhs (2–5%) in the '70s have dwindled to less than 500. The community was spread across Kabul, Jalalabad, Kandahar, Ghazni, Khost, and other cities. As traders, moneylenders, Unani and herbal medicine practitioners, they had endeared themselves to society. More than a dozen gurdwaras have been destroyed in the Civil War. The obvious question is: after the obliteration of the Bamiyan Buddhist relics, are Sikhism and its shrines next on target?

These attacks have been projected as retaliation for unconnected events in India, like J&K and the blasphemous remarks controversy. The offer by the ruling dispensation to repair and protect gurdwaras needs to be backed up by actions on the ground. The Sikh diaspora across the Durand Line has also been facing sporadic attacks. While e-visas were granted by Delhi, lthe ament that these could have been accorded earlier has been articulated. E-visas for 3,000 odd Afghan students also require priority handling.

Terrorist attacks have been owned up by various factions of the ISIS. Perpetrators are recycled inductees from various tanzeems, with multiple affiliations. The 2020 attack was executed by Indian-origin ISIS-Levant Khorasan cadres, Abu Khalid al-Hind, and Murshid Mohammed TKJ from Kerala. However, the mastermind was Abdullah Orkazai alias Aslam Farooqi, having affiliations with the LeT and Haqqani factions. He was among the prisoners released by the current Afghan regime, on taking over. The latest attack has been owned by the ISIS-Khorasan Province faction. The suicide bomber had his roots in **JeM. It bears recalling that Masood Azhar was among the first to visit Kandahar, the spiritual capital, to pay obeisance to the new regime.**

In the complex bevy of multiple groups enjoying sanctuary, in remote areas on the Afghanistan-Pakistan border—Nangarhar and Kunar, exacerbated by internal tussle between Taliban Shuras and factions, it is difficult to resolve 'who and why' of attacks. Behind the cover of IS, many pursue diabolic agendas. **It will be safe to assume that Peshawar Corps Commander Faiz Hameed may know the real answers. With the impending nomination of the all-powerful army chief, it could be his way of staking his relevance.**

There has been a significant move forward in engaging with the Taliban regime, which has been inviting India to reopen embassy. The assessment team, led by the joint secretary, visited Kabul, including the mission premises. It appears that Indian aid has been well received and assets like the embassy have not been vandalised. Dr Abdullah Abdullah returned to Kabul after a 44-day visit to India. The visit, although described as personal, included extensive interactions with the Indian establishment and diplomats from the US and France. It is also relevant that Hamid Karzai, former President, unlike Ashraf Ghani and others, remained in Kabul, through the turbulent phase of transition.

There is speculation that the attack could have been orchestrated by the ISI to stymie the normalisation of relations. The saga of India—from being a hot favourite with the Afghans to being completely left out and now struggling to regain relevance—is indeed interesting. Relations hit the nadir in 1996–99, with the proliferation of Mujahideen terrorists in the valley, defined by sordid hijacking drama at Kandahar in 1999. In this period of internal strife, India chose to support the Northern Alliance and non-Pashtun leaders like Tajik, Ahmed Shah Massoud (Lion of Panjshir), and Uzbek Rashid Dostum. Another rude jolt was the attack on the Indian embassy in Kabul in 2008. The casualties included my NDC coursemate, Brig RD Mehta, press attaché, and two ITBP officials.

While officially treating the Taliban as a pariah, the UPA re-established back-channel links in 2011. Mullah Abdul Salam Zaeef, the Taliban envoy in Islamabad, despite the Guantanamo Bay prison track record, reportedly made numerous visits to India. He was seen in Goa, at a literary event, in November 2013, with then-FM Chidambaram. Repeat mistake of siding with Ashraf Ghani, in the face of imminent US pullout and zero contact with Taliban, completely marginalised India in the Afghan reconciliation process. India was quick to pull out of Kabul in August 2021, but Pakistan, Russia, and China maintained a presence. **Ten months down the line, 15 countries now have missions, and the number is likely to grow. In the recent SCO dialogue, India was conspicuous, as the lone ranger.** In the interim, many of our core concerns, including inclusive democracy, women empowerment, and links with terrorist groups, have not been addressed. Yet, there is a realisation that Panjshir resistance has not gathered traction. The Taliban are unified as fighters, but appear faction ridden in governance. There are openings, with moderates like IMA-educated Sher Mohammad Stanikzai, currently deputy FM. Russia originally worked hard to keep India out, but after the Ukrainian crisis, it seems more chastened.

Afghanistan was jolted by a massive earthquake, with the epicentre in the Southern Khost province. **While diplomatic recognition by India is not in the offing, India has rightly responded to signal commitment and reach out to Afghan society by sending a technical team.** It is good that motivated distractions like the gurdwara attack have not been allowed to derail long overdue corrective steps. Physical presence of even a small team is likely to generate multiple benefits, including better security of the diaspora. Concurrently, the Taliban needs to do much more to protect minorities and address Indian concerns.

12.6 Taliban 2.0 May Just Be Floundering Along (Written in September 2022)

As Pakistan gasps for a fiscal bailout and external assistance from a reluctant IMF, neighbouring Afghanistan has been witnessing much worse. The promised version of Taliban 2.0, after America's hurried exit in August 2021, is yet to find acceptability, with continued denial of official recognition to the regime. Only China, Iran, Pakistan, Russia, Turkiye, Turkmenistan, and Qatar have extended accreditation to Taliban diplomats. India has a non-diplomatic presence in Kabul to coordinate relief assistance. The Islamic Emirate of Afghanistan, in its nineteenth month, is still working with only an interim cabinet, lurching towards theocratic autocracy.

Foreign reserves of $7 billion left by the Ashraf Ghani regime remain frozen, with half of the amount, $3.5 billion, re-appropriated in trust for damages and rehabilitation of 9/11 victims. The US, in the tortuous **Doha dialogue, visualised the new regime to ensure three fundamental objectives—quelling terrorism, basic human rights, particularly for women, and stability in governance. Pakistan had taken on the role of guarantor.** There was an informal understanding with the US to install Ghani and other moderates at the helm. In keeping with his perfidious nature, erstwhile ISI boss Lt Gen Faiz Hameed was in Kabul to oversee the installation of Pakistani nominees.

Power Struggle

Consequently, Mullah Abdul Ghani was not only sidelined but also subjected to physical manhandling by the Haqqani clan. Fisticuff governance was again witnessed last week, when the minister of higher education fractured his arm, courtesy of a senior functionary, resorting literally to 'arm-twisting' during a meeting. The present

Amir-ul-Mu'mineen (a title that means Commander of the Faithful), Hibatullah Akhundzada, initially dismissed as a reclusive theocratic leader, is proving to be the toughest obscurantist. As per sources, he has stymied efforts towards the transition to the Rahbari Shura (a steering high council), for collective leadership. He is being blamed for the denial of secondary and university education to women, as well as employment.

Stability, one of the key desired objectives, should include both rudimentary democracy and inclusivity. Democracy in the form of jirgas/shuras, collective decision-making tribal bodies, remains a non-starter with Akhundzada in Peshawar acquiring an Ayatollah-like veto power. The other metric of inclusivity, which is a critical prerequisite in the diverse Afghan ethnic society, is being only notionally applied. Abdul Salam Hanafi, an Uzbek, has been appointed as the second deputy PM with a peripheral role. Tajiks, the second largest ethnic group, find representation through Qari Fasihuddin as head of the Afghan Army. Hazaras (Shias) have Abdul Latif Nazari as a mere deputy minister. **The real power centres are Sirajuddin Haqqani, the all-powerful interior minister, and Defence Minister Mullah Yaqoob, who is Taliban founder Mullah Omar's son. The Haqqani clan has grabbed control of the Kabul Capital Region, where 25% of the country's population is huddled**. There is an Indian connection too in the form of IMA-trained Sher Mohammad Stanikzai, the spokesman of the high-profile Doha dialogue, has been relegated to deputy foreign minister. The Western desire to accommodate former President Hamid Karzai and Dr Abdullah Abdullah is unlikely to fructify, notwithstanding their continued presence in Kabul.

The major factor aiding the continuity of the Taliban is the inability of the Panjshir Valley-based National Resistance Front (morphed version of late Ahmad Shah Massoud's Northern Front) to find traction and support. Taliban's declaration of zero tolerance to terrorism sounds hollow in the light of Al-Qaeda head Ayman Zawahiri being sheltered in a personal property of the Haqqani clan till his elimination by an American drone. The Taliban Government is half-heartedly battling the Islamic State Khorasan Province (ISKP), which orchestrated attacks on Gurdwara Karte-Parwan in Kabul and has now shifted focus to Chinese and Russian entities to embarrass the regime. The Taliban has promised to prevent the export of terrorism to neighbouring countries by controlling Xinjiang-focused ETIM, Islamic Movement of Uzbekistan (IMU), IS-KP, JeM, and LeT. Calibration of control and sanctuary to these groups acts as a significant leverage for the Taliban, especially in China.

TTP Factor

The most complex and sensitive element is in dealing with TTP, which has an avowed aim to install a Sharia-compliant regime in Pakistan. It also promises an autonomous homeland for Pashtuns, extending on both sides of the Durand Line. **Having been partners in crime for decades, the Taliban has obvious limitations in checking TTP, which has significant tribal support in frontier provinces, on both sides.** There has been an increasing number of cross-border clashes and raids. TTP has increased the targeting of Pakistani personnel, like the recent suicide attack on a police congregation in a Peshawar mosque. Efforts by the Taliban to broker and extend a ceasefire between Pakistan and TTP have not found success. Pakistan has started fencing and fortifying the Durand Line and border posts, notably the Torkham crossing. **The ISI's dream of strategic depth lies in tatters. China, having burnt its hands in the CPEC, remains a reticent player, refusing to get directly involved.** Beijing's current interests are control of ETIM and shepherding commercial mining interests, like the Aynak copper mine, for exploitation after stabilisation.

The Taliban's survival is currently based on the financial drip being administered through international relief agencies. Cash doles amounting to $20 million are being injected periodically to prevent starvation and abject penury. The misery and plight of the populace are another diabolic leverage of sorts, ensuring some succour. Distribution has become a victim of the recent diktat to female aid workers to wear hijab. The measure has since been reviewed, particularly for medical and health workers. The only bright spot in the Taliban report card is a comparative reduction in corruption.

India was kept out of the reconciliation process on Pakistan's insistence and complicity by the US and even Russia. India is now increasingly being courted by the Taliban. **The current Indian focus is on disaster relief and inclusive capability building with local tribal ownership. However, Taliban assurances cannot be taken merely at face value. The way forward is caution and trust after due verification.**

12.7 Taliban at the Helm but Situation Fluid in Kabul (Written in October 2022)

The Doha accord had sought zero tolerance on terrorism, especially providing sanctuary to Al-Qaeda and ISIS. It also expected inclusiveness in society, with fair representation to non-Pashtun ethnic groups. There was optimism about basic human rights. The elimination in August 2022 of Zawahiri in Kabul and in a safe-house provided by the Haqqani clan exposes the hollowness of the Taliban regime, on the most critical parameter.

15 August was declared a holiday in the Islamic Emirate of Afghanistan (IEA) to mark one year of the Taliban rule. **There was little cause for celebration as the Taliban, which promised to transform into a 2.0 avatar, has, at best, crawled to 1.1.** The country continues to languish as a pariah state with recognition from only China, Pakistan, and Russia. Humanitarian crisis in the form of refugees and famine has reduced it to a basket case. Aid is being pumped in by UN agencies and NGOs. **India made considerable contributions in disaster relief during the recent earthquake and famine with wheat shipments. India has even restored the presence of officials in its embassy, terming it a non-diplomatic presence.** Similar ad-hoc set-ups have been instituted by many other countries, primarily to coordinate relief and retain contact with a larger populace. To be fair to the new regime, the overall level of violence has indeed diminished,

though it is because the prime perpetrators are now in the seat of power.

In order to attempt an objective appraisal, it is important to start with the Doha process and its major thrust areas. Even the Taliban regime, after a drone attack on Ayman al-Zawahiri, accused the US of violating it. The Doha accord had sought zero tolerance on terrorism, especially providing sanctuary to Al-Qaeda and ISIS. It also expected inclusiveness in society, with fair representation to non-Pashtun ethnic groups. There was optimism about basic human rights, particularly women's education and employment, coupled with fair justice, without reprisals. The elimination of Zawahiri, so-called Emir of Al-Qaeda in Kabul and in a safe-house provided by the Haqqani clan, exposes the hollowness of the Taliban regime, on the most critical parameter. Apart from this, recent frequent terrorist attacks in the capital, traced to ISIS-KP, validate the presumption that the Taliban is either complicit or not in full control. As per some experts, it may even be orchestrating calibrated attacks by fringe groups. Most terrorist elements have shifting allegiance, driven less by ideology and more by egos, petty personal rivalries, and the urge to control revenue-generating sources like narco-terrorism and protection money for transit. How else can a sudden resurgence of the ISIS-KP faction be explained?

It is important to reiterate that the Taliban has many factions and Shuras, depending on tribal affinities. Mawlawi Haibatullah Akhundzada, the Emir, is confined to spiritual capital Kandahar like Mullah Mohammad Omar. He is the temporal head only, with writ limited to the interpretation and enforcement of Sharia. In the tussle between Shuras, the Haqqani clan, headed by Sirajuddin Haqqani, has cornered most spoils and portfolios. Mullah Hassan Akhund, the Prime Minister, remains in outer orbit. Kabul capital territory, scene of Zawahiri elimination and dastardly Gurdwara attacks, is controlled by the Haqqanis, indicating a serious failure in governance. **The state of the security situation is so tenuous that even the Haqqanis rushed to their cave shelters in Paktika after the drone attack.** The other

Shuras and their leaders, like two Deputy Prime Ministers Mullah Abdul Ghani Baradar and Mawlawi Abdul Salami Hanafi, Uzbek (the most significant non-Pashtun face), are all nationally represented. The alternate power centre in the Rehbari Shura is Defence Minister Mawalawi Yaqoob (Mullah Omar's son). From the Indian and global perspective, the Doha group, anchored by Mullah Baradar and moderates like the IMA-trained Sher Mohammad Stanikzai, remain on the margins.

In the Afghan game of thrones, the ultimate arbiter, the Peshawar Shura (based in HQ 11 Corps) has seen a major shake-up. **The master manipulator and Imran acolyte, Lt Gen Faiz Hameed, ex-ISI chief, has been consigned to the defensive formation, 33 Corps, at Bahawalpur. He has been replaced by Bajwa loyalist Lt Gen Sardar Hassan. Pakistan, despite protracted talks and mediations by a group of clerics led by Muhammad Taqi Usmani, has failed to work out an acceptable deal with the TTP.** There are frequent clashes on the Iran-Afghan border and on the Durand Line. Despite fencing, the TTP continues to operate on both sides. The situation is likely to get vitiated in the run-up to the polls in October.

The National Resistance Front, which had been hibernating in the Panjshir Valley and waiting for an operationally conducive summer, has not found much traction. Consequently, Tajiks, Uzbeks, Hazaras, and Ismailis remain largely unrepresented. The only hope for inclusiveness simmers in the continued presence in Kabul of former President Hamid Karzai and Abdullah Abdullah, but that is subject to the Taliban hierarchy paying some heed to them. The human rights record remains abysmal, with women pushed out of education and employment into veils and mandatory male escorts. Notwithstanding window dressing, flogging and reprisals are back in Taliban Kangaroo courts.

Acting Foreign Minister Amir Khan Muttaqi has been shuttling to Gulf capitals to push for recognition of the IEA. India, with investments of US$2 billion, is under pressure to restart work on development projects like the Shahtoot (Salma) dam. The situation has become more complex with China seeking to include India in the Afghan resolution process, notwithstanding the fact that the China-Pakistan-Russia troika spared no effort to keep India out of the Doha process, the Quadrilateral Coordination Group (QCG), the Ankara dialogue, and even regional initiatives. **Viewing from the Indian perspective, from total abhorrence to the reopening of informal contacts with the Taliban is a major and welcome step in keeping with altered realities.** India has opportunities due to a groundswell of popular acceptance, yet we can proceed only with caution and after due diligence.

Update: May 2025

- The Taliban continues to be in power, having completed two years plus in 1.1 mode. It has failed to implement the three conditions of stable and inclusive democracy, zero tolerance to terrorism, and basic human rights, especially for women and children, as well as no reprisals.
- Taliban affiliated staff have taken over the Afghan embassy in New Delhi, and India maintains a non-diplomatic presence in Kabul.
- Pakistan continues to grapple with the TTP and has lost a significant part of its leverage.
- India has gained some leverage through relief and rehabilitation help. It has also maintained its presence without receiving diplomatic recognition. It has allowed Taliban-affiliated diplomats to assume control by easing out earlier Ashraf Ghani-appointed staff.
- China-Pakistan and Afghanistan, in a trilateral agreement, decided to extend the CPEC to Afghanistan.

Indus Water Treaty

13.1 Leveraging the Indus Water Treaty (IWT): A Realistic Appraisal (Written in 2017)

Update

- After the Pahalgam terror attack, India decided to hold IWT in abeyance.
- India also stopped exchanging hydrological (water flow) data, adding to uncertainty and psychological leverage.
- India also carried out the flushing of the Salal, Baglihar (both on the Jhelum), and Kishenganga reservoirs. Later, it closed the barrage to restrict the supply of water.
- India also decided to expedite projects under construction and revive stalled projects.

For some time, India has been trying a firmer approach with Pakistan to increase the cost it must bear for supporting cross-border terrorism. The surgical strikes, heavier retaliation to cross-border firing, and similar activities are a manifestation of the hard line adopted in New Delhi. However, it doesn't seem to have the desired effect on Pakistan. This article examines the potential of the use of water as a weapon and explains the current arrangements in place, and suggests certain augmentations on the Indian side within the ambit of the IWT.

The Indus Water Treaty (IWT) has been under much debate and is being touted as an ultimate leverage to choke Pakistan, setting the stage for a call for the use of water as a weapon. **Former Pakistani President Pervez Musharraf, in his thesis at the Royal College of Defence Studies (RCDS), had identified water as the most likely flashpoint between India and Pakistan. More than the potential and morality of water as a weapon, it is the attendant capability in terms of dams and storage, which needs to be realistically appraised.** The question that begs an answer is, even if we want to, can we do it? Any renegotiation of IWT is likely to bring in China and Afghanistan, as well as new issues like climate control. The answer lies in an ancient Chinese proverb, 'hide your shine, bide your time', implying work within the treaty norms but utilise in-built provisions.

The Indus River basin comprises Pakistan – 47%, India – 39%, Tibet (China) – 8%, and Afghanistan – 6%. India is really a middle riparian state for the Indus and the Sutlej. The other rivers—Jhelum, Chenab, Ravi, and Beas—originate in India.

The World Bank-brokered treaty signed in 1960 allocated rivers in two groups, i.e., Eastern: Ravi, Beas, and Sutlej, amounting to 33 million acre feet (MAF), which was entirely allocated to India, and Western: Indus, Jhelum, and Chenab, totalling 135 MAF, mainly allocated to Pakistan. India has rights on western rivers in terms of 'run of the river' power projects, irrigation, and flood control upto specified limits, which are shown in the tables. While our share prima facie may appear skewed, the utilisation is even more worrying. With a less water-intensive horticulture-based economy in the Kashmir

Valley, potential really lies in hydro-power and inter-basin transfer to quench water-stressed Punjab and Haryana.

Share: Western Rivers

River	Storage**	Power**	Flood Control**	Total**
Indus	0.25	0.15	Nil	0.40
Jhelum	0.50	0.25	0.75	1.50
Chenab	0.50	1.20	Nil	1.70
Total	1.25	1.60	0.75	3.60

*(** All figures in MAF)*

Power Utilisation: Western Rivers

Executed**	Under Construction**	Planned**	Total Allocated **	Total Utilised and Planned**
3034	2526	5046	18600	11406 (61.33%)

*(*All figures in MW)*

Analysis of eastern rivers reveals that every year, nearly 1 MAF of water flows out from the Ravi to Pakistani Punjab, and 1,000 cusecs (0.0019 MAF) from the Sutlej at Husainiwala. It is important that we build the physical wherewithal in terms of storage for positive control as a strategic capability. This has been grossly lacking because of interstate disputes, and it is to the credit of the Central Government that in March 2017, it pushed the contending parties into an agreement. The dispute over the Ravi has been regarding the Shahpur Kandi dam since 1999. Punjab and J&K governments have not been able to resolve issues of compensation, power, and water distribution. **In a welcome development, the project has been designated as a centrally monitored one, with 90% funding by the**

Centre. Punjab has agreed to provide 180 MW of power at ₹3.50 per unit to J&K. In addition, the Jammu region will get 1,150 cusecs of water, boosting irrigation and enhancing the defence potential of the Upper Tawi link canal. Armed with a positive nod from the new Punjab Government, the Centre needs to ensure fast-track and time-bound execution. We should take this forward by harnessing minor rivers like Degh (Basantar), Ujh, Tarnah, and Bein, as water increases the obstacle potential in the strategically important Shakargarh bulge and aids infiltration into the Samba-Kathua Corridor.

The Sutlej is not a major problem, as the reasons for water flowing to Pakistan include leakage because of the lack of maintenance of antiquated sluice gates at Husainiwala and silting of the Harike reservoir. Once again, the Central Government has brokered a much-delayed agreement, and now, Rajasthan and Punjab have agreed to fund their respective shares. This must be followed up with de-weeding Hycinth from Harike, which has gobbled up approximately 80% of the storage capacity. Repairs of headworks and de-silting of all reservoirs, Gobind Sagar (Bhakra), Maharana Pratap Sagar (Pong), and Ranjit Sagar (Thein) are overdue. There is a strong case for raising Ecology (Dredging) TA battalions for de-silting to augment storage, which can be utilised for inter-basin transfer and flood control. It may be relevant to mention that a push forward on clearances has been assisted by the army flagging the issue repeatedly and providing impartial data with evidence.

The western rivers for us are mainly the Chenab and Jhelum, as the Indus has only limited potential, yet it needs to be optimally harnessed. Dynamism manifesting in recent clearances to Sawalkot, Pakad, Dul, and Bursar on Chenab should lead to a mission-mode approach. The 'go-ahead' to fill Kishenganga storage is another welcome move and is an appropriate message to the Chinese engaged in competitive hydrographic counter-action at the Neelum Valley project for Pakistan. It's time we accelerate the Tulbul project on the Jhelum for flood control and navigation, building on the only issue of convergence amongst opinion makers in the valley. There is a need to improve the silt disposal of existing reservoirs on Chenab, Salal, Baglihar, and Dulhasti, especially Salal, which is because of sub-optimal design agreement.

Mercifully, our hydrographers have catered for such upgradation. Envisaged projects are well within our allocated share, and we should continue to execute our plans, disregarding the delaying tactics by Pakistan. **Despite huge technological challenges, it is time to examine the possibility of inter-basin transfer of some of our balance share (approximately 20,000 cusecs or 0.04 MAF) from the Chenab to Ravi-Beas through tunnels to avert a looming water crisis in the northern region. India, with 17% of the world's population, has only a 4% water share and a storage of barely 90 days compared to two years in some countries.**

A popular Pakistani folk ditty describes the centrality of water in Pak Punjab, '*Ravi vichon waghan teen naharan, do sukiyan, teh teeji waghe hi nah* (from Ravi flow, three canals, two are dry and the third one doesn't even flow).' In a water-stressed economy with groundwater receding to alarming levels, we need to build our capability on a war footing to include dams, reservoirs, and maintain existing ones to harness a legitimate share of water to exercise positive control. While dams are not in sync with new ecological narratives, they have their strategic relevance as China is planning a bouquet of three dams on the Indus for Pakistan as part of the CPEC. **In times to come, for keeping its canals flowing, Pakistan should be forced to introspect and improve its relations with its upper riparian neighbour.**

13.2 Reappraisal of the Indus Water Treaty (IWT) (Written in March 2020)

Update:

- **The IWT meetings and consultation, which had recommenced in March 2020, were suspended again in 2023. Meetings were held** in 2021 and 2022 (22–23 March at New Delhi). The suspension happened after Pakistan insisted on invoking the Permanent Court of Arbitration in The Hague, even when a concurrent mechanism of a neutral expert was initiated. India termed it a dilatory tactic by Pakistan and has boycotted it.

- India issued a notice to Pakistan on 25 January 2023 that it intends to modify the existing IWT as per Article XII (3). India asserted that Pakistan has refused to resolve the Kishenganga and Ratle projects for the last five years.

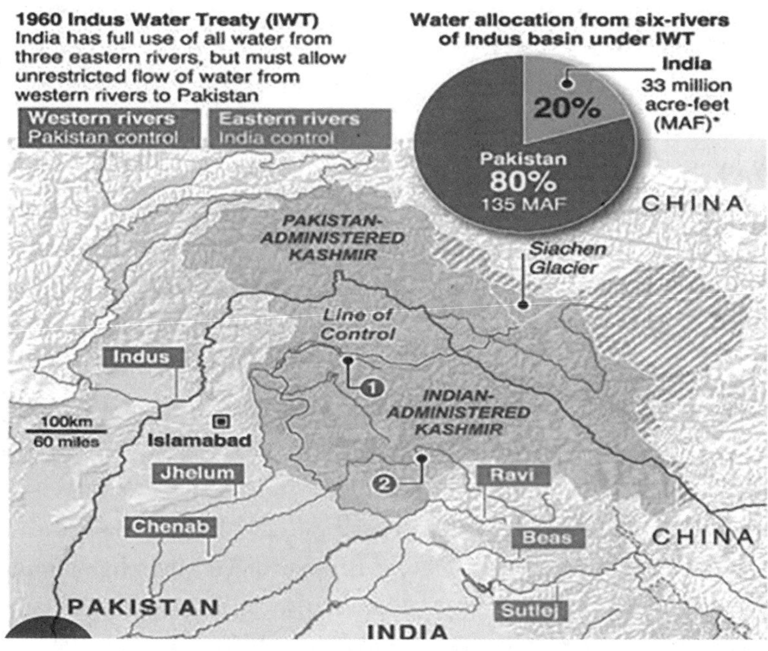

https://images.app.goo.gl/9uk8XB87gxCh42B37 Kishenganga 2- Ratle (Chenab)

India and Pakistan resumed periodic consultations on the IWT after a gap of nearly eighteen months. The last meeting was held on 30–31 August 2018 in Lahore. This gap was officially ascribed to the COVID pandemic. Notwithstanding this explanation, the hiatus was consequent to the Balakot strikes of February 2019, the abrogation of

Article 370, and the recall of High Commissioners by both sides. The 116th meeting of the Permanent Indus Commission, anchored by Indus Commissioners of both nations, met in New Delhi on 23–24 March 2020 and held consultations.

The main item on the agenda was planned by India on the Chenab River and its tributaries. The focus in the last two meetings has been on the designs of Pakkal Dul (1,000 MW) and Lower Kalnai (48 MW). These talks followed an agreement on a ceasefire on the LAC between both sides on 4 March 2020. The obvious question is: is this part of a larger rapprochement or at least recalibration, after relations had touched the very 'nadir'?

The specific issues related to the IWT merit detailed analysis. Can there ever be a 'win-win' formulation under this treaty, originally slanted in favour of the lower riparian state? Alternatively, driven by looming water scarcity in India, with the lowest per capita water availability, will it become a more potent instrument, in the quiver of leverages, for the upper riparian nation? It is relevant to draw attention to the thesis submitted by Brig (later Gen) Pervez Musharraf, during a course at the RCDS, surmising that water will indeed be the primary 'casus belli' for the next round of Indo-Pak conflict.

The mature and compliant Indian response to the IWT needs to be contrasted with reports of Chinese plans of constructing a 1,100 km channel linking the Yarlung Tsangpo (Brahamputra) with the Taklamakan Desert. As an upper riparian state, China has set a very poor example in the Mekong River projects, thereby starving downstream delta countries. China is also anchoring mega hydel projects on the Indus, like Daimer-Basha and Kohala on the Jhelum as part of the CPEC.

The Chinese quest for clean water in Shaksgam for proposed silicon chip projects has been cited, among possible reasons, for the recent incursion in Ladakh. There was also hype on the river manipulation project in Galwan. India had already been administered periodic jolts of Chinese high-handedness as an upper riparian, during the Pare-chu deluge in the Sutlej in 2000, and more recently, the

Brahmaputra floods, even after express agreement and funding on the sharing of hydrological data. After opacity and denials, China seems to be revealing its intentions on a water war with India.

The IWT has survived three and a half wars and an unabated proxy war, logging more than 50 years of uneasy existence. Brokered by the World Bank, supporters of the treaty describe it as 'uninterrupted and un-interruptible'. Like many relics of the Nehruvian era, steeped in liberalism, it was in an era when water wars were not even thought of.

The IWT is a complex bundle of paradoxes. Despite the Kashmir war of 1947–1948 and Pakistan's dalliance with Naga rebels (Phizo escaping to London through East Pakistan in December 1956), the treaty invested in hope, magnanimity, and development to cement relations. **IWT enabled the construction of the Bhakra, Pong, and Ranjit Sagar dams, and the Rajasthan canal. It triggered the green revolution, helping India overcome its 'ship to mouth' and PL-480 existence.** How can we forget the Monday fast in the '60s, when the nation had a serious food crisis?

Critics blame the Indian hierarchy for not leveraging the upper riparian status and bartering away rights of three western rivers (Indus, Jhelum, and Chenab), in lieu of exclusive rights of three eastern rivers (Ravi, Beas, and Sutlej). In effect, it amounted to a 135 MAF (80.2%) share to Pakistan, compared with 33 MAF (less than 20%) for us. India also agreed to contribute 83 crores (in pounds sterling) towards the construction of dams and replacement canals in Pakistan.

Ironically, in Pakistan, surviving on a Punjab-centric, agrarian economy, there were prolonged protests describing the treaty as a complete sell-out. Considering a non-water-intensive, horticulture-based economy in Kashmir, coupled with challenges of tapping western rivers upstream, it was probably logical to tap western rivers through Tarbela and other dams in Pakistan and construct canals to link Marala to the Ravi and Balloki barrage to Suleimanki. Counter viewpoint, to some extent, is driven by hindsight, which comes with 20/20 vision.

Riled by Pakistan's engineered fasaadi agenda and consternation due to lack of dissuasive measures, there have been desperate demands for abrogation of the treaty and sloganeering like, 'terror and water should not be allowed to flow together'. There is a demand for the revocation of the treaty and choking Pak Punjab of much-needed water. **A mini trailer was flashed in 2008 with the filling of the Baglihar reservoir on the Chenab. Though well within the treaty norms, as per Pakistani media, it resulted in an estimated 30% crop loss. We may discount it as Pakistani hype, but it is beginning to pinch, and Sawalkote and other dams may really hurt.** The Indian position is justified by floods in Pakistan and a large amount of water running off through the Indus basin to the Arabian Sea, primarily due to poor basin management. In any case, in a highly skewed treaty, we are entitled to optimise our allocations.

The reality check on emotive exhortations throws up a few interesting pointers on the need for calibration and well-considered actions. The following need careful consideration:

- **Firstly, the treaty has no exit clause and the only remedy lies in invoking, the most rarely utilised provisions of the law of treaties under the Vienna Convention.**
- **Secondly, any attempt to renegotiate requires bipartisan agreement. Pakistan would draw in China and probably even Afghanistan (Taliban controlled) as co-riparian states. The China factor is already manifesting in CPEC hydel projects on the Indus and Jhelum in GB and PoK.**
- **Thirdly, it is elementary that stopping water without building reservoirs can only be an unmitigated disaster. Building capacities in the challenging terrain of the Indus basin, especially western rivers, is a time- and resource-intensive exercise.**
- **Fourthly, hydel dams had literally gone out of fashion after the Tehri dam and other such disasters.**

The most important and harsh truth is that we have failed to utilise the full potential of legitimately allocated eastern rivers and allowed annually approximately 5 MAF of precious water to flow downstream to Pakistan due to inter-state bickering. **However, the saving grace is that the Central Government has stepped in and is working on a much-delayed balancing reservoir at Shahpur Kandi on the Ravi, which has gathered pace and is nearly 60% complete.** It is hoped that the project will be functional by 2023.

Update: The project has missed another deadline, and it appears that it may get completed by mid-2024 only.

It is also heartening that satellite projects on smaller rivers like the Basantar (Degh) and Tarnah are being given the much-needed push. Long overdue repairs of the regulator mechanism at Husainiwala headworks are nearing completion. Hopefully, more water from the Sutlej will reach legitimate recipients, farmers in Rajasthan, rather than being wasted across. In a welcome departure, the Centre has not only given impetus but also assumed ownership through funding.

Our record on western rivers remains uninspiring, primarily due to repeated obstacles created by Pakistan through the IWT, also coupled with a lack of concerted action by us. The IWT permits India to create storage on the western rivers of 1.25, 1.60, and 0.75 MAF for general, power, and flood storage, respectively, amounting to a total permissible storage of 3.6 MAF. It does not stipulate that India deliver assured quantities of water to Pakistan; instead, it requires India to allow flow to Pakistan, the water available in these rivers, excluding the limited use permitted to India by the treaty. There are no quantitative limits to the hydro power generation, utilising the western rivers, nor any limit to the number of run-of-the-river projects upstream. For general, power, and flood storage amounting to a total permissible storage of 3.6 MAF, India has built no storage and is yet to utilise its entitlement, even partially. Further, of the 1.34 million acres permitted for irrigation, India is using only 0.792 million acres. Out of an assessed potential of 18,653 MW, projects worth only 3,264 MW have been commissioned so far.

The Salal project near Reasi, on the Chenab, has serious silting-related issues due to Pakistan's obduracy in design formulation; it is likely to manifest in Baglihar also. Faced with a similar challenge, the iron brother of Pakistan, China, has carried out blasts in the Sanmenxia dam to flush out silt. Notwithstanding Pakistan's obscurantist behaviour, our hydrographic designers have incorporated de-silting plugs in even vintage dams, like Salal, which will hopefully be activated in the future to drain the silt.

The IWT, in its conception, while outlining differing perspectives, mandated the need for sound, economical, and efficient designs, even in an era when issues like climate change, de-silting, livelihood, and non-consumptive usage were not critical. These issues of navigation and livelihood have been highlighted in the stalled Wullar barrage (Tulbul navigation project) for minimum draught in the Jhelum. Notwithstanding Pakistan's delaying tactics, leveraging dispute resolution mechanisms, such as arbitration and even the ICJ, it has only managed some minor tweaks on the run-of-river projects like Kishenganga. In almost all cases, the Indian stand has been upheld; however, this has caused considerable time and attendant cost escalation penalties. **We need to push ahead with Pakkaldul, Lower Kalnai, Sawalkot, Ratle, and Bursar, as even with these projects, total utilisation, out of the potential 18,600 MW of power, will only be enhanced to approximately 62%. Concurrently, India has utilised a very small portion of the agreed storage of 3.6 MAF.**

India, with 17% of the global population, has barely 4% fresh water reserves. Even by optimistic projections, we have only 90 days' reserves compared to many countries boasting of two years' worth of reserves. Reports of Chinese plans to construct a 1,100 km channel linking the Yarlung Tsangpo (the Brahamputra) with the Taklamakan Desert, should inspire us to take on the Chandrabhaga tunnel project for inter-basin transfer from the Chenab. It will be fair to surmise that the IWT, though suboptimal, can be better harnessed to optimise benefits through sustained focus. In sum, we should discard emotive distractions and focus on building hydrological infrastructure to tap our legitimate share of allocations under the IWT. The Central Government has taken appropriate initiatives, and they must be followed through.

13.3 Shahpur Kandi – Inching Towards Indo-Pak Water Wars?

Media reports built great hype on the completion of the Shahpur-Kandi Project (SKP) with a catchy headline of India stopping the flow of water of the Ravi River to Pakistan. Pakistani newspaper Dawn had reported that filling up of the reservoir for the Baglihar dam (on the Chenab) in 2008 had resulted in 30% crop loss in Pakistan. **For Pakistan, the Ravi is the River of Punjab and Lahore.** The famous gazhal by Pakistani singer Sajjad Ali sums it up poignantly, '*Jeh Ravi which Pani koi na, teh apni kahani koi na*', meaning: 'if there is no water in Ravi, we have no story to tell'. The obvious question is: are we heading towards Indo-Pak water wars?

The SKP Project

Objective assessment indicates that 98% work is complete. The filling of the reservoir has commenced, and it will take two to three months to fill up the reservoir, for the projected water level, for power-generation requirements. Recently constructed dams and reservoirs have been the missing parts of the Ranjit Sagar dam (RSD) at Thein. RSD was commissioned in 2001, after an inter-state agreement in 1979. The scheme was upgraded to a national project in 2008, but work commenced in 2013, only to get stalled in 2014. The Centre had to step in in 2018 to resolve a festering dispute between Punjab and J&K.

Balancing reservoirs in a large dam system are an essential pre-requisite for exercising positive control on water flowing downstream. SKP, 11 km from Thein, is a multipurpose project and includes two hydel projects (55.5 m height) with installed capacity of 206 MW. It seeks to check the uncontrolled flow of water (approximately 2 MAF) to Pakistan and harness it for irrigation. It is projected to supply 1,150 cusecs of water for irrigating 32,173 hectares in the Kandi belt of Kathua and Samba through the Main Ravi Canal. The earlier tedious method of lifting water into the Tawi Lift Canal will be simplified with a gravity feed. **Regulated water supply in canals will bolster the defence potential of the vulnerable Kathua-Samba Corridor.** J&K will also get a 20% share of power. Punjab, besides getting 80% power, will draw water to irrigate an additional 5,000 hectares. The balancing reservoir will also optimise water supply to the Upper Bari Doab Canal (UBDC), which was erratic and inefficient, conditioned by power generation considerations.

Ravi River – Water Utilisation

The IWT allows India to utilise the waters of three western rivers: Ravi, Beas, and Sutlej. As per some estimates, 95% of the water would be utilised, but some water, especially in the rainy season, would still flow to Pakistan. The Ravi basin includes many tributaries, like Ujh, which join after transiting through the Shakargarh bulge in Pakistan. A follow-up project at Makaura-Pattan in Gurdaspur is envisaged to further impound approximately 600 cusecs of water for irrigation and drinking water supply. Punjab had asked for central funding of 412 crore in 2019. Haryana has even pitched for an ambitious link canal, like the Sutlej Yamuna Link (SYL), from the proposed dam to Harike to boost water supply downstream.

The Ravi is a trans-border river, defining 70 km of the Indo-Pak border, and is notorious for shifting its course. It is resuscitated in Pakistan by link canals transferring water from the Marala Dam, on the Chenab. It also provides a number of enclaves to both sides. These can be utilised as launch pads, as they obviate the need to fight tricky river-crossing operations. Defences are supplemented with DCBs. **Hydrological control of the Ravi definitely aids operational plans.**

Criticality of Water Management

India has the lowest per-capita fresh water availability, with barely 4% fresh water reserves for 17% of the global population, creating severe water stress. Even by optimistic projections, we have only 90 days' reserves, compared to many countries boasting of two years' worth of reserves. Fresh water is becoming a much sought-after resource as it is required in large quantities for silicon chip fabrication. **Chinese aggressive forays to control the 'Water table of Asia' in Tibet are ascribed to looming water stress and ambitious plans for chip manufacturing.**

China enjoys upper riparian leverage on our major rivers like the Indus, Sutlej, and Brahmaputra. The Dragon has a very dubious record of opacity and refusal to share even mandated data. **It was accused of triggering the Pare-chu deluge in the Sutlej in 2000 and the Brahmaputra floods in 2020.** It is reportedly building the Yarlung-Zangbo dam on the Tsangpo (Brahmaputra) with plans to build a 1,100 km long channel to the Taklamakan Desert. Climate change-induced melting of glaciers is further curtailing the availability of water. Pervez Musharaff, in his RCDS course thesis, had inferred that water will be the next trigger for an Indo-Pak conflict. Both countries face unresolved domestic inter-state water disputes, like the Cauvery and SYL in India, as well as Kalabagh and Kohala in Pakistan. The abysmal track record of water management in Pakistan is reflected in periodic floods, most notably debilitating deluge in 2022, and the build up of salinity in the Indus basin.

Dysfunctional IWT

The IWT mandated 85% share of the Indus basin to Pakistan, with near-total share of the three western rivers, the Indus, Jhelum, and Chenab. **Notwithstanding, pronounced tilt towards Pakistan, mercifully, it allows India to build storage for run-of-river projects for power generation and livelihood issues like the Tulbul Navigation project (Wullar barrage) on the Jhelum, as well as flood control, etc.** India can build a storage of 3.6 MAF and has the potential to generate 18,653 MW power, whereas our current utilisation is barely 0.75 MAF (31%) storage and 3,264 MW (17%) hydro-power. Pakistan's obduracy is resulting in a delay in de-silting operations in existing IWT dams, notably Salal (Reasi) on the Chenab.

Belated Indian efforts like the Kishenganga project and the Ratle dam on the Chenab have been dragged by Pakistan, concurrently before the Court of Arbitration and neutral experts. India has refused to be party to such filibustering and concurrent dispute resolution mechanisms. Resultantly, the annual meeting of the IWT Commission has become irregular since the Uri (2016) and Pulwama (2019) attacks, with demands that the IWT should be scrapped. The last IWT meeting was held in May 2022. In January 2023, India gave the notice for the modification of the treaty. **The key requirement is to convince Pakistan to allow India to harness its agreed potential on western rivers.** India has a number of projects on the Chenab, like Ratle, Pakkal Dul, Kiru, and Bursar in the pipeline. **Even bigger challenge is to convince China to behave as a responsible upper riparian state.** It is time China treats the water table as a global or Asian common and shares it equitably.

13.4 Review of the Indus Water Treaty (IWT)

Participating in seminars on the IWT, I feel that **we still don't take the criticality of water stress as a serious issue. Our thinking is clouded by emotions and spirituality. The harsh reality is that with a 17% and increasing population, India has barely a 4% share of global fresh water resources. We have just 90 days' reserves of water, whereas many countries boast of two years' worth. China, with 16% population, has 6% share and is engaged in unlocking the largest water column in Tibet.** To redress uneven distribution, China is building mega dams and diverting rivers to the Taklamakan Desert. Fresh water is required in copious quantities for chip fabrication. In addition, hydro-power as a clean source of energy, is back in reckoning as long as environmental and seismic hazards are taken care of. The looming water crisis is accentuated by pollution in our rivers and the failure to clean them.

IWT – Historical Context

The treaty signed in 1960 was a continuation of the c... creating two nations, both heavily dependent on agrar... roject of with a marked tilt towards the lower riparian state... omies, **approximately 19.8% (33 MAF), and Pakistan received 80... got 135 MAF). India was given exclusive control over three eastern ...s (the Sutlej, Beas, and Ravi) to cater to the needs of the Chadi... (rising) Punjab. Pakistan was allocated three western ones (the Indus, Jhelum, and Chenab) with India getting just the minimal share in these rivers for domestic, non-consumptive, agricultural use and hydro-power generation.** The share was capped at 3.6 MAF, further sub-divided category-wise in these rivers. The overall theme was 'run-of-river' projects, in a less water-intensive horticulture-based economy of J&K. Pakistan, in turn, constructed dams likeMarala and Panjnad to transfer water through link canals for Lehanda (retreating) Punjab. India even funded 83 crores (in pounds sterling) for canal construction under treaty obligations.

India, battling ship to mouth, PL-480 regime, constructed the Gobind-Sagar (Bhakra-Nangal), Pratap-Sagar (Pong), and Ranjit-Sagar (Thein) dams to usher in the green revolution. **However, considerable water, approximately 2 MAF, continued flowing to Pakistan through the Ravi due to the absence of a balancing reservoir as an adjunct to the Ranjit-Sagar dam. In addition, leaking sluice-gates (now repaired) at Husainiwala barrage added to Pakistan's illegal share. There is considerable progress towards the operationalisation of the balancing reservoir and Shahpur-Kandi dam on the Ravi River.** The reservoir is under testing, and the powerhouse is nearing completion. The issue has such an emotive connection that premature completion was announced last year before elections.

Status of the Treaty

The IWT has been touted as a unique example of hydr... maturity that has survived three and a half conflicts a...

an unending proxy war fueled by Pakistan. India, impor riparian, despite having been forced into an unequal as th displayed significant accommodation. **This stands out in tre ontrast to China, whose hydro-hegemony bordering on st onsibility, manifested in shattering the agro-economy of lower riparian states of the Mekong Delta.** The Indus and utlej originate in Tibet, and India has faced a China-triggered Pare-chu deluge in 2000, besides floods in the Brahmaputra. Apart from this, after the Galwan incident, China rescinded on providing even hydrographic data, despite clear agreement and funding by India. Much bigger hydrographic challenges await us and Bangladesh, with China pushing ahead with the mega Zangbo dam on the Siang tributary of the Brahmaputra (Yarlung Tsangpo). Unfortunately, our defensive measure to create a reservoir to absorb potential hydro-bombs seems to still be caught up in land acquisition hurdles.

Stalled IWT

India served a second notice to Pakistan on 30 August 2024 for reviewing and modifying the 64-year-old treaty. This was the second notice after the first formal one on 25 January 2023, two days before CoA hearings. The trigger for these has been Pakistan, which concurrently invokes the intervention of Court of Arbitration (CoA) even when the matter is under consideration with a Neutral Expert (NE). Pakistan's obduracy has been flagged with the NE ruling on 20 January 2025 that he is competent to adjudicate issues raised by Pakistan, thereby vindicating the Indian stand. Meanwhile, India has been boycotting CoA proceedings. It also raises questions about the World Bank, which has enabled and anchored the treaty. **hy has the World Bank allowed concurrent application of two te resolution mechanisms and not adopted the stipulated ial process?**

The IWT is administered through Permanent Commissions in both countries with annual and periodic meetings, averaging two per year. However, this process got suspended for three years between August 2018 and March 2021, after terrorist attacks, though the hiatus was partially attributed to COVID-19. The mechanism is again stalled after the 118th meeting in May 2022. Notwithstanding the commonly articulated lament about the absence of an exit clause in the IWT, Article XII (3) of the treaty does allow modifications, albeit in the case of significant changes in treaty conditions. **The parliamentary Standing Committee in August 2021 strongly advocated a review of the treaty, flagging climate change, global warming, and advancement in technology as the key drivers.**

India has been forced to seek review due to the dilatory tactics of Pakistan, which have delayed our projects and resulted in cost escalation. Pakistan objected to the Reasi and Baglihar dams on the Chenab, necessitating design modifications. The Tulbul Navigation (Wullar Barrage) project and the Kishenganga project on the Jhelum were also disputed by Pakistan. The latter was even dragged to CoA, where India got a largely favourable verdict. Once again, Pakistan has raised objections to the Ratle and other projects on the Chenab and Kishenganga despite the CoA resolution.

Way Forward

It is time we realise the criticality of water stress and conserve and clean our rivers. We should push forward planned projects on the western rivers under the IWT to utilise our mandated share. The current power generation of 3,200 MW is barely 18% of the planned potential. Finally, in transactional Trump world, a review of unequal IWT is long overdue.

BUCKET LIST

Activities to be taken up on priority

- Flushing and desilting of dams at regular intervals
- Revival of the Tulbul Navigation Project
- Immediately taking up works on Wuller lake and Jhelum for better flood management
- Ensure more water for Jammu region through existing Ranbir and Pratap canals
- Study feasibility of lift projects which may take water quickly and effectively to deficit zones
- Exploring how surplus flows can be redirected from J&K to Punjab, Haryana, and Rajasthan to balance regional water availability

Steps to prioritise hydro-power projects in J&K

Four under construction projects to be taken up as top priority

Project	In MW
Pakal Dul	1,000
Ratle HEP	850
Kiru HEP	624
Kwar HEP	540

Works on clearance bottleneck of three projects through judicious review

Project	In MW
Sawalkote HEP	1,856
Kirthai HEP	930
Uri-I HEP	240

Stepping up survey and investigation

Dulhasti (Stage-II) 260 MW

(Graphic – Courtesy TOI – 23 May 2025)

Proxy War in J&K

14.1 Key Statistical Data

Update: Please read 2.1, 2.2 and 2.3 covering Pahalgam terrorist attack and Operation Sindoor.

Terrorist Attacks

Year	Incidents-Killings	Civilians	Security Forces	Terrorists/ Collaborators	Not Specified	Total
2000**	1910	1260	573	2260	28	4121
2001	2802	1508	883	3005	108	5504
2002	2329	1255	721	2454	181	4611
2003	2321	1280	524	2328	216	4348
2004	1679	849	531	1466	134	2980
2005	1750	1105	439	1584	111	3239
2006	1376	966	400	1283	146	2795
2007	1290	932	439	1219	113	2703
2008	1122	915	366	1232	92	2605
2009	1158	685	435	1112	31	2263
2010	864	757	359	747	21	1884
2011	555	393	199	465	02	1059
2012	539	274	132	429	02	837
2013	442	308	177	386	02	873
2014	523	400	167	441	04	1012
2015	437	176	152	398	03	729
2016	492	204	178	525	00	907
2017	443	202	172	437	01	812
2018	478	217	183	540	00	940
2019	332	159	132	330	00	621

2020	299	100	106	385	00	591
2021	314	116	104	365	00	585
2022	281	99	47	267	01	414
2023	281	151	82	230	06	469
2024	278	165	53	404	04	626
2025££	87	52	28	273	03	356
Total ££	24395	14522	7528	24562	1210	47876

*** – From March 2000 ££ – Upto 17 March 2025*

Source – https://www.satp.org/datasheet-terrorist-attack/fatalities/india

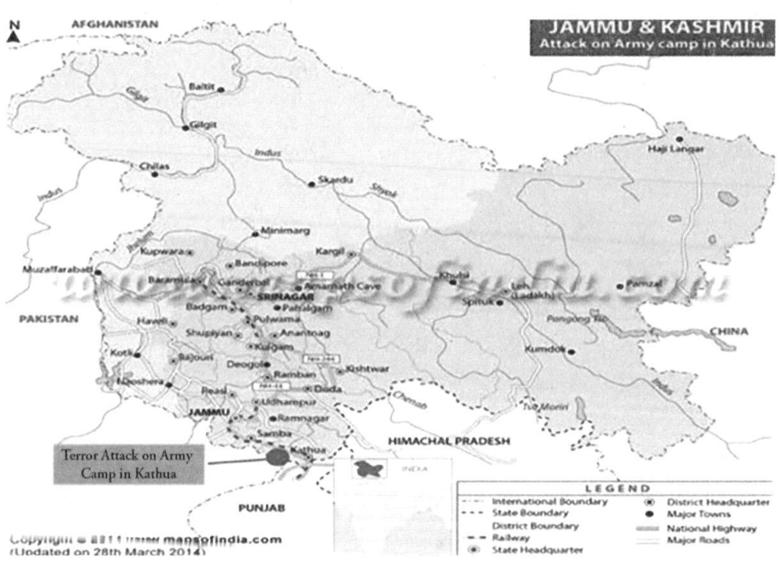

14.2 Mediators Need to Be Experts Sans Government Links (Written in November 2017)

The journey of Indian nationhood has been tumultuous, punctuated by many internal conflicts. The Naga insurgency erupted in the '50s, followed by equally violent movements in the entire North-East. The Naga movement has the dubious distinction of being a perpetually festering problem, which, despite 67 years and three agreements, is still to find closure. The ongoing proxy war in Kashmir is the most severe challenge, keeping the nation literally on the edge with frequent skirmishes in the valley and daily TV encounters.

Separatist elements in peripheral areas leverage centrifugal forces generated by alienation and ethnic as well as theological fault lines. They draw ready sustenance and support from Pakistan and China. Sporadic incidents of Islamist terrorism and still simmering left-wing extremism have kept even the hinterland in a state of turmoil. In this maze of multiple insurgencies, the success rate in terms of conflict resolution remains very poor, and the only notable positives have been Mizoram and Punjab. Putting Laldenga, an insurgent leader, in charge as Chief Minister was an imaginative stratagem.

In Punjab, security forces, especially the Punjab Police, were given a free hand. But regardless of the recent success in Sri Lanka, the hard power-centric model is an extreme option. It is difficult to analyse various conflicts to prescribe a common template for resolution, yet there is a need to have a discussion on an indicative model. Though neither discreet nor well-defined, most conflicts tend to follow stages like initiation, escalation, stabilisation, recession, resolution, and closure. These phases get complicated as they often overlap and stage a comeback, much like the painful relapse after sickness.

Well-synergised security agencies, when given operational freedom, invariably stabilise the situation and put it in a recession loop. The timespan varies as per the complexity, severity of the conflict, and operational parameters. The frustrating reality is that the response to conflict meanders along without a clear-cut road map, especially in the socio-political domain. Often, it is a story of missed opportunities and 'deja vu'. Invariably, after appreciable improvement in the security situation, premature relaxations and a lack of political process led to crises, like those in South Kashmir and North Nagaland, reigniting the escalatory cycle.

The only redeeming feature is that, after twenty odd years of ceasefire in Nagaland, people have become addicted to peace, but the drift of two decades has entailed huge opportunity costs. While Nagaland has seen the demise of two leaders (Issac Swu and Khaplang) out of the original trio, with only Muivah holding the torch, with every death, new challenges spring up. There is a case for replacing the 'drift and tire out' approach with a dynamic conflict resolution model.

Critical enablers are mediators/interlocutors and the time of initiation of dialogue. It would be ideal to keep the mediation window open right from the very beginning. The ideal resident interlocutor can be the governor; hence, the need for an expert with domain competence, no previous baggage, and a father figure image. When I was a colonel in Nagaland, the army had a very meaningful relationship with Shyamal Datta, who was probably the most dedicated and clued-up governor. Yet, Naga leaders could never trust him because of his IB pedigree. Unfortunately, all parties are now using gubernatorial appointments as a sinecure or dumping ground for retired politicians, politically aligned bureaucrats, and security officials. It is axiomatic that in trouble-prone states, merit takes precedence over political affiliation.

Starting with the Naga groups, a number of monitoring mechanisms have been set up to supervise agreements with ultras. Initially, with two National Socialist Council of Nagaland (NSCN) factions, these were termed as ceasefire agreements, thereby giving needless legitimacy to the demand for a Naga nationhood. These bodies, if leveraged properly, have the potential to provide an additional channel for negotiations. While we have refined their nomenclature, there has been inadequate analysis and feedback to evolve effective mechanisms. Initially, retired army generals headed such bodies, but, of late, the police have usurped this space. Unfortunately, some appointees have very limited domain knowledge based on an odd tenure, sometimes of a dated vintage, and in a much junior capacity. Objectivity demands a mention that not all army incumbents measure up to expectations, hence the need for stringent selection.

Last in the negotiation chain are designated interlocutors; the most important ones are handling Nagaland and Kashmir, who, despite their enviable credentials, have an IB tag. The first two interlocutors in the Naga peace process were Indian Administrative Service (IAS) officials and were opposites of each other, underlining the lack of set guidelines for such appointments.

The first preferred Bangkok and visited Nagaland only when forced to accompany Swu and Muviah. The second had been the chief secretary and spoke fluent Nagamese. An interesting, though failed experiment was a three-member team in Kashmir during the UPA regime to balance intellectual, bureaucratic, and theological connections. It is difficult to prescribe a model, especially when 'horses for courses' is being replaced by 'jockeys for seasons' depending on the party in power. Yet, it is an important subject that requires research, refinement, and a national consensus.

14.3 Kashmir – Need for a Full-Spectrum Approach (Written in April 2018)

Last month has seen very intense exchanges, including artillery duels, across the LoC. It has indeed been one of the bloodiest chapters, with considerable damage to civilian lives and property. While an uneasy calm prevails, it appears that we have hit the law of diminishing marginal returns in our much-touted strategy of 'Hot LoC' and in raising the costs of proxy war. However, in the hinterland, security forces had unprecedented success, accounting for 13 terrorists at three different locations.

Every summer, 'mischief diviners' of the ISI roll out new strategies with ploys like stone-pelting (replication of the intifada) coupled with spreading the arc of terrorism to newer areas like South Kashmir and Jammu-Kathua-Samba. **Though rather early this year, a new element is manifesting in the stoning of tourists. This misguided tactic amounts to economic Harakiri and a reprehensible form of fidayeenism, dealing a twin blow to the tourism-based economy and the culture of Kashmiriyat.**

Just before the onset of summer, our think tanks indulge in intellectual 'manthan' (brainstorming) to anticipate and work out options to combat these challenges. In keeping with our reactive character, a full-spectrum, pro-active approach is seldom discussed. Panjab University (PU) organised a national-level seminar attended by the director of the Vivekanand International Foundation, the finance minister of Punjab, two army commanders, veterans, and a large number of academicians. This was followed by serious deliberations by a collegium of very senior veterans of the Tri-City area, from all three services. I found myself as a 'first termer', an army jargon to describe the juniormost, and was asked to project their collective wisdom appropriately, hence this jotting.

There was a unanimous view that the security situation is getting under control; however, significant improvement can only happen if the problem is addressed at its centre of gravity, which is the 'awaam', the people of Kashmir, hence it requires a socio-political approach. While there is a clamour to revive our past glories and legendary heroes, we seem to be missing out on eternal wisdom propounded by Kautilya. Chankaya Neeti has specified Saam (negotiations); Daam (bribe); Dand (punishment), and Bhed (intrigue) as the four essentials. Chanakya also implied that force or Dand is applied selectively by a designated functionary like Dandpal (adjutant). Kings and statesmen are supposed to be more known for Daan (largess) and Khasma (pardon). It appears that everyone has become a victim of a competitive masochistic urge to punish, and our responses, even for serious issues of conflict resolution, are becoming hostage to the TRP factor.

The Arthashastra has suggested that ideally, all instruments should be applied concurrently, and different players should play their varied roles. The optimum solution is like a complex new recipe that requires skill, experience, and a fair degree of intuitive decision-making. We have overestimated the efficacy of our 'stick' as surgical strikes and fire assaults seem to be losing their deterrent value. It is also relevant that at the other end is an obstinate Punjabi Musalman, who is a mirror image of our Punjabis, even bearing common surnames with an additional theological underpinning, which only adds shades of fanaticism to his character. An important spin-off from the recent seminar was the realisation of the imperative to study contemporary realities of the populace across. We need to build our linguistic skills, especially in Shahmukhi, without which it is impossible to understand the dynamics of regional and vernacular dialogue across the Radcliffe Line.

There is also a worrying concern with regard to our fortress mentality to protect our camps and security establishments. While some hardening is desirable, the key lies with the 'awaam', who live around these camps. Fortified by a liberal dose of Vitamin 'N' (Nationalism), the gullible public demands 'zero infiltration', losing sight of the age-old maxim that no defence line can ever stop determined terrorists of the fidayeen genre.

The incorporation of technology in camp security is most desirable, as it reduces the load on already harassed troops; yet, it is not a panacea, as gadgets have limitations. A solution based on physical hardening, surveillance, the involvement of police and the public, coupled with quick reaction teams, is recommended. Other so-called leverages have only limited efficacy. The withdrawal of the MFN status and the designation of Pakistan as a terrorist state are cosmetic measures, unlikely to yield any tangible benefits. **The threat of revocation of the IWT really amounts to playing to the gallery, as we must first create reservoirs to store water.** The recent policy initiative of a time-bound approach to push our projects, especially on the Ravi (Shahpur Kandi dam), and the repair of the leaking Husainiwala barrage, should be implemented relentlessly. In the interim, it is good to keep Pakistan engaged through the IWT to get clearances for our plans for live storage on the Chenab (Sawalkote, Pakal Dul, and Bursar dams) and Tulbul navigation project on the Jhelum River.

It is high time to apply benign and constructive 'Bhed' (intrigue) combined with 'Daam' (money) to help rightly inclined grassroots politicians to resuscitate themselves, as there is a dangerous vacuum, apportioned by anti-national elements. Cyber warfare and covert intelligence operations require long-term commitment and imaginative orchestration. **In the long run, we have to further refine our surgical strike capability to make it more lethal, precise,**

and remote. There is also an inescapable requirement to address 'hollowness' to regain a punitive edge in conventional forces and resuscitate a proactive (cold start) strategy. A full-spectrum approach with concurrent options is indeed long overdue in J&K.

14.4 Jammu & Kashmir – Paradigm Shift in Conflict Resolution (Written in August 2019)

Key Takeaway

- Most acceptable conflict resolution models entail a five-step process: Stabilisation, Engagement, Package Proposal, Negotiation, and Accord, also referred to as SEPNA.

The recent hard-line endeavours in J&K have thrown up pertinent questions on a possible paradigm shift in the application of conflict resolution models. Will a security-centric approach be the new normal? The formation of Nagaland in 1963, literally, unleashed the 'domino effect', resulting in the splintering of Assam into the seven sisters, including the grant of statehood to Union Territories like Arunachal and North-East Frontier Agency. The standard prescription to address regionalism was to create states and a plethora of autonomous regional councils—Bodo, Kachari, Kuki, etc. **Historic amendments in Articles 370 and 35-A, coupled with the downgrading of J&K to a Union Territory, amount to jettisoning the earlier trend of pandering to sub-national aspirations.** While each conflict has its own set of unique challenges, precluding templated solutions, there are a few common parameters that need to be flagged. **Conventional conflict resolution models have been characterised by steps like stabilising the security environment, engagement with groups, proposing a solution package, negotiations (often prolonged ones), and, finally, according—summed up into the acronym SEPNA.**

The Naga insurgency erupted in the '50s, followed by equally violent movements in almost the entire North-East. The Naga movement has the dubious distinction of being the perpetually festering problem. Notwithstanding many agreements, like the 16-point agreement of 1960, the Shillong accord in 1965, and the recent framework agreement in 2014, it is still to find closure. While violence in the North-East simmered down, the proxy war in Kashmir emerged as the most complex challenge, having kept the nation on the edge for three decades with frequent terrorist attacks in the valley, followed by daily court martial on TV and Twitter. Separatist elements leveraged centrifugal forces generated by alienation and ethnic/theological fault lines, drawing ready sustenance and sanctuary from external forces like Pakistan and China. **Special credit must be given to the current governments in Bangladesh and Myanmar for denying bases and flushing out ultras.**

Simmering left-wing extremism combined with the looming threat of fedayeen, has kept even the hinterland in a state of uneasy calm. In this maze of multiple insurgencies, the success rate in terms of conflict resolution remains poor, and the only notable positives have been Mizoram and Punjab—an imaginative stratagem of installing Laldenga at the helm, catalysed by the solving of the Mizo problem. Punjab has been the only successful, hard power-enabled solution, wherein security forces, especially the Punjab Police, were given free rein. Despite success against the Liberation Tigers of Tamil Eelam in Sri Lanka, the use of force remains an extreme option. Its recent application in Kashmir is due to prolonged cumulative frustration built up due to Pakistan, stymying all other options like Sadbhavana. **Yet, this model is restrained and unlike the heavy-handed approach, prevalent in the American and Pakistani armies, where gunships and heavy weapons are used freely.**

Security agencies led by the army, given operational freedom and synergy, invariably stabilise the situation and put insurgencies in a recession loop, as evidenced repeatedly in J&K and the North-East. **The frustrating reality is that the response strategy lacks a clear-**

cut roadmap, especially in the socio-political domain. More often than not, it is a story of missed opportunities and 'deja vu'. Flare-ups in south Kashmir and northern Nagaland are recent examples. The oft-repeated cliché of 'prevention is better than cure' needs to be adopted by creating a separate specialist administrative cadre dealing with national security, also endorsed by former governor, NN Vohra. It can be a contemporary version of the erstwhile Indian Frontier Administrative Services. **More importantly, the CAPFs have proved unequal to the task, forcing the Army to step in; they need to take up this challenge.**

The only redeeming feature in Nagaland is that after 20 odd years of stand-still, the populace has become addicted to peace, and this acts as a restraining influence on insurgents. Drift is also relished by agencies and forces, as it gives them relevance and unaudited funds. But the status quo needs to be broken by innovative initiatives. The impasse of two decades has imposed huge opportunity costs, reducing the 'Act East' policy to a mere paper exercise. The NSCN remains obdurate, insisting on a separate constitution and flag. The biggest challenge is to address these aspirations and yet extend a nuanced interpretation of 'one nation, one constitution' to the North-East. Financial inclusion, dismantling of extortion regime, and enabling genuine economic liberation are key challenges. There is definitely a strong case for replacing the 'drift and tiring out' approach with dynamic conflict resolution initiatives. It will be interesting to see if groups in the North-East draw any lessons from the new hard-line approach in Kashmir.

Critical enablers include mediators/interlocutors and the initiation of dialogue. It would be ideal to keep the mediation window open, allowing moderates to come on board. Nagaland also has a formal monitoring mechanism, headed by an army general. The mechanism has the most inappropriate nomenclature of 'Ceasefire Monitoring Group', giving additional legitimacy to separatists, as a ceasefire is normally between sovereign nations. Ideally, a nominated mediator should operate from the state concerned. The Naga peace process, in earlier years, was steered by a former bureaucrat who preferred Bangkok and rarely visited the North-East. The transition from non-resident Indian to resident mediator, RN Ravi, in his new role as governor, is very welcome. J&K witnessed the failed experiment of a group of interlocutors headed by Dileep Padgaonkar, aided by Radha Kumar and MM Ansari. The current interlocutor, Dineshwar Sharma, seems to have yielded ground to the governor and the National Security Advisor. **Over-reliance on former intelligence operatives requires review and balancing.**

The government, in all likelihood, has an action plan that is yet to be shared, as ambiguity seems to be the current flavour. Transparency and involvement of domain experts will not only result in value additions but will also inject certain amount of peer review and accountability.

14.5 Change in the Terror Template (Written in April 2020)

Key Takeaway

- **Pakistan seeks to retain relevance and control over the narrative to include a mix of 'kinetic' and 'non-kinetic' domains.**

As summer sets in the Kashmir Valley, Pakistan has revived its proxy war, upping the ante. The current summer, the first after the altered constitutional status of J&K, is likely to be a defining one. There is discernible desperation on the part of the ISI to alter the 'terror-scape' in terms of the organisation of tanzeems (terror groups). Concurrently, agencies across seek to tweak the template of waging the Kashmiri struggle. The picture is further bloodied by a chain of incidents in the Afghanistan-Pakistan region, with Indian connection and obvious serious ramifications for us. At this evolving stage, we can only forecast emerging likely scenarios that need rigorous monitoring to shape our response strategies.

The broad contours of underlying macro trends can be gauged from the Pakistan Army's recent publication, Green Book 2020, although such manuals are often also used as part of propaganda, serving as a smokescreen. Unmitigated hostility to India and Kashmir centricity is evident. There is a realisation of strategic milestones of Balakot and revocation of Article 370 and Section 35-A, coupled with India's hardened stance. Gen Bajwa, in his foreword, emphasises that, 'These will have a lasting imprint on the geopolitics of the region.' It chases the dream of getting India bogged down in the Kashmir quagmire. As postulated by Farzana Shah, Pakistan seeks to take the war into the 'non-kinetic domain', characterised by information, cyber, and psychological operations. The book recommends that the struggle should incorporate all these influences and be given an indigenous character, exploiting 'misinformation'.

The first indication of the reordering of structures was provided by Castellium AI, a US-based regulatory company. The internationally monitored terrorist list was halved, from 7,600 to 3,800, without any explanation by Pakistan, in April. Surprisingly, downsizing is yet to be flagged by the FATF. The listing excludes Zaki-ur-Rehman (Lakhvi), the mastermind of the 2008 Mumbai attack. Pakistan could utilises the pandemic or other ISI ploys to account for some of them before the mandated FATF review in June, postponed to September.

The ill-advised US hurry to abandon the elected government under Ashraf Ghani and hand over Afghanistan to the Taliban has opened a few other possibilities for the ISI. The most worrying is the sudden emergence of the Islamic State-Khorasan (IS-K), manifested through the dastardly attack on the historic Guru Har Rai Gurdwara in Kabul on 25 March. It was orchestrated by the newly anointed Amir, Aslam Farooqi Akhundzada, a Pakistan national and a recycled LeT operative. The terror squad purportedly included Abu Khalid al-Hindi, originally Mohammad Muhsin (28), a resident of Kasaragod in Kerala. If verified, this would make him the second Indian IS suicide bomber, after Abu Yusuf al-Hindi or Shafi Amar, eliminated in 2015. Doubts have arisen because the media had reported that

Muhsin was killed in a drone strike in 2019. It could be mischievous attempts to portray the Indian connect, as part of the misinformation campaign. Interrogation of the mastermind, Farooqi, was followed by the nabbing of the elusive Kashmiri recruiter, *Aijaz Aihangar, presumed* to be dead for two decades. The reported concentration of 50 odd Indian-origin IS operatives in the Nanganhar province and hyperactivity of its surrogate, Islamic State Hind Province, on social media is indicative of a plan to proliferate the extremist contagion of Wilayat (IS province) to include India, harking back to Gazwa-e-Hind.

The diabolical attack in Kabul, killing 25 members of the Nanak Naam Lewa sangat, has thrown up disturbing questions regarding the status of the K-2 project, linking Kashmir with Khalistan, through the Pakistan Army-orchestrated Kartarpur Sahib project. Lukewarm response of the pilgrims and the COVID crisis has acted as a dampener. The SFJ-2020 referendum has failed to find traction. Another development has been the damage to all five domes of the gurdwara due to a severe storm. It reinforces the perception of tearing hurry, lack of planning, and non-adherence to the Rehat Maryada by the FWO, in fixing flimsy fibre-glass contraptions.

The ISI controls most events in Kabul, and attempts to explain the attack as a rogue action defies logic. Many unexplained possibilities of developing IS-K as a counterweight to the Taliban, and even the addition of Khorasan in K-2, making it K-3, need monitoring. Attempts to revive militancy and smuggling of drugs and weapons, using innovative delivery means, are likely to continue, notwithstanding the recent nabbing of the Khalistan Liberation Force (KLF) associate Billa Mandiala with a cache of weapons.

LeT has been renamed The Resistance Front (TRF) to meet the twin objectives of escaping FATF scrutiny and delinking from fasaadi roots. The use of 'fasaadi' (strife creator), instead of jihadi, is well considered, as Pakistan has termed its counterterrorist operation as Raad-ul-Fasaad. The incorporation of the term 'resistance' in the TRF is designed to evoke sympathy and repackage it as a localised struggle. The inspiration is probably derived from Palestine, on the lines of stone-pelting and 'intifada'. Earlier, the JeM had renamed itself Majlis Wurasa-e-Shuhuda Jammu-wa-Kashmir (gathering of descendants of martyrs of J&K) for similar reasons. Later, JeM created new formulation of Peoples Anti-Fascist Front (PAFF).

Distinct spurt in attacks in North Kashmir, under the banner of the TRF, can be understood as a new tactic to revive insurgency, in an otherwise stabilised region. It may indicate plans to activate other dormant areas like Doda and Kathua. The morale of the security forces has been boosted by the elimination of Riaz Naikoo, commander of the Hizbul Mujahideen. As terror activities in the valley gather pace, it will be imperative to remain agile to shifting paradigms of the proxy war. It calls for better use of technology, information operations and relentless targeting of key commanders. Concurrently, the socio-political push for conflict resolution is axiomatic.

14.6 Choose 'Smart' Conflict Resolution Strategies (Written in January 2022)

Key Takeaway

- Nagaland remains the Gordian knot, defying solution; at present, insurgents are enjoying de facto powers with rampant extortion.

India is gearing up for Amrit Mahotsava, but notwithstanding celebratory fervour, many conflicts within remain unresolved. The dominant mood being self-laudatory, honest introspection is hardly the flavour of the season. Even the United States of America, despite 245 years of independence, faces new set of challenges. So, it would be appropriate for India to take objective reality check and formulate requisite conflict resolution templates.

Conflict resolution is conceptualised as a combination of methods, structures, and processes involved in the peaceful ending of conflict.

The common strategies recommended are, firstly, in the hard power domain, avoidance (back-burner approach) and quelling. Secondly, in the soft power realm, yielding, conciliation, cooperation, and competitive coexistence. My recommendation is for smart power strategy entailing focused minimal application of hard power, combined with soft power. The foremost requirement is to craft a 'win-win' strategy, based on building long-term trust. Unfortunately, most often, parties to conflict, notably insurgent groups and governments (through interlocutors) try 'smart aleck' approach, derailing the entire process.

India despite 'Bharatvarsha' and 'Akhand-Bharat' projections, suffered constraints of prolonged colonial 'divide and rule' regimes. It will be appropriate to reiterate remarks of national security advisor, Ajit Doval, 'India has always lost due to treachery and enemies within.' The sheer range of diversities and lack of linguistic glue generate fissiparous and centrifugal tendencies. According to accepted classification norms, India can, at best, be designated as a 'nation state' or 'cultural state'.

Hence, the first challenge after independence was to integrate 520 odd princely states. Despite considerable obduracy on the part of many dominions, all four elements of Saam (negotiations), Daam (inducements), Dand (punching), Bhed (intrigue) were utilised by relatively inexperienced rulers. While it has become fashionable to indulge in ruler bashing, aided by hindsight, Plebiscite in Junagarh, Operation Polo (Hyderabad-1948), and the merger of Puducherry and Goa operations (1960), are shining examples of conflict resolution. It is also important to remember that the efforts to project only Sardar Patel need to be rationalised with the fact that Patel passed away in December 1950, within 40 months of independence.

Despite resistance of the government, linguistic states had to be accepted, which nurture seeds of conflicts. The decades of '60s and '70s were dominated by external conflicts of '62, '65 and '71. These conflicts and skilful leveraging by Shastri and Indira Gandhi with slogans like 'Jai Jawan-Jai Kisan' transformed them to people's war.

They played significant cementing role in our troubled journey of forging nationhood.

Two festering fault lines, left wing extremism (LWE) and Naga insurgency, owe their origin to this period. LWE started in 1967 in Naxalbari, and despite being quelled by the army, kept simmering to manifest again in the '90s. Proxy war, often understood to be synonymous with Kashmir and Khalistan, in fact, was initiated with China and East Pakistan, providing sanctuary to Naga rebels in late '50s.

Notable silver linings are the resolution of Mizo and Punjab insurgencies. The former was a classic application of smart power, co-option, by putting Laldenga in-charge. The same has been tried in less critical situations, like Gorkhaland and All Assam Students' Union movements, where Subash Gheising and Prafulla Mohanta were mainstreamed. Ironically, all such leaders, when placed at the helm, have failed to fulfil aspirations, getting consigned to oblivion. Nagaland remains the Gordian knot, defying solution despite passing away of two (Khaplang and Isaac Swu) out of three musketeers, as Muivah continues to hold out. De jure mainstreaming of the NSCN remains the key; currently, insurgents are enjoying de facto powers with rampant extortion.

Punjab is the only example of hard power solution, albeit combined with the support of society. It is also unique because unlike other problems, the state police were empowered and the army remained in the background. It is a pity that despite massive expansion of the CAPFs and the state police, including specialised battalions and intelligence agencies, we remain hesitant to empower the khaki, heavily relying on Armed Forces. The unfortunate reality is that everyone loves simmering insurgency. It ensures flow of funds (many non-audited), rewards, and allowances for forces and agencies, and even insurgents are happy with extortion. Resolution can be expedited if normalcy is incentivised.

It would be appropriate that across the state, the application of the Disturbed Area Act (DAA) is stopped. In each designated disturbed district, the state government should yield control on the posting of deputy commissioner, senior superintendent of police, and other functionaries to joint consultative mechanism and special audit of funds by the Centre. The army should review its statistical (kills-based) citation award process in favour of normalcy parameters.

The role of society has been critical in Punjab, Mizoram, and, to a certain extent, in even Nagaland, where no rebel group can take up arms readily, as populace has literally got addicted to the ceasefire regime since 1997. It will be prudent to avoid the replication of divisive strategies for narrow and immediate political gains. Trust and normative power of societies, like Punjabis, should be consolidated and harnessed.

The creation of states with the splitting of Assam and even unmanageable number of autonomous councils has, to limited extent, satisfied aspirations of tribal satraps. However, the permanent solution lies in economic development and skill-building. The North-East, with collective tribal ownership, reserve forests, and pressure on unexploited resources is witnessing frequent armed clashes. It is imperative that issues of inter-state borders are upfront and on priority, as 'good fences make good borders'.

The functioning of the Ministry of Development of North-Eastern Region (DoNER) and the North-East Council needs to be reviewed, with bottom-up planning and genuine autonomy. The North-East Frontier Agency was managed by the Ministry of External Affairs till the '60s. We experimented with internal security division in the Ministry of Home Affairs (MHA) in the '80s. Is there a need to reorganise MHA to facilitate conflict resolution? We should also consider designating the right kind of interlocutors, as over-reliance on an intelligence background is not working.

Protection of Bases

15.1 Army Camps, Fortresses, Scapegoats, and Accountability (Written in September 2016)

Ancient scriptures articulated realistic wisdom, Veer Bhogya Vasundhara, implying that brave soldiers will enjoy the privileges of the universe. Chanakya, the wise sage, counselled rulers to look after their armies in billeting, emoluments, and privileges. Britishers, abiding by this logic, created quaint but very habitable cantonments like Mhow and Deolali with a micro-climate of their own, facilitating training and recuperation. The issue of military camps and their security has become relevant due to a reported move by the Defence Ministry to compulsorily retire some camp commanders to fix exemplary responsibility consequent to terrorist attacks.

After independence, a new set of 'paper tigers', emerging from files, decided to abandon seminal wisdom, pushing forces to peripheral areas. Consequently, the three largest post-independence military stations, Bathinda, Hisar, and Binaguri, defy all planning parameters. They have an extreme climate, debilitating humidity, and the largest one figures in the old Punjabi expression, '*via Bathinda*'. The land allocated to the army had to be reclaimed to make it even buildable. Unfortunately, after cantonments have been developed as islands of excellence, the desire now is to grab them and push the army into the wilderness.

Most camps came up in the pre-insurgency era, when security was an elementary and routine function. Our military stations have rudimentary protection in terms of cattle fencing, without even boundary walls. Apart from this, they lack a perimeter patrolling track for surveillance and quick reaction. The scenario is grave in stations located in insurgency-affected areas. Army camps are in penny packets, posing challenges in providing a separate, stand-alone security grid for each pocket. In Jammu, the army is in eight pockets, with a highway passing through them. Ill-advised settlement of Rohingyas in proximity of Sanjuwan was flagged, but dismissed; unfortunately, it served as a probable launch pad for a terrorist raid two years later.

Air force stations are comparatively better off with basic boundary walls and Defence Security Corps (DSC) pickets to protect them. The main problem is encroachments, violating statutory, 'no construction' buffer zone with high-rise constructions overlooking these vital stations. Influential parties with the right connections have stymied efforts to remove such encroachments.

A few important **parameters for camp security** are:

- First, **no camp can be impregnable, as history bears testimony to repeated breaches of even the most formidable Berlin Wall.** According to official records, more than 1,00,000 people attempted to breach the legendary wall, 5,000 succeeded, and nearly 150 lost their lives.
- Second, security requires a multi-spectrum response with a combination of technical surveillance and human element, which includes designated security and access control elements, as well as proactive involvement of all inmates.
- Third, **surveillance requires networking with the civilian populace, police, and intelligence agencies. The biggest deterrence is quick reaction and assured neutralisation, which has exponential effect.** It is best to have layered security and ideally neutralise nefarious elements even before they reach their target.
- Finally, **guard against fortress mentality,** which ties down troops in tiring, repetitive activities, thereby deflecting them from their core functions of dominating the environment and training. Such diversion furthers terrorists' design.

The crux of camp security is an inclusive, people-centric approach, which at a macro level translates into the involvement of all agencies and people. The socio-political elements must address the Kashmir problem at its core. In all hybrid war scenarios, the centre of gravity or focus must be on people, but we seem to be getting caught in a quagmire of a fortress mentality, shifting from a proactive to a defensive approach. Border guarding needs major revamping but requires complementing it with a multi-tiered deployment and the participation of all agencies.

As an Army Commander, I had to take up special drives to put together a basic semblance of perimeter security. We had depots and installations swamped by jungles. **These exercises were called Paridhi Suraksha (perimeter security) and Swacch Paridhi (clean perimeter). It simply implies keeping the perimeter clean, developing a patrolling track, dominating the periphery with training, and maintaining quick response teams.** The onerous responsibility of camp security has to be handled in 'mission mode' with all hands on board, yet not allowing it to overtake core functions. Theoretical studies with ambitious budgetary projections and skewed over-reliance on gizmos must be supplemented with short-term jugaad solutions in the current environment of budgetary choke. At best, technical solutions can only be provided in an incremental manner, and these have gestation delays. **Smart fences are effective but certainly not a panacea, and suffer degradation due to weather and require manning by trained personnel.** The need is to motivate Jagruk Hindustanis (citizen warriors) like the carpenter who detected the presence of terrorists much before Samba and vectored army reaction, disregarding personal safety.

Armed Forces, unlike most other agencies, have very rigorous norms of accountability, where justice is quick and punishment severe. In the army, a mere court of enquiry is enough to jeopardise well-honed careers and destroy reputations. Ironically, punishment is invariably diluted or set aside by Armed Forces Tribunals and courts, who give the benefit of the doubt to the accused. **Those at the helm**

must fix incorrigible ones, but more important is to nurture a climate to build leaders and guard against 'zero-error syndrome'. Responsibility in these cases is diffused and shared with elements outside the army with differential levels of accountability. Enough and more has already been meted out to camp commanders in terms of entry in their profiles, likely to impact career progression. Those advocating scapegoating may like to read the story of Col Megh Singh, creator of 'Meghdoot Force', a forerunner of special forces. Despite his court-martial, Gen Harbaksh gave him responsibility and, later, promotion for the execution of successful raids. It is hoped that wiser counsel will prevail and the issue will be left to the discretion of the services.

15.2 No Installation Can Be a Fortress (Written in February 2018)

The recent terrorist attack on the Sunjuwan Army camp on 10 February, in which seven persons were killed, was the second on the same camp, albeit after a gap of 15 years. It brought back painful memories as well as a flood of calls, offers for articles, and TV appearances. My plea has been, let the heat and dust settle to enable a meaningful analysis. During my tenure as Western Army Commander in 2015–16, we faced two attacks on Armed Forces installations (Samba and Pathankot) and two police stations (Kathua and Dinanagar). Each of these had lessons. The most abiding lesson came from Arnia, where a carpenter alerted the army to eliminate four dreaded terrorists in the intermediate tier well before they reached their intended target at Samba.

The Jammu-Samba-Kathua (JSK) belt along the National Highway (referred to as the terror highway) provides ample opportunities for infiltration due to its riverine stretches and proximity of targets with high TRP value. It keeps alive the Pakistani bogey of an unsettled Working Boundary (WB) stretching from Akhnoor to Kathua (termed by us as International Border or IB), thereby seeking to project the entire J&K as disputed.

The attempts at extension of the arc of terror with attacks on Dinanagar and Pathankot in the settled IB sector were most perplexing. The Pakistani establishment tried to explain the Pathankot attack as a rogue action, and that possibly enabled a visit by a Pakistan investigation team to this airbase. A lull of nearly two years seemed to indicate that the plan to extend JSK to Pathankot and Gurdaspur may have been rolled back. Now, an open boast by the Jaish chief portends terror returning to JSK and adjoining areas under tacit ISI patronage. The obvious question is, has Pakistan decided to jettison the previous understanding?

There are numerous small camps in this belt, initially based on the availability of land, dating back to the pre-insurgency era. Most camps have been overtaken by civilian habitations and communication arteries, flouting mandatory safety distances even in the case of sensitive airbases like Pathankot. Jammu itself has seven such camps, including Sanjuwan and Kaluchak, previously targeted in the second biggest attack after the recent one on the Uri camp. In proximity, there have been attempts on Janglot and multiple ones on Samba, a favourite target for fedayeen, who describe it as Maheshwar camp, referring to the temple in the vicinity. While the army has pragmatically yielded land in Jammu for the expansion of the airport and university, response from civilian agencies has been tardy; hence, the relocation of civilian pockets and consolidation of camps is unlikely.

The harsh reality of security is that no installation can be turned into an impregnable fortress. Formidable defence lines, such as the Maginot and Barlev lines, were breached. As per official records, more than one lakh people attempted to breach the legendary Berlin Wall with 5,000 succeeding and nearly 150 losing their lives. Security has two essential and inter-connected dimensions of infrastructure and people. Our committees and armchair experts tend to focus only on the security apparatus and recommend converting every camp into a mini-fortress with high-tech gadgetry and drones.

While surveillance and anti-intrusion devices enhance security appreciably, they are not the magical silver bullets. The recent release of funds for enhancing security is most welcome, but its application on the ground is bedevilled with numerous obstacles like cumbersome procedures, limited availability of expertise, gestation period, and ever-lurking auditors. The crux of camp security is a people-centric approach, which, at the macro level, translates into the involvement of all agencies and instruments of state. As a first step, socio-political elements have to address the Kashmir problem at its core. In all hybrid war scenarios, the centre of gravity or focus has to be on people, but we seem to be getting caught in the quagmire of the fortress mentality, which furthers the aim of proxy warriors, making us defensive and tying down troops.

Border guarding needs to be reinforced further. It has to be supplemented by multi-tiered deployment and participation of 'nagrik yodhas' (citizen warriors), like the carpenter from Arnia. Early indicators in the form of mushrooming mansion of taxi driver Ikagar have to be dealt with and superintendents of police of the Salwinder variety cannot be allowed to run riot in sensitive border districts.

It is considered a belief that most such attacks have a vectoring element and insider support. How else can intruders enter an airbase at its most deserted corner with non-functional lights and over-hanging trees enabling an easy entry? The unfortunate part is that the investigation loop is never completed due to petty and parochial interests, and above all, vested political links combined with the '*chalta hai*' attitude. To add to our woes is inept forensics and 'jugaad' by state police in handling GPS and such devices seen after the Dinanagar incident, resulting in the loss of valuable evidence.

While it may sound pedantic, more attention needs to be given to ensure secure parameters with a track for patrolling and quick reaction. Jungles and nullahs around our military camps have a contributory role in intrusions, as seen in Nagrota and now Sanjuwan. The security routine is repetitive and strenuous. We tried programmes like 'Swacch Paridhi' (clean perimeter) and 'Paridhi Suraksha' (perimeter security) to make the activity more imaginative.

Attacks certainly need to be minimised, and response in each case has to be efficient, backed up by a thorough investigation to identify the insiders and deal with them like Israelis do, closing the loop.

15.3 Approach Towards the Protection of Military Installations

Proxy war manifests in various actions designed to spread terror, in the form of kidnapping, hostage taking, hijacking, attacking and ambushing convoys, planting Improvised Explosive Devices (IEDs), etc. The most audacious form, often involving the application of fedayeen (suicide bombers), is the attack on military installations. These nefarious attacks have been occurring as a global trend, and India has also witnessed a large number of such attacks. The challenge is in preventing them and, on occurrence, minimising their effect, followed by a credible response.

Scope and Terminologies

Strategy Vis-a-Vis Approach: The article attempts to discuss an approach rather than a concrete strategy, as each military base or installation has its own peculiarities, and it is difficult to stipulate a universal strategy or even a template like a one-size-fits-all. However, an approach is more flexible, wherein indicative guidelines can be utilised to evolve a specific action plan or Standard Operating Procedure (SOP), customised to the relevant base.

Base and Installation: The term installation or even base is flexible to cater to small, medium, and large bases or installations, which, in different Armed Forces jargon, are described as Vulnerable Area (VA) and Vulnerable Point (VP). The categorisation of VAs and VPs is customised to targeting parameters, especially for aerial attacks. Consequently, they also help to deduce connected requirements for defenders like air defence cover, size of protection party, and preliminary or reserved demolition plan, in the event of an imminent attack. For the attacker, they help to prioritise targets, explosive load, and other targeting parameters.

Focus: Terrorists choose their targets based on an entirely different set of factors, like possible visibility or Targeted Attack Protection (TAP), or media value of the attack, the chance of success, local support, etc. Repeated attacks in the Samba belt of the Jammu-Pathankot sector are driven by these visibility factors, the ease of infiltration, proximity to the National Highway, and the main communication link to the erstwhile state of Jammu and Kashmir. The focus of this article is on terrorist attacks in the Indian context. However, relevant inferences have been drawn from global and regional scans to devise a recommended approach.

Macro Trends for Protection

Bottom Line Reality: The urge for safety and protection has witnessed the development of fortresses, moats, and barriers in the form of formidable defensive lines and walls. The Great Wall of China, the Berlin Wall, the Maginot Line, and the Barlev Line are relevant examples.

As per official records, more than 1,00,000 persons attempted to breach the legendary Berlin Wall, 5,000 odd succeeded, and 150 lost their lives in the process. The famed multi-layered Barlev defences across the Suez, linking the Sinai Peninsula, were a hybrid of multiple layers of physical and technical means. Though described as impregnable, the Arabs breached them in the Yom Kippur War of 1973 using rudimentary and basic techniques. Defensive barriers are increasingly incorporating technical means like surveillance cameras, CCTV, smart fences, and now, surveillance drones, integrated into automated warning and alarm systems. On balance, technology aids, but is neither the silver bullet nor panacea for assured impregnability. The bottom line and seminal reality are that no wall or fence can stop a determined attacker, especially when aided by collaborators.

Evolving Trends: While defensive means have evolved, concurrently, attackers have kept pace in their tactics, even adopting fedayeen tactics. In certain ways, it is a cat-and-mouse game. The very idea of attacking a protected military camp is based on audacity, regardless of near-certain death, but this generates very high visibility. Often it is timed to commemorate certain notable events in Tanzeem's (terrorist group) calendar, like the death anniversary of a terrorist, wherein the security personnel are aware of a higher probability of attack, yet the attacker chooses a suicidal approach. Desperation or determination has been evidenced in the Germans storming the Belgian fortress of Eben Emael in 1940 with gliders. Drones currently reflect a nuanced progression in the aerial domain in the current context, both for attacks like the Jammu airbase intrusion by mini drones, and for defensive surveillance.

Dynamic Nature of Threats: Starting with the ancient Greek Trojan Horse perfidy in the city of Troy, the threat has now morphed into cyber bugs, also referred to as malware or Trojans. Closer home and in our context, tunnelling is being resorted to by terrorist groups for infiltration, especially in the Jammu-Kathua-Samba sector. Hence, there is a constant need to analyse the dynamics and evolving trends both in the threat matrix and in protection measures. Terrorists keep varying their pattern of targeting, like heightened attacks in the Jammu-Pathankot belt in 2013–16—three years—Samba (twice), Kathua, Arnia (foiled attempt aimed at Samba), Janglot, Dinanagar, and Pathankot. These have now petered off with the current focus in the last two years (2022–23) in Poonch-Rajouri. It seems like going back to Hill Kaka, Operation Sarp-Vinash, and the tumultuous period of 2003. Terrorists also have a choice to shift periodically to attacking convoys and ambushing. In this dynamic flux of varying areas of attack and their methodology, security forces tend to slacken down in out-of-focus areas, treating them as routine, often violating the basic SOPs, resulting in setbacks like the recent ones in the Poonch-Rajouri sector.

Major Fidayeen Attacks on Armed Forces Establishments in J&K

The tabulated data in Section 14 as part of Key Statistical Data lists fedayeen attacks during the last three years, including in areas of J&K. This is the period when most such attacks have taken place. The relevant details of the period from 2016 onwards are tabulated in Section 14 as part of Key Statistical Data. An analysis of the data shows that attacks in the Samba-Pathankot belt, which was the main focus in 2013–16, have reduced from 2017 onwards. These attacks don't consider ambushes like Lethpura (Pulwama) on 14 February 2019 on the CRPF convoy, wherein a lone JeM suicide bomber caused 40 fatal casualties. More recently, on 21 April 2023, five soldiers were killed and one injured in an ambush on a Rashtriya Rifles vehicle by JeM near Bhimber Gali (Poonch). Another dastardly improvised explosive attack was on the District Reserve Guard, the auxiliary force of Chhattisgarh Police, by LWE, leading to the fatalities of 10 jawans and a civilian driver. Fratricide incidents like the recent one in Bhatinda military base on 12 April 2023, leading to four fatalities, are not discussed as they are of different categories, and as these require separate corrective and mitigation measures. **Terrorists have shifted their focus to Poonch-Rajouri from mid-2022.**

Challenges in Camp Security

Locational Challenges: The British planned the first set of cantonments away from population centres, often in climatically suitable hill stations. Hence, stations like Wellington, Simla, Kasauli, Yol, Panchgani, Mhow, Deolali, etc., came up. Even in cities, cantonment areas were sited at the periphery with a clear demarcation of civilian and military pockets. After independence, the land was allotted, often on political considerations, in places like Bhatinda, Hisar, and Binaguri. The primary threat being conventional wars in the proximity of borders, terrorist threats were not given due importance. Hence, local protection considerations got watered down. This unplanned urbanisation has resulted in the following challenges:

- Civilian pockets, encroachments, and residential areas sprout along the periphery of bases.

- In some cases, encroachments have taken place in buffer or no construction zones of sensitive installations like ammunition dumps, airbases, and HQs.
- Highways and communication arteries have been constructed through military areas, providing easy access and observation.
- Dominating high-rise structures have come up in proximity to vital institutions.

Internal Layout of Bases: Most army bases still have only cattle fences and lack perimeter walls provided for airbases and major depots. The Uri and Samba camps had only basic cattle fences when they were first attacked in 2016 and 2013, respectively. Post-attacks, some attempts in hardening fences, with Corrugated Galvanised Iron (CGI) sheets and other contraptions have been made. Bases are very green spaces; some are like biodiversity parks. They often have nullahs, rivulets, and microforests, which are exploited by terrorists to hide, like in the Pathankot and Sanjuwan attacks. Very few bases have continuous and clear perimeter patrolling tracks. Some have overhanging trees providing Tarzan-like entry over the wall or fence, as evidenced in the entry at the Pathankot airbase in 2016.

Satellite and Isolated Pockets: Constraints of land availability have forced the creation of isolated and satellite pockets. As an example, Jammu has as many as eight pockets; each one requires its own security, surveillance, and response mechanisms, imposing huge financial costs and human deployment penalties. Three outlying pockets—Sanjuwan, Kaluchak, and Ratnuchak—have borne the brunt of terrorist attacks. Many of these, due to unplanned urban mushrooming, are in stand-alone mode with little mutual support from other pockets. In some cases, highways further divide these pockets into sectors, like the Patiala and Bhatinda stations.

Night and Bad Visibility Challenges: Almost all bases and perimeters lack night and low visibility surveillance devices, like thermal imaging.

Some bases even lack basic flood lighting, and even where provided, they may be unserviceable, as in the case of the Pathankot airbase.

Proximity to Borders: Bases and military posts in the proximity of borders provide terrorists with an opportunity to infiltrate, strike, and exfiltrate without elaborate logistics support. They also provide opportunities for reconnaissance to detect vulnerabilities.

Criminal Ecosystem in the Border Belt: Criminals often find shelter and operate in border areas due to difficult terrain and a lax law enforcement system. These areas have shady gangs indulging in human and cattle smuggling, particularly on the Indo-Bangladesh border. Other activities include narco-trafficking, arms smuggling, counterfeits, and illegal mining. An informal media survey in 2016 established that very few all-India cadre officers from the IAS and the IPS are posted in such areas. It will be apt to quote examples of sacked SP Salwinder Singh in Pathankot and Inspector Devinder Singh in the Srinagar Airport in this regard.

Repetitive Routine: Security duties entail long tenures of duty, which are repetitive and mundane, causing fatigue.

Coordination: Base security is handled by multiple agencies, which often work in silos, creating issues of coordination and accountability.

Lack of Skilling: Troops employed on security-related duties like Defence Security Corps (DSC) and Territorial Army, are treated as auxiliary forces, which are sub-optimally equipped. They have human resource-related problems of age profile, lack of initiative, and sub-optimal periodic refresher training. These troops seldom get recognition and lack motivation.

High Cost of Modernisation: Technological surveillance and modernisation of equipment entail very heavy expenditure and dictate prioritisation.

Long Gestation: Construction of perimeter and surveillance systems takes time and entails gestation periods.

Foreign Origin of Equipment: Dependence on foreign-origin equipment, especially Chinese cameras, creates vulnerabilities. There is a need to develop indigenous manufacturing and avoid foreign systems.

Collaborators: It is a considered opinion that most attacks are supported or even vectored by local or in-house collaborators. However, in most cases, these collaborators escape investigation and legal action.

Demographic Pockets: Interested parties have allowed the settlement of vulnerable sections of the population in the proximity of military camps. Rohingya pockets have come up adjoining the Sanjuwan Base and Gujjar settlements in the Samba belt, in close proximity to the installations. These have been utilised by attackers for reconnaissance and logistics, including the staging of their attacks. Mazars and such religious shrines have also been misused for access and reconnaissance.

Investigation and Forensic Backup: It has been seen that investigation is often tardy, slow, and the forensic support is inadequate. Evidence, even when available, gets mishandled. For example, the GPS recovered in the Dinanagar attack (on the police post) got mishandled due to tinkering by local jugaad (improvisation) type of experts in Mohali.

Symbolic Scapegoating Approach: The investigation loop, after most incidents, fails to fix full accountability, identify, and book collaborators and often lapses into symbolic scapegoating with the fixing of one odd person in the chain, like the base commander and two lower officials after the Pathankot incident. In this incident, no seniors of police and CAPFs, or even collaborators, were identified and held accountable.

Lack of Transparency and Peer Review in Follow-Up: Most investigation reports are classified and even non-redacted portions are not put in the open domain. There is total absence of peer review. It is indicative of a fire-brigade response and failure to learn long-term lessons for genuine security audits of bases.

Policy Approaches for Protection

Operational: There could be various macro-operational approaches for the protection of bases and installations, like the following:

Defensive or Reactive Approach: This methodology focuses on boosting protection in terms of walls, fences, surveillance devices, and such defensive measures.

Offensive or Proactive Approach: This format seeks to identify the potential source of the threat and nip it at the origin, ideally, or before it impacts the protected installation. This approach is practised, to a certain extent, by the US in its Homeland Security of Continental America. It has been used as a justification for the target of terrorist groups like the Taliban, ISIS, and Somali groups. The concept has obvious limitations, both in the selection of the target and in its efficacy. The Twin Tower attacks on the World Trade Centre, New York, of 9/11, is a relevant example in this context. After the Uri attack and the Pulwama ambush, surgical raids and the Balakot Surgical Strikes were executed. While they delivered a strong deterrent message and reduced the frequency of attacks, the series of recent incidents in Rajouri reflects a continued threat and the need for a hybrid or combined approach.

Hybrid or Combination Approach: This is also termed as offensive-defence and is a balanced combination of strong dissuasive protection and an offensive approach articulated in localisation, neutralisation, and targeted punitive response. The Israelis rely on strong, highly automated surveillance and intelligence system backed with assured offensive surgical response.

Physical vs. Technical: Another set of policy choices is about the physical hardening vis-a-vis reliance on technical aids. It is a decision between a physical wall and a smart fence with electronic surveillance, including a CCTV system. Protection, especially surveillance and technical means, entails considerable expenditure, as well as considerable gestation. Hence, a due cost-benefit analysis and prioritisation are mandatory due to fiscal constraints. In addition, life cycle maintenance and upgradation are due to obsolescence in technology. In sum, both physical and technical could be utilised to complement each other.

Armed Forces Study and Planned Correctives

Armed Forces Study: After the Pathankot Airbase incident in 2016, the government ordered a tri-service study headed by the former VCOAS, Lt Gen Philip Campose. This panel suggested that perimeter security entails three key ingredients, beginning with quality local intelligence gathering, smart technology for fence management, and ensuring a quick response. The report visualised a sort of buffer or no man's land between the boundary and the inner fence. The idea was that in case there was a breach, the response mechanism should be efficient enough to neutralise the intruders in this buffer strip between the first and second layers of the base perimeter.

Financial Dimension: The study made several highly ambitious recommendations, entailing a huge budgetary expenditure. As per media reports and informed sources, the committee had identified a paucity of funds allocated for base security as one of the main reasons for the army's inability to secure its camps by installing high-tech surveillance gadgets, including electrified fences, night vision devices, radars and CCTVs for effective access-control, perimeter security-cum-intrusion detection systems, and better intelligence response mechanisms. As per reliable estimates, there are more than 600 big and small and isolated camps in Kashmir, and every camp needs at least ₹1–2 crores to upgrade its security to acceptable levels. The media also reported that the army, navy, and IAF, in 2017, had sought more than ₹2,000 crores for strengthening perimeter security of their prioritised sensitive bases. There are more than 3,000 such installations, including 600 categorised as sensitive by the three services after the Pathankot airbase attack in January 2016.

Response Mechanisms: The same study had recommended revamping the designated protection force, DSC, with revamped 20,000-strong physically fit soldiers. It also recommended arming them with AK-47s instead of 7.62 mm self-loading rifles (SLRs). The equipment upgrade recommended faster vehicles, bulletproof jackets, and night vision devices.

Follow-Up and Implementation of the Study: The report didn't receive an expeditious response, and it was only after the attacks on the Uri Brigade in September 2016, Panzgam in April 2017, and more importantly, the Sanjuwan base attack on 10 February 2018, that the Ministry of Defence (MoD) belatedly approved ₹1,487 crores budgetary allocation on the same day, probably forced by the increasing media and social media pressure.

VCOAS-Delegated Powers: In July 2017, the government briefed the media, and also built up a narrative that VCOAS has been delegated with substantial financial powers amounting to ₹40,000 crores. It was claimed in July 2018 that out of these allocations, they were allowed to spend up to ₹800 crores annually towards upgrading the perimeter security of sensitive installations. However, the share allocated towards the upgradation of security must be balanced with several critical modernisation requirements like armaments, munitions, and equipment, already with shortfalls in ten types of armament systems and 45 types of munitions.

Recommended Measures

At the macro level, the policy recommended is a balanced combination of a proactive, offensive-defensive approach based on the following:

- **An efficient intelligence and surveillance system to predict threats to enable dissuasive measures and gear up protective barriers.**
- **Defensive measures should be in layers, starting with a likely point of infiltration to provide depth and reaction time.**

- **The base should have a well-organised perimeter and an automated protection system manned by requisite well-trained personnel. There should be a perimeter patrolling track acting as a buffer and providing a second layer within the base.**
- **The aim should be to expeditiously detect the intrusion, localise it, and neutralise it by Quick Action Teams (QATs). Ideally, this process should be completed in the buffer zone.**
- **It is recommended that surgical strike or response capabilities should be built up to deliver a punitive message across borders or the LoC by nuanced targeting of the source of the attack.**

It is necessary that at the base level, the organisation has to be balanced with an optimised and synergistic utilisation of technology and human resources. In a resource crunch reality, at least on an interim basis, hygiene factors and human resources will remain relevant. The following could be considered:

- **Have a people-centric approach to make the population in proximate** areas partners like the Reliance Mitra program. It will be appropriate to recall the contribution of the carpenter in Arnia in 2015, and the residents in Udhampur in 2016, in nabbing terrorists.
- Periodic cyber hygiene exercises like Swachh Paridhi should be undertaken to maintain and reinforce the perimeter.
- The presence and domination of the perimeter should be boosted by regular training activities like physical training, riding, and treks. The Western Command had conducted these as Surakshit Paridhi exercises, wherein intrusions and response were simulated and tested. Local dogs that have been duly vaccinated can be trained and utilised to boost the alarm system.
- Released Agniveers can be inducted into the DSC for a more youthful profile.

In the long term, municipal and civic authorities should play their part by carrying out the demolition of unauthorised structures. They should also create bypasses to reduce civilian traffic and install view cutters, where relocation is not possible. Civil police and intelligence agencies should play a meaningful role in access denial and access control. The government, on its part, should remain committed to upgradation and modernisation by making dedicated budgetary allocations.

Conclusion

The protection of bases will remain a persistent and formidable challenge, which will require modernisation and eternal vigilance. A resource-crunch economy and introduction of technological innovations balanced against an obdurate and desperate set of infiltrators, requires a whole-nation approach. The system has to be based on the prioritisation of bases as per sensitivity and a judicious mix of technology and human resources. The bottom line is that the base must be prepared and ready to take on any threat.

North-East – Challenges and the Way Forward

16.1 Manipur: Disturbing Trends and the Way Forward (Written in May 2023)

The improving situation in the North-East, characterised by a reduction in violence, has been a welcome trend. It had gotten an impetus with the BJP becoming part of the ruling coalitions in most states, providing a 'double-engine' effect in the region. The role of central agencies has always been catalytic and even overriding in the North-East. This gave a much-needed push to policy, which otherwise has gone through only semantic upgrades, like 'Look East', 'Think East', and 'Act East'. It has manifested in enhanced reach to border areas through tunnels, mega bridges, expansion of road, rail, and air connectivity. Unfortunately, ethnic violence in Manipur and violence unleashed in its wake have delivered a reality check, mandating measures to cap the mistrust.

Comprehending North East

It is axiomatic to reiterate a few critical paradigms of understanding the North-East.

- The founding principle is based on an established law of physics, of **centrifugal forces. It implies that fissiparous tendencies are natural in peripheral spaces.** These fuel a desire for autonomy, and if not handled well, can lead to separatist/secessionist yearnings, as seen in multiple insurgencies, like Naga, Mizo, ULFA, etc. The list of all such movements, many unresolved, is indeed long.
- The second principle is that **ethnicity and identity are defining markers.** Identity fixation, manifested in Nagaland's separation

from Assam on 1 December 1963, unleashed a domino effect, with the region splintering into seven states by 1987, giving it the 'one brother, seven sisters' character. These states are complemented by 27 autonomous councils, under the Sixth Schedule, for Bodos, Dimasas, Karbis, and others. Unfortunately, our approach is largely superficial, wherein we brand them as tribes, often condescendingly.

- Three, **traditional landholding norms and nomadic lifestyle, compounded by colonial laws like inner-line and forest areas, complicate the fixation of boundaries** for councils and states. Consequently, violent inter-tribe and even inter-state clashes occur.
- Four, **across the Brahmaputra, life moves 'lahe-lahe' (easy and slow)**. Impatience needs to be curbed by shifting to a lower gear and understanding better. Having served in the North-East, I have imbibed the Zen principle, 'even when hurrying, do it slowly'.
- Five, as a logical corollary to the first four principles, the **desire for integration and mainstreaming needs to be moderated and customised to local aspirations.**
- Six, a **parallel economy in the region is driven by extortion.** Even government employees/contractors contribute to forced levy, euphemistically described as taxation.
- **Most importantly, there is a seminal principle that insurgency is over only when it is comprehensively resolved.** The Naga movement, the mother of all insurgencies, started in the '50s and continues to fester, despite a ceasefire (an inappropriate term) and talks for 23 years. We have numerous suspensions of operations (SOO), a more appropriate term, and ongoing talks with affected groups. The only comprehensive resolution has been Mizoram with the Laldenga model, by putting the rebel leader in chair.
- **Finally, in the long term, it is worthwhile to build mutual dependencies to make the North-East populace realise that India needs them as much as they need India.**

External Drivers

The environment across the Siliguri Corridor is shaped by our neighbours. Unlike the western border with just one inimical Pakistan, the **North-East region has one declared adversary, China, a benign Bhutan, and other three nations in shifting, ambivalent orientation.** The common understanding that a proxy war was initiated in the '80s with the Khalistan and Kashmir movements needs to be corrected.

The real watershed was Phizo escaping to erstwhile East Pakistan and Mowu-Angami to China in the '50s. Bangladesh, under Zia-ur-Rehman, Ershad, and Begum Khaleda Zia, right till the recent clampdown by Sheikh Hasina, remained a hunting ground for ISI. It is to the credit of the present regime that Anup Chetia was handed over, and others were driven out. Myanmar has often facilitated transit and temporary camps. Demographic movement and open borders add complexity to the environment. While we mostly discuss the 'Miya' factor, the influx of Bhupalese, Chakmas, and, more recently, Chins has also created problems.

Complexities of Manipur

In a diversified identity mosaic, Manipur is an apt example of hyper ethnicity, characterised by skewed demographic distribution and rebel groups from all ethnicities. The state has approximately 53% Meitei (Vaishnavite and Sanmahi) population concentrated in the valley, accounting for barely 10% area, open to all. Sanmahi (8%) is the traditional religion of nature worship and animistic traditions. Sharing space with the Meiteis are Panghals (Muslims), who constitute 8% of the population.

Christians (Nagas and Kukis) account for 39%. Nagas are 23% and reside in the upper hills. Kukis, Chins, and Zomis, residing in the lower hills, make up 16%. The Sixth Schedule protection in hills bars settlements by outsiders. Kukis reside in Southern Manipur but exercise a chokehold on communications to Imphal through the Sadar Hills. Apart from the majority of Meitei chief ministers, Manipur also boasts of having two Naga and one Panghal chief ministers. These chief ministers, despite tensions, managed complexities, with odd aberrations like Naga-Kuki clashes in 1998. During peak insurgency, Meitei groups insisted on Meitei-Mayek (script) and traditional dress (the wrap-around Phanek), and Hindi films were banned.

The new disturbances have come when SOO, with Kuki groups, was rescinded, and there was an anti-drug and anti-encroachment drive, Kukis being at the receiving end. **The situation has been exacerbated due to the influx of the Chins from Myanmar into Mizoram and Manipur. The trigger was a high court verdict directing the state government to take up ST status for Meiteis in four months.** The environment, unfortunately, was replete with branding of Kukis as nomadic infiltrators, though some other hill communities like Paities (a Naga tribe) were also targeted. The saving grace has been Assam Rifles and the army providing timely succour and relief. Trust having been severely degraded, Kukis are demanding a separate administration. It will require intervention by the Central Government, wherein mature handling and better perception management are critical.

16.2 Manipur: A Chance Slipping in the North-East (Written in August 2023)

In 2017, I wrote an article titled, 'Manipur Opportunity' highlighting the possibility of using the state as a 'Gateway to the East' and a catalyst for the Centre's Act East Policy. Six years later, on 28 May, another column was titled, 'Eyes on Manipur: Disturbing Trends and the Way Forward'. It has been 66 days since the manifestation of malfeasance, yet we still seem to be groping for some semblance of a resolution. It appears that fatigue is beginning to set in and attention is shifting to riots in France and the Khalistani vandalism abroad. Ironic indeed, but we seem to be lapsing into the age-old malady of keeping the North-East remote and out of focus.

As a measure of gratitude to the wonderful people of the North-East and Manipur, this follow-up is another attempt to continue meaningful discussions to seek normalcy. In this scope, it attempts to skirt the all-pervasive 'whodunit' temptation. The present state of the binary divide in communities is such that any attempt to unravel the plot only adds to the schism and the blame game. A formal inquiry has been ordered. It is hoped that it will help to move forward in the process of truth, reconciliation, and at least some semblance of justice, although the process inspires little confidence, at least currently.

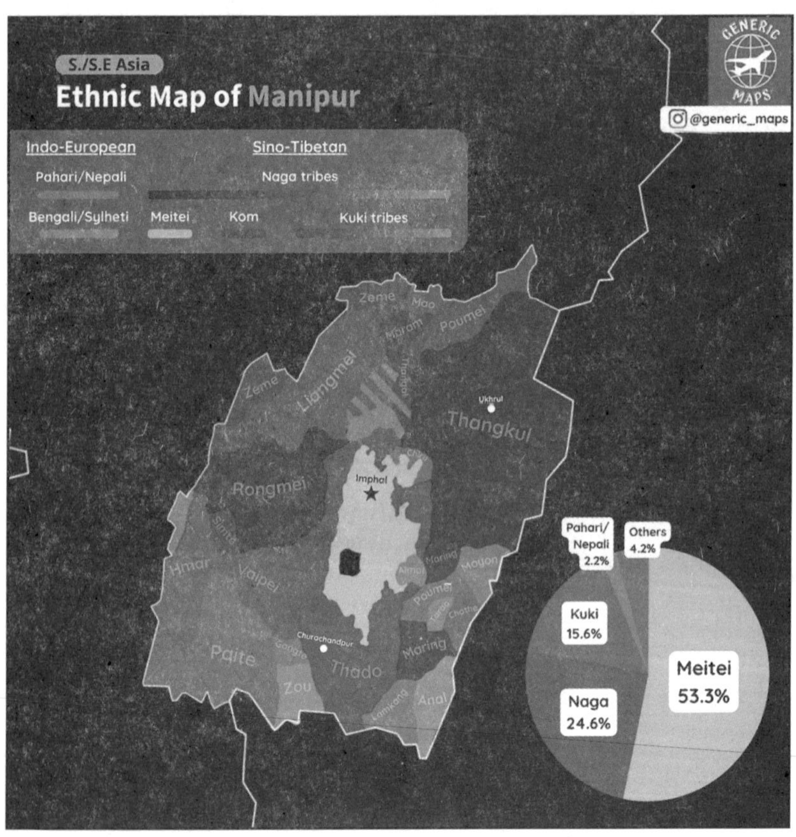

External and Regional Factors

It is indeed ironic that the new US ambassador has strayed into uncharted territory and even offered to help in the Manipur crisis, though he has added the caveat 'if requested for such assistance'. This utterance breaches the established norm of staying clear of domestic issues, and is especially jarring in the current Indo-US bromance. Hopefully, the US will stay away from any forays, but it should bring home the stark realisation that the issue is serious and finding resonance abroad.

In the regional context, even more serious is the Myanmar Government's sharp reaction to the Indo-US joint statement calling for the release of all political prisoners and the restoration of democracy. Myanmar's cooperation is absolutely critical for the resolution of the Manipur quagmire and kick-starting the Act East policy. **More importantly, with the ubiquitous presence of China, do we want another collusive manifestation in the east along with the Sino-Pak one in the west? It is imperative that we find ways to assuage the military junta in Tatmadaw, on priority.**

Drivers for the Reconciliation Process

The process of healing has to start by building on the realisation that we can choose many things but have no choice in our neighbours. Even with the hypothetical scenario of separate administration for Kukis, communities have to co-exist as neighbours. Contentious issues, like ST status, forest, and land rights, need to be put on the back burner till we build inter-community consensus. The root cause of turmoil is fear and uncertainty. **The Meiteis are apprehensive, sandwiched between Greater Nagalim and Kuki-Chin-Zomi homeland demands. The lifelines to Imphal Valley, NH-2 (from Dimapur- Kohima) and NH-37 (from Silchar), are subjected to regular coercive blockades by hill tribes.**

The menace of rooting out illegal poppy cultivation requires to be tackled with a de novo approach. Combating a narco-terrorist economy (approximately ₹40,000 crore), which is larger than even the state budget, requires a multi-dimensional approach. While it is expedient to target small fish (illegal farmers), much more important is to tackle mafias with political connections and linkages with terrorist groups. Concurrently, alternatives in terms of skilling, vocations, and replacement remunerative crops have to be devised. It is equally important that such initiatives are seen to be impartial and avoid stereotyping and targeting any particular community.

Security Matrix and Challenges

Columns of the army, Assam Rifles (AR), CRPF, BSF, ITBP, and SSB, numbering approximately 40,000, are deployed to aid the civil authority, besides the Manipur Police, as per media reports. These have been put under a coordinating HQ led by a former DGP of the CRPF. The initial deployment was more in fire-brigade mode. It is now being rationalised to 'one force, one area', with the likelihood of the BSF being given charge of the most volatile Bishnupur and Churachandpur. **The focus is to stop inter-gang fights and create buffer zones.**

Security forces face multiple challenges. The important ones are:

- The first is the absence of the Armed Forces (Special Powers) Act (AFSPA) regime in the valley, which is used by insurgents as a rest and recuperation base, and eventually as a launch pad, in connivance with sympathisers.
- Two, **the state has gotten nearly 4,000 weapons looted, many of them having found their way to militants.** It would be relevant to quote a Manipuri general: 'In Kashmir Valley, we chased a few hundred, maybe less than 500 weapons; here, numbers are scary.'
- Three, open and porous borders in difficult terrain, coupled with inadequate forces and minimal infrastructure, for border management and controlling narco-terrorism.
- Four, partisan interference of NGOs, especially Meira Paibis.
- Finally, the mischievous narrative of painting the Assam Rifles as a pro-Kuki force.

The problem is likely to foster; hence, a unified command and redeployment of forces, preferably a combination of Assam Rifles and the CRPF, aided by the army, is recommended. The CRPF should even induct three-four mahila (women's) battalions to control Meira Paibis. It may appear retrograde, but AFSPA needs to be re-imposed, at least temporarily, in the valley areas. In the long term, border infrastructure, intelligence, and bodies to control narco-terrorism need major revamping. The information vacuum needs to be bridged to counter divisive narratives.

The Way Forward

The idea of imposing the President's Rule has floundered with the chief minister orchestrating a melodramatic coup. Concurrently, the peace committee has not found any traction, with the Kukis objecting to the chief minister at the helm. The real status is that communities, including even academia, are pushing divisive narratives. The Centre should consider a more proactive intervention with a short-term President's Rule with an unambiguous mandate and authority to recover arms and restore sanity. **Concurrently, much-needed inter-community rapprochement can be initiated by an independent external group of trusted interlocutors to foster bipartisan healing.**

16.3 Looking for Sanity in Manipur (Written in August 2023)

The mayhem in Manipur and simmering chaos rekindles painful memories. The first challenge, on posting to North-East is to comprehend anthropological complexities, as the key to the Gordian knot is ethnic diversity. When posted in a quaint place called Zakhama, near the Nagaland-Manipur border in 2002, it took me nearly six months, to get close to the correct pronunciation of the place, with the right intonation.

As per official accounts, Nagaland has 20 odd tribes, but NSCN groups, rooting for Nagalim (greater Nagaland), put the number at 60 plus. Many, like Koms and Anals, are claimed by both Nagas and Kukis. The movement under Muivah is driven by the Tangkhuls of Ukhrul in Manipur. On the other end, Konyaks and Heimis of Myanmar are pushing for a separate, Eastern Naga Peoples' autonomous council, incorporating North-East Nagaland and Southern Arunachal. Any resolution of the Naga problem is likely to trigger cascading effects in neighbouring states, especially Manipur. The proposed council will bolster the Kuki demand for a separate administrative unit.

The original theological template in the North-East was animism, based on worship of nature and spirits. Though currently on retreat, animism has survived in Manipur as Sanmahi and Donyi-Polo (Sun and Moon worship) in Arunachal, besides a few other minor tribes. The most notable protagonist of animism was Rani Gaidinliu, Padma Shri, freedom fighter, hailing from the Rongmai (Naga) tribe of Manipur. In Kangleipak (modern Manipur), rulers like Pamheiba (referred to as Garibnawaz), followed by Ching-thang Khomba (Bhagyachandra) in the mid and late eighteenth century, adopted Vaishnavism. It is indeed true that beginning in 1871, Baptist missionaries, aided by British rule, altered the theological profile of the hill areas. However, it is to the credit of missionaries that they transformed head-hunting tribes, giving them a common Nagamese language and codified twenty odd dialects. Restrictions, like the inner line permit, prevented access of others in the hills. The Ramakrishna Mission, and recently, the Rashtriya Swayamsevak Sangh (RSS), have tried some rear-guard action.

Like religion, people moved into these areas in waves. The latest and currently in focus are the Kukis, who were settled by the Britishers in the mid-nineteenth century. Hilly areas were their natural habitat as till the recent 'go to hills' movement, nobody wanted to venture there. Employees hired proxies on nominal wages, preferring to remain in Imphal. The police considered armouries unsafe, stocking weapons in the valley, and only the CAPFs carried weapons. **It is ironic that**

5,000 odd weapons, including mortars and machine guns, are still being allowed to be looted, a large portion from Imphal and even Indian Reserve Battalion (IRB) armouries.

Valley, though no longer considered disturbed, is the real nerve centre with bases of insurgent groups of all ethnicities, including Meiteis, Nagas, Panghals, and Kuki/Zomis (though temporarily closed). All leaders have their support structures and sanctuaries, where they descend for collecting extorted bounty, shady deals, treatment, and recreation. **Overall, women were not only respected but their presence in the security convoy obviated terrorist actions. Society was permissive of inter-mingling, unlike khaps in North India.** The red flag was only raised when many Sema women started marrying Miyas, giving rise to fears of a hybrid Semiya tribe. It was most distressing to hear that a Kuki lady married to a Meitei and her ailing son, being transported for treatment, were burnt in an ambulance, in recent mayhem. Are we regressing to the head-hunting era?

Imphal had veteran, Capt Ashok Tipnis and his wife, Mrs Ngam, a Tangkhul from Ukhrul. They were much in the news as their daughter, Madhuri, was engaged to the legendary footballer, Baichung Bhutia. Soccer-crazy Manipuris were literally kicked with the idea of Baichung becoming the son-in-law of Manipur. Capt Tipnis represented few, who not only served in the North-East, married local ladies but also made Manipur their home.

The real example of anthropological blending was Comdt Ratan Singh Jassal. He grew up in Hoshiarpur and had post-graduate degree in Sanskrit. He joined the army in 1962, through emergency commission, and was commissioned in 3/8 Gorkha Rifles. He opted for the Assam Rifles (AR), spending his lifetime in the North-East. His first wife, a Sikh lady, passed away, leaving a son, who is a principal in an educational institution in Punjab. Later, Jassal married Apar Thoubala, a Tangkhul Naga, and they had one son and two daughters. Harkirat, a sales executive, lives in Chingmoirang (Imphal), a Naga-dominated locality, and runs a reputed school with his Meitei wife. Jassal's elder daughter is an educationist, and the younger one is a doctor, both married to Meiteis. Jassal's story has the final twist: after Apar's demise, he married N Kipgen, a Kuki nursing officer, with AR. She is still serving in J&K. Jassal was a prolific writer for regional media, flagging societal fault lines. He passed away in 2016, at 76 years of age. In Chingmoirang, the Jassal household has Apar's grave with 'Ek Onkar' inscribed on it, as per her wish.

Kukis, even with jobs and homes in Imphal, have relocated to safe areas. We hope sanity is restored and they return and rebuild their lives. Manipur needs an urgent healing touch, reconciliation, and many more indigenous Jassal-type stories. The sad part is that the government seems hesitant and content with legitimising buffer zones with both sides armed to the teeth. The recovery of weapons simply cannot be postponed. Dialogue within society is required to define the limits of unbridled activism by Meira-Paibis vis-a-vis law enforcement. The problem of migrants and refugees dictates skilful negotiations with Myanmar to enable the repatriation of refugees. Sensitivities of Mizoram require to be catered for. **In the interim, humanitarian relief in camps is overdue, along with continued education and employment. Concurrently, the border management and free movement regime (16 km) needs to be reviewed. The immediate need is for precipitate action, overhauling of the security structure with DAA/AFSPA and President's Rule for at least a short duration.**

Update: Shri AK Bhalla, former home secretary, was appointed as governor in January 2025, and the state was placed under President's Rule in February 2025.

16.4 Operationalising the Act East Policy Through the North-East

Abstract

The Act East policy of India has been a landmark policy initiative with twin objectives: connecting the Indian economy with the rising economies of the ASEAN region as well as accelerating the rather slow pace of development in the North-East region of India. It also has a geo-strategic dimension with China having made significant inroads in the ASEAN region, leading to supply chain dependencies that give it considerable leverage. The well-intentioned program has completed a decade, and there is some sub-optimal progress, which needs to be ramped up. More importantly, the North-East continues to languish and has failed to draw the full benefits of this policy. Consequently, it is caught up in a vicious cycle of terrorism and lack of development. It is time that the policy is reviewed and recalibrated to achieve its stated objectives.

Introduction

India recently celebrated the tenth anniversary of its decade-old Act East policy. Prime Minister Narendra Modi visited Singapore, Brunei, and Laos in September–October 2024 and also attended the 21st ASEAN-India Summit, followed by the 19th East Asia Summit. This visit was followed by an exchange at the RM level by Rajnath Singh. There has been progress on many fronts, including trade, yet the overall sense is that progress is incremental and much more needs to be done. While concerted effort has been applied, the **worsening and adversarial geo-strategic environment in the neighborhood, especially Bangladesh and Myanmar, is posing worrying challenges.** Internally, continued unrest in Manipur and in pockets of Nagaland mandates a harsh reality check on the current status of this policy. It is relevant to highlight that one of the stated and desired objectives of Viksit-Bharat-2047 relates to the success of the Act East policy. It is appropriate to analyse the evolution of policy, progress, problem areas, and identify mid-course correctives.

Evolution of Policy

India, since independence, has been more focused towards on West Asia, Europe, and the Middle East, despite its ancient history and traditional connection with South East Asia (SE Asia) and East Asia.

India hesitatingly initiated the 'Think-East' policy in the late '80s, which was later upgraded to 'Look-East' by the PV Narsimha Rao regime in 1991. There were many catalysts for this recalibration, including the end of the Cold War, the collapse of the Soviet Union, and the success of ASEAN as a regional forum. Internal drivers included the launch of the policy of liberalisation in the aftermath of a grave fiscal crisis in India, necessitating an IMF bailout. This initiative was followed through in the subsequent Prime Ministers AB Vajpayee and Manmohan Singh governments. **However, in 2014, Prime Minister Narendra Modi sought to revitalise it in a new rebranded format of the 'Act East' policy.** This was coupled with a 'neighborhood first' policy and serious attempts to resolve unrest in the North-East through focused conflict resolution.

The Act East policy, as a spin-off, sought to tap into and integrate with the indigenous geo-economic network of the North-East with the economies of SE Asia. There was realisation that the North-East has lagged behind other regions, and the lack of economic opportunities was fueling separatism and insurgencies. The planned template promoted connectivity, trade, and tourism. Manufacturing hubs and markets exist in the adjoining extended neighborhood. Ideally, it envisages the development of a mutually beneficial economic order and network. Few such formulations include sharing of surplus hydro-power, bamboo, fruits (pineapple), spices (ginger), honey, tea, and leveraging tourism (especially Buddhist circuit). Traditional cultivation methods without inorganic fertilisers make it an appropriate location for organic farming and branding high-value organic products accordingly.

In essence, it aimed to link the North-East region of India, Nepal, Bhutan, Bangladesh, Myanmar, extending to Thailand and other countries of the ASEAN block, dubbed as 'Tiger' economies. Map-1 graphically depicts the linkage. The Bangladesh-China-India-Myanmar (BCIM) Corridor and Trilateral Highway (India-Myanmar-Thailand) were projected as signature connectivity links to develop a shared economic future. BCIM has been re-appropriated by China as the China-Myanmar Economic Corridor (CMEC) due to Indian reservations on account of the China-focused nature of the project and fears of dumping of Chinese goods. However, the Trilateral Highway project is under development, though it is currently stalled due to unrest in Myanmar. Economics apart, the region has had cultural and theological linkages, forged through historic maritime corridors and diaspora reflected in Angkor Wat (Cambodia), Prambanan (Java, Indonesia), and other heritage sites in the ASEAN region. **Historical and cultural connections date back to the fourth century CE, reflected in the spread of the Ramayana, Buddhism, Chola, and Sri Vijaya empires.**

Geo-Strategic Compulsions

India has, to its west, the highly disturbed Afghanistan-Pakistan region, followed by the volatile Middle East North Africa (MENA) region, characterised by multiple ongoing conflicts. **On India's eastern flank is rising South East Asia, with tiger economies in a competitive overdrive.** This dilemma was posed by Japanese Prime Minister Koizumi in his interaction with Indian Prime Minister Manmohan Singh when he compared the two and described them as a disturbed west and a rising east. **The current century is being described as Asia's century, which has been catalysed by the meteoric rise of China, though currently tapering off.** Along with China, there has been impressive progress by India and ASEAN economies. China has extended its footprint in the Indo-Pacific and has displayed aggressive expansionist forays in the South China Sea. Chinese presence is witnessed in Cambodia (Ream naval base), Laos (control of power generation and distribution grid), Thailand (attempts to build Kra Canal), Myanmar (Kyaukphyu), Sri Lanka (Hambantota), Maldives (Feydhoo Islands), and Bangladesh (Cox's Bazar)—please see Map 2. While China seeks to describe them as facilities for civilian use, they can be converted very quickly for prosecuting naval operations. Many countries, especially in India's extended neighborhood, have

Chinese-origin equipment, giving a presence for servicing, repairs, and maintenance. More alarming is the dependence on Chinese manufacturing, supply chains, digital and surface connectivities, giving her considerable leverage. The US has been promoting the China plus One policy to relocate and diversify manufacturing outside China. India is making concerted attempts in this exercise, but Vietnam, Malaysia, Indonesia, and Taiwan seem to have managed to corner a greater share of this pie.

Having realised the dangers of growing Chinese dominance, the US has articulated a marked shift to Asia in 'Rebalancing to Indo-Pacific' and 'Pivot to Asia' policies. The QUAD, comprising the US, Australia, India, and Japan, was established to counter Chinese hegemonic designs. Although described as a non-military grouping, it has facilitated strategic cooperation and interoperability to promote the law of the commons and the open seas regime. There is growing talk of QUAD plus, with New Zealand, South Korea, Vietnam, Brazil, and Israel invited in post-COVID deliberations. Even the Philippines wants to join this grouping. In addition, another grouping, AUKUS (Australia, the United Kingdom, and the US) has been forged to foster strategic cooperation in maritime capability building, especially nuclear submarines for Australia with assistance from the other two, i.e. the US and the UK. Peninsular configuration of India, coupled with Andaman-Nicobar Islands, gives India significant dominance over sea lanes and choke points like the Malacca Straits. The US has renamed the Pacific Command at Hawaii as the Indo-Pacific Command and would want India to play a much bigger role, but India, conscious of China's allegations of ganging-up against China, is proceeding with caution. Consequently, **Prime Minister Narendra Modi in the Shangri-la dialogue, enunciated the policy of SAGAR (Security and Growth for All in Region) to assuage Chinese apprehensions.**

India has been anchoring joint naval exercises like Malabar to promote interoperability, maritime security, freedom of navigation, rule-based order, and the law of the commons for open and inclusive oceans. India has also deployed maritime assets for coordinated patrolling, anti-piracy, and disaster relief missions. **India has also been anchoring initiatives like the Indian Ocean Rim Association (IORA) and Indian Ocean Naval Symposiums (IONS). Another significant step was the establishment of the Information Fusion Centre-Indian Ocean Region (IFC-IOR) to enhance maritime domain awareness.** India has equipped the Philippines with the BrahMos strategic missile system to enable it to stand up to the growing Chinese aggression in the South China Sea. India has collaborated, albeit at a sub-optimal level, with Vietnam, Indonesia, Sri Lanka, and Myanmar in the construction and refurbishment of naval vessels. India has been negotiating with Malaysia and others for the supply of Tejas aircraft, Dhruv helicopters, and other weapons; however, talks have remained at the negotiation level. India aslo has a maritime presence in Can Ranh Bay in Vietnam, Sittwe in Myanmar, and seeks presence in Trincomalee (Sri Lanka) in an attempt to counter the Chinese 'string of pearls'.

Act East Through the North East

The North-East and peninsular India are the geo-economic pivots for the operationalisation of Act East. Out of these pivots, the North-East has primacy and is the main driver due to contiguity. Traditionally, 'Mainland India', a term utilised in limited extent and only to reiterate the critical aspect of this article, has had a rather indifferent record in its dealings with the North-East states. It is very aptly summed up in the omnibus misuse of the term 'Purabaiya', implying a person belonging to the east. All and sundry, starting from Poorvanchal (Eastern UP), have been bundled in this category. The Eastern Command HQ of the army was located in Lucknow and moved to Kolkata only after the Chinese invasion in May 1963. Parts of the North-East, like the erstwhile North East Frontier Agency, later Arunachal and Naga Hills Tuensang Area (NHTA), were governed by the Ministry of External Affairs (MEA) till the creation of Nagaland and Arunachal Pradesh.

The policy aims to act as a catalyst and an enabling mechanism to promote development in the North-East. The first critical requirement is to develop a better understanding and appreciation of the region and its diversity. Winston Churchill's oft-repeated quote, 'It is a riddle wrapped in a mystery inside an enigma', can be utilised to describe the North-East. It has a significant amount of diversity with the rest of India in terms of anthropology, ethnicity, and tribes; theological beliefs and religion; socio-cultural norms, dress, and customs; land ownership and agricultural practices, just to name important aspects. Physical distances are such that tea gardens in the North-East follow their own time zones, more aligned with Bangladesh and Bhutan, which have a variation of 30 minutes from Indian Standard Time (IST). The post-independence formulation devised by noted anthropologist Verrier Elwin, advocating insularity, has given way to increasing integration with the mainstream. **It will be in order to preserve local customs and values, duly modified based on societal consensus. Ideally, the system should transition to mutual dependency from the current patron-client relationship.** The green shoots of this are taking shape through the induction of a large number of people in service, retail, hospitality, and tourism sectors, employed outside in metropolitan cities, leveraging their soft skills.

While looking outwards and on regional plane, the policy pre-supposed stability in the security environment and resolution of ongoing insurgencies. While many movements in Mizoram, Assam (Bodo and ULFA), Tripura, Meghalaya, and Gorkhaland have been capped, the Naga insurgency, the proverbial Gordian knot of the North-East, is still to be fully resolved. Meanwhile, Manipur is witnessing an ethnic war between Kukis and Meiteis. **The situation has been exacerbated by multiple insurgencies in adjoining Myanmar and its attendant demographic outflow in the North-East, with the influx of Chin and Rohingya refugees.** The region has pockets of high-density demography, like in Bangladesh, forcing a sort of lebensraum and illegal economic migration outwards. The influx of refugees and illegal migrants has generated challenges, like altering the demographic balance in sensitive border districts. Frequent cyclones, tsunamis, and the spectre of rising sea levels have added to an adversarial environment and frequent bouts of death and destruction.

Dragon's Shadow – Clash of Connectivities

Chinese revanchist policy, proclaimed by Mao Zedong in the format of Tibetan palm with fingers extending outwards to include Ladakh, Nepal, Sikkim, Bhutan, and Arunachal, threatens the sovereignty of other neighbours. China is yet to settle land borders with India and Bhutan, despite protracted negotiations, and has renamed South Tibet as Xangnan and has included parts of Arunachal as part of its claims. It has made extensive claims, renamed places, and is creating Xiaokangs, border villages. Concurrently, China has tried to build dependencies and leverage by rolling out variants of the BRI in the form of economic corridors like the CMEC and the China-Nepal Economic Corridor (CNEC). The traditional and natural connectivity matrix was based on Kolkata, as a maritime gateway for land-locked neighbours like Nepal and Bhutan. Till the '60s and the Sino-Indian war, rice and other commodities were imported by Tibet from Kolkata. Much has changed with China planning and even executing topography-defying surface (rail/road) corridors from the Chinese hinterland to outlying territories of Tibet, traversing high-altitude regions. It aims to extend these into Nepal, Bhutan, and Myanmar and link them to Chinese supply chains. **India has also operationalised the Chennai-Vladivostok maritime corridor, which cuts transit time from 40 to 24 days and achieves 30% cost savings.**

Accompanying the surface connectivity juggernaut is growing Chinese gridlock in the Bay of Bengal, described as a 'string of pearls'. Cox's Bazar, Kyaukphyu, Ream, Hambantota, and Feydhoo Islands (Maldives) are not only ports of call but also instruments of power-projection. At the very heart is the objective to overcome the strategic vulnerability of the Malacca Straits. China is also pushing for resolving its Malacca dilemma by creating the Kra Canal through Thailand, to bypass this narrow passage. Security situation and the threat of dumping of Chinese products in already Chinese-dominated markets has imposed caution on India. Consequently, India had pulled back from signing the Regional Comprehensive Economic Pact with ASEAN. Does this imply Act East, but set up guard rails against the Dragon's economic domination? The complexity is accentuated with Vietnam despite fighting a war and being at the receiving end of ongoing maritime contestation in the South China Sea, further strengthening supply chains with China. Connectivity is acquiring new variants and is becoming multi-domain, covering facets like digital, power grids, pipelines, health, and tourism.

In the American engineered push-back policy of the relocation of manufacturing through the China plus One policy, Vietnam, Malaysia, and Indonesia are strong competitors, with Vietnam seeming to have an edge over the others currently. Hence, within Act East, it is an uneasy shared space of cooperation, competition, and even contestation amongst member states. It is also the region where regional organisations, except ASEAN, are dysfunctional and literally on a ventilator. The list of these bodies includes Bhutan, Bangladesh, India, Nepal (BBIN), and the Mekong-Ganga Cooperation. Only BIMSTEC spurts to life, but only occasionally and for brief spells. The North-East is also facing prospects of water wars likely to be unleashed with the construction of a mega dam on Tsangpo (Brahmaputra) at Zangbo Yarlung (Great Bend), which has major implications for Bangladesh and India. India is seeking to mitigate potential disaster by building a dam-cum-reservoir on the Subansiri River.

Siliguri Corridor – A Tenuous Link

India's link to the North-East (also described as seven sisters and one brother) is through the narrow Siliguri Corridor (approximately 18 km, at the narrowest) and the Dragon's Dolam (the Chinese call it Doklam), an ominous shadow over the corridor. India's rail-road corridor, pipelines, power, and communication grid runs through the corridor—please see Maps 3 and 4. India had proposed the creation of the Tetuliya surface corridor to create redundancy and reduce vulnerability. The complexity and challenges are magnified due to demography and latent separatist movements like Kamtapur (Rajbongshi) and Gorkhaland. The North Bengal region, with Siliguri as its hub, is emerging as an economic hub with trading, tea, tourism, medical, and education facilities, which have clientele in neighbouring Eastern Nepal, North-Western Bangladesh, and Bhutan. The famous apparel export trade of Bangladesh sources almost all of its raw materials, cotton, and yarn, from India. In addition, it banks on the techno-commercial network of India. Even in Nepal, Chinese-funded and aided power plants utilise Indian power distribution companies. Strategic vulnerability in the North-East besides unresolved border with China is compounded by a difficult-to-manage border with Bangladesh, spanning approximately 1,800 km, and with Myanmar, 1,600 km. The former is 80% fenced, but riverine terrain facilitates trans-border movement. Only 30 km of the Indo-Myanmar border is fenced and runs over difficult and treacherous terrain marked by hills and primary forests. In effect, **Bangladesh makes the North-East land-locked and connected through a tenuous link of the Siliguri Corridor. The current anti-India sentiment in Bangladesh can be exploited by China in collusion or by using Bangladesh as a proxy. On the other hand, Myanmar is the land bridge, which can unlock terrestrial connectivity to the ASEAN region.**

The efforts to forge alternate maritime connectivity between Kolkata and Sittwe port in Myanmar and onwards to Zorakhtwar in Meghalaya, utilising multi-modal (maritime, road, and riverine) Kaladan link, have been stalled for nearly two decades. The project did make some progress recently, but it is currently stalled due to internal chaos in Myanmar. There is also uncertainty on surface connectivity projects, anchored on the restoration of rail links between India and Bangladesh, which were executed only recently. The unfortunate swing between pro-India (Sheikh Hasina) and anti-India regimes (Begum

Khaleda Zia, Gen Ershad, and the current regime of Mohammad Yunus), coupled with instability in Myanmar, mandates building multiple connectivities and creating bilateral/multilateral stakes in these links. **Unfortunately, most plans remain on drawing boards, while China has managed to push its projects through, creating a strong presence in this region.**

Ten Point Plan and the North-East Council Meeting

Prime Minister Narendra Modi, in his recent visit to Laos, has laid out an ambitious agenda with a ten-point action plan under the summit theme of 'enhancing connectivity and resilience'. The action plan includes celebrating 2025 as the ASEAN-India year of tourism, with India providing funding of US$5 million for joint activities. It also proposes the celebration of the decade of the Act East policy with people-centric activities. The proposed list includes Youth Summit; Start-up Festival; Hackathon; Music Festival; ASEAN-India network of think tanks and Delhi Dialogue; ASEAN-India Women Scientists conclave under ASEAN-India Science and Technology Development Fund; doubling the number of scholarships in Nalanda University, and provision of new ASEAN scholarships in agricultural universities in India.

Besides these measures, it is proposed to review ASEAN-India Trade in Goods Agreement by 2025; enhancing Disaster Resilience with US$5 million funding by India; new Health Ministers Track towards Health Resilience; initiating ASEAN-India Cyber Policy Dialogue to strengthen Digital and Cyber Resilience; workshop on Green Hydrogen and invitation to ASEAN leaders to join 'Plant a Tree for Mother' campaign towards climate resilience. Amit Shah, the home minister, recently presided over the 72nd North-East Council at Agartala and outlined a new agenda for the North-East. **He reiterated that there has been a 71% decline in violence and called for Act East-Act Fast-Act First[xiv].** He laid out a rather ambitious plan of the North-East becoming the most prosperous region in India by 2047, as well as an export gateway.

Way Forward

An objective appraisal leads to the inference that the action plan and agenda are loaded with symbolic exploratory initiatives. Most proposals are in the soft power domain and would require backing in ramping up connectivity, trade, and joint ventures. Though symbolic, they hold the promise of opening new avenues. However, on balance, the essence lies in converting promises into time-bound implementation. A complementary plan and agenda for the North-East is warranted, with a focus on the revitalisation of governance structures like the Department of North-East Region (DONER) and the North East Council. It will also be prudent to invest in regional organisations like BBIN, BIMSTEC, and Mekong-Ganga Cooperation. **The recent announcement of Tata wanting to set up a semiconductor unit in Morigaon, Assam, has the potential to kick-start a digital ecosystem around it, extending into the ASEAN region.** Even if symbolic, the President of India, the Prime Minsiter, and other key functionaries can relocate to the North-East for three to four weeks in a period spanning Hornbill Festival and Christmas. A suitable Presidential retreat in Shillong, like Shimla, Hyderabad, and Dehradun, can be considered.

India can emulate the successful Yunnan model being implemented by China, which has expedited development in the underdeveloped region. India has also indicated a desire to review its reluctance to join RCEP. The current flux in the region, characterised by an anti-India environment in Bangladesh and not-so-friendly governments in Nepal, Sri Lanka, and the Maldives, poses complex challenges. It calls for nimble diplomacy, while sticking to a long-term commitment to the Act East policy. Hopefully, a strategic and mature approach will make these countries realise the age-old maxim that 'one can choose friends but not neighbours'. India faces concurrent challenges of multi-domain connectivity with and beyond the North-East. As we strengthen our outreach, concurrently, it is important to expedite conflict resolution in the North-East. Stable North-East with resilient connectivity is strategically critical to checkmate Chinese expansionist policies. **It is also equally critical to resolve the connectivity paradigm to ensure multiple connectivities across domains (surface, maritime, digital, and power grids) with in-built redundancies. The bottom line is Act East through the geo-economic pivot of the North-East.**

References

- USI Strategic Year Books – 2024, Vij Books India Pvt India, New Delhi, 2024.
- USI Strategic Year Books – 2022, Vij Books India Pvt India, New Delhi, 2022.
- USI Strategic Year Books – 2018, Vij Books India Pvt India, New Delhi, 2018.
- https://MEA.gov.in

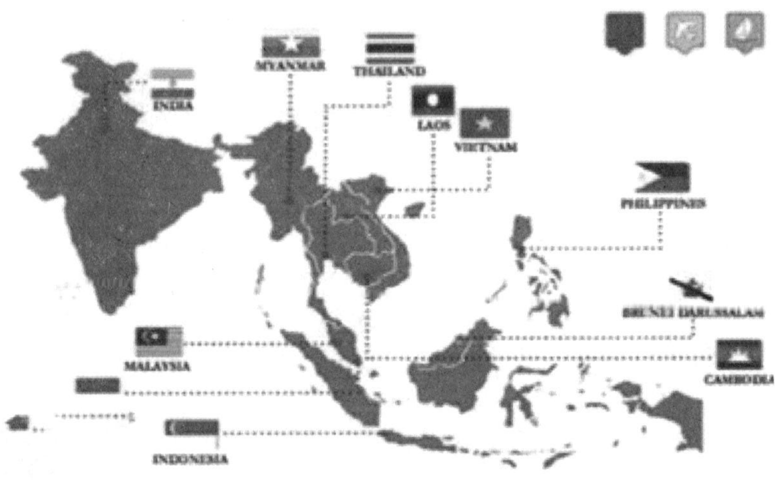

(Map-1 – Source – https://www.indiaasean.org/india/about/overview)

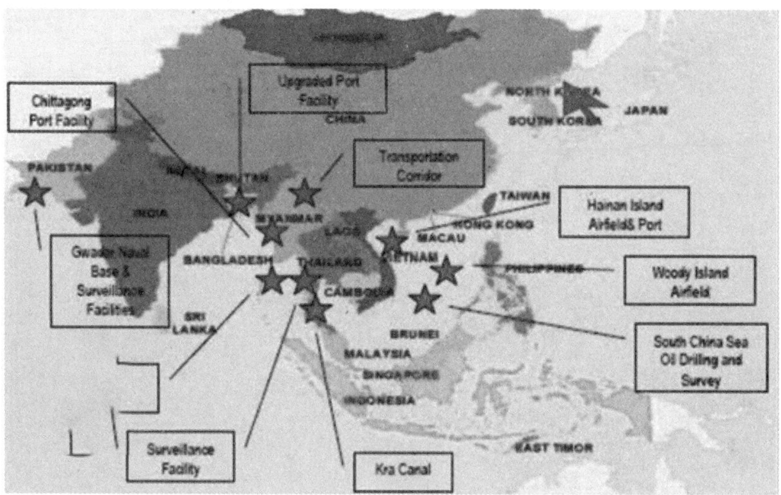

(Map-2 – Source – https:// images.app.goo.gl/iGiJMKDt7Bw822rC6)

(Map-3 – Source – https://images.app.goo.gl/guWhWfSz9HMXKsBX7)

(Map-4 – Source – https:// images.app.goo.gl/TWfbugwZ9j36Sb7n6)

Punjab and the Khalistan Bogey

17.1 Corridor Symbolises Reverence, Aspirations, and Apprehensions (Written in November 2019)

The Establishment of the Kartapur Corridor is partial fulfilment of a long-cherished dream of the Sikh sangat of securing 'khulle darshan deedar' and 'sewa sambhal', implying free, unhindered access and right to look after their shrines. This is an integral part of 'ardas' in gurudwaras all over the world. It is a bit of incongruity (mercifully glossed over) that the focus of the 550th birth anniversary celebrations are two abodes of Guru Nanak, Kartarpur in Pakistan and Sultanpur Lodhi in India, rather than the more appropriate Gurdwara Janam Asthan in Nankana Sahib in Pakistan. While Pakistan exults at this milestone in its revanchist journey, will this quest spread to Nankana Sahib and Panja Sahib, and how will free access be granted to other shrines? These are worrisome and pertinent questions, which may haunt Pakistan.

Kartarpur is the place where Guru Nanak exhibited the most laudable examples of handing over his temporal seat (in his lifetime) on a non-dynastic basis, and then, continued with spiritual work coupled with farming for 18 years. Defying and disregarding this legacy, current political satraps continue to cling to power and nurture their dynasties blatantly. They have further entrenched this malady by matrimonial alliances, amongst influential ruling families, particularly in Punjab, thereby ensuring collective immunity. It is most unfortunate that the slugfest for brownie points has resulted in separate events, superfluous expenditure, confusion, and even tussle for getting the Prime Minister to venues.

While a few want to hog the credit for this historic initiative, it has been possible due to sustained collective yearning, prayers, and untiring efforts of many. It is rather unfortunate that in trying to be the showstopper, Navjot Sidhu seems to have walked into a crafty orchestrated trap. Notwithstanding our reverence, and at the risk of being labelled as spoilers, many, like Punjab Chief Minister Capt Amarinder Singh, have valid apprehensions. These views are prefaced with the assertion that the Sikh community has displayed unimpeachable loyalty and is not known to be naive.

The Current initiative on the corridor project is being anchored by Khaki generals and is possibly part of the ISI's diabolic K2 project. Doubts on this score are reinforced by Gen Asif Ghafoor vetoing concessions announced by Pakistan Prime Minister Imran Khan with regards to waiving off requirement of passport for Sikhs and facilitation fee for two days. The timing of this step has to be seen in the context of mischievous SFJ's 'Referendum 2020' campaign and events like Canadian elections. Inclusion of visuals of the dreaded and controversial trio of Bhindranwale, Amrik, and Shabheg in the official video is indicative of Pakistan wanting to utilise these as tools for psychological war. A similar evil intent is evident in a prominent display of the remains of an Indian shell in the vicinity of the shrine. More of the same must be in pipeline, aimed at encouraging centrifugal forces.

Competitive populism is driving self-appointed guardians of faith towards more extremist postures. It suits the nouveau-rich and politically relevant (kingmaker) diaspora to fund mischief makers to chase the Khalistani mirage. They seemed to be emulating Sheikhs, who have funded jihadi influences and outsourced Wahabi extremism to the subcontinent. Unfortunately, people who want to stoke these fires have forgotten that the last round of extremism had put Punjab irretrievably back by a couple of decades and degraded Punjabiyat. Are Punjabis prepared for another round of senseless terrorism?

Pakistan wants to leverage fault lines between communities by wanting to extend special concessions to Sikhs, ignoring the inclusive culture of the 'Nanak Naam Lewa Sangat', which includes all those who believe in Guru Nanak's teachings. Besides Sikhs, Sehajdharis, Kabeerpanthis, Ravidasias, Sindhis, and even Muslims were treated as one by Baba Nanak. Pakistan should reconsider the levying of facilitation charges of $20, as gurdwaras world over provide not only free access but also free langar and many other facilities. Access and charges, if unavoidable, should be the same for all pilgrims, as envisioned in Guru's inclusive message.

As communities rededicate themselves to Nanak's path, it is time to introspect and reflect on some important questions. Has the overemphasis on 'rehat maryada' (codified norms) articulated through rituals, impacted and diluted the very essence of the original 'Sehaj' path of Guru Nanak? It is also time to jettison the caste system, driving marginal sections to *deras*, which have sprouted all over Punjab.

Pakistan's propensity to push drugs, counterfeit, and arms will require full-body scanners and multiple screenings. The desire to stoke fires in Punjab is very strong, and organizations, like Sikhs For Justice (SFJ), are being propped up by the ISI to orchestrate the demand for Referendum 2020. **The proposed corridor will also trigger the demand for a liberal pilgrim circuit for other gurdwaras and even peeths and temples like the Sharada Peeth, Hinglaj Mata and Katasraj.** While Pakistan has to deal with its share of challenges, the bigger ones for us lie within. Internally, Sikhs, especially those who have usurped the authority to run socio religious affairs, need to be introspective. Sadly, as we get set to celebrate 550 years of Baba Nanak, the overwhelming feeling is that Panthic rigidity has pushed tolerant and liberal Sikhs out. We have strains of fundamentalism that extol deification of Sarup (form) with heavy reliance on external symbols.

Pakistan should also honour collective aspirations of the populace on both sides for peace and reconciliation. **This can happen, only if it gives up its quest to foment trouble in India, including activities like promoting Khalistanis, nefarious designs of crafting 'Udta Punjab', and Drugistan.** Indians, particularly Punjabis and Sikhs, should remain vigilant to defeat these machinations.

Even Pakistan will have to remain on guard as such shrines, with emotive connections, remain potential targets for mischievous elements for taking over as bargaining tools. It should rein in mischievous elements, like Gopal Singh Chawla, and sanitise the Evacuee Trust Property Board (ETPB) and the Pakistan Sikh Gurdwara Parbandhak Committee to keep extremist elements out. Pakistan must also ensure that minorities are given religious freedom and shielded from abduction and forced conversion, as evidenced in the recent case of Jagjit Kaur and numerous other cases.

The abiding wisdom enshrined in 'Baba Nanak Shah Fakir, Hindu da Guru, Musalman da Peer' needs to be carried forward in implementing the historic Supreme Court verdict in the Ayodhya dispute. It is time, the nation focuses on economic empowerment, not allowing divisive religious issues to stymie our progress. The message is 'Keerat Karo, Wand Chako'—(endeavour and share)—besides 'Naam Japo' (recitation).

17.2 The Plan Behind Smart, Secure Headgear for Sikh Warriors (Written in January 2023)

The Indian Army's recent request-for-proposal (RFP), seeking the emergency procurement of 12,730 ballistic helmets in two sizes—8, 911 in large and 3,819 in extra-large—has become mired in an avoidable controversy. Veer customised headgear, designed by the MKU, will include a central bulge to accommodate a *'jura'* (hair bun), with the head wrapped in the form of a *dastar* (turban)-like patka or *parna/kesaki*. These wrappings, worn by the UN forces, are referred to as a semi-turban. Sikh troops have been donning functional head covering during physical training (PT), sports, and maintenance parades.

This is the first time that customised headgear, which seeks to combine protective and smart battle function attributes, is being procured. Sikh troops deployed in CI areas and on the LoC have been using bulletproof patka (BPP). The improvised, unpopular contraption has its share of problems with weight and rigid configuration due to dated technology. The current generation of headgear based on Kevlar and ceramic materials seeks to redress these problems and provide value-added attributes.

The procurement has been criticised by Sikh religious bodies, who have called the helmet a 'loh top' (iron hat). They have termed it as interfering with Sikh rehat maryada (tenets and traditions), and expressed apprehension at the replacement of pagri (turban) with a helmet. They also assert that the turban is not merely a 5–7m piece of cloth, but a 'crown' gifted by Gurus.

The issue needs to be logically analysed. The first requirement is to look at the historical perspective. There are illustrations that show Sikh warriors of Maharaja Ranjit Singh's forces wearing metallic helmets with chain mail for providing protection. A few pieces are displayed in British museums, and were reportedly used in the Anglo-Sikh wars. The evidence is backed up by engravings on the Sutlej Medal awarded in colonial times. This fits into Maharaja Ranjit Singh being far ahead of his time and readily adapting various technologies. The defining trend of pragmatic improvisation, or jugaad, and resilience continue to define Sikh soldiers.

Sikh soldiers used steel rings, called *chakris*, over turbans to ward off attacks by swords and spears. These are still displayed on ceremonial turbans by Sikh regiments. Nihang dastar bunga turbans, in pyramidal, tier shape, include multiple rings and steel contraptions. It is a fact that Sikh regiments refused the offer of wearing helmets in the two world wars and even fought post-independence wars in turbans. Precision and lethality of weapons have, however, altered the basic paradigm of survivability.

Sniper rifles, with single-shot kill capability, are emerging realities. The most vulnerable target is the head of a soldier. A study of ballistic injuries with disabilities is required to objectively analyse the issue. Soldiers in contemporary Armed Forces in the US, Canada, and Australia wear combat helmets. Sikh soldiers in our forces, who have been serving as part of the crew of tanks and armoured fighting vehicles, have been using padded headgear with built-in headphones. Pilots, paratroopers, drivers, and submarine crews have also been donning specialised headgear. Sikh sportsmen in cricket, hockey, and boxing have opted for functional head-wraps, like patka, with protective helmets, to optimise their performance. How can we forget Milkha Singh, the Flying Sikh, with just a rumal (kerchief) covering his hair bun?

Sikhs have five basic mandated tenants, referred to as *kakkars*—kesh, *kada,* kangha, kaccha, and kirpan. All five have become modified and compromised to a considerable extent. *Dastar*, or turban, is an adjunct to maintain kesh, but the original version of rounded *dastar* and *dumalas* have gone through multiple variations, with only a few persisting with the near-original form.

The four dominant types of turbans currently are Vattan Wali, Amritsari Shahi, Barnala Shahi, and Taksali Dumala. The present turban of our Sikh soldiers is an inverted, V-shaped variant, with symmetrical seven folds. In transition, starched turbans have given way to unstarched ones. In civilian society, they have been affected by fashion trends and have been used as regional and even caste/identity markers.

Religious bodies are seeking to discard functional *dastars,* like *kesaki,* patka, and *parnas*. They project it in zero-sum format, whereas both forms can co-exist. Sikh soldiers can continue to wear turbans for ceremonial occasions and switch to much-preferred functional head wrap for operations, sports, and maintenance. These can be combined with the new proposed headgear.

Socio-religious bodies need to focus on critical societal issues, like drug menace, *deras,* and a large number of Sikh youths, especially role models, opting to cut their hair. In network-centric warfare, soldiers would be like plugged entities in battlefield surveillance and management system. Each link would have to be given the requisite processed and synthesised awareness as also protection, as the chain snaps at the weakest link. It would be axiomatic to equip Sikh soldiers with multi-functional gear, which is light, protective and comfortable, and provides hands-free operation. To deny it to the mainstay of our forces (Sikhs make up 8%) is both retrograde and illogical. Bravado and tradition alone cannot compensate for combat realities.

Most importantly, socio-religious bodies should allow forces to devise their own norms as these are generally evolved after due consultation and feedback. However, the proposed customised gear could be renamed as *kesaki-veer* headgear. The government, on its part, needs to put at rest apprehensions, especially with regard to proliferation in the civilian domain.

17.3 Punjab at a Crossroads in the Run-Up to Assembly Polls (Written in January 2022)

Dark ominous clouds are once again looming over impending Punjab assembly elections. Bomb blast at Ludhiana, coupled with sacrilege incident at Harmandar Sahib brought back painful memories of the Maur blast and Baragari incident in the run-up to the 2017 elections. Adding to the complexity are other lynching incidents, sought to be passed off as *be-adbi* (sacrilege), which has emerged as the new tool in cognitive electoral manipulation. The major difference this time is that the blame-game has shifted from *deras* to Khalistanis and elements across the border. However, a spurt in incidents and the timing of these have sprouted conspiracy theories.

K2 is a perennial terror instrument of Pakistan's ISI. Militancy in Punjab originated in the '80s and pre-dates the ongoing proxy war in the valley. It accounted for approximately 20,000 senseless deaths, including then Prime Minister, and both sitting and former chief ministers. Unfortunately, fault lines were shaped by scheming and wily politicians. They unleashed Frankenstein masquerading as a saint, who, like a proverbial genie, refused to heed to facilitators.

Punjab, with strategic significance, will always remain on Pakistan's radar, as unrest here has the potential to wreck agricultural economy and vital national food security. By nature, Punjabis remain fiercely independent, resulting in opposition being at the helm for a prolonged period. Compulsive contrarianism (euphemistically termed as panga-taking) is a natural instinct and is sought to be exploited by the ISI to shape centrifugal forces.

Emotion rules and trick is in reaching out and addressing sensitivities; bullying simply doesn't work. Religion and politics are dangerously mixed up, peppered with a large number of *deras,* engaged in divisive self-serving activities. Most have even acquired their own militias. Riverine terrain, drugs, and gun-running form a complex template for crime in border areas. Drones and tunnels have added third dimension, making-up for, albeit to limited extent, the currently suspended overland rail and road transit.

Punjab and Mizoram are two isolated examples of success in our rather gloomy conflict resolution matrix. It is also relevant that the state police, supported by the populace, defeated nefarious proxy war designs. The unfortunate part is that very few recount this success story. Every time, I complimented Punjabis on this account, hate mail followed. Many mainstream regional parties have countenanced the glorification of terrorists.

Pakistan has been striving to extend the arc of terrorism from Jammu-Katha-Samba to adjoining areas of Punjab. This is part of the obstinate ploy to keep the concept of working boundary alive. Multiple attacks have occurred in Samba, followed by incidents at Dinanagar (Gurdaspur) and Pathankot. In Dinanagar, the army consciously allowed the state police to take the credit, despite a machine gunner from the army being the main enabler in the successful elimination of three terrorists. Notwithstanding recovery of GPS, which was unprofessionally handled (as per media reports), there can be no real closure on route of ingress and the number of terrorists.

The Pathankot incident highlighted the complicity of Salwinder, sacked superintendent of police, and the possibility of a 'diamonds for drug' racket. The mansion of the taxi driver in his village and the involvement of a jeweller raised serious doubts about a well-organised nexus, complete with a logistics chain. Unfortunately, cops like Salwinder and Devinder (of Srinagar airport notoriety) are nurtured and given responsibilities well beyond their competence, overlooking documented red flags and shady dealings.

A rough check of manning the profile of border districts from Jammu to Ferozpur in 2014–16 revealed a few worrying facts. First, the IAS and IPS officers are conspicuous by their absence. Second, the state services officers linked to politicians are posted in border range, on multiple tenures. Third, most are linked with local crime syndicates. Fourth, passing the buck follows after every incident. Intelligence agencies flag generalised warnings, blaming the police for ignoring them. The BSF and police trade accusations. Finally, NIA and Special Investigation Team (SIT) step in, but never achieve closure. Almost all sacrilege and blast cases remain unresolved, eroding trust and fuelling unwanted speculation.

The two confidence builders in citizenry, central agencies and apex police hierarchy, have been politicised completely. Most placements are based on suitability (read pliability) and affiliations, ignoring domain competence. Having served with outstanding officers in Khaki, including central agencies, yearning for reforms is natural. When Ludhiana blast happened, I was in Hoshiarpur, addressing a large youth fest. Almost every one blamed the interested parties and agencies. It will require concerted serious work by parties and agencies to dispel the prevailing notion and regain their credibility. It threw up another disturbing realisation that unfortunately, the youth now believes that all is fair in polls. Amity and tolerance seem to be yielding turf to hate and binaries. Ignoring norms, polls and campaigns are plummeting into a sort of unrestricted warfare.

In sum, nuanced federalism, as enshrined in the Indian Constitution, is critical in border states. Festering disputes, like farmer agitation, are ticking fault lines. Police and administration in border areas need to be revamped, modelled on the erstwhile Indian Frontier Administrative Service (IFAS). Investigations need to be time-bound and findings shared. All parties should reduce electoral temperature. As an eternal optimist, I have faith that the 'Punjabiyat' and 'Nanak Naam Lewa' traditions will defeat diabolic plots.

17.4 Punjab – Seeking a Way Forward in a Simmering Crisis (Written in March 2023)

Introduction

Role models like Rishi Sunak, Prime Minister of the the UK, and Ajay Banga, recently appointed President of the World Bank, bolster Punjab's image, giving it a larger-than-life narrative. The community is characterised by an adventurous and industrious spirit, very visible and known to be punching much above its weight classification, notwithstanding small numbers. Unfortunately, back home, Punjab and Punjabis have been in the news, mostly for the wrong reasons. The unending chase of the self-appointed head of Waris-Punjab-De (WPD), Amritpal Singh, turned into a tragi-comic drama and charade, finally leading to his apprehension after more than a month-long, hit-and-miss chase. Punjabis have been spearheading unresolved farmers' agitation, which has been unfairly dubbed as a Khalistan-linked movement.

Dominant Narratives: The two dominant narratives are drug addiction ('udta' or delirious Punjab) and the threat of revival of the separatist Khalistan movement. This erodes the image of farmers, sportsmen, and enablers of the green revolution as well as numerous much-acclaimed charity initiatives by organisations like the Khalsa Aid. Even abroad, especially in Canada, some Punjabis are embroiled in drug trade and extortion. The recent shooting of a top UN-designated gangster, Amarpal Singh in Canada, attacks on Hindu temples in Australia, and violent protests and attempts to ransack the Indian High Commission in London are ominous trends. The recent report by Colin Bloom, a reputed and independent faith engagement advisor of the UK government, has recommended a detailed investigation into pro-Khalistan activists and the application of necessary correctives. Many such maladies have been soft-pedalled in Canada, the UK, and Australia, allegedly due to the compulsion of vote-bank politics. It will be appropriate to examine emerging challenges and flag appropriate coping strategies.

Challenges

Demographic and Theological Environment: The Punjabi society has traditionally been syncretic with a tolerant, multi-faith character, living in harmony. The approximate demographic distribution is—Sikhs (57%), Hindus (38%), Muslims (2%), and a visibly increasing number of Christians (2%). The culture is referred to as Punjabiyat and the inclusive faith as 'Nanak Naam Lewa', with Sufi influences. **Punjab has approximately 32% Scheduled Caste (SC), Dalit population, divided into Ramdasias Mazhabis Kabirpanthi, Ravidasias and Adi Dharmi sects, often jostling among themselves.** This is the highest percentage of SC in a state. Unfortunately, the Sikh religion has been taken over by gurdwara tussles and competitive extremism, and has become intertwined with mainstream politics. This has resulted in the sprouting of *deras* (seminaries) and *sants* (spiritual heads), some even with private militias. The overarching religious body, Shiromani Gurdwara Prabandhak Committee (SGPC), has been forced to yield control of Nanded Sahib and Patna Sahib, temporal seats, referred to as Takhats. Similarly, Delhi Gurdwara Prabandhak Committee (DGPC) and Haryana Sikh Gurdwara Prabandhak Committee (HSGPC) have come up in Delhi and Haryana. A new trend is fomenting societal tensions, by orchestrating sacrilegious acts (described as be-adbi) like the Baragari incident, wherein the holy book is desecrated by mischievous elements. Another notable phenomenon is the faith healing camps to convert poor Dalits.

K2 Conundrum: Pakistan is reportedly running the Kashmir-Khalistan (K2) project through the ISI, aimed at reviving the Khalistan movement even when the situation in Kashmir is improving. A large number of extremist leaders are operating from Pakistan. The recent shooting down of the dreaded and wanted Khalistan Commando Force Chief, Paramjit Singh Panjwar, in Lahore, corroborates this fact. As a corollary, there are regular reports of sightings and shooting down of drones, by security agencies. The drone-drug combo is being misused by narco-terrorism mafia across the border to drop weapons besides drugs, of course, in connivance with agencies and rangers across. **It is fairly apparent that currently, Khalistan and separatism have no real traction within Punjab. The old generation still recalls the difficult period and '*Santaap*' (suffering) during the '80s and the '90s. The fact that Amritpal and his movement failed to gain traction and he was described as a *bhagoda* (absconder), amply proves their irrelevance.** However, the movement simmers abroad amongst the diaspora with sporadic, high TRP-grabbing incidents, aided by complicit elements in authority.

Agrarian Complexities: Punjab continues to be the granary of the nation, with a record-breaking output. The overflowing granaries enabled the free grain scheme, which provided much-needed relief during the COVID-19 pandemic and the Ukrainian conflict, which had disrupted grain supply. **However, the 'rice-wheat' cropping pattern is an irrigation-intensive process, resulting in the water table receding/depleting and creating a spectre of looming water, stress.** The burning of crop residue along with other factors creates choking environmental pollution in the National Capital Region (NCR). The rampant use of chemical fertilisers and pesticide have poisoned soil and water leading to a high incidence of health hazards like cancer. Land holdings have become smaller, and farming is done by contracted migrant labour, which is creating demographic challenges.

Socio-Political Determinants: The politics are a complex cocktail of theologically inclined parties like factions of the Akali Dal. The unprecedented majority given to the Aam Admi Party (AAP) was essentially a rejection of established parties.

The Punjabi society is characterised by a few defining peculiarities. These include:

- First, **an overbearing sense of scepticism.** This also leads to Punjab being perpetually out of step with the central authority manifesting in non-ruling (opposition) parties, like the AAP, at the helm of state.

- Second, the **youth needs persuasion and sensitive handling,** as Punjabi nature is described in the seminal quote, *'Pyar naal saadi jaan bhi le lo, Jora-Mardi naal, assi pinde di joon bhi nahi deni'*. It means that with love, you can ask for our life but with coercion and force, we shall not part with even unwanted lice, on our body. This often is mistaken as entitlement or bullying, which is avoidable.

- Third, **if convinced about a sense of fair play and the right cause, the very same lot is willing to blindly follow the leader.** The caveat is that leadership has to be earned, as we see in the Sikh soldiers and the response of soldiers and rural peasantry in the 1965 and 1971 wars. Most importantly, the Green Revolution, transforming the starving PL-480-dependent ship-to-mouth national economy into a grain exporting one, bears reiteration on this account.

- Fourth, the **Punjabi youth is aspirational and is willing to live on the edge, and increasingly seeks greener pastures through migration.** This has resulted in the eulogising of gangsters, guns, and even drugs. Ironically, even those aspiring to drive trucks prefer to do it in Canada and the US.

- Most importantly, the **Central Government has undertaken multiple initiatives, including emotive ones, like recognising the martyrdom of Sahebzadas (sons of Guru Gobind Singh), yet, it requires more efforts to overcome persistent scepticism amongst society.**

Way Forward

The solution to Punjab's woes mandates a multi-dimensional and focused long-term commitment. It is high time that the law-and-order mechanism in the border state is sorted out. Pakistan is hell-bent on prosecuting the K2 project, and it is axiomatic that the police and central agencies should be synergistic and stay focused on operations and keep out of partisan politics. The reality is that state administrative and police cadres are divided along political affiliations with incessant inter and intra-cadre tussles. Supreme Court-mandated reforms, outlined in the Prakash Singh Committee report, need to be applied post-haste.

Externally, hierarchy and diplomats have red-flagged extremist tendencies, and pressure has to be kept up, as these governments tend to pander to vote banks. It is also necessary that those identified as dubious are denied reciprocal citizenship benefits, like the Overseas Citizens of India (OCI) and Non-Resident Indian (NRI) privileges. The problem has political dimensions, wherein theologically inclined parties are sprouting factions, which seek recognition by positioning themselves on the extremist fringes. The established parties owe it to Punjab to forge Punjabiyat and an inclusive 'Nanak Naam Lewa' culture. **In the long term, it is all about tackling the socio-economic problems, primarily enabling Green Revolution 2.0, skill-building, and building an ecosystem for employment to reclaim the lost glory of Punjab.**

The bottom line is that problems, although serious, are manageable and flagged. Given the right catalysts—meaningful leadership, commitment, and central initiatives—Punjabis, being self-starters, are blessed with legendary resilience and improvisation (jugaad). They have it in them to rebound. Meanwhile, the diaspora should contribute by anchoring meaningful initiatives back home, but most importantly, desist from supporting malevolent elements and fissiparous tendencies.

Clash of Corridors – BRI, CPEC, and IMEC

18.1 Strategic Appraisal of the Belt and Road Initiative and the China-Pakistan Economic Corridor

> *Chinese infrastructure and connectivity projects around the world have an element of 'national security' and are less of an economic offer for host countries.*
>
> —Mike Pompeo, former US Secretary of State

Update: China has managed to forge a trilateral agreement with Pakistan and Afghanistan for the latter to join the CPEC. This may lead to the Taliban becoming a guarantor for the security of the CPEC.

Introduction

It is now an established and **academically validated conclusion that the building of all-weather roads or transportation corridors by China has catalysed and paved the way for the country's prosperity.** The current Chinese domestic network, linking markets to distribution centres, acted as a pathway to trade, governance, and unprecedented progress. It was described as a hub and spoke model, along with many other similar names. The proof is in lifting 770 million people out of poverty. President Xi Jinping declared in the CCP Congress that China has achieved the first centennial goal of achieving modest prosperity and banishing poverty. This is also documented in the joint book titled *Four Decades of Poverty Reduction In China: Drivers, Insights for the World, and the Way Ahead.* It is important to reiterate that connectivity has always been relevant in great games in the form of Silk Roads and maritime corridors, like spice routes. Many other developing countries are trying to replicate this infrastructure push as a poverty alleviation measure in the form of roads, freight, and maritime corridors, as a sort of panacea or silver bullet. **However, the real challenge lies in the correct initial planning, timely project execution, and, most importantly, corruption-free management.**

China, flush with surplus capital and infrastructure-building capacities, embarked on a global initiative in the form of the BRI in 2017. The Chinese outward reach has been propelled by a desire to present an alternate mode of development. It also has historical drivers, as China, driven by the Middle Kingdom Syndrome, perceives it as the pivot. This is also coupled with the desire to redress alleged historical and colonial wrongs to claim her rightful place on the global stage. The BRI attracted as many as 120 odd countries, and it seemed that every nation wanted to join what was hailed as the 'project of the century'. This much-heralded initiative seems to be floundering, with many dismissing it as a 'road to nowhere'. It is important to take note of the legendary resilience of China, and carry out an objective assessment of the BRI to map the likely trends.

History of Silk Roads – Major Inferences

- The Royal Road of the Persian Empire in the fifth century BC, which predates the Chinese Silk Roads, is the earliest known transport corridor.
- The earliest Chinese transportation corridor initiative was the eleventh-century BC Silk Roads of the Han dynasty, spanning approximately 4,000 miles (6,500 km). Chang'an-Tianshan Corridor in China-Kazakhstan-Tajikistan has been accorded a UNESCO heritage site status.
- Besides terrestrial connectivity, the Chinese invented the mariner's compass, a master instrument for seafaring, in 220 CE. The Chinese had also constructed dry docks and the capability to make large

ships. The Chinese Treasure Fleet under Admiral Zhang earned notoriety for its exploitative voyages.

- **The basic drivers for Chinese outreach are:**
  - **Firstly, the Middle Kingdom orientation or syndrome**
  - **Secondly, the correction of alleged historical wrongs perpetuated by various colonial empires in the 'century of humiliation'**
  - **Thirdly, the desire to build and showcase alternative models of development**
  - **Fourthly, the availability of surplus capital and infrastructure-building capacity**

The Pandemic and the Ukrainian Conflict – Major Lessons

- **Public health is a vital component of CNP**, and well-being can boost the gross domestic product (GDP).
- A pandemic, at best, can be tackled with a scientific and evidence-based approach rather than quick-fix solutions like the failed Chinese Zero-Covid policy of lockdown and selective vaccination.
- The sharing of transparent data and statistics enables peer review, which is vital in tackling pandemics.
- **Dependencies in health-related supplies can create strategic vulnerability**, and this was even used as leverage by China.
- **Self-reliance and decoupling of supply chains** are the new trends.
- Health and vaccination corridors are manifesting.
- The increasing frequency of natural disasters dictates **the need for disaster mitigation, relief, and the creation of disaster-resilient infrastructure**.

- Notwithstanding the pandemic, resilience and innovation can help to persist with limited activity, throwing up new possibilities in remote working and Work From Home (WFH). Some of these are being retained even after the return of normalcy due to cheaper costs and flexibility.
- **The BRI and the CPEC have been significantly impacted by COVID-19.** The BRI's northern links to Europe through Eurasia have been stymied.
- The Ukrainian war has spurred the development of the International North-South Transport Corridor (INSTC) and the improvisation of the Wheat/Grain Maritime Corridor.
- In sum, pandemics are proliferated by **vectors like viruses and bacteria, which travel along transportation corridors. Hence, it is important to deal with them on a global basis with a cooperative endeavour.**

Appraisal of the Belt and Road Initiative (BRI) – Major Inferences

- The concept of mega connectivity was **first propounded in 2013 as One Belt One Road (OBOR) but later renamed BRI in 2017.**
- **Belt and Road, or '*yidaiyilu*' in Chinese, really implies 'a "belt" of overland routes and a maritime "road" connecting Southeast Asia to Eastern Europe and Africa'.**
- The BRI, described as **the 'project of the century' and the '21st Century Silk Road'**, is planned to extend to 65 countries, touch the lives of 62% of the world population, entail an expenditure of 30% of global GDP, and harness 75% of energy reserves.
- BRI summits in 2017 and 2019 were attended by 120 countries, including 29 at the apex level. **India was the most notable absentee.**

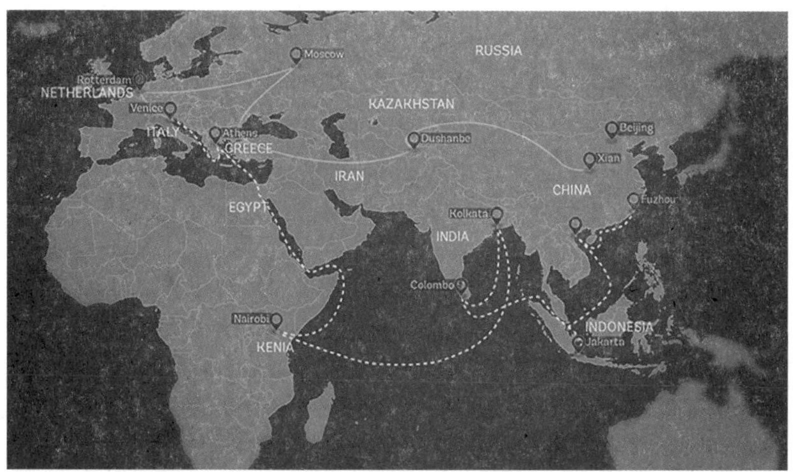

(*Source – Official Website of BRI-https://eng.yidaiyilu.gov.cn/wap/wap.htm*)

- China has a presence in 42 ports in 34 countries with a stated desire to extend to 75 ports as part of the 'string of pearls' or maritime bases.

- As many as **42 countries are currently trapped in a debt repayment crisis**, termed a 'debt trap'. Despite the pandemic-induced humanitarian crisis, China has only agreed to reschedule the debt of the 17 most distressed nations.

- China is attempting to extend her influence and **foster dependencies in cyber and space domains by promoting Digital and Space Silk Roads.**

- **BRI projects are carbon intensive** with large greenhouse gas (GHG) emissions and don't really comply with climate action plan norms.

- BRI projects are encountering multiple challenges, such as debt servicing, corruption, security, inefficient project execution, and opposition from the local populace.

- China has assured and is **attempting to rebrand the initiative as BRI 2.0 after a review.** However, host nations remain largely sceptical. These are being packaged as **Global Development/ Security/Cultural Initiatives in 2021, 2022, and 2023.**

- **America is attempting belated rear-guard action in the form of B3W**, and similar infrastructure initiatives are proposed by multilateral forums like the Quad.

Manifestations of the Debt Trap

- **Sri Lanka** has been forced to yield control and lease **Hambantota for 99 years.**
- **Pakistan** has also handed over **de facto control over Gwadar to China by allowing a 43-year management control.** Pakistan has become **a basket case.**
- **Malaysian Prime Minister** Mohamad had **cancelled the Railways project** amounting to US $20 billion on the grounds that the country could not afford such exorbitant projects.
- **Tajikistan** had to yield control of **1,158 square kilometres of territory to China** in 2010 in lieu of loan waivers. This territory is now being used by **Chinese companies to mine minerals, including gold.**
- **Laos has yielded control of her electricity grid to China for 25 years** as part of debt restructuring.

Analysis of the CPEC

- The CPEC was **first considered in 2003** and offered to Pervez Musharraf but was not progressed. **Nawaz Sharif, in 2013, announced the launching of the CPEC, describing it as game changer.** The project got traction in 2015 with the signing of MOUs.
- Described as a geo-economic oriented project, it is a **manifestation of China-Pakistan collusive linkages and is another addition to the geo-strategic glue after the gifting of the Shakasgam Valley.**

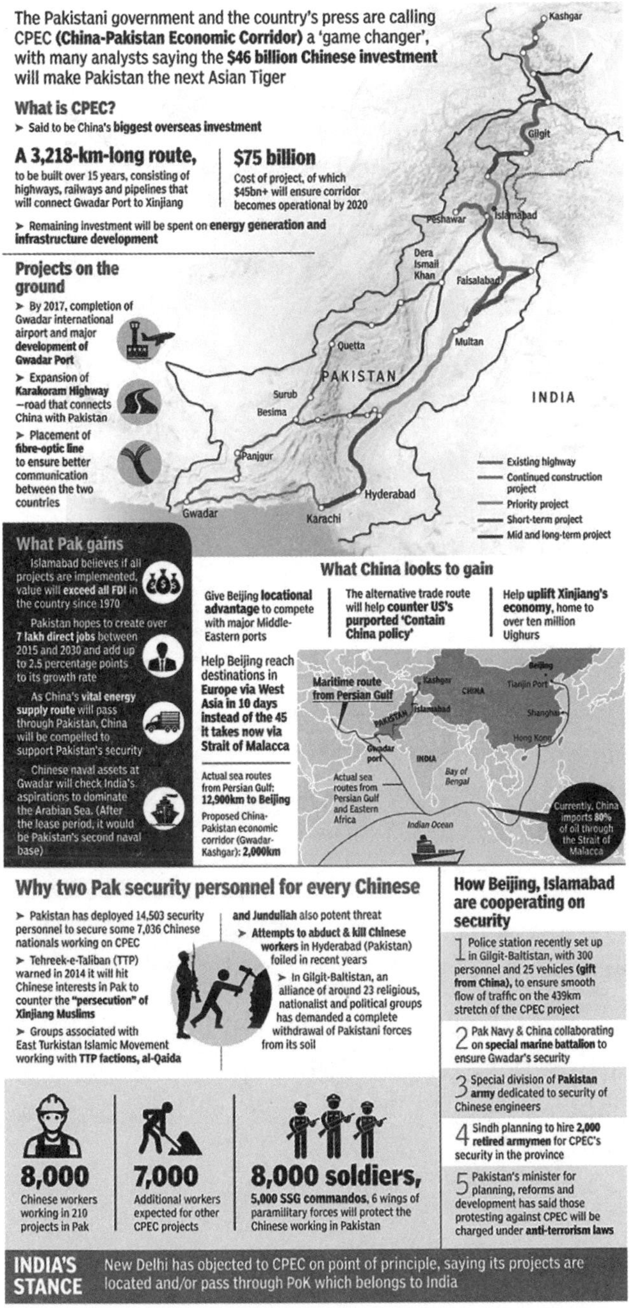

The Pakistani government and the country's press are calling CPEC **(China-Pakistan Economic Corridor)** a 'game changer', with many analysts saying the **$46 billion Chinese investment** will make Pakistan the next Asian Tiger

What is CPEC?

➤ Said to be China's **biggest overseas investment**

A 3,218-km-long route, to be built over 15 years, consisting of highways, railways and pipelines that will connect Gwadar Port to Xinjiang

$75 billion Cost of project, of which $45bn+ will ensure corridor becomes operational by 2020

➤ Remaining investment will be spent on **energy generation and infrastructure development**

Projects on the ground

➤ By 2017, completion of Gwadar international airport and major **development of Gwadar Port**

➤ Expansion of **Karakoram Highway** —road that connects China with Pakistan

➤ Placement of **fibre-optic line** to ensure better communication between the two countries

Kashgar
Gilgit
Peshawar
Islamabad
Dera Ismail Khan
Faisalabad
Multan
Quetta
PAKISTAN
INDIA
Surub
Besima
Panjgur
Gwadar
Karachi
Hyderabad

— Existing highway
— Continued construction project
— Priority project
— Short-term project
— Mid and long-term project

What Pak gains

Islamabad believes if all projects are implemented, value will **exceed all FDI** in the country since 1970

Pakistan hopes to create over **7 lakh direct jobs** between 2015 and 2030 and add up to 2.5 percentage points to its growth rate

As China's **vital energy supply route** will pass through Pakistan, China will be compelled to support Pakistan's security

Chinese naval assets at Gwadar will check India's aspirations to dominate the Arabian Sea. (After the lease period, it would be Pakistan's second naval base)

What China looks to gain

Give Beijing **locational advantage** to compete with major Middle-Eastern ports

The alternative trade route will help **counter US's purported 'Contain China policy'**

Help **uplift Xinjiang's economy**, home to over ten million Uighurs

Help Beijing reach destinations in Europe via West Asia in 10 days instead of the 45 it takes now via Strait of Malacca

Actual sea routes from Persian Gulf: **12,900km to Beijing**

Proposed China-Pakistan economic corridor (Gwadar-Kashgar): **2,000km**

Maritime route from Persian Gulf
Kashgar
CHINA
Beijing
Tianjin Port
Shanghai
Hong Kong
Islamabad
PAKISTAN
Gwadar port
INDIA
Bay of Bengal
Actual sea routes from Persian Gulf and Eastern Africa
Indian Ocean
Currently, China imports 80% of oil through the Strait of Malacca

Why two Pak security personnel for every Chinese

➤ Pakistan has deployed 14,503 security personnel to secure some 7,036 Chinese nationals working on CPEC

➤ Tehreek-e-Taliban (TTP) warned in 2014 it will hit Chinese interests in Pak to counter the **"persecution" of Xinjiang Muslims**

➤ Groups associated with East Turkistan Islamic Movement working with **TTP factions, al-Qaida and Jundullah** also potent threat

➤ **Attempts to abduct & kill Chinese workers** in Hyderabad (Pakistan) foiled in recent years

➤ In Gilgit-Baltistan, an alliance of around 23 religious, nationalist and political groups has demanded a complete withdrawal of Pakistani forces from its soil

8,000 Chinese workers working in 210 projects in Pak

7,000 Additional workers expected for other CPEC projects

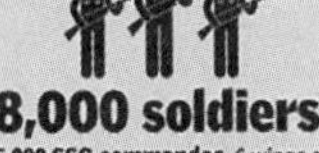

8,000 soldiers, **5,000 SSG commandos,** 6 wings of paramilitary forces will protect the Chinese working in Pakistan

How Beijing, Islamabad are cooperating on security

1 Police station recently set up in Gilgit-Baltistan, with 300 personnel and 25 vehicles **(gift from China)**, to ensure smooth flow of traffic on the 439km stretch of the CPEC project

2 Pak Navy & China collaborating on **special marine battalion** to ensure Gwadar's security

3 Special division of **Pakistan army** dedicated to security of Chinese engineers

4 Sindh planning to hire **2,000 retired armymen** for CPEC's security in the province

5 Pakistan's minister for planning, reforms and development has said those protesting against CPEC will be charged under **anti-terrorism laws**

INDIA'S STANCE New Delhi has objected to CPEC on point of principle, saying its projects are located and/or pass through PoK which belongs to India

(Graphic Source – Times of India – Rajat Pandit)

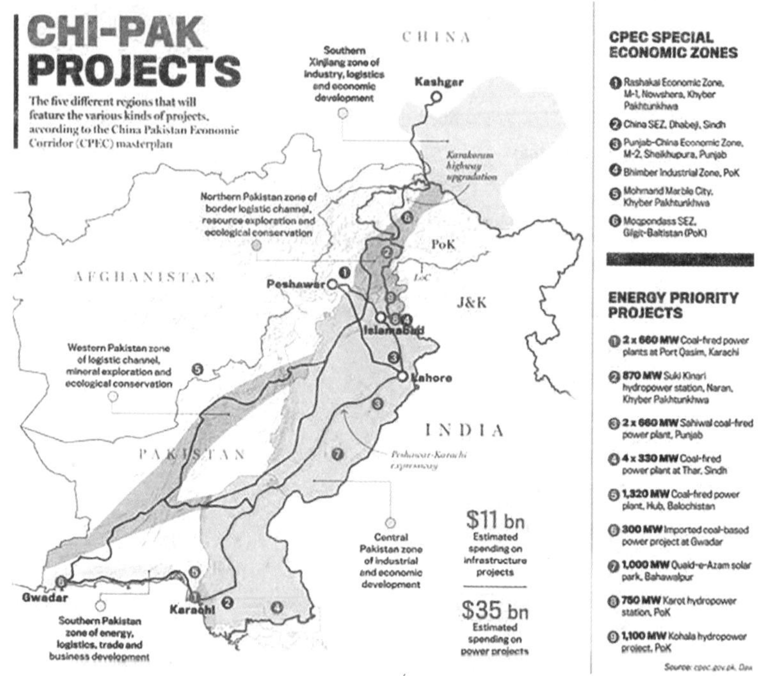

(Source Graphic – India Today – Tanmoy Chakraborty)

- **The project traverses through contested PoK and GB, on which India has de jure territorial claim.**
- The CPEC encompasses **critical strategic spaces like the Shaksgam Valley, Khanjureb pass, located in confluence of multiple civilisations.**
- The project is situated in **highly volatile KPK and Baluchistan affected by insurgencies and terrorism.** The region is **loosely administered with traditional codes** and has a **large number of warlords or self-styled Emirs.**
- **Gwadar on the Makran coast is the pivot with warm water connectivity** and potential to reduce dependencies on sea lanes transiting through **the Malacca Strait.**
- **The ambitious project includes power generation, road**

connectivity, port development, and Free Trade Zones (FTZs) and Special Economic Zones (SEZs) as the focus areas.

- Financial **outlay is pegged at $46 billion, with the possibility of growing to $62 billion** and more. Currently, however, **it is stalled due to the rethink and review** of projects.
- The project, in **more than seven years, has missed deadlines and has made tardy progress.**
- Major gain has been the **addition of approximately 6 GW power generation** out of the projected 12–15 GW, making approximately 45% accretion. The **utilisation and distribution of this power is tardy as the CPEC has only one minor project on the upgradation of the power distribution grid.**
- Most power projects are **coal-based, with GHG emissions and have problems of the availability of coal.** Three hydel projects are still under construction.
- There have been **improvements in the 3,218 km long road corridor,** but **upgradation to all-weather capability at the Khunjerab pass is still underway.**
- While **the ongoing Orange Line Metro project, bundled as early harvest, has been commissioned, other projects, like ML-1 are pending on funding challenges.**
- **Gwadar** has been **notionally activated and lacks infrastructure,** like captive power plant, water supply, and communications. Overall, it is **underutilised and yet to find traction.**
- Security threat to the Chinese workforce and **repeated terrorist attacks have created major concerns.**
- Pakistan has **added two light divisions equipped with sophisticated equipment and other dual use capabilities** in the garb of the CPEC.
- Pakistan is caught in a **debt trap and economic crisis, leading to a**

spectre of Hambantota type of situation and even talk of economic colonisation.

- The project has potential to **escalate regional tension and add to strategic challenges for India.**
- **India needs to be prepared to face a long-term threat posed by China and Pakistan in collusive mode.**

Recommended Indian Response Matrix

- **China is increasing its presence and influence in the Indian Ocean,** using bases like Djibouti, in conjunction with Gwadar, Hambantota, and other bases as part of its **Maritime Silk Road (erstwhile 'string of pearls') and the two-oceans strategy.**
- The Chinese attempt to secure a role in Chabahar after launching Gwadar as well as Kyaukphyu in Myanmar in relation to the Indian venture of Sittwe, is **indicative of the desire to stymie Indian**

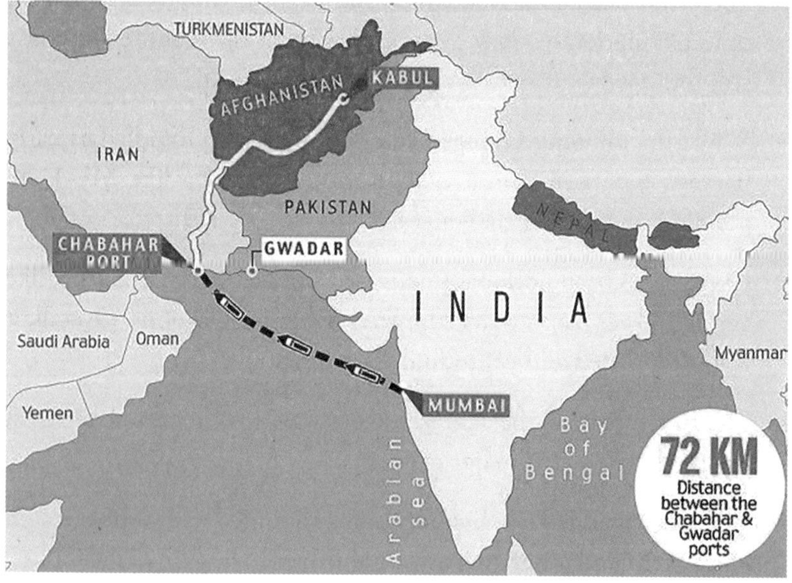

(Source Graphic – ORF report on Chabahar Port)

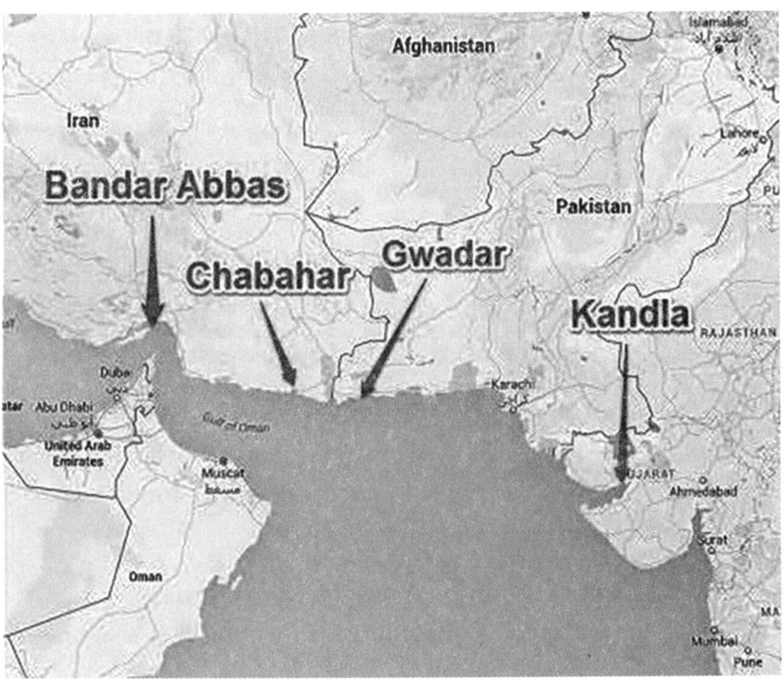

(*Source – Levina, The Chanakya Forum*)

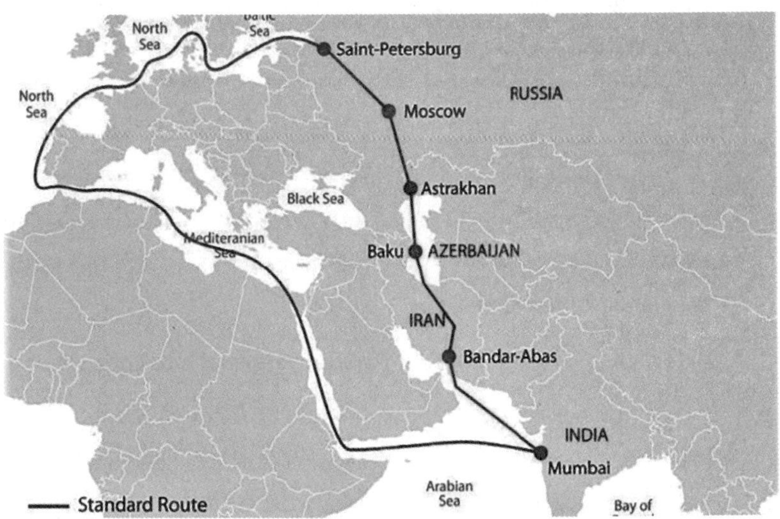

INST (Source – Levina, The Chanakya Forum)

connectivity initiatives. It doesn't fit into **the propaganda narrative of shared prosperity and regional cooperation.** On the contrary, it is more appropriate to read it in the context of the Chinese maxim, '**One mountain cannot take two tigers**'.

- **China** though a **late entrant** is utilising its fiscal clout and port development leverage to **set up forums to counter the already-established ones.**

- The Indian Ocean and Indo-Pacific are becoming **increasingly contested spaces with maritime strategic power games.**

- The Chinese threat must be **viewed in collusive format with Pakistan, and it can manifest in various domains—land air, cyber, besides maritime.** The **CPEC could contribute to this as a flank of application, launch pad, and for logistics.**

- India is looking at a **holistic response** based on alternate connectivity, increased cooperation, tie-ups for access to more bases, and strategic upgradation.

- **India has an indifferent record in its regional connectivity projects and needs to review its project management strategy.**

- **The International North-South Transport Corridor (INSTC) has the potential to negate salience of the CPEC and bypass the Gwadar** maritime choke being attempted by China.

- **Alliances like the QUAD have only limited utility, as partners are reluctant to physically apply forces. India may have to face its threats largely on its own.**

- **India needs to adopt a 'whole-of-nation' approach to cope up with China.**

India, at a defining stage in the journey of its development in '**Amrit-Kaal**' (75 to 100 years), is faced with **complex challenges of balancing its resources**:

- Between development and defence—the '**guns vs. butter**' dilemma.
- Apportioning between **land-based threat and maritime domains.**
- Resolution of tech asymmetry—**current vs. future.**

Concluding Inferences

- Transportation corridors or **connectivities will enjoy seminal relevance and will continue to 'proliferate influence'.**
- There are serious concerns about **the lack of compliance with climate action goals** in most BRI projects. Their carbon audit is warranted.
- China has been forced to review and repackage the BRI and even the CPEC, but **it is unlikely to pull out or foreclose in the short term.**
- The CPEC is currently in a stagnant mode and has made only a marginal difference to the life of Pakistan's population. Pakistan is caught in a fiscal emergency, debt trap, and high inflation. The power situation remains grim.
- **Gwadar, with its strategic location, has major utility for China's Indian Ocean push, but is also a very serious security challenge for India.**
- The success of corridors is conditioned by **'bottom-up' planning based on local aspirations and the environment in a 'win-win' format**, most importantly, in a corruption-free, efficient, and timely project execution.
- The crux is inclusive planning and customisation to enable and trigger economic activity for debt servicing. The CPEC is a prime example of sinking more than $40 billion, spread over nearly a decade, yet Pakistan is caught in a fiscal emergency, food riots, inflation, and a power crisis.

- Projects should **build local competencies and the stake of communities.** They should up-skill and empower the population of host countries.
- Planning, execution, and funding of projects should be transparent and compliant with international norms, including auditing.

18.2 IMEC – Ramping-Up for the Connectivity Game (Written in November 2023)

The real icing of the G20 summit was on the sidelines, in the declaration of the new India-Middle East-Europe-Economic Corridor (IMEC). This initiative, projected as pathbreaking, has the potential to develop a more efficient connectivity ecosystem.

It may also checkmate China's Belt and Road Initiative (BRI) and, more specifically, the China-Pakistan Economic Corridor (CPEC), which have a direct bearing on India. It may sound a bit discordant, but many such lofty projects have floundered after launch, and our track record in the infrastructure realm has been rather uninspiring. It is a must to analyse the issue objectively to ensure that it does not end up as another missed opportunity.

Update: The **project is currently stalled due to the ongoing Israeli offensive in Gaza and only planning and preparatory work is underway.**

Salience of Connectivity Corridors

The salience of connectivity corridors since ancient times, like the fifth century BCE-dated Royal Road of the Persian Empire and the Chinese Silk Roads, have served to bind empires, spanning nations. The alignment of the proposed IMEC links India through a maritime route to Red Sea ports, a freight corridor through the Arabian Peninsula to Israel, and going on to Europe. It brings the focus back to the Middle East or West Asia as a competitive connectivity hub. Iran and Turkiye are already pitching for the revival of a tweaked version of the ancient

Persian Empire's alignment, linking present-day Iran, Iraq, Syria, and Turkiye.

These highways and maritime corridors have served multiple purposes as part of thegeo-strategic powerplay. Objectives have included: first, geo-economics for trade, starting with barter for silk and spices; second, geo-theological for proselytisation and proliferation of religions; and third, geo-political for tax collection, law enforcement, and alliances. On the downside, there is the spread of pandemics, like smallpox in the sixth century CE and then the Black Plague. In the present times, COVID-19 proliferated along these pathways and aerial corridors. Looting and plunder by Mongol and Mughal hordes were also executed through these routes.

BRI and CPEC

The Chinese, flush with surplus funds and infrastructure-building expertise, launched the OBOR in 2013. Stung by criticism, they had to repackage it as BRI in 2017 to make it sound more inclusive.

However, as it happens in translated Mandarin terminologies, 'belt' is terrestrial/surface link and 'road' is a maritime corridor spanning oceans, with a covert aim to have a presence in 95 odd ports.

The Chinese, as per internationally verified estimates, claim to have lifted approximately 700 million people above the poverty line by linking manufacturing hubs with markets. The Chinese model is being replicated in India with projects like the Golden Quadrilateral corridor and freight corridors.

The crucial challenge is time-bound execution, ensuring quality and minimising corruption. Climate change has inducted requirements of disaster resilience and green corridors. In our context, collapsing highways in Himachal Pradesh and Uttarakhand are a stark warning signal. China has also curated newer variants like the Digital Silk Road and space and health roads. Notwithstanding failed projects like Hambantota and a debilitating debt trap, the Chinese footprint is ominous across Africa.

Indian Track Record

Forays in connectivity corridors can be traced back to the stalled Kaladan multi-modal project linking Sittwe in Myanmar to the Zokhawthar border town in Mizoram. Even the India-Myanmar-Thailand trilateral highway has been impacted by the disturbed internal situation in Myanmar. In contrast, China has operationalised the Kyaukphyu project and the China-Myanmar corridor with connectivity and a pipeline to Yunan. China has also muscled its entry into the Chabahar port project in Iran. It is likely to take over a rail link to Hajigak in Afghanistan, usurping the old border road project of Zaranj-Delaram. Another much-acclaimed project, the International North-South Corridor (INST), linking Mumbai to St Petersburg through Bandar Abbas and the Caspian Sea, has become a casualty of power politics. **In sum, tardy project implementation, coupled with instability in the extended neighbourhoods, has made it a litany of languishing, sub-optimal projects.**

The Way Forward

The IMEC is a somewhat belated outcome of the Build Back Better World (B3W) plan announced by the US President Biden in 2020. It has leveraged initiatives of the Abraham accord, I2U2 (India-Israel-US-UAE) and India-US-Saudi Arabia negotiation, to put together this project. The transit time from Mumbai to Port Suez, using the clogged Suez route, is approximately 11 days. The IMEC is likely to take six days to reach the Dammam/Jebel Ali Red Sea ports. Added with one–two days of transhipment and rail freight to Haifa, **it saves three–four days in transit and 20–25% in cost.**

The big advantage is that major building blocks of Indian and European legs (from Port Piraeus in Greece) are already in place. The main requirements are a rail link in Jordan, connecting it with the Saudi rail corridor (currently under modernisation) and Israel on the other end. The rail corridor is based on uniform standard gauge, obviating transhipment. Saudi Arabia has committed $20 billion, and the rest should be possible through a multilateral lending forum. India has already acquired a presence in the Haifa port and has shown interest in Port Piraeus, especially in keeping the Chinese out.

Various stakeholders have their own interests, such as the US wanting to promote decoupling from the Chinese supply chain. India will have to step up its manufacturing base. Considering our domain competence, we should also bid for a role in rail infrastructure creation. Saudi and Israeli interests include the resolution of the Palestinian issue. Saudi Arabia also seeks guarantees against Iranian nuclear bombs. Concurrently, China has been actively promoting rapprochement between Iran and the Gulf states. In this age of multi-polarity, the Gulf countries are playing a balancing game by joining BRICS with China, the Organization of the Petroleum Exporting Countries Plus (OPEC+) with Russia, and IMEC. The challenge is to keep the focus on our interests in this new complex game. For India, Russia, Iran, and Central Asia remain strategically relevant. **In our plurilateral template, it is not a zero-sum game of corridors but a multiplicity of connectivity and redundancies, which is important to cater for strategic flux.**

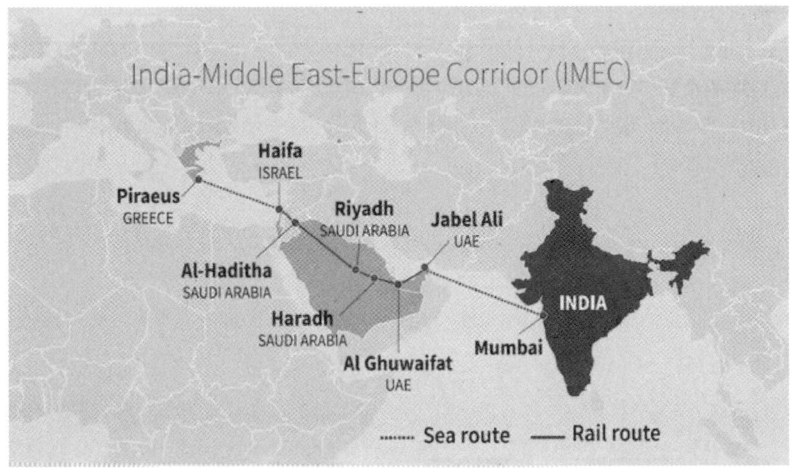

Parting Shot

May I extend my sincere gratitude to all the readers of the first edition of *General's Jottings*, which has resulted in selling out of all copies of the limited print run.

This and your feedback has given me an opportunity to update the revised edition and include the latest trends in the ever-dynamic geo-strategic flux.

The ultimate joy for an author is not only in readers buying or reading the book but in readers imbibing the mantra of **LED-P^2A^2L**, which translates to Location, Economics, Demographics, Past, Power Balance, Alliances/Adversaries, and Leadership to make sense of the evolving situations in the strategic environment.

National security mandates a 'whole-of-nation' approach and participation by all citizen warriors/nagrik yodhas, as we face the challenges of the BANI (Brittle, Anxious, Non-linear, and Incomprehensible) or VUCA (Violent, Uncertain, Complex, and Ambiguous) global order.

May I request you to please continue to share your valuable feedback and comments through e-mail (singhkayjay3363@gmail.com) or even social media (X-@kayjay34350; LinkedIn, or Facebook).